S0-FJU-670

UT VIDEAM

UT VIDEAM

CONTRIBUTIONS TO AN UNDERSTANDING OF LINGUISTICS

For Pieter Verburg on the occasion of his 70th birthday

edited by

WERNER ABRAHAM

LISSE/NETHERLANDS
THE PETER DE RIDDER PRESS
1975

Printed in Belgium by N. I. C. I., Ghent

A WORD IN EXPLANATION OF THIS BOOK

Launching a Festschrift is no longer the simple scholarly undertaking, that it once was. In the first place, a *receuil* of articles by the friends of the recipient is invariably too heterogeneous in content to attract consistent scholarly attention. The recent inflation of literature in linguistics has made us all sensitive to this difficulty. Moreover, there has been a decline in belief in the *raison d'être* of such works as such. A new array of social and political convictions, especially *intra muros universitatis*, have eroded confidence in the competence and moral dignity of the individual. The Socratic teacher-disciple relation is no longer generally accepted as an ideal. Will the masterless scholars of the future compile Festschriften?

For the first reason cited, we cannot hope that all the different linguistic specialists who take this volume in hand will be equally stimulated by all of the diverse contributions contained therein. It is noteworthy, however, that the singular diversity of topics does reflect the wide-spread scholarly interests of the Festschrift recipient.

That this volume exists testifies to the role that personal relations still play among scholars. The articles here offered to Pieter Verburg are tokens of friendship for him as a person and respect for him as philosopher, linguist, educator, and scientific organizer. Emeritus at seventy, Verburg can look back on a life and an academic career which, while not exempt from moments of crisis, is remarkable in its exemplary interweaving of essential principles of human conduct with academic responsibility. It would, finally, be an omission not to take note of those special qualities of courage and endeavour, especially as a scientific organizer and entrepreneur, for which international linguistics owes him recognition.

For diverse reasons, some of the invited scholars were unable to submit their contributions in time for inclusion in this volume. While no tabula gratulatoria was initiated, Verburg will take enjoyment from the express wish of the following persons to be included in such a list: Francis Dinneen, Morris Halle, Dell Hymes, Roman Jakobson, Berta Siertsema, Frits Staal, Don Graham Stuart, and John Verhaar. Last, but pragmatically by no means least among the expressions of esteem for Verburg should be mentioned the grants-in-aid of the Groninger University Fund, the Harmannus-Simon Kamminga Fund, and the Freseman Gratama-Fund, which have contributed to the cost of producing this volume.

W. A.

TABLE OF CONTENTS

A Word in Explanation of this Book 5

A Brief Biography of Pieter A. Verburg, Professor of General Linguistics in the National University at Groningen 9

Bibliography of P. A. Verburg 13

WERNER ABRAHAM
A Linguistic Approach to Metaphor 17

EUGENIO COSERIU
'Taal en functionaliteit' bei Fernão de Oliveira 67

SIMON C. DIK
Universal Quantifiers in Dutch 91

F. G. DROSTE
On Saying 107

ERIC P. HAMP
The Gothic Rune Name *chozma* 133

PETER HARTMANN
Dimensionierung als wissenschaftliche Teilaufgabe in der Textlinguistik 139

HENRY M. HOENIGSWALD
Schleicher's Tree and Its Trunk 157

J. H. HOSPERS
Some Observations About Semitics and General Linguistics ... 161

W. J. M. LEVELT
What Became of LAD? 171

BENSON MATES
On the Semantics of Proper Names 191

J. J. A. MOOIJ
On Reference 211

HERMAN PARRET
Idéologie et sémiologie chez Locke et Condillac: La question de l'autonomie du langage devant la pensée 225
W. KEITH PERCIVAL
On Plagiarisms in the *Minerva* of Franciscus Sanctius 249
H. SCHULTINK
Output Conditions in Word Formation? 263
A. G. F. VAN HOLK
Semiotic Aspects of the Interrogative 273
WIECHER ZWANENBURG
Ambiguïté dans le lexique 289

A BRIEF BIOGRAPHY OF

PIETER A. VERBURG

PROFESSOR OF GENERAL LINGUISTICS IN THE NATIONAL UNIVERSITY AT GRONINGEN

Born in Amsterdam on the 27th of July, 1905, Pieter A. Verburg grew up attending elementary and secondary school in that city. In 1920, he obtained employment as a junior clerk in the Amsterdam office of a Rotterdam firm dealing in tropical produce. After three short and successful years, in which he rose to a position of some responsibility as foreign language correspondent in the service of his firm, he decided, under the influence of the philosopher and theologian Prof. A. H. de Hartog, to abandon this career to pursue his studies.

Having successfully presented himself for the State Examination in Letters ('Staatsexamen Alpha') he was able to enroll in the Faculty of Letters of the Free University of Amsterdam in 1925, as a student in Classics. Here he studied under the classicist J. Woltjer and the logician-philosopher H. J. Pos — from the latter he received his indoctrination in General Linguistics and, especially, in the history of this science. At the Municipal University of Amsterdam he followed the lectures of Cohen. He continued his studies in Germany, first in Freiburg, under Immisch, Fränkel and Schadewaldt, and, then, in Berlin where he followed Norden and Lietzman.

After his doctoral examination, he passed approximately a year in London as a private tutor, where, using the library of the British Museum, he elaborated a plan for a dissertation on metaphor as an essential factor in language. Back in Holland, he was to hear from Prof. H. J. Pos, when he laid before him his outline and the material he had collected, that this topic has already been pre-empted by another of his students, C. F. P. Stutterheim, later to become Professor of the Dutch Language and Literature at Leiden.

Shortly after, in 1936, Pieter Verburg was appointed Classics Master charged with the organization of the municipal grammar school section of the Wagenings Lyceum in Wageningen. In the same year, he married Miss Cora de Boer, instructor in pedagogy, and settled down in Wageningen.

In consultation with Dr. A. J. B. N. Reichling, at that time 'privaat-docent' in the Municipal University of Amsterdam, whose own dissertation on the word had made a deep impression on him, Pieter Verburg undertook in 1938 a new dissertation project on the concept of lexical roots.

This project was nearing completion when the war brought work on it to a complete stop. Verburg became involved in the Resistance, and early in the war had to go underground. He started a series of clandestine pamphlets entitled *De Nieuwe Wijnzak* (The New Wine Sack), in which articles from his hand appeared arguing for two major initiatives. The first of these was for the care of victims of the occupation and the relatives of men in the Resistance; the second was a national organization for education and information to promote a deeper consciousness of national cultural identity.

In order to guard his most valuable possessions from possible confiscation, he stored everything, dissertation manuscript, notes, books, and materials, in the custody of trusted friends; on the 17th of September, 1944, all of these were destroyed by aerial bombardment.

After the liberation, at the request of the Minister of Education, Art and Science at that time, G. de Leeuw, Verburg became the director of the National Institute Foundation (Stichting 'Het Nationaal Instituut'), created at his initiative with a subsidy from the state, of which H. R. H. Prince Bernhard had accepted to be President. In this capacity, Verburg organized the first general post-war cultural conference which met under the chairmanship of the Prince, as the Congress on the Future of Dutch Culture, in August, 1946, in Nijmegen.

Several weeks before the Nijmegen Congress, Verburg's health failed and he was obliged to undergo treatment in Switzerland until the end of 1947. In his absence, the activities of the National Institute stagnated and came to an end, so that in the middle of 1948, after an interruption of some six years, he returned to his teaching post in Wageningen.

Through the loss of his manuscripts and materials and the diversion of his energies to the activities that war time and immediate post-war circumstances forced upon him, his scholarly work had come to nothing. It was Professor Anton Reichling who persuaded him in 1948 to take up his research again and begin a new dissertation. In 1950, he published an article in *Lingua*, based mainly on recollections of the lost pre-war dissertation. Then, in 1951, Verburg defended an entirely new dissertation entitled *Taal en functionaliteit: Een historisch-critische studie over de opvattingen aangaande de functies der taal* ... (*Language and Functionali-*

ty: An Historical-Critical Study of Views Concerning the Functions of Language ...). His defence was accepted *cum laude.*

In 1955, he was appointed Rector of the Municipal Gymnasium in Hilversum. For two years this responsibility occupied all his time and energy.

In 1957, Verburg accepted appointment to the newly created chair of General Linguistics at the National University of Groningen. In his inaugural oration on "General Linguistics and Liberal Education" ("Algemene taalwetenschap en encyclopaedie") we see already his broad vision of how and in what directions the new chair should be developed.

When, in the mid-sixties, the Central Interfaculty was constituted to satisfy the needs of all faculties for instruction and research in philosophical-methodological background questions, Verburg was selected by the Faculty of Letters to teach the Philosophy of Language in the new framework.

Early in 1970, on the occasion of the inauguration of new quarters for the Institute for General Linguistics and the twelfth-and-a-half aniversary of his chair, Verburg organized a symposium, the first of the Groningen Linguistic Round Table Conferences, to discuss the 'state of the art' in linguistics.

In the years of his leadership at Groningen Professor Verburg represented his department in many international gatherings. In 1962, before and after the Ninth International Congress of Linguists at Cambridge, Mass., he spent nearly a half year in the United States, where he visited some forty institutions and gave lectures at several different universities. In 1964, he was invited to take part in a small symposium on the theme "Continuity vs. Revolution in the Study of Language" organized by the Wenner-Gren Foundation at Burg Wartenstein in Austria.

Since its organization, he has been a member of the International Committee on Computational Linguistics and an active participant in its activities.

In 1961, together with Father John Verhaar, S.J., at that time still preparing a dissertation under his supervision, Verburg drafted plans for the creation of a new international journal to be devoted to questions of language and philosophy. From these plans emerged at the beginning of 1965 the now well-known journal *Foundations of Language*, of which Verburg is one of the editors and president of the foundation.

Verburg contributed significant articles to the fields of General

Linguistics and Philosophy of Language. His book *Language and Functionalism*, revised from his dissertation, has been translated into English. An Italian edition is likewise in preparation. His interests include not only general linguistic theory but also the history of theories of language – a dual specialization in which he follows the example of his teacher H. J. Pos. His orientation and position he describes as 'personalist – functionalist' and his own highly integrated theory he calls *Delotics* (Delotiek) from Greek *dèloun* 'to explain or clarify'.

He is a member of many learned societies, among them the Linguistic Society of America, the Societas Linguistica Europaea, the Association for Computational Linguistics, and various local Dutch associations in the field of linguistics, the Genootschap voor Wetenschappelijke Philosophie (the Society for Scientific Philosophy), and the Calvinistische Vereniging voor Wijsbegeerte (Calvinist Association for Philosophy). As far as his professional responsibilities leave him time, he takes part in religious and oecumenical activities on both a national and international level.

D. G. S.
W. A.

BIBLIOGRAPHY OF P. A. VERBURG

1941 Review of C. F. P. Stutterheim, *Het begrip Methaphoor, een taalkundig en wijsgerig onderzoek* (Doctoral dissertation Amsterdam 1941): *C.V.C.W.* (Corr. bl. Ver. v. Calv. Wijsb.), 1941/4.

1942 Review of K. Bühler, *Sprachtheorie*, Jena, 1936: *C.V.C.W.*, 1942/3/4.

1950 "The Background to the Linguistic Conceptions of Bopp", *Lingua*, 1950/2, 438-468. Reprinted in Thomas Sebeok, ed., *Portraits of Linguists*, Bloomington, 1966, 221-250.

1951 "Enkele lijnen en feiten in de ontwikkeling der taaltheorie", *Wetenschappelijke Bijdragen door Leerlingen van Prof. Dr. D. H. Th. Vollenhoven*, Franeker, 1951, 13-32.

1952 *Taal en functionaliteit: Een historisch-critische studie over de opvattingen aangaande de functies der taal* (Doctoral dissertation), Wageningen, 1952, I-XVI, 1-490 (see also 1975).

1952 "De humanistische taaltheorie van Juan Luis Vives (1492-1540)", *Handelingen v. h. XXIIe Ned. Philologenkongres te Utrecht* (Abstract).

1952/'53 Series "Taal en wet" (Language and law), *C.V.C.W.*, 1952 nov./'53 dec..

1954 "Model-gedachte, sub-functie, betekenis", *Handelingen v. h. XXIIIe Ned. Philologenkongres te Nijmegen* (Abstract).

1957 *Algemene taalwetenschap en encyclopaedie* (Inaugural oration), Groningen, 1957, 1-23.

1959 "Grondtrekken der moderne Amerikaanse linguistiek", *C.V.C.W.*, 1959 sept.

1961 "Bacon als vernieuwer van de encyclopaedische idee" (Commemorative oration held for the Alg. Ver. v. Wijsb.), *Alg. Ned. Tijdschrift v. Wijsb. en Psych.*, 1961/4, 169-180.

1961 “Het optimum der taal bij Wittgenstein”, *Phil. Ref.*, 1961, 161-172.

1961 “Het schaakspel-model bij F. de Saussure en L. Wittgenstein”, *Wijsgerig Perspectief*, 1961, 227-234.

1961 “Hearer-Speaker Relation in Language Theory”, *Proceedings of the 2nd International Course in Paedo-Audiology*, Groningen, 1961, 29-35.

1962 “Een boek over moderne Engelse taalfilosofie” (Review of M. J. Charlesworth’s *Philosophy and Linguistic Analysis*, 1959): *Bijdragen*, 1962, 12-22.

1962 “Some Remarks on ‘Communication’ and ‘Social’ in Language Theory”, *Lingua*, 1962/XI (*Studia Gratulatoria A. W. de Groot*), 453-468.

1963 Review (first part) of Arno Borst, *Der Turmbau von Babel, Geschichte der Meinungen über Ursprung und Vielfalt der Sprachen und Völker*, Stuttgart, 1957-1963: *Lingua*, 1963/3, 309-317.

1964 “Vicissitudes of Paradigms” (Contribution to the 25th Burg Wartenstein Symposium on the theme: “Revolution vs Continuity in the Study of Language”, August 15-25, 1964), Stenciled, Groningen, 1965, 1-31 (see also 1974).

1965 “Delosis and Clarity”, *Philosophy and Christianity: Essays Dedicated to Prof. Dr. H. Dooyeweerd*, Kampen, 1965, 78-99.

1965 “In Memoriam Albert Willem de Groot” (prepared in collaboration with G. F. Bos), *Jaarboek 1964-1965 v. d. Maatschappij der Nederlandse Letterkunde*, Leiden, 1965, 66-74.

1967 Review of J. A. Hutchison, *Language and Faith, Studies in Sign, Symbol and Meaning*, Philadelphia 1963: *Linguistics*, 1967/34, 118-123.

1968 “Ennoësis of Language in 17th Century Philosophy”, *Lingua*, 1968 (*Festschrift* for Reichling), 558-572.

1968 Review of N. V. Banerjee, *Language, Meaning and Persons*, London 1963: *Linguistics*, 1968/39, 109-113.

1969 “Computational Linguistics en de buitenlandse samenwerking”, *Universiteit en Hogenschool*, 1969/16/1, 77-82.

1969 “Hobbes’ Calculus of Words”, Contribution to the 3rd International Conference on Computational Linguistics, Sanga Säby, 1-4 sept.

1970 "Hobbes' Calculus of Words", *I.T.L.* (*Tijdschrift v. h. Inst. v. Toegepaste Linguistiek te Leuven*), Vol. 3 (1970), 62-69, and in *S.M.L.* (*Statistical Methods in Linguistics*, Stockholm), Vol. 6 (1970), 60-65.

1971 "De mens in de taalkunde", *Truth and Reality, Dedicated to Professor H. G. Stoker*, Bloemfontein (Trvl), 1971/3, 156-158.

1971 "Het lege woord", *De Gids*, 1971/3, 156-158.

1974 "The Idea of Linguistic System in Leibniz", to appear in: *History of Linguistic Thought and Contemporary Linguistics*, ed. Herman Parret.

1974 "Vicissitudes of Paradigms" (see also 1964), rewritten and expanded, to appear in: *Studies in the History of Linguistics: Traditions and Paradigms*, ed. Dell Hymes, Indiana University Press, Bloomington, Ind.

1975 *Language and Functionality* (English translation of *Taal en functionaliteit*; see 1952), to appear in 1975.

A LINGUISTIC APPROACH TO METAPHOR*

WERNER ABRAHAM

"780. – Quand quelqu'un me demande si un mot est français, j'y puis répondre. Quand on me demande si une diction est bonne, je n'y puis répondre, à moins qu'elle ne choque la grammaire. Je ne puis savoir le cas òu elle sera bonne, ni l'usage qu'un homme d'esprit en pourra faire: car un homme d'esprit est, dans ses ouvrages, créateur de dictions, de tours et de conceptions; il habille sa pensée à sa mode, la forme, la crée par des façons de parler éloignées du vulgaire, mais qui ne paroissent pas être mises pour s'en éloigner. Un homme qui écrit bien n'écrit pas comme on a écrit, mais comme il écrit, et c'est souvent en parlant mal qu'il parle bien."

(*Montesquieu*: *Oeuvres complètes I.* Texte présenté et annoté par Roger Caillois. Paris: Editions Gallimard, 1949 [n r f: Bibliothèque de la Pléiade], p. 1216.
Mes Pensées: *Quelques Réflexions ou Pensées detachées que je n'ai pas mises dans mes Ouvrages.*)

ABSTRACT

An intensionalist position is taken in the discussion of metaphorical use of language The concept of meaning (refuted by extensionalism as being unclear and hence methodologically unacceptable; compare, for example, Quine 1961, Cohen 1962) is developed by integrating both the meaning postulate approach (Carnap) and the componential analysis approach (which plays a decisive role in the semantic theory introduced by Katz and Fodor 1964 and is most prominently advocated by Katz 1972).

The basic thesis is that among the possible associations (meaning components) that verify the proper use of a lexeme only those are conditions for the normal use of the lexeme that have top priority (are the strongest, or necessary, associations). Metaphors are explained on the basis of a reordering of those components such that associations of low priority in the meaning analysis gain prominence (high priority). In principle, every attempt at metaphorical interpretation presupposes some inferential operation of the traditional sort.

Since there are metaphors of a more universal (etymologically and typologically recurring) sort and those of a highly context-specific kind, pragmatic categories and rules of discourse add to what can be generally called an approach of *semantic pragmatics*. The senses of lexemes are elicited by interaction with other lexemes syntactically connected, as well as by situative conditions. The phenomenon of the metaphor is thus not distinct from any other lexematic occurrence the sense of which is established by *interaction* with its context (conversational meaning; cf. Cresswell 1973:239); rather, it is a separate type only insofar as the metaphorizing intention of the speaker is explicit.

0. 'Nonliteral' meanings of words in phrases such as *the foot of the piano*, *the neck of a bottle*, *the head of the bed*, *the leg of the table* occur frequently in everyday usage.

These uses of *foot*, *neck*, *head*, *leg*, may, to a certain extent, be fixed or lexicalized. Besides them there are new metaphoric meanings we keep inventing, maybe without our always being aware of it: Thus, instead of *He rolled into the room like a ship with a broken rudder in a wildly moving sea* we simply say *He rolled into the room*; instead of *The girl was wilted like the petals of a flower* we simply say *The girl was wilted.* The suggestion that for each of such metaphoric uses of lexemes or combinations of lexemes a separate description in the lexicon of a generative grammar should be provided would certainly be a far too simplistic approach. It would only be applicable in the case of the *frozen* metaphor. Furthermore, while we are interested in describing the strategies that underly such meaning transfers in metaphoric language, the rules governing the relation between the literal and metaphorical uses of an expression can be omitted only where such relations are not retraceable, i.e. where the relation between the metaphoric and the literal use of an expression is one of *definiendum* and *definiens*, in which the meaning relation does not become obvious. The latter, however, are the uninteresting cases. What we want to simulate is the creative step from the generally accepted literal use of a word to the unexpected, but nevertheless understood and, what is more, pointedly illustrating transferred use of the word. It should be clear that, with any such transfer conditioned by human encyclopedic knowledge (knowledge of different possible worlds), metaphoric word meanings of this interesting sort cannot be embodied in the static lexicon. To establish what precisely its relation to this lexicon is I consider the prime task of this paper.

At this initial point I provisionally adopt a naive attitude as far as the term 'metaphor' is concerned. That is to say, I shall not settle for a particular definition of the term, first because there exist quite a number of controversial attempts at such a definition and secondly because I do not know how to meet Harweg's quite acceptable requirement that a definer of metaphor has to consider the usefulness to be expected from his explanation of the term. Much rather I shall use 'metaphor' in the sense of 'transfer of meaning' restricting this wider sense, that embraces allegory, simile, symbol, fable, etc., to mean 'use of words in well-formed sentences or syntactic phrases in a non-literal sense'. I hereby exclude that type of metaphor which is manifested not within one single sentence, but in text portions, in that specific expectations with regard to descriptions of the world are established by means of several specific lexical elements; these expectations are not satisfied at a given point of the text, thus necessitating a change in the interpretation of the world that has to underly the attempt to understand the text correctly. Compare, for example, Robert Musil's *Der Mann ohne Eigenschaften*, 1st chapter, 2nd paragraph, in which a distant bird's eye view of the city of Vienna is created by such items as *tiefe Straßen* – *Seichtigkeit heller Plätze* – *Fußgängerdunkelheit bildete wolkige Schnüre* – *Striche der Geschwindigkeit*, etc. (For further discussion of this concept of 'text metaphor' and of the consequences for an instrumentarium of description, see Siebert 1973.)

With this I find that my use of the term comes close to what are traditionally classified as *metonomy*, *catachresis*, *synecdoche*, etc., as well as to Chomsky's *semi-grammaticality*. Thus, the sentence *Green ideas sleep furiously* may indeed be meaningful in a certain context provided the violation of the selection rules through personification of *ideas*, the association of physical concreteness, and thus the property of being coloured, with *ideas* as well as the association of 'active' with *sleep*, are sanctioned within this context. Granted that on the basis of our encyclopedic knowledge we find a compatible context, any violation on the level of selection rules (i.e. the 'most semantic' of all grammatical rules) has to be interpreted as metaphor.[1] This conclusion is not reversible: We cannot say that every metaphor can be explained as resulting from a violation of selection rules. The meanings of *Man is a wolf* or *The black people are the poor of Europe* cannot be interpreted by means of such inconsistencies of selection constraints. As for the first mentioned Chomskyan example, however, it is true for all metaphorical meanings of sentences that they are syntactically well-formed constructions. This can be demonstrated by an extreme example, say *de-de-de*. It is only if we can state a structure definable in terms of syntactic categories and their interdependence relations (as in (1)) that interpretation becomes possible

(1)

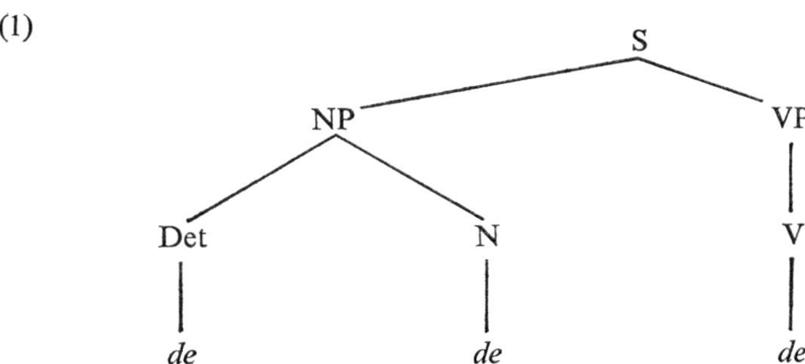

– provided that we have a context that permits association of nominal, article, and verbal categories with *de*.

This is a condition that has to be met also in the case of the 'grammatical' metaphor, which has been intriguing many linguists. I think it provides a simple explanation of this phenomenon. Thus, *you calls* is simply a change from formal to material supposition which has not been made explicit and at once becomes transparent by meta-marking it as '*you*' *calls* represented as follows:

(2)

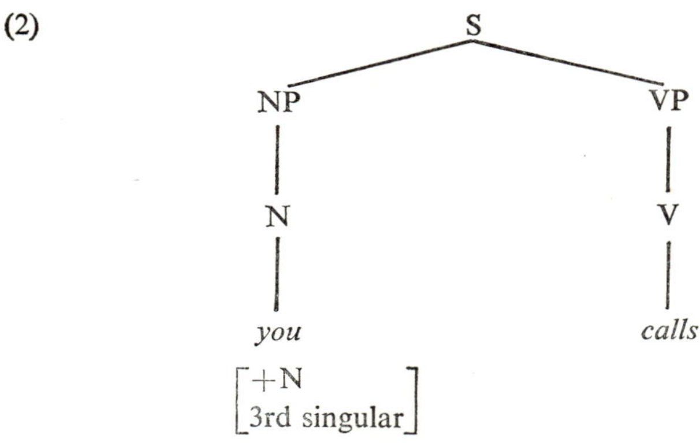

The following considerations are divided into five main sections:

(1) A short discussion of the pragmatic conditions that have to be met in order that a structure be called 'metaphor'.

(2) Conditions for the use of language in metaphoric function: a survey of the research done in this field.

(3) Substitution hypothesis, comparative hypothesis, and interaction hypothesis: a review of philosophical aspects.

(4) Remarks on the roles which the terms 'literal meaning' and 'acceptability' play in the explanation of metaphors: topicalization of components in the decomposition of lexical meaning, different degrees of acceptability, and possible worlds.

(5) Some illustrations.

1. PRAGMATIC CONDITIONS

I shall adhere to the following terminological framework (see also Black 1962:47):

(3) E ... expression (utterance)

(4) F ... verbal 'frame' (context)

(5) F(E) ... E within a context F that is not compatible with E
(6) m'(E) ... meaning of E within F(E)
(7) m(X) ... meaning of X

where:

(7.1.) m'(E) = m(X) such that X ist the *substituens* (substitute) for E within F(E), and E within F(E) is the *substituendum* (substituent);
(7.2.) m'(...) = metaphoric usage (characterized by nonliteralness and other properties), thus: transferred meanings;
(7.3.) m(...) = literal usage

Obviously it is above all two problems that seem of particular interest:

(a) What linguistic tools are there for describing F(E) in such a way as would make a meaningful interpretation of E (in the sense of X) possible?

(b) What are the limits and conditions for E becoming interpretable in an incompatible context?

(a) is a problem of linguistics and logic (in the sense of strict, scientific systems of description); (b) is a problem of philosophy and of the social sciences, and also of pragmatics as one of the disciplines which determine the form of this discussion.

Among the categories that are introduced by pragmatics we are interested above all in *speaker* (Sp) and *addressee* (Addr). Suppose we take for granted that the meanings of some of the words which are used by Sp and Addr are not identical; then we have to add to (3)-(7) above:

(8) m_{Sp} (X)
m_{Addr} (X)

The meaning of X common to both Sp and Addr is represented by

(9) R [m_{Sp} (X), m_{Addr} (X)]

where R indicates the intersection of the conditions governing the use (the semantic properties) of X. For R we can assume the following extreme possibilities:

(10) $\{m_{Sp}(X)\} \cap \{m_{Addr}(X)\} = \emptyset$
wholly different meanings;
$m_{Sp}(X) = m_{Addr}(X)$
identical meanings

Between these extremes, there are degrees of intersection of semantic features.

Note that this pragmatic characterization of the substituens (substitute) for the metaphorically used lexeme also covers the literal meaning of E outside F (i.e. m(E) $\neq$ m(X)). In order to be able to distinguish within all F(E) between (more or less acceptable) metaphors and meaningless (uninterpretable) incompatible structures it is useful to look at some of Grice's discourse implications (see Apostel 1971:13ff.):

(11) Sp knows that Addr is attaching a meaning to E that does not differ greatly from the meaning which Sp attributed to E: $m_{Sp}(X) \cong m_{Addr}(X)$.
(12) Sp wants Addr to attribute this meaning to E.
(13) Addr knows that it was Sp who uttered E, which he (Addr) has perceived.
(14) Sp knows (or believes) that Addr when perceiving E knows (or believes) that Sp knows m(E) (or thinks he knows it).
(15) When Addr perceives E, he (Addr) knows (or believes he knows) that Sp knows (or thinks he knows) m(E).

The following relation holds between (14) and (15):

(15.1.) KNOW (x, m) *implies* m
(15.2.) BELIEVE (x, m) *does not imply* m

with m representing the conditions governing the use of the sign E (that is those characteristics or properties that guarantee the correct use). In other words, (15) is not necessary if in (14) only the epistemic operator KNOW is used. Condition (15) excludes lying and pretending of Sp as well as general misunderstanding on the part of Addr.

(16) Sp has the intention that Addr should know (think he knows) that Sp knows (thinks he knows) m(E).
(17) What has been described in (11) through (16) is that epistemic state that the perception of E creates in Addr about Sp; for Addr thinks that E belongs to a set {E} with a structural description such that only systems which comply with the rules of a certain language create elements of {E}, and he believes that the rules of this language are such that only on the basis of the knowledge of m(E) and the intention that others too should know m(E) such an E can be produced.
(18) *Under normal conditions* it can be taken for granted (it is true) that (a) Sp acts in accordance with these rules of the language, R, and

that (b) Sp believes that Addr thinks that Sp thinks he knows m(E).

Violation of the conditions (a) and (b) leads to one of two situations:

(18.1.) Misunderstanding: e.g. if (a) is violated or if Addr thinks that Sp knows (thinks he knows) m(E), whereas Sp wants that Addr should believe that Sp believes (knows) m''(E), where $m(E) \neq m''(E)$. This is also true for that case of non-equality where $m(E) \cap m''(E)$ equals m(E) or m''(E), i.e. where a relation of inclusion or implication holds between m(E) and m''(E).

(18.2.) Understanding: either if Addr notices (expects) the deviation from R, or if Sp (thinks he) knows that Addr (thinks he) knows that Sp does not believe (does not know) m(E), but knows m'(E) or m''(E).

(15) and (18) are conditions describing 'honest talking': that is to say, it is the intention of Sp to be understood by Addr in the way intended by Sp, which is in accordance with the rules of the language Sp and Addr are both familiar with. This situation, however, involves a certain amount of idealization, since it presupposes a level of *language norms* to be shared by Sp and Addr (cf. above: $m_{Sp}(X) \cong m_{Addr}(X)$).

Furthermore this restriction excludes attitudes of the speaker such as the intention to deceive; pretence (Sp wants Addr to think that Sp thinks (knows) m(X), whereas Sp actually thinks (knows) m''(X)); non-sense talk; confusion on the part of Sp (Sp does not know that Addr does not know that Sp knows m(E); ignorance of Sp as to the normality of $m_{Sp}(X)$ or as to the rules for the use of E resulting in use without any meaning); and, generally, manipulation of the communication (Sp does not want Sp to know m(E)).

Irritation and dissociation from the normal use of language – attitudes to be found in modern literature – have to be explained on the basis of this second assumption (18.2.). Metaphoric use presupposes the intention on the part of the Sp (user of the metaphor, creator of the metaphor) that Addr understands what Sp wants to express. Generally this is true for the type of language use where Sp is conscious of the recipient of the communication and his possible expectations, i.e. in discourse, letters, lectures etc. If Addr fails to understand F(E), he will try to recover from Sp more information on $m_{Sp}(E)$ or on such implications as render an analogy between m(X) and m'(E) possible. The use of metaphoric language in dialogue or discourse is, therefore, commonly governed by other strategies on the part of Addr as when metaphoric language is used under conditions which do not allow for checking, e.g. in the case of written language. There Addr depends on nobody but himself to discern the implications necessary to find the *substituens*, m(X). Furthermore, he has to find out whether m(X) was in fact intended by Sp to figure as a *substituens*.

How this last question is decided by Addr depends not only on the relation between the alternative worlds of Sp and Addr, but also on whether or not the following premiss is valid in the discourse:

(19) Addr knows/believes/doubts that Sp does in fact mean something by E.

This premiss (which differs from (15) in that it is more general) can be generalized as follows:

(19') Addr knows (thinks he knows) that Sp wants to get E across to Addr in such a way that Addr thinks that Sp knows (thinks he knows) m(E).

The decision as to whether (19) holds, depends on the expectations Addr has about the credibility of Sp.

Metaphorical use of language by definition presupposes this latter discourse implication, (19). It is the primary state of recognition which precedes any attempt to interpret semantically incompatible, but grammatically well-formed structures. (19) or (19'), respectively, also ensure that, if Addr wants to accept an as yet uninterpreted structure as metaphorical, Sp consciously draws the analogy between m'(E) and m(X). Consequently, 'figurative speech' of children, catachresis, abnormal use of words with aphasics etc. are not to be understood as (possible) metaphors but as speech conventions with no analogue m(X) underlying (and being consciously attributed to) the function of F(E) and thus m'(E).

2. CONDITIONS FOR THE USE OF LANGUAGE IN METAPHORIC FUNCTION: A BRIEF SKETCH OF RESEARCH TO DATE

While the literature on metaphor has concentrated on the question 'What is a metaphor?' and 'What does a metaphor do?', Helmer (1972) takes up the question which has above all interested psychologists: 'Under which conditions can a person use a metaphor?'. Answers to the first question are attempted by investigations in the domains of philosophy and aesthetics (Black (1962), Goodman (1968)). They are concerned with the meaning of words or groups of words, i.e. with the relation between symbols and the object referred to. The psychologically oriented investigations, on the other hand, aim at accounting for metaphor as dependent on certain attitudes, experiences or dispositions, generally speaking as dependent upon reactions of both speaker and addressee.

Although my own attempts go mainly, but not exclusively, in the first direction outlined above, it appears to me of value to touch sketchily on the second sort of problems. Among these, the question which group of people are more or less unable to use or understand metaphoric language has been in the centre of interest. Jakobson and Halle (1956) have described that type of aphasia which confines the aphasic's grasp of the meaning of words to their literal meanings, excluding an interpretation of words used metaphorically. Since the meaning of a word is co-determined by its context (the linguistic context into which it is placed, and the situational context to which it refers), the inability to interpret metaphors correctly must be taken to imply that the context makes available for the aphasic just one single word meaning. Where this one context for one specific meaning of a word symbol is not present, the aphasic cannot produce the sentence (phrase). The similarities between uses of one and the same word in different contexts referring to different objects, and between different words, used in similar contexts in order to signify similar objects, remain obscure to him. Jakobson (1960:356; I follow Helmer's quotations (1972:9)) characterizes this difficulty in its most general form as the loss of the ability for metalinguistic operations: the aphasic has lost the ability to use words which refer to other words or which signify other words.

This very inability to distinguish the metaphorical and literal use of language is reported also of schizophrenics and acute suicidal cases. With the latter it should of course not be identified with a pathological disability, but rather understood as a form of communication, which, under pressure from the suicidal state of mind, does not employ the stylistic means of the metaphor (Osgood 1960). Likewise, children up to the age of 11 and 12 generally do not use words metaphorically unless the metaphor is a well-established cliché. In the latter case, however, the child does not associate the literal meaning of the word and the meaning transfer that is inventional in the cliché; in other words, no transfer rule is operative between the two uses of the word, rather its use merely derives from isolated storage in the memory (in the lexicon). Thus, while a child may refer to solid objects as well as to his friend's father as *hard*, he does not associate these two uses of the word with one another (Asch/Nerlove (1960)). The intensions of these two meanings have no non-empty intersection, and this entails that no proximity of meaning can be construed.

Such findings are contradicted by speculations of Cohen/Margalit (1970:470): "Children do not learn to speak metaphorically as a kind of crowning achievement in the apprenticeship of language-learning. Rather they use metaphors naturally from infancy onwards, and have gradually to learn – with respect to each noun, verb, adjective or adverb – how to speak literally." Quite obviously, however, Cohen/Margalit use a concept of metaphor which is not in line with traditional ones, nor with any other concept that is interesting: In the tradition of the term, *metaphor* (just like *symbol, allegory, simile*, concepts that Cohen/Margalit seem to use without much distinction) signifies *conscious* meaning transfer. And as far as I can see, Cohen/Margalit's own words, by implication, permit no other interpretation. What else can 'metaphorical' mean but the *conscious* deviation from the 'literal' use of the word-symbol – controlled by further constraints which we have subsumed under the term 'transfer of meaning'? To use an example that Cohen/Margalit give: If the child says 'the car shouts' (instead of 'hoots') he does so with his *literal* understanding of *shout*, where obviously *shout* is less constrained selectionally than in normal usage. We can exclude, in this context, the case where the child uses *shout* consciously as a kind of bad, but just tolerable, substitute simply because his memory fails him momentarily with regard to the correct *hoot*. To speak metaphorically presupposes that one has the option to speak literally and that the deviation of the metaphoric use from the literal receives weight with stylistic purport. However, if we speak about 'literal meaning' we will have to clarify what 'normal' meaning is (see an attempt toward a definition p. 23), a concept that has not been considered by Cohen/Margalit at all and which seems to be of utmost importance in this context.

In his brief presentation of the second complex of questions, Helmer points out the parallel between 'metaphoric incompetence' and 'metalinguistic incompetence'. This can be diagnosed as the incompetence to use words in order to signify other words. This, in turn, clearly implies the view that metaphor is a process in which the meaning of a particular word is mediated, under certain regular restrictions, by a different word. In the literature pertaining to question 1 above, this view is presented under the label 'substitution hypothesis' or 'comparison hypothesis'.

3. SUBSTITUTION HYPOTHESIS – COMPARISON HYPOTHESIS – INTERACTION HYPOTHESIS

3.0 Whatever definitions of 'metaphor' we look at, we find that, despite all the controversial details, they have one thing in common: they all take metaphor to involve a transfer of meaning. In this sense, metonymy, synecdoche (*pars-pro-toto* structure), simile, imagery, allegory, etc. all describe similar types of meaning transfer without being clearly distinguishable from one another. I do not want to go into problems of defining metaphor here; to me they are not of central interest. Rather, I shall bring into focus two interpretations of Black (1962) and discuss their (micro-)linguistic aspects. I think Black's basic classification covers the essential part of all processes of the transfer of meaning. I therefore do not actually have to restrict myself to metaphor; rather, it is only the starting point of my discussion.

3.1 *Substitution Hypothesis*

The following examples illustrates the assumption that a *substituens* with a literal meaning, m(X), is necessary for the transfer of meaning to become understandable.

(20) *He ate his way through the mountain of letters.*
(21) *He trumpeted out the news.*
(22) *The rain was drumming on the roof.*
(23) *Man is a wolf.*
(24) *The poor are the black of Europe.*
(25) *Light is but the shadow of God.*

In the first three examples literal interpretations of the sentences can be produced by substituting a synonym or a synonymous combination of words. Thus, the verbs in (20)-(22) can be replaced by *work*, *tell to anyone who wants to listen*, *knock at short, regular intervals*. Such cases of transferred meaning are covered by the substitution hypothesis.

3.2 *Comparison Hypothesis*

In these first three cases obviously we can also establish LIKE-relations: *the knocking of the rain on the roof* is LIKE *the drumming of the rain on the roof.* Interestingly enough the LIKE-relation in some cases seems to be supported by *topoi* from our encyclopedic knowledge: thus, the LIKE-relation between *trumpet out* and *broadcast the news so that everybody can hear it* is associated with the image of the royal herald or the nomenclator, while the analogy between *work through* (or *dig one's way through*) and *eat one's way through* brings to one's mind the *topics* of the mountain of semolina pudding in (the German) cloud cuckoo land. However, this does not seem necessary for the explanation of how the transfer of meaning comes about. In other words, the metaphors can also be interpreted without associating them with exactly these topoi. I shall take up this question once more, during the discussion of 'acceptability' and 'state of the lexicon' (chapter 4.2.).

Note that all those cases which can be explained by substitution can also be accounted for by comparison.

3.3 *Interaction Hypothesis*

Black (1962:38ff.) has claimed that there is a separate class of metaphors which cannot be explained by either the substitution test or the comparison test. Cases like

(24) *The poor are the black of Europe*

cannot, according to Black, be interpreted literally by substituting a certain word or combination of words for elements in (24). Black sees the explanation of (24) in the assumption that our 'ideas' about *the poor of Europe* and *the black people in the USA* are in a kind of attraction or 'interaction' which generates the common meaning as in (24).

In the following I shall try to demonstrate that this observation alone is not sufficient evidence for a specific class of metaphors. I shall try to explain the production and interpretation of metaphors more generally by means oi the comparison hypothesis. However, the observations made by Richards and Black as to the interaction of the lexical elements involved in a metaphor are important for the linguistic explanation of the metaphoric process. I thus claim that it is possible to establish a LIKE-relation for (24) just as in the case of the rest of the examples (compare for example '*The poor of Europe are* LIKE *the American black*'). By showing that the LIKE-relation underlies the general process of meaning transfer I have, however, not indicated why this comparison between the poor of Europe and the American black can legitimally be made. In other words, what remains to be found (or plausibly deduced) are those characteristics that are common to the semantics (or encyclopediae) of the concepts *the black of the US* and *the poor of Europe* such that a comparison of other wholly arbitrary elements will yield a different interpretation, or none at all.

4. 'FOCUS' AND 'CONTEXT'

4.1 All metaphors have their origin in a violation of the compatibility of lexemes in a syntactic structure. The syntactic regularities (constituent structure rules of base and derived structures), on the other hand, remain unaffected. In such a grammar, which interprets also violations of a syntactic nature (cf. Abraham 1970; Abraham/Braunmüller 1971 and 1973), the rules of strict subcategorization and selection rules will thus mark distinctly syntactic non-interpretability (not excluding, however, 'possible' semantic interpretations; cf. Abraham/Braunmüller 1971) on the one hand and metaphoric interpretability on the other. As Matthews (1971:416) has rightly observed, such a marking serves only as a *sufficient*, but not as a *necessary*, condition for the distinction of metaphorical utterances and those which cannot be interpreted at all.

The selectional restrictions attached to the verb are, as it were, included in the set of compatibility rules which, unfortunately, never have received attention in modern linguistics (the only exception that I know of is Lang 1974). Violations of the selectional restrictions have to be subject to certain limitations if meaningless sentences are to be precluded. Let us look at (26):

(26) *At night all cats are black.*

The problem lies in the contingent non-compatibility of 'cat', or rather its quantification by means of 'all', with the predicate 'are black'. A semantic description of 'cat' in the framework of componential analysis would yield the colour feature '(White) ∨ (Brown) ∨ (Spotted) ∨ (Black) ...', and certainly not '(Black)'. This, however, contradicts the 'all' in the combination of features above, a contradiction which has to be resolved unless we accept the sentence as meaningless, which is counter-intuitive. Generally it would seem that meaninglessness is indeed attributed in a great number of cases, unless the speaker of the utterance warrants certain expectations with the observer such as to make him look for a 'deeper', i.e. non-literal, sense, which might be intended and which is compatible and informative in a certain context. In our example, (26), it is from 'at night' that we can unravel this contradiction. What happens is similar to phonological neutralization: within the context of 'at night', analytically marked '(Dark) $\wedge$ (Colourless) $\wedge$ (Black)',[2] etc., the disjunction '(White) $\vee$ (Brown) $\vee$ (Spotted)', being but complement of any features of '(Black)', is neutralized to '(Dark)' or '(Colourless)' both of which are compatible with '(Black)'.

(27) '(((White) $\vee$ (Brown) $\vee$ (Spotted) $\vee$ ... $\vee$ (Black)) / (Cat))' in the context '(Black) / (Night)' $\Rightarrow$ '((Black) / (Cat))'
'/' is the functor representing the relation between the grammatical attribute and its head. Note that logical conjunction, under the law of commutativity, would allow for ambiguous surface derivation of such a semantic analysis. For arguments see Abraham 1973.

Obviously, acceptance of the predicate 'is black' requires its interpretation as 'appears black' or 'looks black'.

What we have considered so far makes plausible the following thesis. It is the very coincidence of 'contradiction' and a somehow legitimate claim to meaningfulness that justifies the characterization 'metaphorical' (and likewise such attributes as 'simile, allegory, imagery'). Depending on the type of operation by which this contradiction is eliminated, in other words depending on the procedural type of interpretation, the label 'metaphor', 'simile', 'allegory', etc. can be applied. At the moment, however, my ideas as to how these types are to be distinguished from each other are not developed enough. (A quite comprehensive, but in many respects unsatisfactory survey is given in *Communication* 16 (1970).)

4.2 *Excursus on the Notion "Incompatibility"* [2a]

Lang (1974:45) discusses the following relations and their interdependencies:

(1) *non-distinctiveness* as holds between synonyms (lexical variants of one and the same meaning); meaning postulate universal: $F(x) \leftrightarrow F(x)$

(2) *implication* holding between two events where the acceptance of one necessarily, or normally, associates the acceptance of a second event but not the other way round; meaning postulate: $F(x) \rightarrow G(x)$

(3) *contradictory opposition* as holds between two events such that their relation can be described as: $F(x) \rightarrow \neg G(x)$

(4) *contrary opposition* as holds between two events such that their relation can be described as: $F(x) \rightarrow G(x)$ and $G(x) \rightarrow \neg H(x)$

(5) *compatibility* which holds between two events if and only if they are distinct, non-implicative (non-inclusive), and non-contradictory or non-contrary.

The interdependencies are illustrated conveniently by means of the natural integers above 2 ($n > 2$).

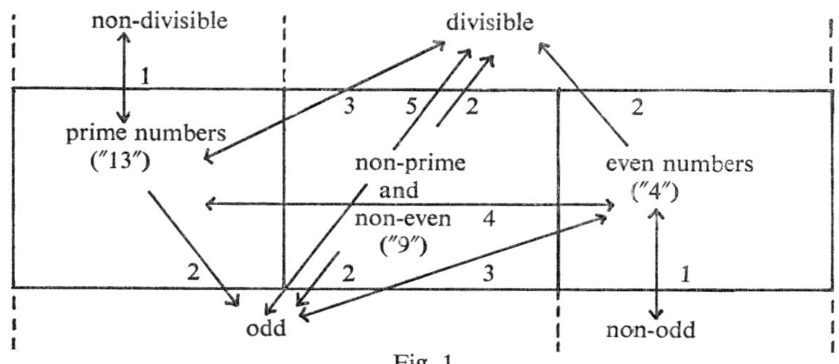

Fig. 1

Each arrow or double arrow corresponds to one of the five relations above as is indicated by the integers alongside each arrow. The arrow-relations are to be read as follows: 'if x is a prime number, then it is non-divisible, and conversely' (non-distinct (1)); 'if x is non-prime and odd then it is divisible (but not conversely)' (implicative (2)); etc. If we consider these relations as truth functions the conditions for the semantic (extensional) well-formedness of two events that are dependent upon one another on the basis of one of the first four relations above can be stated in the following manner:

ad (1) F(x) and G(x) are semantically non-distinct iff either T-T or F-F (i.e. either if F(x) is true then also G(x) is true, or if F(x) is false then also G(x) is false; no other possibility is determined by the relation of non-distinctiveness ('synonymy', 'equivalence')).

ad (2) F(x) semantically implies G(x) iff

(a) if $F(x) \rightarrow G(x)$ (F(x) is the *implicator*), either T-T or F-T or F-F;
(b) if $G(x) \rightarrow F(x)$ (F is the *implicatum*), either T-T or T-F or F-F.

ad (3) F(x) contradicts G(x) iff T-F or F-T (contradiction is characterized by binary disjunction of the universe of discourse).

ad (4) F(x) is in contrary opposition to G(x) iff either T-F or F-T or F-F (contrariness is characterized by ternary disjunction of the universe of discourse in the sense that both events can be rated false and the relation is still determinable; see the diagram above).

ad (5) F(x) is semantically compatible with G(x) iff any combination of truth functions is admitted (either T-T or T-F or F-T or F-F). This seems to be the general characterization of compatibility. Note, however, that under the restriction of the discussion of natural integers to $n > 2$ the combination F-F must be disallowed since only '2' is neither odd nor divisible.

As has already become clear from (1) to (5), only events with the characteristics of (5) (and, by that token, of 'ad (5)') are independent of one another (i.e. their truth values are independent); the rest are dependent in that some sort of implicative relation holds (the truth values of x and y are not independent of one another).

From this follows that we can speak of different types of *incompatibility* all of which, however, share one feature, namely that of dependency of some sort ('compatible (x,y) $\rightarrow$ independent (x,y)' and, by the law of contraposition, 'dependent (x,y) $\rightarrow$ incompatible (x,y)').

The types of incompatibility are the following:

(A) *dependencies stated in terms of meaning postulates with the implicator or implicator negated*

(a) $F(x) \rightarrow \neg G(x)$ as the relating meaning postulate (T-F)
(b) $\neg F(x) \rightarrow G(x)$ as the relating meaning postulate (F-T)
(c) $F(x) \leftrightarrow \neg G(x)$ as the relating meaning postulate (T-F or F-T)

In addition to an implicative connection of some sort (a) through (c) have in common heterogeneity of the attributable truth values. Let us call this truth-functional (or extensional) incompatibility (*Unverträglichkeit* in Lang's terminology). Consequently, truth-functional compatibility requires sameness of truth values.

(B) *dependency stated in terms of inclusion or deduction*
A second type of interrelation of events can be stated by means of the inclusion relation. Incompatibility as caused by inclusiveness can be defined in such terms as 'there must not hold an inclusion relation such as $F(x) \subset G(x)$'. Note that this definition is subject to intensional interpretation in that inclusion relations can be established with respect to very idiosyncratic evaluative systems ('y deducible from x' instead of 'x included in y').

It would seem that incompatibility as caused by redundancy would have to be included under (B) in the case of tautological but not of deducible redundancy. Note, however, that the term 'redundant' is applicable only on the basis of what can be presupposed from speaker and addressee and their systems of knowledge. It is thus a criterion that plays a role in the conversational postulate 'be relevant' which, among other things, is as much as 'do not be redundant'). It will hence be an important criterion within the grammar of conjunctions (*but*, *and*, etc.; see Lang 1974:184ff.), but I have no clear notion what its import is in the discussion of metaphor.

(C) Distinctiveness and non-distinctiveness do not help to decide between compatibility and non-compatibility. In other words, there is room for distinct and non-distinct meanings in both dependent (and thus incompatible) and independent meaning relations.

The range of dependent (incompatible) meanings is determined by the following relations (Lang 1974:173):

(d) incompatible (x,y) → dependent (x,y)
(e) independent (x,y) → compatible (x,y) (from (d) by the law of contraposition)
(f) incompatible (x,y) → distinct (x,y)
(g) non-distinct (x,y) → compatible (x,y) (from (f) by the law of contraposition)

What status have violations of subcategorization rules in this framework, and inhowfar is this type of deviation included in that of the more general deviation of 'non-compatibility'? What both strict subcategorization and selectional rules state – explicitly as minus-features, or else implicitly, i.e. by redundancy rules which have the general form '+X → —Y' – is that, given a number of properties in the form of grammatical categories or semantic features, a number of other properties are excluded. These restrictions are further characterized by being bound to the syntactic-logical frame of the verb. What this amounts to can be explained more generally by restrictions on the logical rule of predication thus leaving open a much wider field of application: The restriction on *read*, in one of its meanings, to [+[+Human] — ...] is to be understood as 'among the predications that the grammatical subject of *read* can receive there must be none that is [-Human], directly or by implication'. It goes without saying that this rule of predication tolerates definitions of compatibility of any grammatical relation in the sentence, not just of the verb-dependent ones. Thus, *the legible amoeba* is highly unacceptable because 'among the possible predications of the grammatical attribute of *amoeba* there is none that can be deduced as [+Legible]', a restriction which is better treated as deriving from 'among the predications that the grammatical object of *read* can receive there is none that is [+Amoeba]'. I will discuss below that it seems to be a universal characteristic of the interpretation of such a structure that the normal reading of the predicate remains unaffected whereas the predicated arguments are subject to a change of properties such that the incompatibility relation is suspended.

4.3 The thesis as stated in 4.1 requires some modification in the light of the discussion in 4.2. 'Contradiction' in its non-technical sense is rendered more adequately by 'non-compatibility' – non-compatibility, that is, between the semantic characteristics of one part of the sentence and the remainder: in the example above, incompatibility between 'all cats' and 'are black'. As far as I can see this 'part' and 'remainder' resembles Black's metaphorical *focus* and the *complementary frame* of the sentence (Black 1962:28). As we have seen from (20), this focus can, but need not, be one single word. Black's example is:

(28) *The chairman plowed through the discussion.*
(which is as much as 'The chairman presided over the discussion with complete disregard for the opinions of other participants')

Here the focus is the single *plowed.*

As far as I can see, the meaning of the metaphor in (23) has to be analyzed similarly.

(23) *Man is a wolf.*

The topic in (23), *man*, raises a particular expectation regarding the selectional features of the predicate of the rheme which follows. Among these features there are some which are incompatible with those of *man.* Because of the expectation that the utterance in question must have some meaning (one of the prime conversational postulates, cf. Grice (1970)) we search for possibly low-priority (and possibly not even lexically, but just encyclopedically contingent) features of *man* which are compatible with the lexical features of *wolf* (in Black's terminology: 'common places' in the *wolf*-system) – thus: (Wild) ∧ (Voracious) ∧ (Bloodthirsty)). The search proves successful: Our knowledge permits association of these *definientes* with the *definiendum* MAN. Obviously there are limits to such associations: Presupposing for the moment the system of knowledge that we have intuitively established about this world, both (Animal) and (Plant) would be contradictory to MAN (see figure next page).

I assume that the use of such metaphors as 'the man is a wolf' presupposes the following: Not only is the grammatical subject the theme of the sentence, but it also picks up what has been referred to in the situation which has preceded the speech act 'metaphorical commentary'. One can interpret the application of the rule of identification as re-reference

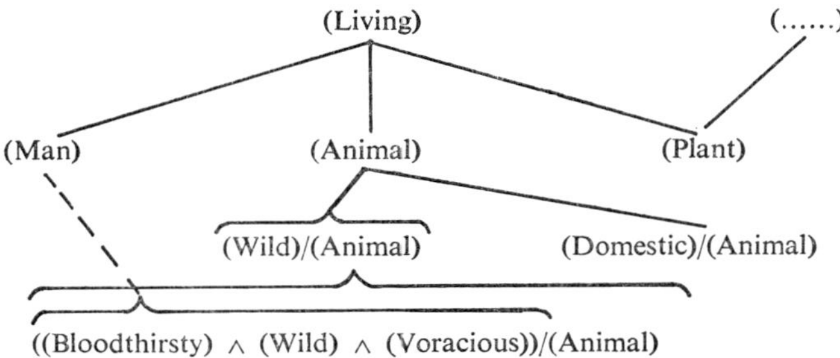

(The unbroken branches are meant to mirror 'semantically implicative' ('normally' associative) relations, whereas the broken branches render encyclopedic (contingently deducible) relations which can be established in particular worlds.)

Fig. 2

to what is contextually known (either situative or uttered), whereas the rule of predication attributes a new property to an object thus identified. This new property serves as a parameter in the search for compatibility with the argument which may be contrary to what is manifest in the lexical semantics (cf. ((Bloodthirsty) ∧ (Wild) ∧ (Voracious)) / (Animal) in semantic relation to (Wild) / (Animal), ((Bloodthirsty) ∧ (Wild) ∧ (Voracious)) in the newly elicited (encyclopedic) relation to (Man)). This explains why one would reject a seemingly meaningless utterance (one for which one has not established associations that make incompatible predications compatible) with words such as '(Non-sense!) Man is no wolf', which is to say as much as 'I have checked the predicate which has been attributed by you to the argument, and found it not correct: *man* must receive a different predicate'.

What is this operation of 'making compatible' on the basis of the parameter 'is a wolf'? As far as I can see it has two main characteristics. One is the 're-topicalization' of features within the semantic analysis of a particular concept (this can also be regarded as shifting a feature of thematic dominance from the head of such a semantic concept (in Fig. 2, this would be (Animal)) to one of the satellite (determining) features (like (Bloodthirsty) above). The second is an operation which might be called 'short circuiting' chains of implication in the sense that to establish an association between a 'topicalized' feature in one chain ('(Bloodthirsty)') and a feature in a different chain ('(Man)'), for the time of this operation, the old semantic hierarchy (i.e. the chain of implication concepts from the bottom to the top ((Living) in Fig. 2) is partially upset.

Under this interpretation, any metaphor – in contrast to the literal use of the utterance – is a world creating relation: 'world creating' because it posits new conceptual structures (involving encyclopedic features, establishing new priorities in the structure of the literal meaning), 'relation' because this reorganization of concepts which yields the metaphorical meaning is elicited by the relation with the literal meaning of the metaphorical frame. Black (1962:41) says about the *wolf-man* metaphor: "... any human trait that can without undue strain be talked about in the 'wolf-language' will be rendered prominent, and any that cannot will be pushed into the background. The wolf-metaphor suppresses some details, emphasizes others – in short, *organizes* our view of man" [my italics – W. A.]. Quite obviously, in the transfer of features of *wolf* onto *man*, the latter does not receive *all* properties of *wolf*: The feature (Animal), for example, is excluded since incompatible with (Man). Thus, the production of metaphors as well as their interpretation are subject to conventions which relate to our systematic knowledge of the world. It would require a very particular effort (i.e. the constitution of a particular possible world, quite different from the world of our normal experience) to deduce (metaphorical) meaningfulness for 'the mess-tin is a wolf', simply because the encyclopediae of the two concepts have no obvious compatible decompositional entities in common – outside the uppermost common implicate (Physical Object), which seems trivial and cannot account for compatibilities within this range.

5. REMARKS ON THE ROLE OF THE CONCEPTS 'LITERAL MEANING' AND 'ACCEPTABILITY'

5.1 *The Notion '"Re-topicalization" of Features'*

I would first like to make a few remarks on the term 'priority of a semantic feature'. The argument and the illustrations are borrowed from linguistic and technical considerations about information retrieval systems. The non-technically minded reader might want to skip this discussion up to the point where the conclusions for the problem of metaphor are drawn (p. 38 bottom).

The following noun phrase is a descriptor taken from the vernacular of criminal law which was analyzed with the aim of setting up an information retrieval system (cf. Abraham 1973b).

(31) UNZUCHT MIT ABHÄNGIGEN: (Geschlechtlich) / (Tun) ∧ (Sittlichkeit) / (Fehlen) ∧ (Selbständigkeit) / (Fehlen) / (Beziehung)

[Translated for illustration only:

(31') IMMORALITY WITH DEPENDANTS: (Sexual) / (Activity) ∧ (Morals) / /(Lack) ∧ (Independence) / (Lack) / (Relation)]
'/' is a functor mediating between the preceding modifier and the head which is modified, as in 'sexual activity', 'lack of morals', 'relation of dependence'; in our analysis above, the first two conjuncts correspond to the meaning of *immorality*; *with dependants* is rendered by the third conjunct.

Now, according to the axiomatics of canonical logic, the conjuncts of '∧' are commutable, i.e. none has priority over the rest. On the other hand, the scope relations of the functors '/' und '∧' are such that the scope of the logical conjunctor is more general than the scope of the '/'-functor. Quite obviously, however, we shall have to set priorities among the complex components connected by the logical conjunctor. Note that if we tried to provide hyperonyms of the conjuncts in accordance with functional priority (the scope of '∧' ranges over the scope of '/') we would be left with (Fehlen) in the second conjunct as the hyperonym over the more complex component (Sittlichkeit) / (Fehlen). Although formally correct this would be a very unsatisfactory result. For in the representation of the meaning of 'Unselbständigkeit' the 'semantic head' ('core', 'theme'; in the terminology of retrieval systems: the 'descriptor' which subsumes the meaning of its privatives and of accepted meaning complexes which further modify the descriptor, and which is therefore the trigger element for all derived elements in the retrieval system) is not the privative feature (Fehlen), but rather (Selbständigkeit). This is one of the reasons why, within our formal system, features like (Fehlen) are elements of a class of 'function words'. The latter are deleted whenever hyperonyms are derived. In accordance with this principle, the first step in the process of 'hyperonymizing' yields:

(31a) (Geschlechtlich) / (Tun) ∧ (Sittlichkeit) ∧ (Selbständigkeit) / /(Beziehung)
[(Sexual) / (Activity) ∧ (Morals) ∧ (Independence) / Relation)]

And the last step finally yields:

(31b) (Tun) ∧ (Beziehung) ∧ (Sittlichkeit)
[(Activity) ∧ (Relation) ∧ (Morals)

Clearly this is not satisfactory either since (Activity) and (Relation) are but weak semantic constituents of the definienda IMMORALITY and

DEPENDENCY, respectively. Therefore two more types of priority are introduced: one which topicalizes on the level of components and a second which topicalizes on the level of the single feature.

An example of topicalization *on the level of components* (the higher the integer preceding the component the higher its priority):

(32) UNZUCHT MIT ABHÄNGIGEN: 2 (Geschlechtlich / Tun) ∧ 2 (Sittlichkeit / Fehlen) ∧ 1 (Selbständigkeit / Fehlen / Beziehung)

An example of topicalization *on the level of features*:

(33) UNZUCHT MIT ABHÄNGIGEN: 1 Geschlechtlich / Tun ∧ 1 Sittlichkeit / Fehlen ∧ 2 Selbständigkeit / Fehlen / 1 Beziehung

Consequently we have three types of topicalization (priority) the cyclic application of which yields intuitively correct hyperonyms:
(a) topicalization on the level of the single features;
(b) topicalization on the level of components;
(c) formal priority.

By virtue of the feature priorities, the elements of the class of 'function words' receive zero-priority and are thus ranged lower than the other elements. In what follows I illustrate the derivation of the intuitively correct hyperonym which results from the cyclic application of the three types of topicalization:

(34) UNZUCHT MIT ABHÄNGIGEN:
(34a) 2 (1 Geschlechtlich / Tun) ∧ 2 (1 Sittlichkeit / Fehlen) ∧ 1 (2 Selbständigkeit / Fehlen / 1 Beziehung)
(34b) 2 (1 Geschlechtlich / Tun) ∧ 2 (1 Sittlichkeit / Fehlen) ∧ 2 Selbständigkeit / 1 Beziehung
(34c) 2 (1 Geschlechtlich / Tun) ∧ 2 (1 Sittlichkeit / Fehlen) ∧ Selbständigkeit
(34d) 2 (1 Geschlechtlich / Tun) ∧ 2 (1 Sittlichkeit / Fehlen)
(34e) 1 Geschlechtlich / Tun ∧ 1 Sittlichkeit / Fehlen
(34f) Geschlechtlich ∧ Sittlichkeit
[(Sexual) ∧ (Morals)]

What all this amounts to is that the ordering of the feature components in a list of descriptors of the thesaurus type – the basis for a retrieval system – is not arbitrary. Representation of this ordering by means of numerals is but one of several possibilities. What this example from information retrieval should demonstrate is the plausibility of the assumption that different priorities apply among the logical conjuncts.[3]

In our last example this assumption serves to show which steps are necessary in the derivation of hyperonyms. Applied to the interpretation of a metaphor this is a process which must depart from the normal ordering of (complex) features of a lexical meaning: Features with low priority in the normal meaning of a lexeme (which contribute only marginally to the meaning of a lexeme or which do not contribute to the 'normal' meaning at all) have to be given higher priority (have to be 're-topicalized') in a semantic analysis that remains unchanged otherwise. This seems necessary if compatibility between the normal meaning and the derived (metaphorical) meaning of one and the same lexeme, and thereby understandibility, are not to be lost.[4]

Provided that the following is an adequate inductive assumption about how the meaning of a word constitutes itself: *the normal word meaning (the meaning of a lexeme) is an ordered set of hypotheses with respect to the proper use of this word, i.e. hypotheses which are not contradicted and which do not become irrelevant for the constitution of this meaning, within a non-irrelevant time span in which the word sign is exposed to communicative use within one speech community*; then the interdependency between this definition in inductive terms and our terms for the semantic analysis of natural language amounts to this: The hypotheses can be considered as options between pairs of predicates, where the single elements of these pairs are mutually exclusive. The predicates can be seen as confirmatory of the property which is predicated of the thing that is signified by the word (lexeme). Note again that such pairs of predicates are contradictory, i.e. they are realized either as antonyms such as *fast / slow*, or else they are made mutually exclusive by means of negation, such as [$\pm$ Human] (see Cohen/Margalit for this line of reasoning). This is in line with the insight prevalent in the traditional linguistic view that 'literal meaning' (= normal meaning) is not immutably manifest, but is quite obviously inferred inductively by the single speaker of a language in the course of his linguistic development and is (consciously or unconsciously) subject to continuous verification. Catechresis, diachronic change of meaning, etc. result when the normal status of words or lexicalized phrases is lost.

It seems that this type of norm can be adequately applied only to names or relators of classes of things which are used with considerable frequency by a considerable class of speakers within a linguistic society. In contrast to this norm based on frequency of use, there is the norm based on definition such as is found in purely artificial languages, and possibly (more or less strongly) in partially defined languages (professional vernaculars) in proportion to the extent that natural language is involved. Now, what is the philosophical basis of the 'explanation' given above that *semantic features are replaced by encyclopedic features*? The direction in which an answer can be found is outlined by Black (1962:40). This is what we can conclude from his argument for the concept of the *system of associated common places*: The literal use of a word (the standard meaning, the meaning in the lexicon) is a set of opinions about (attitudes toward) the *designatum* of the lexeme which becomes manifest in continuously reiterated, and thus continuously verifying, situations. Such sets of opinions must be typical of coherent groups of speakers and will, in a naive sense, be statistically significant of these groups. It goes without saying that these opinions can contradict opinions shared by other groupings: for example, those using a professional vernacular. The set of opinions of this characterization, within the particular group of communicators, is that set which can be evoked under the fewest possible restrictions (as to contexts, situations, etc.). It corresponds to that set of opinions which can reasonably be supposed to be held by every other representative of the communication group. (This concept is equivalent to the notion *expectancy norm* which has been used for a theory of style: see Abraham/Braunmüller 1971.) It is for this reason that one can plausibly speak of the meaning of a lexeme in isolation and contrast it with meanings that are evoked only by specific contexts or situations. The search for an interpretation of a word which is incompatible with its frame, verbal or other, is the search for a context (manifestable within a world which is (partially) distinct from the original world) within which it is compatible.

In what follows the process of communication of priorities ('re-topicalization') is illustrated. Each semantic feature is placed in parentheses; '$\wedge$' is the logical conjunctor, '$\vee$' stands for 'and / or'. – I do not avoid redundancy of features, since my only aim is to illustrate the association of the use of the word with reference to a particular world (the world of standard German as I use it). – The colon divides the *definiendum* and the *definiens* which is made up of semantic features. The features need not necessarily be primitives.

ad (26) (I leave undecided whether or not this example is to be counted as a metaphor. In fact, it will be my argument that such processes as the following are necessary to explain compatibility of words quite beyond, or below, the extreme of the metaphor):
KATZE(x): (Säugetier(x) $\wedge$ Haustier(x) $\wedge$ Felltier(x) $\wedge$ Mäuse-

fresser(x) ∧ .... ∧ (Weiß(x) ∨ Braun(x) ∨ ∨ Gefleckt(x) ∨ .... ∨ Schwarz(x) ∧ ...) in the context ((Schwarz) / (Nacht) (y))

⇒

(Schwarz(x) ∧ ....)

[The semantic feature *Schwarz*(x) belongs to the *common place associations* of *Nacht*; it must be retrievable by means of a redundancy rule of the following sort: (Nacht(x) → Schwarz / Nacht(x)].

ad (23) MENSCH(x): Säugetier(x) ∧ Mensch(x) ∧ Zweibeinig(x) ∧ ∧ Sprache(x) ∧ Vernunft(x) ∧ Verstand(x) ∧ ... in the context WOLF(x) ⇒ Wild(x) ∧ Aggressiv(x) ∧ ∧ (Gefräßig(x) ∧ Blutrünstig(x) ∧ ...)

where WOLF(x): Wild(x) ∧ Aggressiv(x) ∧ Gefräßig(x) ∧ Blutrünstig(x) ∧ Säugetier(x) ∧ Hund(x) ∧ Vierbeinig(x) ∧ ∧ ...

[The incompatibility in the relations Mensch(x) → ¬Hund(x) and Hund(x) → ¬Mensch(x) is cancelled by re-topicalization].

ad (20): SICH DURCHFRESSEN(x,y): (Mensch(x) ∨ Tier(x)) ∧ Kauen(x) ∧ ∧ Verdauen(x) ∧ (Eßbar / Nahrung(y) ∧ ∧ (Sehr viel / Nahrung(y)) ∧ (Mühevoll / Arbeit(x) ∧ ...) in the context BERG VON KORRESPONDENZ(y)

where BERG VON KORRESPONDENZ(y): (Brief(y)) ∧ (Viel / Arbeit(y)) and where furthermore the following meaning postulate must be valid: (Viel / Arbeit(x)) → (Mühevoll / Arbeit(x))[5], the compatibilities for sentences (21), (22) and (24) are to be derived in a similar way. (25), however, is more complex in that at least two incompatibilities are involved: for one the inherent 'HELL(Licht) : DUNKEL(Schatten)', and secondly the explicit identity relation *Licht* = *Schatten* which is contradicted by the following meaning postulate:

Schatten(x) > Licht(y,x) ('>' ... 'presupposes')

where *Licht* has the interpretation of *Lichtquelle* (source of light). In both cases the non-compatibility can be cancelled by reference to *Gott*: in the first case by means of the re-topicalized complex feature (Absolut / Klarheit(x)) for Gott(x) – possibly with the further presupposition postulate *Klarheit*(x) > *Sichtbarkeit*(x) > *Helligkeit*(x); in the second case, a characteristic like *Quelle allen Lichts*(x) [source of all light], inferable from the feature *Weltschöpfer*(x) [creator of the world], must be retopicalized for *Gott*. Under my interpretation there is a third non-compatibility to be resolved: in contrast to *Licht*, *Schatten* has the feature *Kontour eines Objekts*(x); this feature is given higher priority the semantic analysis by a predicate like *ist die Quelle allen Lichts*(x) for *Gott*(x). (It is unclear to me whether this observation is of any general value.)

5.2 *Remarks on Acceptability and Grammaticality*

Metaphors are interpretable sentences or syntactical structures of otherwise diminished acceptability. It is not implausible to assume that an important factor in the interpretability of an utterance is the degree of its acceptability.[6]

One can consider acceptability as a kind of grammaticality in so far as grammatical sentences or complex constituents (e.g. *the leg of a table*, *the leg of the girl*) can be thought of as those sentences or complex constituents that are stored in a state of memory at a particular point of time, plus the sentences or constituents which are derivable through all generative rules which operate recursively on the set of the stored sentences (Kintsch 1972:278ff.). The semantic consistency of these sentences is controlled by a set of meaning postulates which is non-open at this particular time. Every time the generative rules operate under control of a particular set of meaning postulates a set of semantically acceptable sentences is produced. That is to say, given $\{p^t\}$, the set of sentences generated by the recursive rules operating at a particular point in time and consistent with a particular set of meaning postulates, an arbitrary sentence q at that point in time is *semantically acceptable* iff $q \in \{p^t\}$, and it is *semantically unacceptable* at that point in time iff $q \notin \{p^t\}$.

(35) $(\forall q)\ [q \in \{p^t\} \leftrightarrow$ ACCEPTABLE$(q)]$

Assume now that, given the set of well-formed (= stored and derived) and consistent sentences $\{p_o^t\}$, we have to change (expand or restrict – this is what every alteration can be brought down to) the range of underlying meaning postulates such that new criteria arise for semantic acceptability; then, in every alternative world (i.e. under every set of meaning postulates which differs from the original one) a loss of acceptability results in contrast to the primary world. The loss of acceptability increases gradually as more shifts in possible worlds are necessary in order to make interpretable a particular proposition which is not an element of $\{p_o^t\}$. The set $\{p_i^t\}$ is then of *i*th degree of non-acceptability if *i* denotes the number of meaning postulates which have to be changed in the primary set, with $i = 1, 2, \ldots, n$. ($\{p_o^t\}$ is the set of sentences which is stored in the state of memory at the time t, where $\emptyset > i$.)

All this amounts essentially to saying that the directly stored sentences together with those sentences which are derivable by grammatical processes and which are not ruled out as inconsistent with a particular view of the nature of things, $\{p_o^t\}$, are generated on the basis of a state of the lexicon which has been constituted at some point in time *t*. In this state the lexicon will include the following meaning postulates:

(36) Trommeln(x) → [Dumpf / Ton](x)
[Trommel / Schlagen(z) ≡ Trommeln(z)] } lexical rules

To make interpretable the metaphorical use as in (22) (see p. 11f.) a new rule derived from encyclopedic knowledge must be added. By encyclopedic knowledge I mean those parts of our individual private experience which have somehow become intersubjective and which we share.

(37) *Der Regen trommelt auf das Dach*
(38) [*Das harte und schwere Fallen des Regens auf das Dach*](x) → [*Dumpf* / *Ton*](y)

If this rule is instantiated frequently enough and can therefore be anticipated it enters the rules of the temporary lexicon at a particular point of time.

At this point such a metaphorical use must be listed in the dictionary. Any other metaphorical interpretation has to be found by way of new encyclopedic rules (see chapter 5.1.).

In what follows, these assumptions are further illustrated. Quite obviously, (35) is more acceptable than (36).[7]

(35) FRESSEN (Katze, Maus) $\in \{p_o\}$
(36) FRESSEN (Mann, Katze) $\in \{p_k\}$
where 0, 1, ..., k, ...

One can think of the following meaning postulates to account for the gradual decline in acceptability:

(37) for p_o: *Maus*(x) → [*Futter für Katze*](x) → *Eßbar*(x)
for p_k: *Katze*(y) → ¬[*Futter für Maus*](y) ∧ [*Futter für größere Tiere als die Maus*](y) → *Eßbar*(y)

To these we must add the redundancy rule: *Tier*(x) $\rightarrow$ $\neg$*Mann*(x), *Mann*(x) $\rightarrow$ $\neg$*Tier*(x). What makes a sentence such as may be derived from (36) still acceptable, though to a lower degree, is that it can be given an interpretation on the basis of the sameness of the *implicate*, *Eßbar*(x), in the two meaning postulates of (37). Let us now look at sentences of even lower acceptability:

(38) *Die Katze frißt die Wolle.* [The cat devours the wool.]
(39) *Die Maus verschlingt das Haus.* [The mouse devours the house.]

Any attempt to interpret these sentences must presuppose the following meaning relations:

(38') for p_{k+n}: *Wolle*(z) $.\rightarrow.$ $\neg$*Eßbar*(z) $\wedge$ *Verschlingbar*(z) $.\rightarrow$ $\rightarrow.$ *Verschlingbar*(z)

(39') for p_{k+r}: Haus(u) $.\rightarrow.$ $\neg$Eßbar(u) $\wedge$ $\neg$Verschlingbar(u)$_{[\text{für } W_1]}$ $\wedge$ $\wedge$ Verschlingbar(u)$_{[\text{für } W_2]}$
where: 1, ..., k, ..., n, ..., r, ...; and where: W_1 = Mäuse von normaler Größe, W_2 = Riesenmäuse

In ordinary discourse such a lower acceptability is indicated by commenting on (38) and (39) with 'under certain circumstances', and possibly (38) 'she was half starved' and on (39) '... in a Micky Mouse adventure'. Beyond p_o we had to add extra features for *Katze*, *Wolle*, and *Haus* to make (38) and (39) interpretable. These extra encyclopedic features characterize a new state of the lexicon, t_i. The decreasing acceptability is mirrored in the analysis by the increasing rate of specification that is necessary to arrive at the eventual sameness of one feature.

If one takes deviation (from normality) as a case of a particular, i.e. *marked*, property, in contrast to non-deviation characterized by unmarkedness, then markedness in this sense of decreasing acceptability will be characterized by *imbalances between states of lexicons* of the sort illustrated above. It should be noted that the notion *imbalance* is crucial here in that it relates a set p_o^t with other sets, p_k^t, p_n^t etc.

In what follows I would like to summarize these assumptions and include observations of the more recent literature on metaphor.

5.3 *Summaries of the Assumptions*

5.3.1 There exists no stable lexicon in the sense that acceptabilities cannot change. Rather, the lexicon depends on mobile encyclopedic knowledge.[8]

By '(systems of) knowledge' I mean the systems of those relations established by meaning postulates and possible extensions of the sort illustrated by (35) through (39), i.e. the inferences necessary to set free an interpretation as metaphorical. Note that along with this assumption the distinction between 'analytic' and 'synthetic' truth of such meaning postulates is dropped. Compare, among others, Quine (1961, chapter 2), who argues that the distinction between 'analytic' and 'synthetic' truth is a gradient rather than an all-or-none distinction. Such a concept is contested in Katz' semantics (see, most recently, Katz 1972:250ff.). Strangely enough, the problem is not at all appreciated in generative semantics.

5.3.2 The characteristics of an unstable lexicon of this sort is such that consistency applies only partially, i.e. to restricted areas of the lexicon, namely those that can be recalled at once. In extreme cases this consistency is restricted to a few single binary oppositions. In particular, there is a great variance within the hierarchies of meaning postulates ('meaning nets'): The number of implicational elements between the 'least upper bound' and 'greatest lower bound', in the terminology of the theory of lattices, varies considerably (see Kintsch 1971 and 1972 for arguments in this direction; see also Abraham 1973a).

5.3.3 The question of the metaphor (like that of deviation from selection rules) can only be solved if metaphor is considered as a contextual phenomenon, while the problem of literal meaning is *also* a problem of the lexeme in isolation (of the 'core meaning').[9]

If metaphor is a phenomenon of context, then metaphorical meaning, in contrast to mere syntactical deviation, can only be elicited by reference to some context within the sentence borders as well as beyond them. In order to motivate the search for an interpretation of any seeming incompatibility it is necessary to expect from the speaker that his communication has meaning and to believe that he expects his utterance to be understood (see the discussion in chapter 1).

5.3.4 Among all possible categorical distinctions the following seem to bear on the problem of metaphor: the distinction between *deviant* and *non-deviant* utterances, on the one hand, and that between *meaningful* and *meaningless* utterances on the other. Only in those cases where 'deviant' and 'meaningful' are likewise applicable can we speak of *transferred meaning* (not necessarily metaphor).

5.3.5 If the feature 'deviant' (= 'not of high acceptability') is attenuated, through frequent use of the deviant element, and provided a different, normal, meaning of the lexical item remains manifest, then the transferred meaning (metaphor) becomes a cliché ('frozen metaphor').

Note that this does not imply that any *tertium comparationis* (based on a LIKE-relation) need be stored in the memory although there should not be any difficulty in retrieving the steps of deduction. It does seem reasonable to make a distinction in principle between metaphorical clichés and metaphorical innovations. What has been understood by a metaphorical cliché ('frozen metaphor') must be described as a meaning transfer that is either directly recallable from memory, or deducible in a straightforward way – more often than not, both possibilities will be present. In the case of metaphorical innovations, it is only by means of usually less straightforward deductions that a common *implicatum* is arrived at. If this does not yield a result, an interpretation on the basis of meaning transfer is excluded.

		highly non-deviant (= normal)	deviant	meaningful: meaning transfer	
				directly recallable from memory	recallable by deduction
metaphorical meaning	metaphorical cliché ('frozen metaphor')	–	+	+	+
→ transfer →	metaphorical innovation	–	+	–	+
normal meaning of a lexeme		+	–	+	–

The two characteristics 'deviant' and 'meaningful' have a certain interrelation in that deviance is a function of meaningfulness if it is to be interpreted as metaphor. In other words, this function will be tested as to its possible results depending on verbal and situative contexts and 'expectancy norms'.

5.3.6 Within the structure of a lexicon, the following assumptions will be found to hold:

5.3.6.1 On the question of the ontological status of semantic components – and, by the same token, on the question where consistency or inconsistency are to be taken as constitutive features of the actual world: The view is taken, in the absence of any convincing counter-argument, that neither components ('conditions of verification of the use of the analyzed linguistic item'; cf. p. 23) nor meaning postulates and the relations which can be found to hold between them are aspects of the *reality* or *constitutive features* of some world (i.e. discovered by experience, and therefore descriptive characteristics of this world); rather, they are our *conception* of what some such world (some such meaning) is like (is conventionally adequate) if minimal intelligibility were not to be impeded. The characteristic of these devices (semantic adequacy, non-contradictoriness) of language analysis is therefore not ontological but epistemological and conceptual (this is what we have learned to call a Kantian view; cf. Rescher 1973:91f., in the chapter "What would an inconsistent world be like?"). It is in harmony with the concept of an at least partially unstable state of the lexicon that meaning components can be considered as conditions of verification for the most frequent uses of lexemes. The specific features and their internal structures are therefore generalizations about the use of the lexeme in contexts which fit respective generalizations. Consequently, the meaning components can also be regarded as predicates with whose help the use of the lexeme can be verified with reference to the context (see Bartsch 1971; Abraham 1972:6).

5.3.6.2 Similarly, I see very little justification for assuming that *universal primitive* meaning concepts can be found. Indeed, from the practice of decompositional analysis it is more realistic to conclude that such an analysis cannot do better than to have the lexemes, and eventually also their meaning components, define one another mutually, as is the case in traditional lexicons.

5.3.6.3 Every state of the lexicon must specify the semantic-logical relations which are found intuitively to hold among the lexical items. In a componential analysis these relations must be mirrored in a systematic way. A theory of metaphor working with unstructured clusters of meaning features (as conceived by Matthews (1971)) lacks essential assets of explanatory power.

5.3.6.4 For Matthews (1971:423) violation of selectional rules is a necessary condition for any metaphorical interpretation. Consequently

Matthews regards 'the rock is becoming brittle with age' as not metaphorical, which, however, is counterintuitive and certainly not in line with any traditional interpretation of the concept of metaphor.[10]

The violation of selectional rules is probably a sufficient, but certainly not a necessary condition for the predicate 'metaphorical'. That Matthews' criterion is not tenable is further illustrated by *is*-predications as in 'Man is a wolf' or 'The sound is chilly'. Such violations are not definable in terms of selectional rules, but only in terms of the more general *compatibility* rule. Beyond that Matthews' conditions are not sufficient since expectation and contexts (alternative worlds) determine the type of reorganization of the semantic features and consequently also the compatibility or incompatibility of lexical elements.

5.3.7 "Metaphorical meanings of a word or phrase in the natural language are all contained as it were, within its literal meaning or meanings. They are reached by removing any restrictions in relation to certain variables from the appropriate section or sections of its semantical hypothesis" (Cohen / Margalit 1970:482). This means that while constituting the normal (literal) meaning of a word one would have to include all those features ('pairs of variables' in the inductive approach of Cohen and Margalit) which at some time can become relevant for a metaphorical interpretation – provided certain associations with parts from alternative worlds, i.e. from encyclopedic knowledge, are established. The argument of Cohen / Margalit does seem circular since it is the interpretability or contextual compatibility which is not *a priori* lexicalized that makes the metaphor. Cohen / Margalit speak about the order of the meaning components which, for a metaphorical interpretation of a lexeme, is restructured: "Note that in all such cases the variable or variables that have their restrictions removed may be expected to be fairly near the beginning of the ordered sequence of relevant variables. Any such variable must be a fairly important one." This is what was already assumed in Cohen 1971 (684): "... an order of relative importance has in any case to be supposed for the set of distinctive features that characterize a particular meaning. So the less important features will normally be the ones that are exposed to cancellation or deletion in literal usage."[11] But clearly such an order (topicalization, or priority of features over others in our terminology) cannot involve encyclopedic components such that they merge into the constitution of the meaning proper of a particular lexeme since metaphorical interpretability, as we have argued, is more or less dependent upon the system of knowledge that the interpreter has acquired. Clearly also under an assumption like that of Cohen / Margalit it would be difficult, if possible at all, to explain different metaphorical readings that stem from one non-literal, meaningful use of a lexeme, as asserted by different addressees. Cohen / Margalit (1970:485) conclude that there are no semantically deviant sentences in natural languages. Obviously this can only mean that for every semantic anomaly a context can be found which warrants a metaphorical interpretation. Consequently they classify all syntactically well-formed sentences into either *but metaphorically interpretable ones* or *metaphorically as well as non-metaphorically (literally) interpretable ones.* In other words, they exclude meaningless utterances (utterances which are not or cannot be understood). Regardless of whether such an assumption is trivial or not it is certainly wrong under the pragmatic point of view which I have adopted: If the metaphorical interpretability of the use of a word is dependent on the quality of a particular context (a particular world) that can be found then it cannot be excluded that certain users of the language have no knowledge of such alternative worlds (encyclopediae) and consequently cannot interpret meaningfully this use of the word. Unless we want to sacrifice reality for the sake of purely deductive reasoning I think it is necessary to consider also a class of syntactically well-formed, but meaningless (semantically deviant) sentences. Unless we do just that our theory cannot account for the pragmatic truth that very often it is tedious, or impossible, to detect the intended sense behind a deviant structure.

5.4 *Alternative Worlds, Truth, and Metaphorical Processes*

In 5.2 we developed the fundamental assumption that metaphorical processes (more generally, processes of the transfer of meaning) are accounted for in that particular meaning postulates conceived to hold for a particular state of the lexicon are cancelled. Some, or all, of these eliminated postulates can be replaced by meaning postulates which are contradictory to those of the original state of the lexicon.

States of the lexicon establishing relations between lexical items can be compared with *state-descriptions* in the Carnapian sense (*mögliche Welten* in Leibniz' philosophical system, *possible states of affairs* in Wittgenstein's analytic philosophy (*Tractatus Logico-Philosophicus*)). Such a state can be described in the framework of symbolic logic, e.g. of the type that has been developed by Carnap (1958). That is to say all the relations that hold between the lexical meanings that characterize a particular state-description are represented by means of the connectors and operators that are customary in such a symbolic language. Since these meaning relations hold only for particular state-descriptions (particular alternative worlds) it must be determined under which conditions a particular simple statement (an atomic sentence in Carnap's own terms) is part of such a state-description. Such simple statements (atomic sentences) consist of *n*-place predicates followed by *n* individual constants: P(a,b) provided P is a two-place predicate. The state of a whole world is to be described by means of such simple statements. A state-description comprises the totality of atomic sentences which describe the entire world. These sentences are thus true in this world. In how far can the concept of possible worlds add to the explanation of semantic anomalies and meaning transfer? Consider the following example:

(40) *The bachelor is unmarried.*

Provided (40) is an analytic sentence the following meaning postulate must be assumed:

(41) $(\forall x)$ (Bachelor (x) $\rightarrow$ Unmarried (x))

Every anomaly or meaning transfer contradicting this meaning postulate permits two types of explanation:

(a) a sentence, e.g. (40), is analytic and (necessarily) true in the world of (40), (W_{41}). It will then not be analytically true in the world of (42), (W_{43}) (that is it is either synthetic (undeterminable) or else analytically false).

(42) *The bachelor is married.*
(43) $(\forall x)$ (Bachelor(x) $\rightarrow$ Married(x))

(b) a semantic anomaly in W_{41} – which in W_{41} can be accounted for by an atomic sentence with the predicate 'false' – receives a semantic interpretation (= becomes W_{41}-true) of such meaning postulates as (41) or (43) are not valid any more. However, cancellation of such meaning postulates in cases of semantic incompatibility (as between *married* and *bachelor*) is not only interpretable on the basis of a change from W_{41} to W_{43}, but also, as has been explained in chapter 4, by a change of the intensions of one of the incompatible words, which I have described as 're-topicalization of meaning components'.

Let us consider the assumptions (a) and (b) as applied to (44).

(44) *He is a married bachelor.*

Although *married* and *bachelor* are in 'semantic' opposition to one another one can deduce the following as a possible reading for (44): 'He is married, and one would expect him to take over certain obligations with regard to his family, but nevertheless he continues to behave like an independent bachelor.'

If explanation (a) is valid, then the one possible relation underlying (44),

(43) $(\forall x)\ (\mathrm{Bachelor}(x) \rightarrow \mathrm{Married}(x))$

is either not determinable (let us call this case 'C'), that is to say, we must not assume that this relation holds since we do not know whether (44) is analytic or synthetic, or else (43) is determined in that world in which (44) is a statement of analytic validity (case 'D'), that is to say it would contradict (41), i.e. it would not be possible in the world in which (40) is valid (the two worlds are not compatible with one another: their semantics are contradictory, at least within the range of the state-descriptions of (40) and (44) of these alternative worlds, as well as within the range of all necessary inferences about these state-descriptions). From 'D' it follows that (44) is not a meaning transfer of (40); that is to say it cannot be a meaningful sentence with reference to the world of (40). We see, further, that either, in case 'C', Carnapian *L-determinacy* (intersection of all determinacies in all state-descriptions) does not hold, or else that, in case 'D', *L-truth* (truth in all state-descriptions) does not hold for (40) and (44).

Given the metaphorical interpretation of (44) as above I would like to demonstrate that, for an explanation of the metaphor and more generally of the transfer of meaning, it makes sense to depart from the Carnapian concept of L-relations and the relations in alternative worlds. We shall see that this concept will have to be seconded by another concept, namely that of the *(re-)topicalization of meaning components*. To account for the metaphorical interpretation of (44) we can cancel case 'D' since given this alternative no meaningful interpretation of (44) is possible – case 'D' and the analytic meaningfulness of (44) presuppose totally different languages (in other words, *bachelor* and *married* simply do not mean relative to one another what they mean in current English). Any inference from this state-description is idle matter.

Any attempt to make (44) meaningful and interpretable has to proceed from the 'normal' meanings (cf. p. 23) of *married* and *bachelor*. Meaning postulates like (41) are then cancelled; however, the meaning analyses of the two words (the properties or 'intensions', following Carnap's terminology) do not change regarding the set of predicable meaning features but only regarding their relative topicalization. One would have to assume the following topicalization of features in order to account for the analyticity of (40) and (42):

(45) $\text{BACHELOR}_{40}(x)$: Man(x) ∧ Adult(x) ∧ ¬Married(x) ∧ ... ∧ {Single(x) ∧ ... ∧ ¬Monogamous(x) ∧ Home-loving(x) ∧ ...}
(45') $\text{BACHELOR}_{42}(x)$: Man(x) ∧ Adult(x) ∧ Single(x) ∧ Home-loving(x) ∧ Monogamous(x) ∧ ...

(The subscript to the capitalized descriptor lexeme indicates the world in which the meaning postulates hold: '40' for the world in which (40) is necessarily true, and '42' for the world in which (42) is not contradictory.) The intension of *bachelor* is analytic with reference to (41) and (43) (it is *L-true*). If we tried to verify the extension of *bachelor* in W_{4U} we would not encounter any human to whom we could equally assign the two predicates (Bachelor) and (Married). However, if we presuppose an alternative world such that (42) is not meaningless then the intension of *bachelor* must alter in such a fashion that (Married) and (Bachelor) become compatible, or more precisely that BACHELOR can be assigned the predicate (Married); this is brought about by re-topicalization of the semantic components of BACHELOR_{42} and is in line with our intuition. The property (not-Married) has no longer semantic priority within (42), and consequently (43) does not hold any longer. In other words, provided we could vindicate empirically the concept of '(re-)topicalization' of meaning components in the cognitive process, meaning postulates will be functions of the relative priority in which the components appear in meaning analyses like (45) and (45').

Given the status of such features, namely that they have to be assigned to a name (lexeme) in order to verify the use of this name, then we can conclude that the relevance of these features in a particular state-description as conditions of verification for that lexeme decreases the farther we move from left to right. Meaning postulates in the Carnapian sense will then be statements about high-priority components of the meaning analysis of lexemes. It is to be added that despite the cancellation of (41) in the world which assigns meaningfulness to (42) and (44) there remains reference to the L-truth of (41). In other words, it is the never fading consciousness that a cancellation of an analytic system is but short-lived that warrants the status of a metaphor. This is also the basis of every explicit and implicit comparison. In the following descriptive section this is accounted for by the LIKE-relation. Where such a consciousness or fades is missing (*historically*: once such meaning postulates are cancelled in that one or other lexeme associated by virtue of the meaning postulates loses its original conditions of usage; genetically: in the case that interrelated postulates like (41) and (43) have not been constituted yet) we shall have to speak about 'changes of meaning' of a less specific sort, i.e. about 'new' lexical meanings, but not about transferred meanings. The latter, in any case, are characterized by particular reference to some L-determinacy accounted for by a LIKE-relation.

One more remark about the distinction between metaphor and other types of meaning transfer on the basis of the considerations above. It seems that in contrast to metaphor, non-metaphorical meaning transfers such as allegory, fable etc. are based not only on the cancellation of original meaning postulates (such as (41) and (43)) but also on the substitution for them of new postulates. In other words, metaphorical processes are characterized by the restitution of the normal meanings of lexemes whenever the process of compatibilization is run through. However, within an allegory or another type of symbolism which ranges over a whole text ('text metaphor'; see fn. 1) the new alternative world (established by means of new meaning postulates which make equally meaningful a whole sequence of metaphors) is maintained throughout the required text.

5.5 *Induction as the Principle of All Semantic Interpretation*

As will be dealt with in detail below (see section 6) *any* interpretation of a collocation of words in syntagmatic structuring, not only that in metaphor, is based on a hypothesis about the compatibility of the concepts of the words. The compatibility potential of any such collocation is predetermined, and consequently restricted, by the syntactic relations into which the words enter. This assumption, together with that previously proposed on the basis of intuitive, empirical grounds that there is a gradual system of acceptabilities ranging from low to high not to be identified with the categorial bi-modality of syntactic well-formedness, supports the general assumption that any operation of interpretation employs the type of processes which we have provisionally called *interaction* and which later (see 5.2 and 6) will be shown to consist of inductions. That metaphors as wel as other types of meaning transfers are constructions of 'lower face value acceptability' implies that inductive processes (forming hypotheses and trying to verify them) are the determining factor in any kind of semantic interpretation, the differences lying in the number of inferential steps that need to be taken to arrive at some plausible understanding of the structure in question. Only where constructions with a high frequency are employed can one do without the inductive process (i.e. there need be no hypothesizing about the most plausible reading since the construction approaches the status of a cliché).

The concept of metaphor, although not without practical utility for the purpose of intuitive classification of utterances, is better understood as a linguistic phenomenon which, just as in the case of any other *not readily interpretable* linguistic construction, requires us to set in action a *search* for an interpretation. It should be noted that this is in agreement with what cognitive psychologists believe to be the essence of gaining experience or, in other words, 'coming to grips' with the raw sensory data.[12]

6. OBSERVATIONS ABOUT THE 'DEEP STRUCTURE' OF METAPHOR

6.0 The only formally explicit observations about the production and interpretation of metaphor that I know of have been made by Kintsch (1972).[13] I follow Kintsch basically, although not in detail, and attempt to illustrate the formalism with a number of examples. Kintsch's basic assumption is that metaphors can be explained by rules of analogy cast into a format of quasi-predicate logic. This assumption is well founded: It is more or less accepted among those linguists who in their field aim at describing natural language by means of axiomatic systems that a certain, somewhat modified, predicate and relation calculus could yield semantically adequate descriptions of sentence structures. In particular this approach was taken by, among others, Weinreich (1966) and Bierwisch (1969) (see also Abraham (1972)) in an attempt to understand the status of semantic features within the analysis of lexical items. Beyond that, there are observations of a psychological sort which make it probable that the organization of thinking has great affinity to the properties that are characteristic of the predicate calculus (Wygotsky 1962). And, last not least, computational linguistics also simulates natural language by means of logical calculi (Winograd 1972).

In order to account for metaphorical processes (*reception* as well as *production*) the following two steps have to be taken: First, a relation has to be established to sentences of high acceptability, and secondly additional rules have to be presented that describe the type and degree of deviation from these sentences. Consider the following sentence:[14]

(46) *Der Regen trommelt auf das Dach.*[15]

The type of rule violation becomes apparent if we look at the lexical entry: TROMMELN [+ [+ Agent] ___ ...], [where: (Agent) $\neq$ (Caus), but (Agent) $\rightarrow$ (Caus). The attempt to interpret metaphorically a sentence of somewhat less high acceptability than (46) will have to comprise intermediate analytic steps of the following sort:

(47) *Wenn der Regen kurz und periodisch auf das Dach schlägt, dann produziert dies dumpfe Töne so wie jemand, der auf eine Trommel schlägt* ($\equiv$ *der* TROMMELT).

This is a directly acceptable proposition. It is a *metaphor 'in absentia'*, that is to say the substitute is not overt in the metaphorical sentence. We assume then that TROMMELN (*drum*) can only be inserted for SCHLÄGT KURZ UND PERIODISCH in (47) by analogy. This analogy can be expressed in the form of the following inferential schema:

(48) 1st premiss: (*jemand schlägt auf die Trommel*) $\rightarrow$ (*dies erzeugt dumpfe Töne*)
2nd premiss: (*der Regen schlägt kurz und periodisch auf das Dach*) $\rightarrow$ (der Regen trommelt auf das Dach) $\rightarrow$ (*dies erzeugt dumpfe Töne*)

$\therefore$ (*jemand schlägt auf die Trommel*) IS LIKE (*der Regen trommelt auf das Dach*)

Since (47) and (48) are equivalent to the less explicit (47), (47) as well as (48) can be considered as the meaning of (47). The general hypothesis then is this: Given a sentence of low acceptability this sentence is interpretable (understandable) only if an analogy of type (48) can be formed. This type of analogy, then will be taken to be the 'deep structure' of a metaphorical expression.[16]

The following examples (again taken from Kintsch) receive interpretations on the basis of the analogy structure on the right-hand side (after the equivalence symbol. '—' in front of a sentence indicates low acceptability, '+' indicates higher acceptability).

Metaphor "in praesentia":

(49) *Der Nebel kommt auf den Pfoten einer kleinen Katze* $\equiv$ +*Der Nebel kommt, und dies geschieht so weich und unhörbar, wie eine Katze auf ihren Pfoten kommt*

(50) *Der Nebel hüllt die Brücke ein wie ein nasses Tuch* $\equiv$ +*Der Nebel hüllt die Brücke ein, und dies macht sie naß und unsichtbar, wie wenn ein nasses Tuch sie einhüllte*

Metaphor 'in praesentia' means that the substitute as well as the substituted are present in the overt structure.

The more explicit analogy structure of this somewhat compressed form of (50) is this:

(50') *Der Nebel umhüllte die Brücke wie ein nasses Tuch* ≡ *Was von einem nassen Tuch oder Nebel umhüllt wird, wird naß* (≡ *Wenn etwas von einem Tuch oder Nebel umhüllt wird, dann wird es naß*) ∧ *die Brücke wird vom Nebel umhüllt*

The notation in the predicate calculus is this:

(51) [UMHÜLLT($\hat{x}$,nT) .→. NASS($\hat{x}$) ∧ UNSICHTBAR($\hat{x}$)] ∧ (UMHÜLLT(B, N)] where: nT ... nasses Tuch, B ... Brücke, N ... Nebel

The analogy is motivated by the following inferential scheme:

(52) UMHÜLLT[$\hat{x}$,nT N] .→. NASS($\hat{x}$) ∧ UNSICHTBAR($\hat{x}$)
UMHÜLLT[B, N]
―――――――――――――――――――――――――――――――
∴ NASS(B) ∧ UNSICHTBAR(B)

Let us briefly consider once again the question of the order of the meaning components in the semantic analysis of a lexeme in the framework of such inferential schemata. What happened in the case of the metaphorical use of *trommeln* (*drum*) in the frame [*der Regen* _____] ([*the rain* _____]) was a generalization insofar as the restriction of high acceptability, characterizable by the feature [+ Human], was cancelled. Compare with (53) where the topicalization is different:

(53) *Flußbett* = ⁻*Bett des Flusses* (*bed of the river*)

(54) *Inference*: BETT(x) = *A*: zum Liegen(x) ∧ zum Schlafen(x) ∧ für den Menschen(x) ∨ für Tiere(x) ∧ ... ∧ *B*: damit man gegen unbeabsichtigte Bewegungen in der vorhergesehenen Position bleibt(x) ∧ ....
Z DES FLUSSES(x) = [damit Wasser in der vorhergesehenen Position bleibt](x)
―――――――――――――――――――――――――――――――
∴ Z = *Bett*

(where under *A* those conditions of use are indicated which are of higher priority than those preceded by *B*).

This example of analogy in the form of an inferential process illustrates the *production of metaphor*. The production of metaphor, in the most general terms, can thus be thought of in the following way: First of all a *tertium comparationis* must be derivable from our empirical knowledge so as to permit a LIKE-relation; such *tertium comparationis* characteristics are compatible with the rest of the meaning components in the semantic analysis of a lexeme such that they can be posited as meaning components of lower priority. Regardless of whether we have to analyze a metaphor 'in absentia' or 'in praesentia', analogy by virtue of a LIKE-relation is a *prerequisite for understandability*. In the case of metaphor 'in absentia' (i.e. where the *comparatum* is not overt) the features to the right of B in (54) are re-topicalized so that they receive the status of high priority components ('*A*-components').

In the case of the *reception of metaphor* this process is obviously inverse to that of production: Given that somebody is confronted with a case of lexical incompatibility; then what he has to assess is a Z as in the inferential scheme above, (54), and what the interpreter of the metaphor has to do is to find those implicates which are likewise valid for the substitute and for the substituted. These considerations have led to the ensuing distinction of *the production* and *the reception* of metaphorical structures.

6.1 *Analogy Rules for the Production of Metaphor*

Let us take again the afore-mentioned example *Regen trommelt auf das Dach* ((46)).

(55)	$Q = R(a,b) \rightarrow S(c,d)$	'wenn Regen auf das Dach fällt, entsteht ein dumpfer Ton'
(56)	$Q' = T(e,f) \rightarrow S(c,d)$	'wenn jemand trommelt, entsteht ein dumpfer Ton'
(57)	$P^* = \text{LIKE}[Q, Q']$	'wenn Regen auf das Dach fällt, ist es, wie wenn jemand trommelt'

The process of searching and explaining in the case of the production of metaphor departs from R and leads from S to T with the test instance P*. The latter function, P*, has to satisfy the following conditions:

(58) $P^* = \{x | x \rightarrow S(c,d)\}$
$T(e,f) \in P^*$
$R(a,b) \in P^*$

(58) states that there is an equivalence class, P*, such that all elements of this class (propositions of the form T, R) satisfy the condition '→ S(c, d)'. (It is only for the sake of the simplicity of presentation that the propositions have only two arguments.) Obviously this class need not be confined to one element; in other words, there may well be more than one metaphorical realization. However, through hypotheses about the elements of this class (here, for example T and R), the set of possible metaphorical realizations is structured in such a way that, in accordance with our empirical knowledge, the adequacy of these realizations is assessed along a *graded scale of equivalences*. In our attempt to evaluate the adequacy of the inference, S(c,d), we can arrive at some equivalences that range lower on this scale, and some that range higher depending on how many of the hypotheses about the correctness and directness of 'R → S' and 'T → S' are in agreement with one another. This is connected with the question of priority in the feature analysis as discussed in chapter 4.

6.2 *Analogy Rules for the Reception of Metaphor*

The schema of inference in the case of the reception of a metaphor (where the *substituendum* is given whereas the *substitutum* is not) involves the same steps as are necessary in the production of metaphor taking except that the conclusion and the first premiss are exchanged for one another. The reason why the reception of metaphor meets with greater difficulties than the production is that especially cases of low acceptability permit a large set of hypotheses which give rise to distinct implicates and which in turn constitute different equivalence classes. Each of these distinct equivalence classes permits the deduction of implicators (substitutes, normal lexical items) of a more or less heterogeneous nature.

The number of possible solutions is enlarged by uncertainty as to the difference or likeness of the equivalence classes and, to a minor extent, as to what the hypotheses of the producer of the metaphor were. I am not able to illustrate the very general remarks made above (most of which are obvious anyway). In what follows I present one possible process of deciphering the meaning of the figurative phrase *schwarze Milch der Frühe* (taken from the *Todesfuge* by Paul Celan).

(59) ⁻(*schwarze* ⁻(*Milch*: *der Frühe*))

lexical hypotheses .... {(weiß) / (ohne Farbgliederung)}

encyclopedic hypotheses .... { (Helligkeit)
(Sichtbarkeit oder Preisgabe alles Wahrnehmbaren) }

⁻(*schwarze: Milch der Frühe*)

encyclopedic hypotheses .... { (unbekannt)
(traurig)
(gefährlich)
(todbringend) }

The low acceptability of this complex metaphor can be located in two positions (':' indicates the positions of incompatability). Compatible (interpretable) structures are yielded by associating certain hypotheses about the (possible) senses of *Milch* and *schwarz*. The features in brackets, which in an inductive approach as is necessary for the interpretation of metaphorical utterances are equivalent to hypotheses about the possible senses of the words in interaction, represent implicates (S) as well as substitutes (R) in the framework of the schemata for the analogy relations.

6.3 *From Deep Structure to Surface Structure*

Given the deep structure of a metaphorical expression, P*, represented by the LIKE-predicate, the problem remains how to arrive from the deep structure at the overt structure of the metaphor. Kintsch (1972) has made very lucid, although far from comprehensive, suggestions which boil down to certain types of *merging rules*. I have nothing original to add to Kintsch's observations.

In the first step, (60), the common implicate of Q and Q' is cancelled (compare (55)-(57)):

(60) $$\left.\begin{array}{l} Q = {}^{+}R(a,b) \\ Q' = {}^{+}T(e,f) \end{array}\right\} \leftrightarrow \not{S}\,(\not{c}, \not{d})$$
$$\Rightarrow \text{LIKE}[T(e,f), R(a,b)]$$

The LIKE-comparison is thus reduced to

(61) LIKE (Regen fällt auf das Dach, jemand trommelt)

6.3.1 Now let us consider the case in which the predicates in Q and Q' are identical:

(62) Q = R(a,b)
Q' = R(e,f)
P* = LIKE(R(a,b), R(e,f))

The first conflation rule (CR_1) has the following format:

(63) CR_1 : P = LIKE[R[(a,b), (e,f)]]

This rule is operative in the case of metaphorical phrases like *Der Nebel kommt auf den Pfoten einer kleinen Katze* where the predicate *kommt auf weichen Pfoten* is common to both arguments, *Nebel* as well as *Katze*. This conflation process doubtless has a number of sub-types all of which are comparable to the type of transformation that Ross has called 'gapping'.

6.3.2 In the case of distinct predicates a different type of conflation has to be considered:

(64) Q = R(a,b)
Q' = T(e,f)
⇒ P* = LIKE[R(a,b), T(e,f)]
(65) CR_2 : P = LIKE[T[(a,b), (e,f)]]

CR_2 is operative in the drum metaphor: *Regen* as well as *Trommler* (*rain*, *drummer*) have *Trommeln* (*drum*) as their predicate.

6.3.3 To keep distinct the metaphors 'in absentia' and 'in praesentia', an optional CR_3 must be added in which the explicit LIKE-comparison is cancelled:

(66) CR_3 : P = T[a,b]

The application of this rule cancels the WIE(LIKE-)comparison in *Der Nebel hüllte die Brücke ein wie ein nasses Tuch* to yield the metaphor 'in absentia' *Der Nebel hüllte die Brücke* (*naß*) *ein.*

6.3.4 In addition to these conflation rules the descriptive operators will have to comprise a number of typical rules which take care of changes of deep cases. The following *rule of personification* (0 ⇒ A) is just one among a great number of possibilities.

(67) Q = KOMM(O: Nebel) .→. [WEICH ∧ GERÄUSCHLOS] (KOMM)
Q' = KOMM(A, I: auf den Pfoten einer Katze) .→. [WEICH ∧ GERÄUSCHLOS] (KOMM)
P* = LIKE[KOMM(O), KOMM(A, I)]
P = KOMM(O, I)

University of Groningen

REFERENCES

Abraham, W.

1971 "Stil, Pragmatik und Abweichungsgrammatik", *Beiträge zur generativen Grammatik*, hrsg. von A. von Stechow, 1-13. Braunschweig.

1972 "The Necessity of Inserting 'Speaker' and 'Hearer' as Basic Categories in a Practicable Grammatical Model", *Theoretical Linguistic Models in Applied Linguistics*, ed. by P. Corder and E. Roulet, 31-47. Brussels.

1973a "Einige formale Eigenschaften von Komponentialanalysen", *Linguistische Perspektiven*, hrsg. von A. P. ten Cate/P. Jordens, 160-78. Tübingen.

1973b "Komponentialanalyse als Übersetzungssprache in einem Dokumentenretrieval", *Praktische Fälle über Aufbau und Funktionsweise betrieblicher Teilinformationssysteme*, hrsg. von H. F. Preiß, 56-113. München, Verlag Moderne Industrie Wolfgang Dummer/Co.

1974 "Deutsch *aber*, *sondern* und *dafür* und ihre Äquivalente im Niederländischen". Forthcoming in *Studien zur deutschen Grammatik*, 2.

Abraham, W./Braunmüller, K.

1971 "Towards a Theory of Style and Metaphor", *Foundations of Modern Poetics*, ed. by S. J. Schmidt (= *Poetics*, 7), 103-48. The Hague, Mouton.

Apostel, L.

1971 "Further Remarks on the Pragmatics of Natural Languages", *Pragmatics of Natural Languages*, ed. by Y. Bar-Hillel, 1-34. Dordrecht, Reidel.

Asch, S./Nerlove, H.

1960 "The Development of Double-Function Terms", *Perspectives in Psychological Theory*, ed. by B. Kaplan/S. Wapner. New York.

Austin, J.

1962 *How To Do Things With Words*. Oxford.

Bartsch, R.

1971 "Semantische Darstellung von Prädikaten", *Linguistische Berichte*, 13, 33-42.

Bickerton, D.

1969 "Prolegomena to a Linguistic Theory of Metaphor", *Foundations of Language*, 4, 34-52

Bierwisch, M.

1969 "On Certain Problems of Semantic Representation", *Foundations of Language*, 5, 153-84

Bierwisch, M./Kiefer, F.

1969 "Remarks on Definitions in Natural Language", *Studies in Syntax and Semantics* ed. by F. Kiefer, 55-79. Dordrecht, Reidel.

Black, M.

1962 *Models and Metaphors*. Ithaca, N. Y.

Carnap, R.

1958 *Meaning and Necessity*. Phoenix.

Chomsky, N.

1964 "Current Issues in Linguistic Theory", *The Structure of Language*, ed. by J. A. Fodor/J. J. Katz, Englewood Cliffs, N. J., Prentice-Hall.

Cohen, L. J.

1962 *The Diversity of Meaning*. London.

1971 "Some Remarks on Grice's Views about the Logical Particles of Natural Language", *Pragmatics of Natural Languages*, ed. by Y. Bar-Hillel, 50-68. Dordrecht, Reidel.

Cohen, L. J./Margalit, A.
1970 "The Role of Inductive Reasoning in the Interpretation of Metaphor", *Synthese*, 21, 469-87.

Communication
1970 *Communication*, 16: *Recherches rhétoriques* [with contributions by J. Cohen, T. Todorov, a.o., and a selected bibliography]. Paris.

Cresswell, M. J.
1973 *Logic and Languages*. London.

Goodman, N.
1968 *Languages of Art: An Approach to the Theory of Symbols*. Indianapolis.

Gregory, R. C.
1970 *The Intelligent Eye*. London, Weidenfeld/Nicolson.

Grice, P. H.
1968 "Logic and Conversation". William James lectures at Harvard. Duplicated.

Helmer, J.
1972 "Metaphor", *Linguistics*, 88, 5-14

Jakobson, R.
1960 "Concluding Statement: Linguistics and Poetics", *Style in Language*, ed. by T. A. Sebeok. New York.

Jakobson, R./Halle, M.
1956 *Fundamentals of Language*. The Hague, Mouton.

Kamlah, W./Lorenzen, P.
1967 *Logische Propädeutik*. B. I. Hochschultaschenbücher.

Katz, J. J.
1972 *Semantic Theory*. New York.

Katz, J. J./Fodor, J. A.
1964 "The Structure of a Semantic Theory", *The Structure of Language*, ed. by J. J. Katz/J. A. Fodor, 479-518. Englewood Cliffs, N. J., Prentice-Hall.

Kintsch, W.
1971 "Notes on the Semantic Structure of Memory", *Studies in Mathematical Learning Theory and Psycholinguistics* (= *CLIPR Publication*, 4). University of Colorado, Computer Laboratory for Instruction in Psychological Research.
1972 "Notes on the Structure of Semantic Memory", *Organization of Memory*, ed. by E. Tulving/W. Donaldson. New York/London.

Lang, E.
1974 *Studien zur Semantik der koordinativen Verknüpfung*. Doctoral dissertation, Berlin/DDR. [Spirit duplicated.]

Leech, G. N.
1969 *Towards a Semantic Description of English*. London.

Levin, J. I.
1970 "Ob odnoj gruppe sojuzov russkogo jazyka", *Mašinnij perevod i prikladnaja lingvistika*, 13, 64-88. [German translation to appear in *Studien zur deutschen Grammatik*, 2, 1975.]

Matthews, R. J.
1971 "Concerning a 'Linguistic Theory' of Metaphor", *Foundations of Language*, 3, 413-26

Osgood, C.
1960 "Some Effects of Motivation on Style in Encoding", *Style in Language*, ed. by T. A. Sebeok. New York.

Price, J. T.
1974 "Discussion: Linguistic Competence and Metaphorical Use", *Foundations of Language* (to appear)

Quine, W. V. O.
1961 *From a Logical Point of View*, 2nd, revised ed. Cambridge, Mass.
Reddy, M. J.
1969 "A Semantic Approach to Metaphor", *CPLS*, 5, 240-50.
Rescher, N.
1973 *The Primacy of Practice*. Oxford.
Richards, I. A.
1936 *The Philosophy of Rhetoric*. Oxford.
Sampson, G.
1975 Review of K. J. J. Hintikka et al., '*Approaches to Natural Language* (1973), *Foundations of Language*, 12, 4.
Siebert, H. J.
1973 "Isotopie der Metapher". Duplicated. Bielefeld. [See also Chapter 6.7.2, "Die isotope Struktur der Metapher", *Lektürekolleg zur Textlinguistik*, von W. Kallmeyer/W. Klein/R. Meyer-Hermann/K. Netzer/H. J. Siebert, I: *Einführung*, Frankfurt/M., 1973 (= FAT 2050).]
Strawson, P. F.
1952 *Introduction to Logical Theory*. London.
Thomason, R. H.
1972 "A Semantic Theory of Sortal Incorrectness", *Journal of Philosophical Logic*, 1, 209-58.
van Fraassen, B. C.
1971 *Formal Semantics and Logic*. New York.
Vygotsky, L. S.
1962 *Thought and Language*. Cambridge, Mass., MIT Press.
Wason, P. C./Johnson-Laird, A. N.
1972 *The Psychology of Reasoning: Structure and Content*. London.
Weinreich, U.
1966 "Explorations in Semantic Theory", *Current Trends in Linguistics*, 3, 240-51. The Hague, Mouton.
Winograd, T.
1972 *Understanding Natural Language*. Edinburgh.

NOTES

* I am indebted to D. Graham Stuart, J. de Mey, and E. Reuland for valuable criticism of an earlier version. I am grateful for the help I received from A. Tomberg in preparing this English version. – A somewhat shortened German version is to appear in *Poetics*.

1 This is NOT identical with saying that all violations of selectional restrictions are potential metaphors, as has been argued by Cohen/Margalit (1970:485) and Reddy (1969:241). As far as this assumption can be understood, it is empirically empty and practically without any value. It seems safe to assume that among the worlds constituting compatible contexts for particular non-literal word uses there are less and more probable ones (worlds that one has less or more difficulty to imagine) as well as those of utmost improbability. It is this sliding scale of probability that makes some poetry obscure upon the first attempt at interpretation, and more understandable, on second thoughts, later.

2 I disregard any redundancy relation since, for the purpose of my argument, completeness of description is more relevant.

2a The subsequent remarks can be considered as a partial instantiation and exemplification of what in formal semantics has been treated as the semantics of *sortal specifica-*

tion (see, among others, Thomason 1972). In the formal semantics of the type van Fraassen (1971) has developed a sentence receives a meaning interpretation in two phases: first, it is evaluated what its sortal selection is and, second, which further conditions make the sentence true or false. Sortal selectivity boils down to what I have called the problem of compatibility (i.e. selectional rules formulated not only for verbs and their arguments, but also between all other clause constituents). The claim is made that Lang's 'postulate approach', on which my exposition is based, can be interpreted in terms of the theory of sortal semantics, whereas sortal semantics has not developed the insights which are expounded here and without which a theory about this sort of problems remains fragmentary.

3 This amounts to saying that the axioms of commutativity and association do not apply to the use of *and* (and *or*) in our retrieval system or in natural language, i.e. that (p *and* q) does not have the same value as (q *and* p) and that (p *and* (q *and* r)) does not have the same value as ((p *and* q) *and* r). For arguments concerning the difference between the logical conjunctor and that of natural language see Cohen 1971 and Strawson 1952 (80).

4 This is in line with the distinction of *nuclear* and *peripheral* semantic features made by Bierwisch and Kiefer (1969:72). What Cohen/Margalit (1970, especially 476ff.) say about the ordering of hypotheses with respect to the proper use of a lexical element is in fact an inductive formulation of the principle of topicalization among semantic features. See also the discussion of some pertinent literature in 5.2.

5 This implicational relation is not reversible, at any rate not in the world which is the basis for an interpretation here: (Mühevoll/Arbeit (y)) → ¬ (Viel/Arbeit (y)).

6 There is an obvious inference to be drawn from this. The use of acceptability (even in this intuitive, otherwise unsupported way) as a criterion to decide whether a lexeme (group of lexemes) within a context is metaphoric or uninterpretable, precludes the distinction between *competence* and *performance*, in the sense, at least, in which Chomsky has introduced it. There is no way of denying that the capacity for metaphorical innovation in language use (both in producing and understanding) has great affinity to, or is even identical with the creative nature of natural language. 'Creativity' is the crucial term here and in dealing with this notion here we do not mean rule-governed creativity 'that leaves the language entirely unchanged (as in the production – and understanding – of new sentences ...)' (Chomsky 1964:59); rather, creativity as it underlies the interpretation of metaphorical productivity in this context, is something 'that actually changes the set of grammatical rules (i.e. analogic change)' (Chomsky 1964:59). Consequently, if rule-governed creativity is seen to belong to the dimension of linguistic competence, as is usually held in generative grammar, then the scope of our observations is definitely not within linguistic competence, but is marked also by features that cannot be thought of otherwise than as belonging to performance. The mere distinction between the different strategies of speaker and hearer in the encoding and decoding of 'interpretable deviations' would suffice to support this conclusion. Note, first, that the speaker of a metaphorical utterance has the intention of being meaningful. Secondly, he takes recourse in different possible worlds (as constituted by atomic sentences and meaning postulates structuring the field of the meaning postulates). Thirdly, he constantly needs to make reference to different levels in attempting to make a deviant utterance meaningful: to different levels of sophistication or to different systems of experience (as in the case of children's utterances), to knowledge of diachronic processes in the language (catechresis), etc. See also Price (1974) for a brief discussion of this.

7 Since I use the orthographic form of words and sentences to indicate semantic categories and propositions I follow the practice of using appropriate German expressions.

8 Such a dependency is also assumed by Bickerton (1969).

9 This is only an expression of awareness of the seeming contradiction between the notion of componential analysis by means of semantic descriptors (or with some kind of 'semantic markers' which are different from lexical items) and the contention that the distinction between analytic and synthetic truth be dropped. This paradox has been pointed out by Sampson (to appear): 'analytic inference' is one which is valid by virtue of the meanings of lexical items occurring in the utterances that express the inference; a 'synthetic inference' is valid only by virtue of hidden premisses which are inferred to be true but are not made explicit. Any 'logical', or 'analytic', decomposition of a lexical item would then be valid by virtue of meaning, thus satisfying the definition of 'analytic inference' and contradicting the definition of 'synthetic inference'. Thus it seems the distinction has to be and can be made after all, irrespective of the context in which a lexical item appears.

It appears to me that this contradiction can only be resolved by assuming also that a lexical item in citation 'carries with it' an operational meaning, i.e. the meaning of the most frequent contexts in which this item would appear and from which the intensional meaning constituents can be derived. This is what one understands by the 'normal' use of a lexical item, and there are indeed heuristic tests to discover these normal meaning constituents: the different meaning components may be concatenated by the 'and/or'-disjunction to verify the necessary and sufficient conditions for the use of a lexical item (see for similar devices Levin 1971, Lang 1974, Abraham 1974, all in connection with the 'typical use' of sentence conjunctions). There is good reason to assume that such 'core intensions' of lexical items exist in memory; were this not so all our lexicons would simply not fulfil their purpose. But it is another question whether the assumption of such normal readings of lexical items have any bearing on the categorical mutual exclusiveness of analytic and synthetic inferences. I believe that the one does not preclude the other in that the normal, implicit verification context for a lexical item is subject to change in all sorts of processes: diachronic, social, genetic – all of which can be subsumed under the term 'isotopy': think, for example, of a fable or an allegory where particular worlds are constituted which, once understood, give rise to particular expectations deviant from the non-allegorical norm.

10 Reddy (1969:240ff.) is critical of the very same point.

11 By the same argument I cannot see in how far the distinction between semantic *core* and *semantic periphery of a lexical entry* made by Bierwisch/Kiefer (1969:72) is necessarily equivalent to the distinction between linguistic and encyclopedic knowledge. As will be shown later in chapter 6, the association between *core-components* as well as *peripheral components* of the meaning of a word, on the one hand, and such meaning elements as would trigger a metaphorical interpretation, on the other hand, can generally only be realized by way of inference.

12 See, for example, Gregory 1970 and Wason/Johnson 1972. My insight into the theses made by cognitive psychology goes back to a discussion with Pit Corder, Edinburgh.

13 I have not been able to get a copy of Altmann's unpublished work on the metaphor which is conceived in the framework of Fillmore's deep case categories.

14 It will turn out that we are inclined to speak about metaphorical use of a word only when a certain threshold of deviation is crossed. While, up to this point of awareness, we would not tend to apply the term metaphor to a particular use of a word, this word use can nevertheless turn out to stray quite a bit from its normal use. On the whole the following observations describe what in chapter 3 had been called 'interaction' – the influence that words within a sentence excercise upon each other to yield the most probable reading of the whole sentence given a particular context.

15 The major part of the illustrations are German versions of Kintsch's examples. See Kintsch 1972.

16 This is where my general analysis of metaphor differs crucially from Kintsch's.

Note, first, that any LIKE-relation that is espoused in the analysis of metaphor just begs the question unless the otherwise recondite reason for assuming this relation is elucidated. Note secondly that Kintsch's LIKE-relations suffer from a serious deficiency in that rules of extensional and intensional format are not distinguished. Of course, the assumption of analogy by way of a *tertium comparationis* for the intensions of metaphorical processes has always played a crucial role, also in traditional literature on this topic. There is nothing original just about this.

'TAAL EN FUNCTIONALITEIT' BEI FERNÃO DE OLIVEIRA

EUGENIO COSERIU

1.1 Der portugiesische Grammatiker Fernão de Oliveira (1507-1581), obwohl in den Geschichten der Sprachwissenschaft, bzw. der romanischen Sprachwissenschaft gelegentlich erwähnt, ist eigentlich fast nur den Lusitanisten bekannt.[1] Und auch die Lusitanisten haben sich bisher fast ausschließlich darauf beschränkt, seine Bedeutung auf dem Gebiet der portugiesischen Phonetik hervorzuheben und seine Angaben zum Zwecke der Rekonstruktion des phonologischen Systems des Portugiesischen in der ersten Hälfte des 16. Jahrhunderts auszuwerten.[2]

1.2 Es stimmt nun zwar, daß uns Oliveira an erster Stelle als Phonetiker, bzw. Phonologe entgegentritt. Von den 50 meist sehr kurzen Kapiteln (eigentlich Paragraphen) seiner 1536 in Lissabon erschienenen *Grammatica da lingoagem portuguesa* (oder: *Primeira anotação da lingua portuguesa*)[3] widmet er in der Tat nicht weniger als 24 (6-29) der Phonetik

1 Der sonst so ausgezeichnet informierte G. Gröber, "Geschichte der romanischen Philologie", *Grundriß der romanischen Philologie* I², Straßburg, 1904-1906, S. 34, verzeichnet seinen Namen ohne Kommentar und dazu noch irrtümlich (als "*Francisco* de Oliveira"); A. Vàrvaro, *Storia, problemi e metodi della linguistica romanza*, Neapel, 1968, S. 28, erwähnt sein Werk neben anderen Renaissancegrammatiken, die "calate negli schemi ereditati dalla tradizione grammaticale classica" und "fondate quasi esclusivamente sulla lingua letteraria e orientate in senso normativo" seien, was für Oliveiras Grammatik kaum oder nur mit beträchtlichen Einschränkungen vertretbar ist.

2 So insb. I. S. Révah, "L'évolution de la prononciation au Portugal et au Brésil du XVIe siècle à nos jours", *Anais do Primeiro Congresso Brasileiro da língua falada no teatro*, Rio de Janeiro, 1958, SS. 387-399 (zu Oliveira: SS. 393, 398), und "Comment et jusqu'à quel point les parlers brésiliens permettent-ils de reconstituer le système phonétique des parlers portugais des XVIe-XVIIe siècles?", *III Colóquio Internacional de Estudos Luso-Brasileiros, Actas*, I, Lissabon, 1959, SS. 273-291 (insb. SS. 281, 286-289); J. Herculano de Carvalho, "Nota sobre o vocalismo antigo português: valor dos grafemas *e* e *o* em sílaba átona", *RPF*, 12, 1962, SS. 17-39 (insb. SS. 5-10, 16). Cf. auch: S. da Silva Neto, *História da língua portuguêsa*, Rio de Janeiro, 1952-57, S. 482.

3 Das Werk wurde in den letzten beiden Jahrhunderten dreimal neu herausgegeben. Hier benutzen wir die Ausgabe von O. Guterres da Silveira, *A "Grammatica" de*

und Orthographie, 13 der Lexikologie (30-42), und nur 6, bzw. nur ein einziges Kapitel, der Morphologie und der Syntax (43-48, bzw. 49). Aber er erweist sich nicht *nur* als Phonetiker, denn seine Ideen im Bereich der Lexikologie und der Morphologie, ja sogar der einzelsprachlichen Linguistik im allgemeinen, sind nicht weniger interessant und originell als diejenigen, die er im Bereich der Phonetik vertritt. Und auch auf dem Gebiet der Phonetik nimmt er eine ganz besondere Stellung ein, wenn wir ihn im weiteren Kontext der Grammatik und Phonetik der Renaissance in der Romania betrachten. Herculano de Carvalho schreibt in bezug auf die Autoren, deren Angaben er sich zu interpretieren vornimmt: "esses gramáticos e ortógrafos não eram foneticistas nem fonólogos (embora talvez mais isto do que aquilo)", und daß ihre Perspektive "predominante e explìcitamente ortográfica" war.[4] Dies gilt sicherlich als allgemeine Charakterisierung auch für Oliveira wie für fast alle Grammatiker und Phonetiker der Renaissance in der Romania (vielleicht mit den beiden einzigen Ausnahmen von J. Rhys und Giorgio Bartoli). Auch stimmt es, daß es sich bei all diesen Autoren um eine methodisch nicht gesicherte 'Beobachtungsphonetik' handelt. Oliveira übertrifft jedoch bei weitem alles, was uns heute für seine Zeit und zum Teil sogar bis viel später auf diesem Gebiet in der ganzen Romania bekannt ist. Durch seine klare Intuition der sprachlichen Funktionalität und der von ihm auch mehrmals in der konkreten Beschreibung angewandten Unterscheidung zwischen den funktionellen, zum Teil nur virtuell gegebenen einzelsprachlichen Schemata ('Sprachsystem') und ihrer Realisierung ('Sprachnorm') geht er andererseits in der Sprachbeschreibung im allgemeinen seiner Zeit weit voraus und erscheint uns als einer der originellsten Grammatiker der ganzen Renaissance.

Den Anstoß zu seiner Beschreibung des Portugiesischen erhielt Oliveira sicherlich von der 48 Jahre früher erschienenen spanischen Grammatik von Antonio de Nebrija,[5] auf den er sich in seinem Werk auch ausdrücklich bezieht; dies beeinträchtigt jedoch kaum seine Originalität, denn er folgt Nebrija keineswegs als bloßer Nachahmer, wie dies einige Jahre später João de Barros[6] meistens tut. Diese Originali-

Fernão d'Oliveyra, Rio de Janeiro, 1954; die in Klammern angegebenen Zahlen beziehen sich auf die jeweils zitierten, bzw. gemeinten Kapitel. In den Zitaten lösen wir die Abkürzungen auf, heben die Beispiele und die Termini durch Kursivschrift hervor und fügen Satzzeichen und bisweilen Akzente hinzu.

4 *Art. cit.*, SS. 19, 20.

5 *Gramática castellana* [*Arte de la lengua castellana*], Salamanca, 1492.

6 *Grammatica da lingua Portuguesa*, Lissabon, 1540.

tät soll eben im folgenden festgestellt, abgegrenzt und hervorgehoben werden[7] in der Hoffnung, eine solche 'Wiedergutmachung' sei im Sinne unseres Jubilars, der mit seinem meisterhaften Buch *Taal en functionaliteit* der Geschichte der Sprachwissenschaft neue Wege geöffnet und uns alle auf so viele zu Unrecht vergessene oder verkannte Namen aufmerksam gemacht hat.

1.3 Freilich ist nicht alles, was bei Oliveira erscheint, positiv zu bewerten. So z.B. natürlich nicht die phantastische Vorgeschichte Portugals, zu der er sich in den ersten Kapiteln seines Werkes bekennt, und die z.T. auf den im 16. Jahrhundert auch in anderen romanischen Ländern so einflußreichen Annio da Viterbo zurückgeht. Außerdem ist Oliveira, wie dies auch bei anderen ausgezeichneten Synchronikern nicht selten ist,[8] ein schlechter Etymologe, und seine sprachgeschichtlichen Vorstellungen sind meist entweder naiv oder irrtümlich. Er lehnt zwar die pseudoerklärenden Etymologien vom Typ *homem* 'porque é *o meio* de todas as cousas, ou porque está no *meio* do mal e do bem', *molher* [*mulher*] 'porque é *molle*', *velho* 'porque *vio* muito', *tempo* 'porque *tempera* as cousas', *pássaro* 'porque *passa* voando' als Unfug ('patranhas') ab (31). Zugleich aber ist ihm die lateinisch-romanische Kontinuität trotz seiner ausgezeichneten humanistischen Ausbildung keineswegs klar und auch in so offensichtlichen Fällen wie *mesa, lume, homem, mulher, livro, porta, casa, parede* ist er nicht ohne weiteres bereit, lateinische Herkunft anzunehmen, denn, wenn so viele portugiesische Wörter auf das Latein und dazu noch andere auf das Griechische, das Arabische, das Kastilische, das Französische zurückgehen sollten, "então que nos fica a nos?", was bleibt uns übrig? Für die portugiesisch-lateinischen Entsprechungen möchte er die Erklärung vielmehr darin sehen, daß die Römer den Portugiesen zwar gewisse Wörter gegeben, andererseits aber auch von diesen bei Bedarf gewisse Wörter übernommen haben (*ibid.*). Auch in diesem Bereich hat Oliveira trotzdem manchen

[7] Für verschiedene seiner Ideen und Fragestellungen zitiert selbsverständlich Oliveira 'Autoritäten' aus der Antike (insb. Cicero, Varro, Quintilian), aber auch dies vermindert kaum die Originalität seines Denkens: In der Renaissance besteht die Originalität eben auch darin, *welche* Ideen man von der Antike übernimmt, bzw. für welche Ideen man Unterstützung in der Antike sucht (Nebrija z.B. folgt vor allem Priscianus, Donatus, und Diomedes; Oliveira hingegen zeigt eine besondere Zuneigung für Varro). Auch allgemein betrachtet darf übrigens der Bezug auf die Antike nicht ohne weiteres als 'Nachahmung' bewertet werden, wie dies leider gerade in der Geschichte der Sprachwissenschaft so oft geschieht. Die Antike stellt nicht eine bestimmte Auffassung, die man als solche übernehmen könnte, sondern eine komplexe Kulturwelt dar.

[8] Man vergleiche z.B. den Fall von L. Meigret in Frankreich oder denjenigen von Gonzalo Correas in Spanien.

guten Gedanken; so bemerkt er, daß es äußerst schwierig ist, die jeweils ursprüngliche Namengebung zu motivieren, denn man müßte dafür auch wissen, wo die entsprechenden 'Sachen' zuerst entstanden sind und jeweils bis zur namengebenden 'pessoa particular' vordringen: "assi que é trabalhoso e pouco çerto querer saber os naçimẽtos particulares das diçōes" (32).[9]

2.0 Die Stärke Oliveiras liegt jedoch, wie schon angedeutet, auf dem synchronischen Gebiet, und hier sicherlich vor allem im phonischen Bereich. Seine unmittelbaren Vorbilder sind in diesem Bereich, abgesehen von Nebrija, höchstwahrscheinlich die verschiedenen Werke zur spanischen Orthographie, die z.T. gerade in der oder um die Zeit erscheinen, in der er sich in Spanien befindet,[10] d.h. diejenigen von Vanegas, Busto, und Robles.[11] Bei all diesen Autoren – die in Spanien eine mit Nebrijas Grammatik sowie mit dessen Orthographie[12] und z.T. noch früher[13] einsetzende und sehr lebhaft gepflegte Tradition[14] fortführen –, und insbesondere bei Busto, findet man in Einzelfällen ziemlich genaue Beschreibungen spanischer Laute in artikulatorischer Hinsicht.[15]

[9] Vgl. auch: "para saber todas estas cousas requere-se ler e ver muyto; e ainda assi alcançaremos pouco, porque avemos de preguntar isto a cada tempo e terra e pessoa muito pello miudo" (31).

[10] Oliveira verläßt nämlich sein Dominikanerkloster in Évora im Jahre 1532 und flieht nach Spanien, wo er sich einige Zeit aufhält. Es wird sogar vermutet, daß er seine Grammatik in Spanien, vielleicht in Toledo, verfaßt hat (so P. Galindo Romeo und L. Ortiz Muñoz in ihrer Ausgabe von A. de Nebrija, *Gramática castellana*, Madrid, 1946, I, S. XL).

[11] A. Vanegas, *Tractado de Orthographia y accentos en las tres lenguas principales*, Toledo, 1531; B. Busto, *Arte pa[ra] aprender a leer y escrevir perfectamente en romance y latin*, o. O., o. J. [aber 1533]; Fr. de Robles, "Reglas de ortographia", Anhang zu seinem Werk *Copia accentuum omnium fere dictionum difficilium...*, Alcalá, 1533.

[12] *Reglas de Orthographia de la Lengua castellana*, Alcalá, 1517.

[13] Schon bei Enrique de Villena, *Arte de trovar*, 1433, erscheinen einige höchst interessante phonische Beobachtungen; vgl. La Viñaza, *Biblioteca histórica de la filología castellana*, Madrid, 1893, SS. 387-391.

[14] Spanien ist nämlich unter den romanischen Ländern im 16. wie auch noch im 17. Jahrhundert das Land der Phonetik. Nach dem einmaligen Nebrija und bis J. P. Bonet hat es zwar keine Persönlichkeit vom Niveau eines Rhys oder eines G. Bartoli auf diesem Gebiet zu verzeichnen, in Spanien ist aber das Interesse für die Orthographie und ihren Unterricht, und dadurch für die Phonetik, sehr weit verbreitet, die orthographischen Werke sind erstaunlich zahlreich und die spanischen Grammatiker bieten nicht selten sehr sorgfältige phonische Beschreibungen und wertvolle Hinweise z.B. zu regionalen Unterschieden in der Aussprache für das Spanische und erstaunlich genaue phonische Beschreibungen für verschiedene Fremdsprachen (insb. Indianersprachen Amerikas).

[15] Vgl. La Viñaza, *op. cit.*, SS. 552-553 (zu Vanegas), 413-421 (zu Busto), 553-555 (zu Robles).

Oliveira übertrifft jedoch alle, selbst Nebrija, durch die Akribie seiner Beobachtungen und durch die Ausführlichkeit und den systematischen Charakter seiner Beschreibung der portugiesischen Laute.[16]

2.1 Die phonischen (oder, besser gesagt, die Ausdrucks-) Einheiten des Portugiesischen identifiziert Oliveira in Übereinstimmung mit der Tradition und mit der Terminologie seiner Zeit als 'letras' ('Buchstaben'). D.h. er gebraucht *littera*, wie dies seit der Antike üblich war, für die phonischen Einheiten und zugleich für ihre graphische Darstellung.[17] Dabei unterscheidet er aber sorgfältig zwischen der graphischen Darstellung als solcher (*figura*, *sinal*) und der entsprechenden phonischen Einheit (*pronunciação*, bzw. *força*, *virtude*): "As figuras destas letras chamão os Gregos *caracteres* e os latinos *notas*, e nos lhe podemos chamar *sinaes*. Os quaes hão de ser tantos como as *pronũçiações*, a que os latinos chamão *elementos* e nos as podemos interpretar *fundamẽtos* das vozes e escritura" (6). Auch diese Unterscheidung ist als solche nicht neu. Sie geht bekanntlich auf die Antike zurück[18] und ist bei den Grammatikern der Renaissance durchaus üblich.[19] Oliveira wendet sie jedoch mit einer Folgerichtigkeit an, die vor ihm nur bei Nebrija und nach ihm im 16. Jahrhundert nur selten anzutreffen ist, und bei verschiedenen 'letras', so insbesondere bei den Vokalen, beschreibt er *figura* und *pronunciação* (die er gelegentlich auch *voz* nennt) jeweils getrennt. Die phonischen Einheiten, die er im Portugiesischen identifiziert, sind im allgemeinen die Phoneme als Segmente, in einem Fall – demjenigen der Nasalität – handelt es sich jedoch um einen unterscheidenden Zug.

[16] Nebrija beschreibt zwar, wenn auch sehr kurz, in seiner "Grammatik" (I, 4) die Aussprache des Lateinischen, nicht aber eigentlich die des Spanischen, die er vielmehr durch Beispiele verdeutlicht; das gleiche gilt für seine "Orthographie".

[17] Es ist dies die sogenannte 'Nichtunterscheidung' bzw. Verwechslung von Buchstabe und Laut, die so oft, jedoch, abgesehen von Einzelfällen, zu Unrecht der älteren Sprachwissenschaft vorgeworfen wird. In Wirklichkeit handelt es sich nicht um eine 'Nichtunterscheidung' bzw. 'Verwechslung', sondern um eine höhere Abstraktionsstufe: *littera* ist nämlich in der älteren Sprachwissenschaft die phonische Einheit, soweit sie durch einen Buchstaben darstellbar ist, und, umgekehrt, die graphische Einheit, soweit sie einer bestimmten phonischen Einheit einer Sprache entspricht, d.h. eigentlich ein Oberbegriff für Laut + Buchstabe (bzw. Phonem + Graphem). Wenn etwas in der modernen Sprachwissenschaft dem alten Begriff *littera* bis zu einem gewissen Punkt entspricht, so ist dies nicht unser Begriff 'Buchstabe' (bzw. 'Graphem'), sondern vielmehr der Hjelmslevsche Begriff 'Kenem'.

[18] Cf. D. Abercrombie, "What is a "Letter"?", *Lingua* 2, 1949, jetzt in: D. A., *Studies in Phonetics and Linguistics*, London, 1965, SS. 76-85.

[19] So unterscheidet Nebrija *figura* und *voz* (oder *pronunciación*); für die Funktion der *figura* in bezug auf die Aussprache gebraucht er *fuerza* bzw. *oficio* (cf. bei Oliveira: *força*, *virtude*).

2.2 Im Vokalsystem seiner Sprache identifiziert Oliveira zunächst acht Oralvokale, indem er bei den 'letras' *a*, *e*, und *o* jeweils das offene und das geschlossene Phonem unterscheidet, die er 'groß' und 'klein' ('grande' – 'pequeno') nennt (8).[20] Er stellt fest, daß das Portugiesische für diese acht Vokale nur über fünf 'Figuren' verfügt ("temos oyto vogaes na nossa lĩgoa mas não temos mais de çinco figuras") und schlägt deshalb für 'a pequeno', 'e grande' und 'o grande' auch neue 'Figuren' vor (α, ε, ω). Ferner identifiziert er als einfache Vokaleinheiten die Nasalvokale: Die Tilde ('o til', d.h. das Zeichen ~), die man zur Kennzeichnung solcher Vokale gebraucht, entspreche keinem 'Wortbauelement', d.h. keinem phonematischen Segment ("mas ãtre nos claro está que não temos voz a qual se forme cõ este elemẽto ou fundamẽto til"), sondern sei eben nur ein Zeichen der Nasalierung: "assi como fazemos do til nas vo-

[20] Diese Termini hängen höchstwahrscheinlich damit zusammen, daß Oliveira die Opposition geschlossen/offen vielmehr als kurz/lang interpretiert (vgl. 27). Barros, der dieselben Termini verwendet, folgt hierin – entgegen der von M. Carvalhão Buescu in ihrer Ausgabe von João de Barros, *Gramática da língua portuguesa*, Lissabon, 1971, SS. LXI-LXII, vertretenen Meinung – nicht irgendwelchen Italienern und einer angeblichen italienischen Terminologie, die in dieser Form einfach nicht vorhanden war, sondern natürlich Oliveira. Unter den früheren italienischen Grammatikern behandeln G. F. Fortunio, *Regole grammaticali della volgar lingua*, Ancona, 1516, und P. Bembo, *Prose della volgar lingua*, Venedig, 1525, die Phonetik als solche überhaupt nicht. G. G. Trissino, *Epistola de le lettere nuωvamente aggiunte ne la lingua italiana*, Rom, 1524, unterscheidet die *e*- und *o*-Vokale nicht als 'groß' und 'klein', sondern als 'offen' und 'geschlossen' und verwendet für ihre Darstellung ε – *e*, ω – *o* (vgl. S. X: "Le lettere adunque, che io primieramente aggiunsi a l'alfabeto latino, furono ε aperto, ed ω aperto"). In späteren Werken (*Dubbii grammaticali*; *Grammatichetta*: beides Vicenza, 1529) verwendet Trissino die Termini 'chiaro, et acuto'/ 'grave, et ottuso'. Den Ausdruck 'grande' gebraucht er in bezug auf das Graphem ω, indem er sagt, daß er 'l'ω grande de i Greci', das er zuerst für das *o* 'chiaro, et acuto' (d.h. /ɔ/) gebraucht hat, nunmehr umgekehrt für das *o* 'grave, et ottuso' (d.h. /o/) gebrauchen werde: Es handelt sich also einfach um den alten und gutbekannten griechischen Namen des Buchstabens ω. Der Vorschlag von Cl. Tolomei, für /ε/ und /ɔ/ die Großbuchstaben E, O zu gebrauchen, ist ebenfalls kein terminologischer und hat auch sonst mit den von Oliveira gewählten Namen nichts zu tun, zumal dieser Vorschlag zu seiner Zeit nicht einmal bekannt war. Der Gebrauch von E, O mit dieser Funktion setzt erst bei G. A. Gilio, *Dialoghi*, Camerino, 1564, ein, und daß dieser Gebrauch einem Vorschlag von Tolomei entspreche, erfährt man erst von G. Ruscelli, *Commentario della lingua italiana*, Venedig, 1581 (d.h. 28 bzw. 45 Jahre nach dem Erscheinen der Grammatik von Oliveira). Vgl. dazu L. Kukenheim, *Contributions à l'histoire de la grammaire italienne, espagnole et française à l'époque de la Renaissance*, Amsterdam, 1932, SS. 37-38. Die Termini, die Tolomei in seinen – allerdings nur handschriftlich überlieferten – phonetischen Abhandlungen verwendet, sind auch nicht 'grande' und 'piccolo', sondern *chiaro* und *fosco*. João de Barros, der – und zwar wiederum entgegen der Ansicht seiner allzu wohlmeinenden Herausgeberin – ebenso offensichtlich wie skrupellos Nebrija abschreibt, indem er von diesem auch zahlreiche Beispiele, darunter sogar Autorenbeispiele, wörtlich übernimmt, ohne ihn jedoch auch nur ein einziges Mal zu erwähnen, muß übrigens stets und grundsätzlich

gaes quando ... mudão sua voz; digo que mudão a voz porque não hé a mesma voz *vila* e *vilã*, mas o til que lhe posemos muda a calidade do *a* d'clara voz em escura e mete-o mais pelos narizes; outro tanto nas outras vogaes como *e* e *ẽ*, *i* e *ĩ*, *o* e *õ*, *u* e *ũ*, onde o til faz alghũa cousa e tem poder alghũ; o qual sintem as orelhas" (16). Als 'elemento' sei also die Tilde nur eine Modifizierung der Vokale, d.h. eben die Nasalität selbst (vgl. auch 14: "sua força é tão brãda que a não sentimos se não mesturada cõ outras").[21] Es darf nun nicht übersehen werden, daß diese Identifizierung der Nasalvokale als einfacher Vokallaute eine besondere Leistung Oliveiras darstellt, denn dies ist das erste Mal, daß die Nasalvokale als solche in der Romania 'entdeckt' werden (und vielleicht auch das erste Mal überhaupt).[22]

---

als verdächtig angesehen werden. Er folgt zwar Nebrija und gelegentlich, wie eben in diesem Fall, Oliveira, er ist aber inkohärent und unkritisch, und oft versteht er seine Vorbilder einfach nicht. Nachdem er im ersten Teil seiner Grammatik, wie Nebrija und Oliveira, bei den 'Buchstaben' zwischen *figura* und *potestas* ('figura' und 'poder') richtig unterschieden hat, verwechselt er immer wieder die beiden Begriffe: So schreibt er z.B. (Ausg. Carvalhão, S. 296), das Portugiesische besitze 23 "lêteras em poder e trinta e quátro em figura", womit natürlich genau das Gegenteil gemeint sein sollte, und im Teil über die Orthographie (ibid. S. 370) spricht er von 26 'poderes', was Nebrija, *Gram. cast.*, I, 5, 2, zwar mit Recht annimmt, jedoch natürlich für das Spanische, nicht für das Portugiesische. Auf einen italienischen Einfluß auf Barros deutet auch sonst in seiner Grammatik absolut nichts hin. Eine Beeinflussung Oliveiras durch italienische Grammatiker (und dafür käme sowohl zeitlich als auch wegen des Gebrauchs von ε und ω nur Trissino in Frage) ist hingegen möglich – wenn auch freilich nicht, was die Termini 'groß' und 'klein' angeht –, sie ist jedoch nicht nachweisbar. Zu einem direkten Kontakt mit dem italienischen Kulturmilieu kommt allerdings Oliveira erst nach dem Erscheinen seiner Grammatik, nämlich um 1540, als er eine Italienreise unternimmt.

21 Oliveira möchte sogar die Nasalvokale stets nur mit der Tilde kennzeichnen und auf Graphien wie *am*, *an*, *em*, *en* usw. verzichten, da in solchen Fällen kein konsonantisches Element, sondern nur ein 'til' zu hören sei: "e eu digo que [o til] é neçessareo todas as vezes que despoys de vogal em hũa mesma syllaba escrevemos *m* ou *n*" (14); "o qual [til] cõ a boca e beiços muy soltos tambẽ soa na mesma forma em todas as syllabas em cujos cabos nos escrevemos *m* ou *n*, errando cõ o costume, porque as letras mudas, de cujo numero são *m* e *n*, ãtre nos nũca dão fim a dição alghũa nẽ syllaba; e isto a esperiençia e propriedade das nossas vozes no-lo ensinão; e por tanto não escreveremos *ensinar* com *n* na primeira syllaba nem *embargar* cõ *m* a imitação dos latinos, poys nos taes lugares antre nos não sentimos essas letras, mas nessas e outras muitas partes escrevamos til" (19). Dieses Prinzip wendet er im Text seiner Grammatik auch meist an, indem er in den erwähnten Fällen, wenn auch nicht völlig folgerichtig, *ã*, *ẽ*, *õ* usw. schreibt.

22 Die im Französischen wahrscheinlich schon im 15. Jahrhundert entstandenen Nasalvokale findet man während einer langen Zeit in Grammatiken und Orthographiehandbüchern als Nexus von Vokal + Nasalkonsonant dargestellt. Sie werden erst von L. Chiflet, *Essay d'une parfaite grammaire de la langue françoise*, Antwerpen, 1659, und von diesem auch nur beiläufig, als 'de vrayes voyelles' angesehen, und erst von Dangeau [L. de Courcillon], *Essais de grammaire*, Paris, 1694, als einfache Vokal-

Schließlich identifiziert Oliveira fast alle Oraldiphthonge und Nasaldiphthonge des Portugiesischen[23] und stellt fest, daß bei letzteren die Tilde (d.h. die Nasalität) jeweils "auf beiden Vokalbuchstaben lautet".[24]

2.3.1 Was das Konsonantensystem betrifft, so gibt Oliveira für die meisten portugiesischen Konsonanten zwar knappe, jedoch im wesentlichen vollständige artikulatorische Beschreibungen. Verschiedene dieser Beschreibungen sind überraschend genau und, abgesehen von der Terminologie, sogar heute noch annehmbar. So zum Beispiel:

Pronũçia-sse a letra *b* antr'os beyços apertados lançãdo para fora o bafo com impeto;
c. Pronunçia-sse dobrãdo a lingua sobre os dentes queyxaes: fazendo hũ çerto lombo no meyo della diante do papo, casi achegando cõ esse lõbo da lingua o çeo da boca e empedindo o espirito, o qual per força faça apartar a lingua e façes e quebre nos beyços com impeto;
A pronũnçiação do *f* fecha os dẽtes de çima sobre o beiço de bayxo ...;
A pronũçiação do *l* lambe as gẽgibas de çima cõ as costas da lingua achegãdo as bordas della os dẽtes queyxays;
Pronũçia-se o *r* singelo cõ a lingoa pegada nos dẽtes queyxaes de çima e sae o bafo tremendo na põta da lingua. Do *rr* dobrado a pronũçiação é a mesma que a do *r* singelo, se não que este dobrado arranha mays as gẽgibas de çima; e o singelo não treme tãto;
x ... pronunçia-sse cõ as queixadas apertadas no meyo da boca, os dẽtes jũtos, a lingua ancha dentro na boca, e o espirito ferve na humidade da lingua;
A pronũçiação do *z* zine antr'os dentes çerrados com a lingua chegada a elles e os beyços apartados hũ do outro (13).

Die Palatalkonsonanten – und dies ist einer der wenigen Fälle, in denen er sich von der Graphie irreführen läßt – nennt Oliveira wegen der Schreibung mit *h* (*ch*, *lh*, *nh*) 'letras aspiradas' (14). Er kommt jedoch darauf zurück und stellt fest, daß diese Laute keine Nexus, sondern einfache Konsonanten sind, die deshalb auch getrennte einfache 'figuras' benötigen würden, und daß es sich dabei nicht eigentlich um Aspiration, sondern um eine andere 'mudança' (Modifizierung) handelt, die er aber

laute ausdrücklich 'entdeckt'. Vgl. M. Ekman, *Opuscules sur la grammaire par l'Abbé de Dangeau*, Uppsala, 1927, insb. SS. 203-207.

23 "Os ditõgos que eu achey antre nos portugueses são estes: *ae* como *tomae*, *ãe* como *pães*, *ao* como *pao*, *ão* como *pão*, *ãy* como *mãy*, *ei* como *tomei*, *eo* como *çeo*..., *eu* como *meu*, *io* como *fugio*, *oe* como *soe*, *oi* como *caracois*, *õe* como *põe*,... *ou* como *dou*, *ui* como *fuy*" (19).

24 "E nos ... sentimos cõ as orelhas que soa ali hũ til sobre ambas as letras vogaes do ditongo: como *escrivão*, *escrivães*" (19).

nicht näher zu bestimmen vermag.[25] Trotz dieser Unzulänglichkeit und einiger anderer geringfügiger Inkonsequenzen im Detail ist die Beschreibung Oliveiras – die erste systematische und ausführliche artikulatorische Beschreibung des Konsonantensystems einer romanischen Sprache – nicht nur bei weitem die beste für seine Zeit, sondern auch eine der besten für eine längere Zeit nach dem Erscheinen seiner Grammatik.[26] Es sei ferner bemerkt, daß Oliveira, wie schon Nebrija, *i-j* und *u-v* auch orthographisch trennt und daß er zudem [j] in Wörtern wie *meio*, *moio* als konsonantischen Laut ("porque não faz syllaba por si") identifiziert und dafür die Schreibung *y* vorschlägt (14).[27]

2.3.2 Noch interessanter als die artikulatorische Beschreibung – und in funktioneller Hinsicht viel bemerkenswerter – ist jedoch die Tatsache, daß Oliveira im portugiesischen Konsonantensystem funktionierende Korrelationen regelmäßig feststellt. In allen Fällen, in denen die Artikulation zweier Konsonanten bis auf die Stimmhaftigkeit die gleiche ist, wird dies von ihm auch ausdrücklich vermerkt; so für die 'Buchstaben' *c-g*, *p-b*, *t-d*, *ss-s*, *ç-z*, *f-v*, *x-j*, d.h. für die Phoneme k/g, p/b, t/d, ś/ź, s/z, f/v, š/ž.[28] Und es ist wiederum das erste Mal, daß diese

[25] "As letras consoantes aspiradas que são *ch*, *lh*, *nh* não tem propria figura ainda ategora ... mas que seria se dissessemos não aver antre nos aspiração? ... das cõsoãtes eu diria que sem aspiração fazẽ alghũa mudança cujo sinal é aquella figura de letra *h* que lhe mesturamos" (16).

[26] Die italienischen (toskanischen) Konsonanten werden erst von G. Bartoli, *Degli elementi del parlar toscano*, Florenz, 1584, ausführlich beschrieben. Die Beschreibung des Walisers Siôn Dafydd Rhys [engl. John David Rhoese oder Rhese; lat. Rhoesus], *Perutilis exteris nationibus de Italica pronunciatione, et orthographia libellus*, Padua, 1569, ist zwar oft sehr genau und in praktischer Hinsicht fast immer ausgezeichnet, sie erfolgt jedoch vor allem kontrastiv, d.h. durch Vergleich mit anderen Sprachen (Englisch, Deutsch, Französisch, Spanisch, Portugiesisch, Polnisch, Walisisch) und berücksichtigt die italienische Artikulation vor allem, wenn diese von der in anderen Sprachen üblichen abweicht. In Spanien findet man eine mit derjenigen von Oliveira vergleichbare Ausführlichkeit und Systematik erst bei J. P. Bonet, *Reductión de las letras y arte para enseñar a ablar los mudos*, Madrid, 1620; in Frankreich muß man dafür bis Cordemoy (1668) und Dangeau (1694) warten.

[27] Damit kommt Oliveira auf 32 oder 33 portugiesische 'letras' (6, 10, 14). Die Schwankung ist darauf zurückzuführen, daß er sich in bezug auf den Status von *q* und vor allem von *y* doch nicht völlig sicher ist. Die Nasalvokale übernimmt er nicht als solche in sein Alphabet, wohl aber die Tilde als zusätzliches Zeichen.

[28] "A pronũçiação do *g* é como a do *c*, cõ menos força do spirito"; "A força ou virtude do *p* é a mesma que a do *b*, se não que traz mays espirito"; "O *ss* dobrado pronũçia-sse como o outro pregãdo mais a lingua no çeo da boca"; "O *t* tẽ a mesma virtude do *d*, com mays espirito todavia tira o *t* pera fora" (13); "*ç* tẽ a mesma pronũçiação que *z*, se não que aperta mais a lingoa nos dẽtes"; "*j* cõsoante ... a sua pronũçiação é semelhante à do *xi* cõ menos força, e esta mesma virtude damos ao *g* quando se segue despoys delle *e* ou *i*"; "A força de *v* consoante é como a do *f*, mas cõ menos espirito" (14); "antre as consoantes *b* e *p* são muy semelhantes, e *c* com *g* tem muita vezinhença, e *d* com *t*, *f* com *v*, ... *ç* com *z*, e *s* com *ss*, *j* e *x* tambẽ" (18).

Korrelation für ein romanisches Konsonantensystem so vollständig und zugleich so klar und so präzise dargelegt wird;[29] die entsprechenden Oppositionen interpretiert Oliveira allerdings nicht als Oppositionen der Sonorität, sondern stets als Oppositionen der Stärke, bzw. der Spannung (vgl. die in der Fn. 28 angeführten Charakterisierungen).[30] Außerdem stellt er eine Opposition der Quantität zwischen *r* und *rr*, d.h. /r/ und /r̄/ fest (vgl. in 2.3.1 die Beschreibung von *r* und *rr*), sowie eine nicht weiter bestimmte Affinität zwischen *r* und *l*: *r* sei nämlich "semelhãte ao *l*" (13; vgl. auch 17: *l* habe große Ähnlichkeit "com *r* singelo").[31]

2.4 Sehr genau ist bei Oliveira auch die Beschreibung der Phonemdistribution im Wort und in der Silbe (20-23). Dafür konnte er zwar dem

[29] In Italien wird die Sonoritätskorrelation (wenn auch nicht in dieser Form: vgl. Fn. 30) für p/b, t/d, k/g, č/ǧ, f/v, s/z, ts/dz erst von G. Bartoli eindeutig festgestellt. In Frankreich wird die gleiche Korrelation von Bovillus [Ch. Bovelles] *Liber de differentia vulgarium linguarum et Gallici sermonis varietate*, Paris, 1533, sogar zum Gestaltungsprinzip des Konsonantensystems erhoben: Man müsse sie für alle Konsonanten annehmen, denn alle Konsonanten könnte man entweder als *molles* oder als *duriores* klassifizieren (Kap. 26); jedoch sind die Oppositionen, die Bovillus feststellt, nur zum Teil richtig (so z.B. D/T, Kap. 29), und oft sind sie ungenau: *B* z.B. sei 'mollis' gegenüber *P*, aber 'dura' gegenüber *V* (Kap. 27); im Gesamttableau von Bovillus erscheint *F* als die 'mollis' von *V* und *M* als die 'mollis' von *N*, und verschiedene Konsonanten erscheinen in demselben Tableau zugleich als 'molles' und als 'duriores'. Kohärenter und präziser, wenn auch nicht völlig eindeutig, ist in dieser Hinsicht Théodore de Bèze, *De Francicae linguae recta pronuntiatione*, Genf, 1584. Eindeutiger sind die Feststellungen von G. de Cordemoy, *Discours physique de la parole*, Paris, 1668 (zumindest für p/b, k/g, f/v); man muß jedoch bis Dangeau warten, damit man für das Französische so eindeutigen Darlegungen wie denjenigen von Oliveira begegnet.

[30] Dies ist übrigens allgemein in der Romania in der Renaissance und sogar auch bis viel später. Die gleiche Interpretation findet man z.B. bei Bovillus, bei Rhys, bei Th. de Bèze und bei G. Bartoli (der 'suoni rimessi' und 'suoni intensi' unterscheidet; *op. cit.*, S. 23). Die Stimmhaftigkeit wird erst sehr spät als solche identifiziert. Sie wird zwar von J. P. Bonet intuitiv erfaßt und mehr oder weniger eindeutig festgestellt (z.B. für *d*, *g*, *m*, *n*); cf. T. Navarro Tomás, "Doctrina fonética de Juan Pablo Bonet (1620)", *RFE*, 7, 1920, SS. 150-177. Die Beobachtungen und Beschreibungen von Bonet haben jedoch in dieser Hinsicht keine Wirkung auf die weitere Entwicklung der Phonetik in den romanischen Ländern. Cordemoy, Dangeau und das ganze französische 18. Jahrhundert bleiben nämlich bei der Opposition *stark – schwach* (bei Dangeau z.B. findet man die stimmlosen Konsonanten als *fortes* und die stimmhaften als *faibles* klassifiziert; so auch bei Duclos, in dessen *Remarques* zur *Grammaire Générale*, 1754, und bei Boulliette, *Traité des sons de la langue française*, 1760).

[31] Auch Bovillus (*op. cit.*, Kap. 35) nimmt für *r*/*l* eine Opposition *durior – mollis* an. Und merkwürdigerweise möchte auch G. Bartoli für ital. *r*/*l*, wenn auch nicht völlig entschieden, eine solche Opposition annehmen; nachdem er ital. *r* beschrieben hat, schreibt Bartoli nämlich: "il suo rimesso pare che sia lo L bēche lo R si diversifica più da lo L; che gli altri intensi da i loro rimessi; essendo che lo R ripercuote cõ reiteramēto tremulo il medesimo luogo, il che non fa lo L" (*op. cit.*, S. 37).

Vorbild Nebrijas folgen, der die spanische Phonemdistribution ebenfalls sehr genau und sehr ausführlich beschreibt.[32] Oliveira versucht jedoch, seine Feststellungen in diesem Bereich auf allgemeinere Regeln als diejenigen von Nebrija zurückzuführen. Da im Portugiesischen im Wort- und Silbenauslaut nur Vokale bzw. Diphthonge (einschließlich der Nasalvokale und Nasaldiphthonge) und *l*, *r*, *s*, *z*, zugelassen sind, setzt er – z.T. durch einen Zirkelschluß, indem er gerade deshalb *l*, *r*, *s*, *z* "semivogaes ou quasi vogaes" nennt (20) – mehr oder weniger eindeutig die Regel, daß die portugiesischen Wörter und Silben nur auf ein 'vokalisches' Phonem auslauten können, unter Ausschluß der 'letras mudas', d.h. der eigentlich 'konsonantischen' Phoneme, und natürlich der Konsonantennexus (20, 23). Was den Silben- und Wortanlaut betrifft, stellt er fest, daß in dieser Stellung im Portugiesischen [abgesehen von den Vokallauten] nur einfache Konsonanten oder Nexus von muta cum liquida, sonst aber keine Konsonantengruppen erscheinen dürfen (21). Nur Fremdwörter können von diesen Regeln abweichen, und auch diese nur solange sie so 'neu' sind, daß sie dem portugiesischen System noch nicht angepaßt werden ("se não quando ainda forem tão novas antre nos que seja neçessareo pronunçia-las cõ a melodia de seu naçimento").[33] Die portugiesische Tendenz sei aber, solche Wörter anzupassen und z.B. die 'letras mudas' im Silbenauslaut zu vokalisieren (24).

2.5 Ebenfalls sehr genau sind Oliveiras Angaben zu den im Portugiesischen eintretenden Assimilationen (18, 26, 28) – obwohl er in diesem Zusammenhang die Personalpronomina *o*, *os* irrtümlich als 'Artikel' interpretiert – sowie zur Wortbetonung (28-29), was zumindest von bemerkenswerter Beobachtungsgabe zeugt.[34]

2.6 Kennzeichend für die Beschreibungen und Interpretationen Oliveiras im phonischen Bereich ist jedoch vor allem, daß er dabei stets – wie eben im Falle der Distributionsregeln – das Sprachsystem im Auge hat und offensichtlich, wenn auch natürlich mehr oder weniger intuitiv, eben den dem Sprachsystem entsprechenden funktionellen Gesichtspunkt einnimmt. Auf letzteres deuten verschiedene Fakten hin. Erstens entsprechen seine 'Buchstaben' so gut wie genau den phonematischen

[32] *Gram. cast.*, I, 9.

[33] Vgl, die Ausführungen von Nebrija, *Gram. cast.*, I, 9, 5, zu den *diciones* (oder *palabras*) *peregrinas*, in denen Konsonantennexus vorkommen können, die im Spanischen sonst nicht zugelassen sind.

[34] In der vier Jahre später erschienenen Grammatik von João de Barros werden die Assimilationen überhaupt nicht behandelt, und dort, wo sie beiläufig erwähnt werden (Ausg. Carvalhão, SS. 382-383), werden sie falsch interpretiert. Auch die Betonung wird von Barros nicht berücksichtigt.

Einheiten des Portugiesischen und im Falle der Nasalvokale sogar einer funktionellen Analyse vom Typ: V + Nasalität. Zweitens gibt er für seine Unterscheidung von *α* - *a*, *e* - ε, *o* - ω als Begründung an, daß diese Laute jeweils in gleichen phonischen Kontexten erscheinen können und daß sie deshalb nicht als kontextbedingte, automatisch eintretende Realisierungen interpretiert werden dürfen: "E isto porque nos não podemos salvar cõ os latinos dizendo que a consoãte ou consoãtes e letras que vão adiante fazem grande ou pequena a letra vogal que fica, mas vemos que cõ hũas mesmas letras soa hũa vogal grande as vezes e as vezes pequena: segundo o costume quis e não mays" (8). Man wird in dieser Begründung leicht eines der Kriterien erkennen, die viel später im Strukturalismus, insbesondere in der Bloomfieldschen Schule, zur Abgrenzung phonematischer Einheiten verwendet werden.[35] Am klarsten erscheint jedoch die funktionelle Fragestellung in Oliveiras Interpretation von [i], [u] in unbetonter, insbesondere in vorvokalischer Stellung (wo im Portugiesischen die Oppositionen e/i, o/u aufgehoben werden). Oliveira interpretiert nämlich diese Laute als *e* bzw. *o*, trotz ihrer von ihm selbst ausdrücklich zugegebenen materiellen Ähnlichkeit mit *i* bzw. mit *u*, und schlägt entsprechend vor, auch *memorea*, *neçessareo*, *continoar* (also nicht: *memoria*, *neçessario*, *continuar*) zu schreiben: Es handele sich in solchen Fällen jeweils nur um eine durch den phonischen Kontext bedingte Variation, was übrigens auch bei den anderen Vokalen feststellbar sei, und nicht um verschiedene Vokaleinheiten.[36]

35 Bei den von Oliveira für die Oppositionen *e* – *ε*, *o* – ω angeführten Beispielen (*festo* – *fεsta*, *fermoso* – *fermωsos*) könnte man zwar, wenn man zum phonischen Kontext auch die auslautenden Vokale, bzw. das auslautende *-s* rechnet, doch eine kontextbedingte Variation annehmen. Das von ihm angegebene Kriterium gilt jedoch auch für diese Oppositionen (wenn auch freilich nicht für den von ihm gemeinten Quantitätsunterschied), zumal es im Portugiesischen zahlreiche Fälle – und auch Minimalpaare vom Typ *peso* – *pεso*, *porto* – *pωrto* – gibt, in denen sie nicht als kontextbedingt interpretiert werden können.

36 "Não pareça a alguem que nos confundimos *i* pequeno cõ *e* pequeno, nem *o* pequeno com *u* pequeno; porque ellas não são diversas vozes e tam pouco não temos ahi neçessidade de diversas letras; mas é desta maneira que antre *i*, que é letra delgada, aguda e viva, e antre *ε* grande, soa na nossa lingua hũa outra voz mais escura, e não mais que hũa; e a este chamamos *e* pequeno, o qual em hũas partes soa mays e em outras menos, como fazem as outras vogaes; e õde soa mais podemos dizer que é mais vezinho do *e* grande, onde tambẽ menos soa, será isso mesmo mays vezinho de *i*; mas não por isso dizemos que são duas letras, porque não muda a voz se não por respeito das consoantes mais ou menos; ou por qualquer outra vezinhẽça de letras que se cõ elle ajũtão, gasta mais ou menos tempo e apareçe mais ou menos a sua voz, como *escreveste* – *memorea*: mais soa *e* pequeno na penultima de *escreveste* que de *memorea*" (27).

3.0 In den Abschnitten zum Wortschatz ('Das dições') legt Oliveira auf wenigen Seiten – ausgehend von gewissen Ansätzen bei Varro[37] und von dem, was in den lateinischen Grammatiken und bei Nebrija als *species* und *figura* bei den verschiedenen Redeteilen (insb. beim Nomen und beim Verbum) behandelt wird – einen Entwurf der Lexikologie und darin eine Theorie der Wortzusammensetzung vor, und zwar den ersten – und in gewisser Hinsicht den einzigen – Entwurf dieser Art und die erste uns bekannte Theorie der Wortzusammensetzung in der Geschichte der romanischen Sprachwissenschaft.

3.1 Die *dições* – d.h. jeweils den GANZEN Wortschatz – einer Sprache unterteilt Oliveira in Kategorien aufgrund von fünf verschiedenen Kriterien (30). Die *dições* seien nämlich, je nach dem eingenommenen Gesichtspunkt:

a) *nossas* - *alheias* - *comuns* ('unser' - 'fremd' - 'gemeinsam');[38]
b) *apartadas* - *juntas* ('einfach' - 'zusammengesetzt');
c) *velhas* - *novas* - *usadas* ('alt' - 'neu' - 'geläufig');
d) *próprias* - *mudadas* (d.h. nicht-übertragen bzw. übertragen);
e) *primeiras* - *tiradas* (Grundwörter und Ableitungen).

Das erste Kriterium ist ein etymologisches und sprachvergleichendes, jedoch sozusagen vom synchronischen Gesichtspunkt aus angewandt. Die *dições nossas* sind die einer Sprache spezifischen Primärwörter und die in dieser Sprache durch Komposition und Ableitung entstandenen Wörter (31). Die *alheias* sind die in einer Sprache erkennbaren Lehn- und Fremdwörter; diese können mit der Zeit zu 'dições nossas' werden (32). Die *comuns* sind die verschiedenen Sprachen gemeinsamen Wörter, bei welchen die Herkunft aus der einen oder der anderen Sprache nicht erkennbar ist.[39] Zum zweiten Kriterium s. 3.2. Das dritte Kriterium betrifft die Diachronie des Wortschatzes innerhalb einer historischen Sprache. Die *dições velhas* sind die Archaismen; solche könne man auch bei Betrachtung von relativ kurzen Zeitstrecken erkennen, und gewisse

[37] *De lingua Latina*, V, 6 und V, 10.

[38] Vgl. die Unterscheidung von Varro zwischen *verba nostra* und *verba aliena* (*De lingua Lat.*, V, 10).

[39] "Dições comũs chamamos aquellas que em muitas linguas servem igualmente e o tempo em que se mudarão d'hũa lingoa para outra fica tão lõge de nos que não podemos façilmente saber de qual para qual lingua se mudarão, porque assi as podião tomar as outras linguas da nossa como a nossa dellas" (33). Zu diesen Wörtern rechnet Oliveira im Falle des Portugiesischen auch so offensichtliche Arabismen wie *alfaiate*, *almoxarife*, und sogar die aus dem Lateinischen ererbten Wörter (cf. 1.3).

Archaismen können sogar älteren Sprechern noch bekannt sein;[40] außerdem könne man feststellen, daß alte Wörter der Gemeinsprache in den Mundarten oft weiterleben. Die *dições novas* sind die Wörter jüngeren Datums, die vor allem zur Bezeichnung neuer 'Sachen' entstehen und sich mit den bezeichneten Sachen selbst verbreiten (37). Die *dições usadas* sind die Wörter, die weder als Archaismen noch als Neuwörter erkennbar sind, d.h. zu jeder Zeit die meisten Wörter einer Sprache.[41] Das vierte Kriterium (39) bedarf keiner weiteren Erklärung. Das fünfte Kriterium betrifft das Ableitungsverhältnis, so wie dieses z.B. zwischen *tinta* und *tinteiro* ('Tinte' - 'Tintenfaß'), *velho* und *velhice* ('alt' — 'Alter') besteht (39); in diesem Zusammenhang behandelt Oliveira kurz die Frage der relativen Motivation: Das Ableitungsverhältnis sei nämlich ein außersprachlich motiviertes, da es jeweils einem Verhältnis zwischen den bezeichneten 'Sachen' entspreche.[42]

3.2 Am interessantesten ist hier jedoch die Theorie der Wortzusammensetzung, die Oliveira in Zusammenhang mit seiner zweiten Einteilung des Wortschatzes entwickelt und die er auch etwas ausführlicher behandelt (34-35). Diese Theorie ist durch das Suchen nach einem brauchbaren Kriterium zur Abgrenzung der Komposita gekennzeichnet. Anfangs nimmt Oliveira offensichtlich als Kriterium das getrennte Vorkommen der Bestandteile des Kompositums an. Als Beispiel dafür gelte *contrafazer*, wo sowohl *contra* als auch *fazer* getrennt vorkommen (30, 35). Dies sei hingegen bei *fazer* nicht der Fall, da *fa-* und *-zer* nicht als selbständige Wörter vorkommen ("porque *fa* por si não diz nada e *zer* tampouco" (34)), und deshalb sei auch *fazer* eine *dição apartada*, ein einfaches Wort. Die Trennbarkeit der Bestandteile des Kompositums müsse allerdings das signifiant und das signifié zugleich betreffen: *amaríamos* z.B. ('wir würden lieben') bestehe nicht aus *ama* ('Amme')

[40] "As dições velhas são as que forão usadas mas agora são esqueçidas ... e não somẽte de tãto tẽpo, mas tãbẽ antes de nos hũ pouco nossos pays tinhão alghũas palavras que ja não são agora ouvidas, como *cõpẽgar*, que queria dizer comer o pã cõ a outra viãda, e *nemichalda*, o qual tanto valia como agora *nemigalha*" (36).

[41] "As dições usadas são estas que nos servem a cada porta (como dizẽ), estas, digo, que todos falão e entendẽ, as quaes são proprias do nosso tẽpo e terra, e quẽ não usa dellas é desentoado, fora do tom e musica dos nossos homẽs d'agora" (38).

[42] [Die *dições tiradas*] "tẽ muita parte assi na cousa como na voz; e, a meu ver, não digamos que foy isto defeito de não acharẽ vocabolos, mas é cõforme a bõa rezão que aja e se guarde a semelhãça das cousas nas vozes e assi são mais claras e dizẽ milhor seus sinificados, porque a diversidade das vozes mostra aver diversidade nas cousas e tãbẽ a semelhãça por cõseguĩte das vozes faz entẽder que as cousas não são diferẽtes" (39).

und *ríamos* ('wir lachten').[43] Dieses erste Kriterium kann jedoch Oliveira nicht für alle von ihm gemeinten Fälle anwenden, denn die Analysierbarkeit eines Kompositums, die er offensichtlich im Auge hat, schließt nicht unbedingt das getrennte Vorkommen seiner Bestandteile ein. Deshalb gibt er dieses Kriterium auch gleich auf, und schon in seiner Definition der Komposita spricht er vorsichtig von Bestandteilen, "die getrennt bedeuten oder bedeuten *können*" und von "Wörtern oder *Teilen von Wörtern*, die zusammengesetzt werden".[44] Es genüge auch, daß nur einer der Bestandteile als selbständiges Wort existiert, wenn der andere (bzw. die anderen)[45] als virtuelles Wort (bzw. als virtuelle Wörter) angesehen werden können, d.h. wenn ihnen eine lexikalische Bedeutung zugeschrieben werden kann; so z.B. im Falle von *refazer*, *desfazer*, wo *re*- und *des*- getrennt nicht vorkommen.[46] Es gebe sogar 'vozes', die ausschließlich in der Komposition vorkommen, wie eben *re*-, *es*-, *des*-, und die deshalb 'ursprünglich' ('de seu naçimento') [virtuelle] einfache Wörter seien.[47] Ja, es sei sogar möglich, daß keiner der Bestandteile eines Kompositums als selbständiges Wort vorkommt, wie z.B. im Falle von *nelhures*, *algures* ('nirgends', 'irgendwo').[48] Das Kriterium, zu dem Oliveira schließlich gelangt, ist also die segmentarische Analysierbarkeit der lexikalischen Bedeutung, d.h. die Möglichkeit, Segmenten einer Wortform lexikalische Bedeutungen zuzuschreiben,

43 Vgl. die Definitionen von Nebrija, *Gram. cast.*, II, 6, 1: "Senzillo nombre se llama aquel que no se compone de partes que signifiquen aquello que significa el entero", "Compuesto nombre es aquel que se compone de partes las cuales significan aquello mismo que significa el entero".

44 "As dições apartadas ... são aquellas cujas partes não podẽ ser dições inteiras" (34). "As dições juntas, a que os latinos chamão cõpostas, são [aquellas] cujas partes apartadas sinificão ou podẽ sinificar e são dições por si ou partes d'outras dições ẽ que premeiro servião e donde tẽ seu primeiro e proprio naçimẽto ... ou as dições jũtas são aquellas ẽ que se ajuntão diversas dições ou suas partes fazẽdo hũa so dição" (35).

45 Oliveira nimmt nämlich an, ein Kompositum könnte auch aus mehr als zwei Bestandteilen bestehen: "As dições juntas as vezes se ajuntão de duas partes e as vezes de mais; de duas pella mayor parte, como *empedir*, *encolher*; d'mais como *desempedir*, *desencolher*; e as mais não serão mais que tres como aqui são: *des*, e *em*, e *pedir* ou *colher*" (35).

46 "E ẽ *refazer* se ajũtão *se* e mais *fazer*; e em *desfazer des* e mais *fazer*; e posto que cada hũa destas partes não sinifique apartada por si, como *re* e *des*, que apartadas não dizẽ cousa alghũa, abasta que hũa qualquer das partes da cõposição possa sinificar como aqui sinifica *fazer*" (35).

47 "Alghũas partes ou vozes temos na nossa lingua, as quaes são partes por si, mas não sinificão cousa alghũa, e por tãto não lhe chamaremos partes da oração ou da lingua, como são o nome, e verbo, e outras; mas todavia fazẽ ajũtamẽto ou composíção, porque de seu naçimento ellas são apartadas, mas tẽ por offiçio servir sempre em ajũtamẽto e nũca as achamos fora delle; e são estas as partes *re*, *es* e *des*" (35).

48 "e cõ tudo pera mais abastança se se achar alghũa dição junta cujas partes apartadas nenhũa dellas por si sinifique" (35).

die als Bestandteile der lexikalischen Bedeutung dieser Form im ganzen angesehen werden können. Diese Analysierbarkeit ist einzelsprachlich offenbar durch Proportionsgleichungen wie *con-chegar/con-juntar*, *re-fazer/des-fazer*, *nelh-ures/alg-ures* gegeben, und zwar unabhängig davon, ob die dadurch identifizierten Bestandteile der Komposita als getrennte Wörter vorkommen oder nicht. Dieser Auffassung entsprechen in der Tat die Beispiele und Analysen Oliveiras, obwohl er bisweilen immer noch von einem getrennten Vorkommen der Bestandteile spricht. So seien *a-correr*, *a-conselhar*, *en-carregar*, *es-guardar* – bei denen die Analyse möglich ist – Komposita, *apanhar*, *açoutar*, *ensinar*, *esperar* hingegen nicht (35). Und Bestandteilen wie *re-*, *des-*, *com-* könne man jeweils eine bestimmte Bedeutung zuschreiben.[49]

Man wird bei dieser Fragestellung Oliveiras leicht die Ähnlichkeit mit modernen Fragestellungen gerade in bezug auf die Komposita feststellen, insbesondere mit denjenigen von Bloomfield und seiner Schule, und zwar eine Ähnlichkeit, die bei Oliveira denselben Konflikt zwischen der rein materiellen und der inhaltlichen Analyse und dieselben damit verbundenen Schwierigkeiten einschließt, denen der moderne Strukturalismus in Fällen wie engl. *cranberry* und noch mehr in Fällen wie *conceive – deceive – receive* begegnet ist.

4.0 Die Grammatik im engeren Sinne ('Morphosyntax') behandelt Oliveira wie schon anfangs angedeutet nur sehr kurz, und zwar das Verb noch kürzer als das Nomen und die Satzsyntax fast nur andeutungsweise unter Verweis auf andere Werke, die er zu diesen Gebieten in Vorbereitung habe. Jedoch kann man auch bei dieser knappen Behandlung sein Bemühen feststellen, sich von den Schemata der lateinischen Grammatik zu befreien und die im Portugiesischen funktionierenden grammatischen Kategorien als solche abzugrenzen. Und es muß gesagt werden, daß es ihm auch gelingt, auf wenigen Seiten eine von den lateinischen Mustern in nicht unerheblichen Maße unabhängige portugiesische Grammatik zu entwerfen.[50]

49 "esta parte *re* no ajuntamẽto tem virtude de acreçẽtar; e estoutra *des* tem virtude de desfazer ou diminuir ou fazer o contrario; e ... esta parte *com* sinifica muitas vezsə cõpanhia, cujo exẽplo seja *conchegar* e *conjuntar*" (35).

50 Daher, und – wenn man von Nebrijas Einfluß absieht – meist sicherlich nicht wegen irgendwelcher direkter Zusammenhänge, die vielen Übereinstimmungen Oliveiras mit anderen romanischen Grammatikern der Renaissance, die sich ebenfalls von den Mustern der lateinischen Grammatik zu lösen suchen. Schon L. B. Alberti erkennt in seiner um 1450 geschriebenen (jedoch bis zu unserem Jahrhundert im Manuskript gebliebenen) Grammatik kein Neutrum für das Italienische an und stellt Kasusdeklination nur bei einigen Pronomina fest (cf. L. B. Alberti, *La prima gramma-*

4.1 Diese zumindest relative Unabhängigkeit zeigt sich schon in der Auffassung der beschreibenden Grammatik, die Oliveira in dieser Sektion seines Werkes an den Tag legt: Er verzichtet nämlich ausdrücklich auf jegliche Definition der grammatischen Kategorien und möchte sich darauf beschränken, die *Formen*, die diese Kategorien ausdrücken, als solche zu identifizieren und zu beschreiben.[51]

4.2 Was den Stoff dieses grammatischen Entwurfs betrifft, so begnügen wir uns damit, auf einige im Rahmen der Geschichte der romanischen Grammatik besonders auffallende Aspekte hinzuweisen. Oliveira erkennt als erster für das Portugiesische den Artikel als getrennten Redeteil (43). Die Kasus beim Nomen behält er nur noch als Typen von Satzfunktionen bei – jedoch auf nur vier reduziert (Nominativ, Genitiv, Dativ, Akkusativ) und mit neuen Namen versehen: Präpositiv, Possessiv, Dativ, Postpositiv (43) –, nicht aber als morphologische Kategorie: Kasusdeklination gebe es im Portugiesischen nur bei einigen Personalpronomina (46).[52] Zeichen der Kasus als Satzfunktionen seien die Artikel, z.B. beim Maskulinum Singular: *o, do, ao, o*; jedoch seien die Formen vom Typ *do, ao* nicht nur Kasuszeichen, sondern auch Kombinationen von Präposition und Artikel (so z.B. in einer Konstruktion wie: *venho do paço* 'ich komme vom Palast'), und in diesem Fall sei der Kasus, mit dem sie konstruiert werden, der Postpositiv.[53] Die Genera des Portugiesischen seien das Maskulinum, das Femininum, das 'Unbestimmte' (*indeterminado*: z.B. *isto* 'dies') und das Commune (z.B. *maior, menor*); ein Neutrum gebe es nicht (44). Von Deklination des Nomens könne man

tica della lingua volgare, a cura di C. Grayson, Bologna, 1964, SS. 40, 46). Fortunio, Bembo, und Trissino nehmen ebenfalls kein Neutrum an. Fortunio spricht nicht von Kasus für das Substantiv, wohl aber für das Pronomen. Der Artikel – abgesehen vom so lange unbekannt gebliebenen Alberti – wird zuerst von Nebrija als getrennter Redeteil angenommen; in Italien erkennt ihn als solchen Trissino (1529), für das Französische Palsgrave (1530). Gegenüber den besten unter den ersten Grammatikern der Renaissance stellt man bei vielen der späteren – so wie im 17. und im 18. Jahrhundert – nicht, wie man annehmen könnte, einen Fortschritt, sondern vielmehr einen Rückschritt und eine Rückkehr zu den lateinischen Mustern fest. Dazu trägt – trotz ihrer bisweilen ausgezeichneten funktionellen Fragestellungen – auch die *Grammaire Générale* durch ihre falsch verstandene 'allgemeine' Komponente bei.

[51] "Porque aqui não falamos se não das formas ou figuras das vozes ou diçóes" (43); "porque do intento desta parte da grammatica que agora tratamos não hé mais que só dar notiçia das vozes, e não difinçóes ou determinadas declaraçóes das cousas" (44).

[52] João de Barros bedeutet auch in dieser Hinsicht einen Rückschritt gegenüber Oliveira, da er für das portugiesische Nomen die sechs lateinischen Kasus annimmt.

[53] Diese merkwürdige Unterscheidung von 'Kasuszeichen' und 'Präposition + Artikel' ist fast für die ganze romanische Grammatik bis zum 18., z.T. sogar bis zum 19. Jahrhundert charakteristisch und bereitet eine unendliche Reihe von Schwierigkeiten.

im Portugiesischen nur in bezug auf Genus und Numerus sprechen; die Genusdeklinationen (Typ: *moço* – *moça*) seien zahlreich und nicht bestimmbar (44); die Numerusdeklinationen seien vier: Pluralbildung auf *-s* (*moço* – *moços*), auf *-es* (*pavês* – *paveses*), mit Änderung einer 'letra' (*animal* – *animais*), und mit Änderung einer Silbe (*almeirão* – *almeirões*) (45).[54] Bei den Nomina auf *-ão* weist Oliveira auf die Besonderheit hin, daß diese im Plural drei verschiedene Formen aufweisen (*grão* – *grãos*, aber *melão* – *melões* und *cão* – *cães*) und führt dies zutreffend auf die Verschiedenheit der älteren Formen des Singulars zurück: im älteren Portugiesisch lauteten diese Nomina im Singular auf *-ão*, *-õ*, *-ã*, und diese Verschiedenheit sei nur im Plural erhalten geblieben.[55] Beim portugiesischen Verb stellt Oliveira eine einzige Diathese (47) und drei Konjugationen (Typen: *falar*, *fazer*, *ouvir*)[56] fest.

5.1 Wir haben anfangs darauf hingewiesen, daß Oliveira, zumindest intuitiv, die Unterscheidung zwischen den beiden Ebenen der einzelsprachlichen Strukturierung macht, die wir 'Sprachsystem' und 'Sprachnorm' nennen, d.h. zwischen der Ebene der funktionellen Oppositionen und derjenigen ihrer traditionell gegebenen Realisierungen[57] und daß er diese Unterscheidung mehrmals in seiner Beschreibungspraxis anwendet. Schon im Falle seiner Interpretation der unbetonten [i] und [u] könnte man von dieser Unterscheidung sprechen, zumal er in diesem Fall für das portugiesische Sprachsystem /e/ und /o/ annimmt, obwohl er weiß, daß es sich in der Realisierungsnorm vielmehr eben um [i] und [u] handelt (cf. 2.6). Viel klarer zeigt sich jedoch die angedeutete Intuition Oliveiras im Bereich der grammatischen und lexikalischen Morphologie, und zwar im Rahmen seiner Auffassung der 'Analogie'.

5.2 Oliveira geht diesbezüglich von der Unterscheidung Varros

54 Vgl. Nebrija, *Gram. cast.*, III, 6, 4: "Declinacion del nombre no tiene la lengua castellana, salvo del numero de uno al numero de muchos, pero la significacion delos casos distingue por preposiciones. Assi que puedense reduzir todos los nombres a tres formas de declinacion".

55 "Os outros nomes que fazem o plural em *ãos*, como *cidadãos*, *cortesãos*, assi teverão sempre o seu singular acabado ẽ *ão*, como agora tẽ: *cidadão*, *cortesão*; estes guardão sua antiguidade em tudo, e aquelloutros só no plural" (45).

56 So schon Nebrija für das Spanische, *Gram. cast.*, III, 1O, 9. João de Barros folgt hierin nicht dem 'sistema inaugurado por Trissino' (das übrigens nicht von Trissino 'inauguriert' wurde), wie M. Carvalhão Buescu, *op. cit.*, S. 331, annimmt, sondern wiederum Nebrija und Oliveira.

57 Zu dieser Unterscheidung vgl. unsere Studie *Sistema, norma y habla*, Montevideo, 1952, jetzt in *Teoría del lenguaje y lingüística general*³, Madrid, 1973.

zwischen *declinatio naturalis* und *declinatio voluntaria*[58] und von dem als dieser Unterscheidung parallel interpretierten Gegensatz von Analogie und Anomalie (Regelmäßigkeit – Unregelmäßigkeit)[59] aus, wobei er in diesem Zusammenhang wie Varro unter 'Deklination' die Flexion und die Wortableitung versteht. Auch sind die Beispiele, die er für die 'declinação voluntária' und ihre 'Anomalien' anführt, denjenigen von Varro sehr ähnlich. So bemerkt er, daß unter verschiedenen an sich gleichwertigen Ableitungsverfahren im Sprachgebrauch von Fall zu Fall ein bestimmtes bevorzugt bzw. fixiert wird: Von *sarna* habe man *sarnoso*, nicht *sarnento*, von *sarapulhas* jedoch *sarapulhento*, nicht *sarapulhoso* gebildet, und von *pó* weder *pooso* noch *poento*, sondern *empoado*;[60] von einer Frau sage man *pescadeira*, von einem Boot hingegen (*barca*) *pescaresa*; das Verbalnomen von *orar* sei *oração*, dasjenige von *amar* jedoch *amor* (41; vgl. aber w.u.). Trotz der Ähnlichkeit der Fragestellung geht Oliveira, wie uns scheint, über Varro hinaus, da er nicht bloß Analogien und Anomalien des Sprachgebrauchs feststellt, sondern die Sprache als System von Möglichkeiten erfaßt, die im Sprachgebrauch mit Einschränkungen realisiert werden. Varro spricht zwar auch von nicht realisierten Regelmäßigkeiten ("analogia quae in consuetudine non est"), jedoch behandelt er die Analogie und die Anomalie als zwei auf derselben Ebene des Sprachgebrauchs konkurrierende Verfahrenstypen. Die nichtbeachteten Analogien, die er als Beispiele für die Unregelmäßigkeit anführt, sind jeweils einzelne Proportionsgleichungen vom Typ *vinum – vinaria/caro – *carnaria, ovis – ovile/avis – *avile, canto – cantitans/amo – *amitans*. Außerdem neigt Varro dazu, die Derivation als das Gebiet der Unregelmäßigkeit, die Flexion als dasjenige der Regelmäßigkeit anzusehen, und die dem Sprachgebrauch widersprechenden Regelmäßigkeiten lehnt er ausdrücklich ab.[61] Anders ist die Haltung Oliveiras, der Regeln und Realisierungen gegenüberstellt. Die Analogie und die Anomalie betrachtet nämlich Oliveira nicht als gleichberechtigte Verfahren, denn die Sprache ist für ihn an erster Stelle System von Regelmäßigkeiten. Die Bezeichnung 'natürlich' der

[58] *De ling. Lat.*, VIII, 21-22: "Declinationum genera sunt duo, voluntarium et naturale; voluntarium est, quo ut cuiusque tulit voluntas declinavit. ... Contra naturalem declinationem dico, quae non a singulorum oritur voluntate, sed a communi consensu".

[59] Varro selbst stellt übrigens die Analogie und die Anomalie als in gewisser Hinsicht seinen beiden 'Deklinationen' entsprechend dar: In der 'declinatio voluntaria' stelle man vor allem Anomalie, in der 'declinatio naturalis' vor allem Analogie fest (*De ling. Lat.*, VIII, 23).

[60] Im heutigen Portugiesischen sind allerdings *sarnento* und *poento* durchaus üblich.

[61] *De ling. Lat.*, VIII, 33 ff., 54, 55, 60.

declinatio naturalis, die er auch für die Regeln verwendet, interpretiert er in dem Sinne, daß die Regeln tatsächlich eher dem Wesen der Sprache ('natureza da língua') entsprechen.[62] Auch die Wortableitung sei weniger willkürlich als man denken könnte, denn sie müsse der 'Melodie' der Sprache angemessen ("conforme") sein (41). Verschiedene Derivationsverfahren folgen übrigens bestimmten Regeln oder 'Bildungsgesetzen' ('regras', 'leis de formação': 41, 42) und gehören deshalb seines Erachtens zur 'declinação natural'; so im Portugiesischen die Diminutivbildung auf *-inho*, die Augmentativbildung auf *-az* oder *-ão*, die der nomina agentis auf *-dor*. Ja sogar für begrenzte Ableitungsverfahren könne man allgemeingültige Muster annehmen; so entspreche die Bildung auf *-eiro* für Namen von 'ofícios mecánicos' (*pedreiro*, *carpinteiro*, *sapateiro*) einer 'regra geral' trotz der Gegenbeispiele wie *alfaiate* und *ferrador*; und der Typ *sapateiro* – *sapataria* sei ein regelmäßiger trotz *telheiro* – *telheira*. Auch die Inexistenz von gewissen regelmäßigen Formen – d.h. ihre Nichtrealisierung im Sprachgebrauch – gewinnt in dieser Perspektive einen neuen Sinn. Diese Inexistenz kann einfach zufällig sein: Sie kann Lücken in der Realisierung des Systems entsprechen; so in dem von Oliveira angeführten Fall der Adverbialbildung auf *-mente*, wo, wie er bemerkt, *raramente*, *prestesmente*, nicht, bzw. nicht mehr gesagt werden. In anderen Fällen können gewisse Möglichkeiten deshalb nicht realisiert werden, weil die entsprechenden Stellen in der Sprachnorm schon anders besetzt sind; so entspricht nach Oliveira die Bildung von Verbalnomina auf *-ção* (Typ: *orar* – *oração*) zwar einer 'regra geral', diese Regel könne man aber nicht bei allen Verben anwenden, so z.B. nicht bei *amar*, wo man als Verbalnomen *amor* hat (42). Die Sprachregeln gelten also für Oliveira als solche, auch wenn sie in Einzelfällen nicht angewandt werden, denn diese Nichtanwendung hebt sie nicht auf. Sie dürfen folglich auch für virtuelle, im Sprachgebrauch nicht existierende Formen behauptet werden, und gewisse nicht 'normale' Formen können gerade als die sprachlich richtigen angesehen werden. Nachdem er die Regel formuliert hat, daß die ethnischen Namen auf *-ão* wie *africão*, *indião* im allgemeinen – und zwar trotz der Gegenbeispiele wie *alemão* – *alemães*, *bretão* – *bretões* – den Plural auf *-ãos* bilden, bemerkt Oliveira, daß man auch *romãos*, *italiãos*, *valenciãos* sagen würde, wenn man die entsprechenden Singularformen auf *-ão* hätte;[63] so

[62] "As quaes [regras], porque aqui são mais gerais e comprendem mais, chamamoslhe naturaes; e de feito pareçẽ ser mais proprias e consoãtes à natureza da lingua" (42).

[63] "e se fosse em costume tambem diriamos *Romão* – *Romãos*, *Italião* – *Italiãos*, *Valençião* – *Valençiãos*" (45). Die 'normalen' Singularformen sind in diesen Fällen

würde man auch von *castelão*, wenn es diesen Singular gäbe ("se o ouvesse no mundo") den Plural *castelãos* bilden (45). Mit ähnlicher Begründung betrachtet Oliveira die Form *el-rei* (d.h. gerade die 'normale' Form für die Bezeichnung des Königs von Portugal) als unportugiesisch: Die Spanier, wenn sie die Portugiesen nachahmend für *el-rei de Portugal* '*o rei de Portugal*' sagen, in der Annahme, dies sei 'portugiesischer', täuschen sich eigentlich nicht, denn tatsächlich entspreche nicht *el-rei*, sondern *o rei* dem 'Wesen' des Portugiesischen.[64]

6.0 Schon in der Beschreibungspraxis Oliveiras sowie in ihrer jeweiligen Motivierung scheint also eine weitgehend selbständige und kohärente Sprachauffassung durch. Oliveira äußert sich jedoch auch ausdrücklich zu verschiedenen Problemen der Sprachtheorie und der Theorie der Sprachen, und zwar mit stets bemerkenswerten und oft ausgesprochen originellen Ansichten. Seine wichtigsten sprachtheoretischen Stellungnahmen betreffen: a) das Wesen der Sprache und der Sprachen; b) den Sprachwandel; c) die Vielfältigkeit der historischen Sprache.

6.1.1 Als Eigenschaft der 'almas racionais' (cf. Fn. 67) ist die Sprache für Oliveira eine geistige Erscheinung; in ihrer Realisierung sei sie jedoch biologisch, durch 'die Gesetze des Körpers' bedingt.[65] Daher wahrscheinlich auch sein Interesse für die Lautphysiologie und sogar für Realisierungsgewohnheiten wie den Sprechrhythmus.[66]

6.1.2 Die Sprache im allgemeinen, besser gesagt die Sprachfähigkeit – die Fähigkeit zu sprechen und Gesprochenes zu verstehen – betrachtet

im Portugiesischen *romano, italiano, valenciano* (heute übrigens auch *africano, indiano*, nicht die von Oliveira angegebenen *africão, indião*).

64 "para que seja *o rey* mais nosso dizer que *el-rey*, ajuda-me muito o natural da nossa lingua, o qual imitão os castelhanos quando nos querem arremedar dizẽdo "Manda o rey de Portugal", e não dizẽ "Manda el-rey de Portugal", que a elles era mais proprio dizer, mas isto fazem, cuidãdo que assi falão mais portugues; e de feito não se enganão" (43).

65 "Porẽ não é tã espiritual a lingua que não seja obrigada às leys do corpo" (1). Der Körper sei seinerseits durch die Umwelt ("as condiçóes do çeo e terra") bedingt. Auf diese biologische und indirekt ökologische Bedingtheit möchte Oliveira im Grunde die wesentlichen Unterschiede zwischen den Sprachen im phonischen Bereich zurückführen (ibid.).

66 Cf. seine Feststellung zum portugiesischen Sprechrhythmus (die allerdings für das heutige europäische Portugiesisch nicht mehr stimmt): "e outras nações cortão vozes apressando-sse mays em seu falar, mas nos falamos com grande repouso como homẽs assentados" (1). Vgl. auch seine Bemerkung zur Sprechweise der Spanier und der Portugiesen (7).

Oliveira als Gabe Gottes, d.h. als naturgegeben.[67] Eine bestimmte Sprache sei jedoch menschliches Werk ("Die Menschen machen die Sprache, nicht die Sprache die Menschen"), und ihre Gestaltung hänge deshalb mit der kulturellen Entwicklung der Menschen zusammen.[68] In dieser Hinsicht sei eine historische Sprache 'Usus', traditionelle Einrichtung ('costume'),[69] und auch die Regeln einer Sprache seien Regeln und Gesetze des 'costume', d.h. soziale, historisch gegebene Normen.[70] Folglich sei die Grammatik ihrem Wesen nach nicht normativ, sondern deskriptiv; ihre Aufgabe sei einfach, den 'costume' festzustellen, nicht etwa, dem 'costume' Regeln vorzuschreiben. Sie beinhalte als solche keine Einschränkung der Freiheit der Sprecher, sie könne aber auch nichts Neues denjenigen beibringen, die die Sprache schon beherrschen.[71] Die Grammatik [einer Nationalsprache] müsse allerdings den 'bom costume' feststellen, d.h. die 'exemplarische' Form dieser Sprache beschreiben, was sich Oliveira in seinem Werk auch vornimmt.[72] Die exemplarische Sprache, zu deren Vorzügen er die Klarheit und die allgemeine Verständlichkeit rechnet, ist nun für Oliveira nicht etwa die Sprache des Hofes oder der Hauptstadt, sondern diejenige der besten Sprecher, und diese sind für ihn diejenigen, die durch Bildung und Lebenserfahrung hervorragen und traditionsbewußt sind.[73]

6.2 Den Sprachwandel betrachtet Oliveira nicht wie so viele andere Theoretiker der Renaissance als 'Korruption' (Verfall), sondern wie Varro und Dante als der Sprache natürlich, d.h. als im Wesen der Sprache

[67] "este [das Sprachvermögen] só é hũ meyo que Deus quis dar as armas raçionaes para se poderẽ comunicar antre si e com o qual, sendo spirituaes, são sentidas dos corpos" (1).

[68] "E não desconfiemos da nossa lingua, porque os homẽs fazem a lingua, e não a lingoa os homẽs. E é manifesto que as linguas Grega e Latina primeiro forão grosseiras e os homẽs as poserão na perfeição que agora tem" (4).

[69] Dieser Begriff, auf die Sprache bezogen, kommt in der Grammatik Oliveiras immer wieder vor (Vorwort, 8, 36, 41, 42, 45).

[70] "As regras ou leys que digo são como disse anotações do bõ costume" (42).

[71] "ca esta arte de grammatica em todas as suas partes, e muito mais nesta da analogia, é resguardo e anotação d'esse costume e uso, tomada despois que os homẽs soberão falar, e não lei posta que os tire da boa liberdade quando é bẽ regida e ordenada por seu saber; nẽ é divinidade mãdada do çeo que nos possa de novo ensinar o que já temos e é nosso" (41).

[72] "eu não presumo ensinar aos que mays sabem, mas notarey o seu bõ costume" (Vorwort); vgl. auch das Zitat in der Fn. 70.

[73] "a primeira e principal virtude da lingua é ser clara e que a possão todos entender, e pera ser bem entẽdida ha de ser a mais acostumada antre os milhores della; e os milhores da lingua são os que mais lerão e virão, e viverão continoando mais antre primores, sisudos e assentados e não amigos de muita mudança" (38).

gegeben. Mit Bezug auf Varro erklärt er ihn einerseits eben wie Dante[74] ganz allgemein durch die Veränderlichkeit alles Menschlichen, aller menschlichen Einrichtungen.[75] Andererseits geht er jedoch darüber hinaus und erklärt den Sprachwandel im Zusammenhang mit den Grundfunktionen der Sprache: Als Ausdruck des Denkens und Kommunikationsmittel verändere sich die Sprache durch Anpassung an die Denkformen und an die wechselseitigen Beziehungen ('tratos') der Menschen.[76]

6.3 Wie mehr als zweihundert Jahre vor ihm Dante und wie sein Zeitgenosse Bovillus verweist Oliveira wiederholt auf die Vielfältigkeit, d.h. auf die innere Differenziertheit der historischen Sprache. In seinen diesbezüglichen Betrachtungen ist er jedoch ausführlicher als Dante und Bovillus und zudem viel genauer als letzterer.[77] Er begnügt sich nicht damit, die diachronische und 'diatopische' Differenziertheit (Differenziertheit in der Zeit und im Raum) festzustellen, sondern betont zugleich nachdrücklich die soziale Vielfältigkeit des Sprechens und der Sprache und stellt sogar, zumindest für den Wortschatz, die Existenz von 'Sondersprachen' fest. "Jeder spricht als der, der er ist",[78] "die Menschen sprechen von dem, was sie tun", und deshalb sprechen auch die verschiedenen sozialen Schichten und Gruppen nicht gleich.[79] Seine 'diçōes

[74] Cf. *De vulgari eloquentia*, I, 9, 6: "[Cum] homo sit instabilissimum atque variabilissimum animal, nec durabilis nec continua esse potest [loquela], sed sicut alia quae nostra sunt, puta mores et habitus, per locorum temporumque distantias variari oportet."

[75] "porque tambẽ o falar tem seu movimẽto, diz Marco Varrão, e muda-sse quando e como quer o costume" (45).

[76] "e muy poucas [são] as cousas que durão por todas ou muitas idades em hũ estado, quanto mais as falas que sempre se conformão cõ os conçeitos ou entenderes, juyzos e tratos dos homẽs; e esses homẽs entendem, julgão e tratão por diversas vias e muytas, as vezes segundo quer a neçessidade e as vezes segundo pedem as inclinações naturaes" (36).

[77] Die Originalität und Genauigkeit dieser Betrachtungen Oliveiras wird mit Recht von S. da Silva Neto, *op. cit.*, SS. 489-491, hervorgehoben. Dante (*De vulgari eloquentia*, I, 9, 4 und I, 9, 7) beschränkt sich in seinen ansonsten sehr scharfsinnigen Beobachtungen auf die räumliche und zeitliche Differenziertheit der Sprache, und Bovillus (*op. cit.*, Kap. 16 und 48-49) bezieht sich trotz des Titels seines Werkes nur auf die räumliche Differenziertheit und trennt übrigens die innere Vielfältigkeit der historischen Sprache und die Verschiedenheit der Sprachen in einem gegebenen Raum nicht voneinander: Die 'varietas Gallicis sermonis', von der er spricht, ist für ihn nicht nur die innere Differenziertheit des Französischen, sondern zugleich die Verschiedenheit der in Frankreich gesprochenen Sprachen.

[78] "Cada hũ fala como quẽ é" (1).

[79] "os homẽs falão do que fazẽ, e por tanto os aldeãos não sabẽ as falas da corte, e os çapateiros não são entendidos na arte do marear nẽ os lavradores d'Antre Douro e Minho entendem as novas vozes que est'ano vierão de Tunez com suas gorras" (32).

usadas' (cf. 3.1) teilt Oliveira dementsprechend in 'gerais' ('allgemein üblich', d.h. allen Sprechern einer Sprache gemeinsam), und 'particulares'. Letztere seien je nach den Gegenden und den sozialen Gruppen verschieden, denn, wie jede Gegend, so habe auch jede soziale Gruppe – Ritter, Bauern, Hofleute, Geistliche, Handwerker, Händler – ihre besonderen Wörter.[80]

7. Es darf, wie uns scheint, abschließend behauptet werden, daß Oliveira ein nicht unwichtiger Platz in der Geschichte der romanischen Sprachwissenschaft und der Sprachwissenschaft überhaupt gebührt. Er ist nach Nebrija einer der originellsten, in gewisser Hinsicht sogar der originellste Grammatiker, und vor Rhys und G. Bartoli der wichtigste Phonetiker der Renaissance in der Romania. Seine Ansichten zur Lexikologie und zu dem, was man heute 'Soziolinguistik' nennen würde, sind höchst bemerkenswert, sein Beitrag zur funktionellen Fragestellung in der deskriptiven Linguistik unverkennbar. Angesichts der Originalität seiner Ideen kann man nur bedauern, daß er nicht dazu kam, die anderen Werke (zur grammatischen Theorie, zum Verb, zur Satzsyntax) zu schreiben, die er als geplant, bzw. als schon begonnen angibt (Vorwort, 43, 46, 48, 49) und auf die er in seiner Grammatik mehrfach anzuspielen scheint (35, 44, 47); oder, wenn er sie geschrieben hat, daß uns diese Werke nicht erhalten geblieben sind.

Universität Tübingen

[80] "e porẽ de todas ellas [gemeint sind die 'dições usadas'], ou são *geraes* a todos, como *Deus*, *pão*, *vinho*, *çeo* e *terra*, ou são *particulares*. E esta particularidade ou se faz ãtre offiçios e tratos, como os cavaleiros que tẽ hũs vocabolos, e os lavradores outros, e os cortesãos outros, e os religiosos outros, e os mecanicos outros, e os mercaderes outros; ou se faz ẽ terras esta particularidade, porque os da Beira tem hũas falas e os d'Alentejo outras e os homẽs da Estremadura são diferentes dos d'Antre Douro e Minho, porque, assi como os tẽpos, assi tãbẽ as terras crião diversas cõdições e cõçeitos" (38).

UNIVERSAL QUANTIFIERS IN DUTCH

SIMON C. DIK

0. INTRODUCTION

This paper discusses some differences between the Dutch universal quantifiers *alle* ('all'), *iedere* ('every'), and *elke* ('each').[1] In the first section it will be shown, following Vendler (1967), that the difference between *alle* on the one hand, and *iedere/elke* on the other, can be explained in terms of the distinction between the COLLECTIVE and the DISTRIBUTIVE application of a predicate to a set, if, at least, these terms are suitably defined. In the second section it is argued that further differences between quantified constructions depend on the status of the set quantified over. A distinction is made between UNRESTRICTED and RESTRICTED sets, and between INTRODUCED and UNINTRODUCED sets, and these distinctions are shown to be relevant for the different uses of quantified expressions. Section 3 discusses the relations between universally quantified constructions and the PARTITIVE construction. It is shown that in Dutch these relations are much weaker than in English, and Jackendoff's (1968) proposals for describing quantifier constructions are discussed in this light. In the final section an attempt is made at differentiating between *iedere* and *elke*.

1. THE DIFFERENCE BETWEEN *ALLE* AND *IEDERE/ELKE*

In his stimulating paper "Each and every, any and all" Vendler (1967) has discussed a number of differences among universal quantifiers in English. In this section I will show that most of the properties differentiating *all* from *each* and *every* are also relevant for the differences between Dutch *alle* on the one hand, and *iedere* and *elke* on the other. Since these same properties do not differentiate between *iedere* and *elke*, I will leave their possible differences for later discussion and treat them as if they were completely synonymous in the present section.

A first rather obvious difference between *alle* and *iedere/elke* lies in the type and the number of the noun with which they can combine. The situation is as follows:

(1)

	+N −Count	+N +Count Sing	+N +Count Plur
alle	+	−	+
iedere/elke	−	+	−

Thus, in combinations of the type Quantifier + Noun, *alle* and *iedere/elke* are in complementary distribution with respect to the features ±Count and Singular/Plural: *iedere/elke* require a singular count noun, *alle* requires a mass noun or a plural count noun.

One way to combine *iedere/elke* with a plural count noun is to use a partitive construction.[2] Such a partitive construction is not possible with *alle*, in contradistinction to English *all*:

(2)a. Elk van die blokken is geel
Each of those blocks is yellow

b. Al die blokken zijn geel
All those blocks are yellow

c. *Alle van die blokken zijn geel
All of those blocks are yellow

The distribution of *alle* and *iedere/elke* as indicated in (1) suggests that *iedere/elke* have specific reference to individual countable entities, whereas *alle* can be applied to sets of individuals or to quantities. This initial characterization is corroborated if we have a look at the type of predicates with which noun phrases quantified by *alle* and *iedere/elke* can be combined. There is no clear semantic difference between (2a) and (2b), where the predicate *geel* 'yellow' designates a property of individual entities. Differences come to light, however, when we consider predicates which require an argument consisting of more than one individual. Such predicates can combine with noun phrases quantified by *alle*, but cannot combine with noun phrases quantified by *iedere/elke*. This comes out quite clearly with predicates containing the reciprocal *elkaar* 'each other':[3]

(3) Alle kollega's haten elkaar
All the colleagues hate each other

(4) *Elk van de kollega's haat elkaar
*Each of the colleagues hates each other

(5) Al die blokken passen in elkaar
All those blocks fit into each other
(6) *Elk van die blokken past in elkaar
*Each of those blocks fits into each other

The same applies to other types of predicates requiring more than one individual:

(7) Al die lijnen lopen parallel
All those lines run parallel
(8) *Elk van die lijnen loopt parallel
*Each of those lines runs parallel
(9) Alle touristen gingen gezamenlijk naar het museum
All the tourists went together to the museum
(10) *Elk van de touristen ging gezamenlijk naar het museum
*Each of the tourists went together to the museum

When, on the other hand, the predicate is specifically restricted to individuals, it can not only take noun phrases quantified with *iedere/elke* as subject, but also noun phrases quantified with *alle*:

(11) Elk van de touristen ging afzonderlijk naar het museum
Each of the tourists went separately to the museum
(12) Alle touristen gingen afzonderlijk naar het museum
All the tourists went separately to the museum

It is thus clear that *iedere* and *elke* single out every single individual from among a certain set, and require predicates designating properties of such individuals. *Alle* also tolerates individual predicates and in such cases the difference between *iedere/elke* and *alle* is slight. *Alle* can also combine, however, with predicates which require more than one individual in the argument.

Vendler (1967:74) explains this difference in terms of the traditional logical distinction between the *distributive* and the *collective* application of a predicate to a set. His explanation of these notions, however, requires some comment. Relations such as those of 'similarity' and of 'fitting together', he says, "can apply to the whole set in a *collective* sense, or to subsets (couples) of the whole group in a *distributive* sense. ... We can safely conclude then that, at least with respect to a given group of individuals, the reference appropriate to *all* is collective, and the reference appropriate to *each* and *every* is distributive."

However, when *each* and *every* (or Dutch *iedere/elke*) are used, the predicate never applies to subsets (or couples) from among the total set, but always to the individual members of the set taken one by one. We can here speak of a distributive use of the predicate only when we define the term 'distributive' accordingly.

In the second place, the term 'collective' is not quite unequivocal: there are at least two ways in which a predicate can apply to 'the whole set': (i) it can apply to all the members of the set, or (ii) it can apply to the set as such, taken as a totality. In the latter case, as I have suggested elsewhere (Dik 1974) one could speak of 'set-predicates'. These can be one-place or more-place. We would then have: (a) one-place individual predicates such as 'be ill', (b) more-place individual predicates such as 'be taller than', (c) one-place set predicates such as 'be numerous', and (d) more-place set predicates such as 'be more numerous than'.

Certain predicates, moreover, can either function as individual predicates or as set-predicates. A one-place predicate ambiguous in this way is 'be large', as used in:

(13)a. That cupboard is large (individual)
b. That group is large (set)

And an example of a two-place predicate ambiguous between application to individuals or to sets is 'be similar':

(14)a. John and Harry are similar (individual)
b. This group and that group are similar (set)

Now it should be noted that English *all* and Dutch *alle* do not or not easily combine with real set-predicates, which assign properties to sets taken in their totality. Consider the following sentences:

(15)a. Those blocks are numerous
b. *All those blocks are numerous
c. *Al die blokken zijn talrijk
d. ??The number of all those blocks is 17
e. ??Het aantal van al die blokken bedraagt 17

(15d) is judged grammatical by Vendler (1967:72) in the sense of 'the total number of those blocks is 17'. Sentences similar to (15e) are judged grammatical by Van Langendonck (1973:282). In my opinion, however, these sentences are of very doubtful grammaticality in the intended interpretation.[4]

Consider also:

(16)a. These boys are similar to those boys
b. All these boys are similar to all those boys

(16a) is ambiguous between a reading in which the similarity is established between individual boys, and a reading in which the similarity holds between the set of 'these boys' and the set of 'those boys'. But (16b) only has the reading in which the similarity holds between individual members from the two sets.

Van Langendonck (1973:281) rightly shows that noun phrases quantified with *alle* can take set-predicates if *samen* 'together' is added. The same applies to English:

(16)c. *Alle jongens vormden een bonte bende
*All boys formed a mixed pack
d. Alle jongens samen vormden een bonte bende
All the boys together formed a mixed pack

On the basis of these facts we can say that *alle* alone does not tolerate set-predicates. Only the combination of *alle* and *samen* does.

The matter is complicated further in that sets can themselves be quantified over as if they were individual entities. In that case, not only *all*, but also *each* can be used as a quantifier and combine with set-predicates (the same applies to Dutch):

(17)a. All those groups are big
b. Each of those groups is big

It is evident, however, that in such uses it is each individual set from among a collection of sets to which the predicate applies.

From these considerations it appears that the difference between *all* and *every/each* (and their Dutch counterparts) does not lie in their capacity or incapacity to combine with set-predicates: if they are used to quantify over individuals, neither *all* nor *each/every* tolerate set-predicates; and if they are used to quantify over sets, both of them do.

What we might say, then, about the difference is the following: a noun phrase quantified by *each/every* (*iedere/elke*) presents the members of the set in question as items which can be predicated one by one, each separate from the other. A noun phrase quantified by *all*, however, offers the whole collection of individuals for predication.

Thus predicates to be applied to noun phrases quantified by *each/every* can be any predicates applicable to single items of the type in question.

Predicates to be applied to noun phrases quantified by *all* can be any predicates applicable in the case of *each/every*, plus any predicates applicable to pairs, triples, etc. of items of the type in question. If one wishes to use the terms *distributive* and *collective* for this difference, these terms should be defined accordingly. *Collective* should then be taken to mean 'applying to the full range of individuals in a set', not 'applying to a set considered as a totality'.

2. DIFFERENCES RELATED TO THE STATUS OF THE SET TO WHICH QUANTIFICATION APPLIES

Further differences between the universal quantifiers are connected with differences in the status of the set to which the quantification applies (the domain of quantification). We can approach these differences as follows: any count noun can be regarded as a predicate which defines the set of all entities to which that predicate applies. Thus, the noun *dog* defines the set of all entities to which the predicate 'dog' applies, i.e. the set of dogs. In certain uses of the universal quantifier, we make statements about such all-inclusive sets. E.g.:

(18) All dogs are mammals

The set defined by an expression like *all dogs* in (18) may be called *unrestricted*, since a statement like (18) is meant to apply to anything to which the predicate 'dog' is applicable. It is, in general, not possible to specify the number of members of such a set.

In many cases, however, we want to talk about *restricted* subsets of such unrestricted sets. We can do so by adding information such that the addressee is able to identify the particular subset that we want to talk about. This can be either descriptive information, specifying the subset in question in terms of properties independent of the immediate situation of the speech act, or pragmatic information, relating the subset to the immediate situation. In many cases, both descriptive and pragmatic information will serve to specify the restricted subset that we want to identify. The difference between unrestricted and restricted sets comes out in the following examples:

(19)a. All dogs are mammals (unrestricted)
b. All those dogs over there are mine (restricted)
(20)a. All cars are unreliable (unrestricted)
b. All the cars I ever had were unreliable (restricted)
(21)a. All men are equal (unrestricted)
b. All the men in the room were non-smokers (restricted)

In the case of restricted sets, it is in principle possible to add a specification of the number of its members: *all those five dogs over there, all the six cars I've had*, etc.

We shall see that the universal quantifiers behave differently when they are used to quantify over a restricted set than when they quantify over an unrestricted set.

A second important difference relevant only for restricted sets, depends on the question whether the set referred to has or has not been introduced earlier in the discourse. All the quantified noun phrases in (19)-(21) are such that they could be used to start a new discourse (i.e., they could be used as first utterance in a conversation, first line in an article, etc.). This is not the case with expressions like:

(22)a. All the dogs are terriers
b. Each of the dogs gets his own food

(22a-b) cannot be used unless the identity of the subset referred to has been established beforehand. I.e., a speaker can only use expressions like (22a-b) when he has reason to presume that the subset he wants to say something about is known to the addressee, either from the preceding context or from self-evident features in the immediate situation. I shall call a set which is presumed to be known beforehand an *introduced* set, and a set which is not, an *unintroduced* set. Thus, by means of expressions like the quantified noun phrases in (19)-(21) we can talk about unintroduced sets. In fact, these sets *are* introduced by means of the expressions themselves. By means of the quantified noun phrases in (22a-b) we can talk about introduced sets, the identity of which has been established beforehand in some way.

The difference between introduced and unintroduced sets is not relevant in the same way in the case of unrestricted sets. In a certain sense, such sets always have the character of 'introduced sets': knowledge of the meaning of the noun phrase itself is enough to establish the unrestricted set in question as a set which can be talked about. The introduction of such a set equals the introduction of a new term. Cf. the following discourses:

(23) Arab leaders are called 'emirs'. *All emirs* are believed to be descendants of Mohammed.

(24) At the oil conference there were six Arab emirs. *All the emirs* wore their ceremonial dress.

In (23) an unrestricted set is introduced through the introduction of the term *emir*. It is then possible to go on talking about this unrestricted set by means of a quantified noun phrase without definite article. In the first sentence of (24) a restricted set is introduced. One can then go on with a quantified noun phrase with definite article. The second sentence of (24) could not open a discourse unless the speaker had reason to presume that the addressee knew the particular set in question. The second sentence of (23), however, can open a discourse if only the speaker has reason to believe that the addressee knows what an emir is. Thus, the use of an expression referring to an unrestricted set never requires that this set as such has been introduced beforehand.

For the purposes of the present discussion, therefore, we can distinguish three types of sets: restricted introduced sets, restricted unintroduced sets, and unrestricted sets. Let us now see what the relevance of these distinctions is for the use of the different universal quantifiers. In order to show this, we must first have a closer look at the various syntactic constructions in which these quantifiers can occur. We find the following constructions:

(25)a.	alle honden	all dogs
b.	elke hond	each dog
c.	iedere hond	every dog
d.	al de honden	all the dogs
e.	de honden (...) allemaal	the dogs (...) all = all the dogs
f.	elk van de honden	each of the dogs

These are the main possibilities for using *alle*, *elke*, and *iedere*. There are certain further constructions which can be used when the number of members of the set in question is explicitly indicated, or when the complement is pronominal. These possibilities will be discussed later. Let us first see how the constructions (25a-f) can be used with respect to the different types of set which we have just distinguished.

In the case of unrestricted sets we get the following paradigm:

(26)a. Alle mensen zijn sterfelijk
All men are mortal
b. Elk mens is sterfelijk
c. Ieder mens is sterfelijk
d. *Al de mensen zijn sterfelijk
e. *De mensen zijn allemaal sterfelijk
f. *Elk van de mensen is sterfelijk

As is clear from the examples, all constructions containing the definite article are ungrammatical in this case.[5] With restricted unintroduced sets the situation is different:

(27)a. Alle deelnemers aan het symposium houden een lezing
All participants at the symposium hold a lecture
b. Elke deelnemer aan het symposium houdt een lezing
c. Iedere deelnemer aan het symposium houdt een lezing
d. Al de deelnemers aan het symposium houden een lezing
e. De deelnemers aan het symposium houden allemaal een lezing
f. Elk van de deelnemers aan het symposium houdt een lezing

In this case, all the constructions mentioned are grammatical. In the case of restricted introduced sets, the possibilities are a little less clear. Still, it seems that the following paradigm can be set up:

(28) Er lagen vier appels in de mand
There were four apples in the basket
a. ?*Alle appels waren rot
All apples were rotten
b. ?*Elke appel was rot
c. ?*Iedere appel was rot
d. Al de appels waren rot
e. De appels waren allemaal rot
f. Elk van de appels was rot

In this case, then, the constructions with the definite article are grammatical, while the other constructions are of doubtful grammaticality.

Summarizing these facts, we can set up the following scheme:

	Construction:	The set in question is: Unrestricted	Restricted Unintroduced	Restricted Introduced
(a)	*alle* Npl	+	+	?–
(b)	*elke* Nsg	+	+	?–
(c)	*iedere* Nsg	+	+	?–
(d)	*al de* Npl	–	+	+
(e)	*de* Npl *allemaal*	–	+	+
(f)	*elk van de* Npl	–	+	+

It is evident, therefore, that (i) the difference between restricted and unrestricted sets, and (ii) the question whether or not the set is known beforehand, are relevant for describing the properties of the different quantified constructions.

On the basis of these data we can say that the presence of the definite article implies restrictedness (and therefore identifiability) of the set involved, but we cannot say that restrictedness requires the presence of the definite article: the constructions (a)-(c) are possible even in the case of restricted unintroduced sets. The value of the definite article comes out more clearly, however, when the number of members of the set spoken about is made explicit. In that case the constructions (a)-(c) are ungrammatical:

(29)a. *Alle vier bomen in onze tuin zijn doodgegaan
All four trees in our garden have died
b. *Elke vier bomen in onze tuin zijn doodgegaan
c. *Iedere vier bomen in onze tuin zijn doodgegaan
d. Alle vier de bomen in onze tuin zijn doodgegaan
e. De vier bomen in onze tuin zijn allemaal doodgegaan
The four trees in our garden have all died
or:
De bomen in onze tuin zijn alle vier doodgegaan
*The trees in our garden have all four died
f. Elk van de vier bomen in onze tuin is doodgegaan

One should of course expect (29b) and (29c) to be ungrammatical, since *elke* and *iedere* cannot combine with plural noun phrases.[6] But it is rather strange that (29a) is ungrammatical, although the corresponding construction without explicit number is grammatical:

(30) Alle bomen in onze tuin zijn doodgegaan

3. RELATIONS WITH THE PARTITIVE CONSTRUCTION

The quantifier constructions discussed so far have certain semantic and syntactic relations with the partitive construction, in which a proper subset is singled out from a more inclusive set:

(31)a. Drie van de vier bomen zijn doodgegaan
Three of the four trees have died
b. *Vier van de vier bomen zijn doodgegaan
*Four of the four trees have died
(32)a. Alle vier de bomen zijn doodgegaan
*All four the trees have died

b. De bomen zijn alle vier doodgegaan
*The trees have all four died

(33) Elk van de vier bomen is doodgegaan
Each of the four trees has died

(31a) is a partitive construction singling out a subset of three members from among a more inclusive set of four members. This more inclusive set must be expressed by means of a definite description:

(34)a. *Drie van vier bomen zijn doodgegaan
*Three of four trees have died

b. *Drie van bomen zijn doodgegaan
*Three of trees have died

This is presumably because it would be difficult to conceive how one could single out a subset from a set which itself is not presumed to be identified.

The partitive construction can only be used to define *proper* subsets: the number of the subset must be smaller than the number of the including set. (31b), although it could easily be interpreted, is not grammatical. Instead of (31b), one can use (32a-b) or (33). The latter construction is obviously modeled on the partitive construction, and should be described as a link between that construction and universal quantification.

This is not so clear, however, for constructions (32a-b) and here we find some interesting differences between Dutch and English, where the relations with the partitive construction are much stronger:

(35)	English	Dutch
a.	each of the trees	elk van de bomen
b.	each one of the trees	*elk een van de bomen
c.	every one of the trees	*ieder een van de bomen
d.	all of the trees	*alle van de bomen

There are some further constructions where English has a partitive possibility not existing in Dutch:

(36)	English	Dutch
a.	both of the trees	*beide van de bomen
b.	the trees, {all / each} of which	*de bomen, {alle / elk} van welke
c.	the trees, both of which	*de bomen, beide van welke

On the basis of the English data, Jackendoff (1968) suggested a partitive source for constructions with quantifiers. An *of*-deletion transformation would then lead to the non-partitive variants. Jackendoff further suggested that quantifiers like *all*, *each*, and *every* could be treated as articles to the indefinite noun *one* which appears in (35b-c). Without going into the possible merits of these claims for the description of English, it is clear that they would have no or much less justification in the case of Dutch. In the constructions dealt with there is never a possibility of inserting an element like *een*, the Dutch equivalent of English *one*. We have the combinations *iedereen* and *elkeen* 'everyone', but these can only be used substantively, and never in the constructions discussed above. In Dutch, then, there is no basis for classifying these quantifiers as articles. In general, given the specific status of quantifying elements, I believe that questions like 'are quantifiers articles, pronouns, or nouns?' cannot be answered in a sensible way, because they in fact constitute a category of their own.

In the second place it appears that a general partitive-like source for all the quantifying constructions is much less attractive for Dutch than it is for English. As far as the universal quantifiers are concerned, this would imply that the partitive marker *van* ('of') would have to be deleted in all cases except in the presence of *elke*. There is only one other partitive construction containing a universal quantifier. This is when *iedere* is combined with a plural pronoun:

(37) ieder van ons / jullie / hen
each of us / you / them

In all other cases the partitive construction signals that a proper subset is isolated from a more inclusive set:

(38)a. sommige van de bomen — some of the trees
b. veel van de bomen — many of the trees
c. een deel van de bomen — a part of the trees

That *alle* cannot occur in a partitive construction, although this is possible in the case of *elke* and (in special circumstances) *iedere*, may be explained, perhaps, in the light of the differences between *alle* and *elke*/*iedere* discussed in section 1 of this paper. For although quantification with *elke* and *iedere* ranges over the whole set in question, it focusses on every single member of that set, and thus in a certain sense singles out every single member from among the total set. We saw that this is not so when *alle* is used.

4. THE DIFFERENCES BETWEEN *IEDERE* AND *ELKE*

As is the case with English *each* and *every*, *elke* and *iedere* can be interchanged in many contexts:

(39)a. Hij komt elke dag
He comes each day
b. Hij komt iedere dag
He comes every day
(40)a. Elke deelnemer moet een lezing houden
Each participant must hold a lecture
b. Iedere deelnemer moet een lezing houden
Every participant must hold a lecture

There are, however, a number of differences between *elke* and *iedere*, some of which have been mentioned in the preceding sections.

When the complement of the quantifier is non-pronominal, and non-human, only *elke* can be used in the partitive construction:

(41)a. Elk van de vier bomen is doodgegaan
Each of the four trees has died
b. *Ieder van de vier bomen is doodgegaan

We saw that in Dutch there is no construction comparable to English:

(42) Every one of the four trees has died

If, however, the complement is pronominal, *iedere* is possible in the partitive construction, and even more natural than *elke*:

(43)a. Ieder van ons / jullie / hen
*Every of us/ you / them
b. ?Elk van ons / jullie / hen
Each of us / you / them

This suggests that *iedere* has a preference for human complements. This is corroborated by the fact that the normal word for 'everyone' is *iedereen*, whereas the corresponding *elkeen* is rather archaic. There is further some evidence that even in the case of non-pronominal complements the use of *iedere* in the partitive is more grammatical when that complement designates human beings than when it does not:

(44)a. Elk van de deelnemers moet een lezing houden
Each of the participants must hold a lecture

b. ?Ieder van de deelnemers moet een lezing houden
*Every of the participants must hold a lecture

But judgements of grammaticality appear to vary here. The affinity of *iedere* with human complements is demonstrated further by the fact that by the side of *iedereen* 'everyone' and its more archaic variant *een ieder, ieder* by itself can function as the antecedent of a relative clause:

(45)a. Iedereen die deelneemt moet een lezing houden
b. Een ieder die deelneemt moet een lezing houden
c. Ieder die deelneemt moet een lezing houden
Everyone who participates must hold a lecture

(45c) is possible only when human beings are involved. In these same constructions *elkeen* would be archaic, and **een elk* and just *elk* would be ungrammatical.

One difference between *elke* and *iedere*, then, would appear to be the fact that *iedere* has a tendency to be preferred when the set quantified over consists of humans. There are some other differences, however, which cannot be explained in terms of the human/non-human opposition. When the set in question consists of just two entities, only *elke* can be used:

(46)a. elk van beide jongens
*each of both boys
b. *ieder van beide jongens

The ungrammaticality of (46b) is comparable to the ungrammaticality of English:

(47) *every one of the two boys

Again as in English, the Dutch reciprocal is *elkaar* or archaic *elkander* 'each other', whereas **iederander* is impossible. It must be added that especially in *elkaar* the element *elk-* can hardly be said to function independently. In this respect the English reciprocal *each other* is much more transparent. These differences seem to show that when very small sets are quantified over (no matter whether they consist of humans or non-humans), *elke* is preferred to *iedere*.

Vendler (1967:78) explains similar differences between English *each* and *every* as follows: "*every* stresses completeness or, rather, exhaustiveness (...); *each*, on the other hand, directs one's attention to the individuals as they appear, in some succession or other, one by one." It appears that a difference of this kind cannot be established between Dutch *elke* and *iedere*. At least, if present at all, it is less prominent than it is in English.

It seems, then, that we cannot get further than the statement that *elke* is preferred when the set quantified over is small (especially when it consists of only two members), and that, if the set in question is not small, *iedere* has a tendency to be preferred when the set consists of human beings. It is clear that the difference between *all* on the one hand, and *elke/iedere* on the other is much greater than the difference between *elke* and *iedere*.

Institute for General Linguistics
University of Amsterdam

REFERENCES

Dik, Simon C.
1974 "Sets in semantic structure", to appear in the *Proceedings of the Eleventh International Congress of Linguists, Bologna* (= Publication no. 4, Institute of General Linguistics, University of Amsterdam, 1972).

Jackendoff, Ray S.
1968 "Quantifiers in English", *Foundations of Language*, 4, 422-42.

Van Langendonck, W.
1973 "Singulariteit, pluraliteit en kollektiviteit in het licht van de kwantorenteorie", *Handelingen der Koninklijke Zuidnederlandse Maatschappij voor Taal- en Letterkunde en Geschiedenis*, 27, 273-89.

Vendler, Zeno
1967 "Each and every, any and all", *Linguistics in Philosophy*, 70-96. Ithaca, Cornell University Press.

NOTES

1 Each of these quantifiers occurs in two variants: *al/alle, ieder/iedere, elk/elke* depending on certain properties of the noun phrases in which they occur. This automatic alternation will be disregarded here, since it is not semantically relevant. For practical use in paraphrases and translations, the English glosses 'all' (for *alle*), 'each' (for *elke*), and 'every' (for *iedere*) are given. This should not be taken as implying that the English and Dutch quantifiers have precisely the same properties. In fact, I shall point to some differences below. Some of the Dutch sentences are provided with a literal version in English, which often does not result in a grammatical English sentence.

2 There is one other possibility of combining *iedere* and *elke* with plural noun phrases, *viz.* in sentences like (a) *Hij komt iedere drie weken* 'He comes every three weeks', or (b) *Drie van elke vier werknemers waren ziek* 'Three out of every four employees were ill'. This possibility exists only when the noun phrase contains a numeral,

and the group designated by the combination of numeral + noun is interpreted as a unit. I.e., in (a) it is *periods* of time that are quantified over, and in (b) *groups* of four employees.

[3] Cf. also Van Langendonck (1973:275).

[4] As Vendler (1967) rightly notes, (15d) is of course grammatical when it is taken to apply to a set of blocks, each of which has the number 17 on it.

[5] This is my judgement, at least. However, judgements about sentences such as these differ rather strongly. Many speakers of Dutch consider (26d-f) acceptable, though less so than (26a-c). It appears that Belgian speakers use (26d-f) without appreciable difference with (26a-c), perhaps under the influence of French constructions like *Tous les hommes sont mortels* 'All men are mortal', where the definite article is standard

[6] Although, with sufficient contextualisation, an interpretation in the sense of note 2. could be imposed on (29b) and (29c).

ON SAYING*

F. G. DROSTE

I. It's generally known, though not always explicitly stated, that the verb *say*, together with a small group which could be regarded semantically related to it (cf. Rätsep 1973:391), has two distinct syntactic frames and a third one connecting both. We allude to complement structures such as

(1) He says that he'll come tomorrow
(2) He says: "I'll come tomorrow"
(3) He says he'll come tomorrow

Since the third frame can be considered a variant, esp. of (1) but in certain respects of (2) as well, we shall further disregard this bastardy phenomenon and concentrate on the two remaining ones. This one-sided concentration may also explain why we do not start, directly, from Zwicky's 1971 paper; while he analyses the phenomenon of reported speech, we want to restrict ourselves to the relation indirect-direct speech, esp. in regard to the verb *say*. Although the different uses of *say* are respectable enough to have earned a classification in different groups, they are less transparent than this distinction suggests. Cf., e.g.,

(4) He says that I have a beautiful mistress
(5) He says: 'I have a beautiful mistress'

It is clear that (4) and (5) are not related to a degree where one underlying structure would suffice. This is remarkable, at least on face value, since both (6) and (7) could be argued to have the same underlying structure as (4), though they differ from it much more than (5), at least superficially:

(6) He says: 'You have a beautiful mistress'
(7) He says: 'He has a beautiful mistress'

* I'm grateful to my colleagues Emma Vorlat and Guido Geerts for friendly criticism of the first draft of this paper.

To complicate things a bit more it is worth stating that (4), or rather the subject of 'have', can refer to the same 'referent' as (6) and (7), to the same as (6) but not as (7), to the same as (7) but not as (6), and it could also refer to situations (6) nor (7) could refer to. But a relation to (8), although markedly different in form, is quite feasible, at least on referential grounds:

(8) He says: 'Mr. D. happens to have a beautiful mistress'

As regards (5) this could possibly be related to

(9) He says that he has a beautiful mistress

but since the latter is ambiguous, it has to allow also for a reading which excludes coreferentiality of both 'he's'. The way out of this complicated situation, i.e. by stating that this is a matter of deictic functions only, is an overt simplification. For also in

(10) He says that the neighbor's wife is a most beautiful woman

the necessary transparency is failing. The talkative 'he' in fact could as well have exclaimed

(11) 'The neighbor's wife is a most beautiful woman'

as

(12) 'Mrs. K. is a most beautiful woman'

not knowing, in the latter case, that Mrs. K. happens to be the wife of the speaker's neighbor. It should be mentioned that by referring to 'the speaker', we do not aim at the 'he' of (10) but at the person (the underlying 'I') who reports the other's confidences.

The problems we are confronted with, difficult to solve within the limitations of syntax, are not unknown in philosophical quarters. Mediaeval philosophical linguists, e.g., distinguished between an 'interpretatio de dicto' – for (12) – and one 'de re' for (10) (cfr. McCawley 1971:224). This distinction covers what Quine has named the transparency-opacity domain. "Quotation," according to Quine, "gives rise to non-referential positions" (1960:143), which happens to be irrefutable since

(13) Tom believes that Cicero denounced Cataline

(Quine's example) may as well refer to Cicero as to Tully (also if Tom never knew that both names refer to one and the same person). It is proved, furthermore, that verbs such as *look for* also have an opaque reading in certain contexts, i.e. at least two readings can be attached to its object, as is demonstrated by

(14) The commissioner is looking for the chairman of the hospital board

Although Quine is correct in signaling phenomena of opacity, and also in constituting classes of verbs whose objects in one way or another are not transparent, he has not discovered the whole truth. For no double readings are connected with these verbs as soon as they have a first-person subject:

(15) I am looking for the chairman of the hospital board

The problem, therefore, although pertaining to a special class of verbs indeed, should rather be related to what is called: reported speech. It is only in reported speech – number (1) through (10) as well as (13) – that opacity problems may arise, i.e. only in those instances where speaker and subject of the main verb *say* do not coincide. To avoid problems of territorial trespassing ('What is reported speech?', 'Is the speaker part of the utterance?', etc.) we better presuppose a typological frame, basic to every utterance in accordance with the Austin-Ross doctrine (but see section II). All the above examples (1) through (10), then, could be schematized as

(16) *I say to you that* (S (S'))

and problems of opacity rise only where the subject of S is not coreferential with the subject of the typological frame. Now (14) offers a remarkable difficulty. If speaker and addressee both notice the commissioner without having talked to him, the speaker may utter (14), which then in no way is opaque. If the speaker reports (14) under different conditions, it immediately gets its opacity back. This is remarkable for the following reason: in (16) the embedded S necessarily dominates an embedded S' since the opacity results from a relation passing over the NP⁀VP of S: the typological 'I', in other words, may be considered responsible for the surface shape of the NP in S', independent of the *ad hoc* knowledge of the subject in S. The only way out – but the correct way out, for the matter – is offered by the assumption that a verb of *saying* is implicitly present in underlying structure. This is a more acceptable explanation than Quine's (dividing the verb *look for* into two components, viz. *endeavor* and *find*) since it is valid also for verbs such as *wonder, admire*.

Returning now to more technical problems relating to (10) on the one hand and (11)/(12) on the other, one wonders whether it is possible to transformationally relate those surface forms. Is it correct to simply assume that (10) has the same underlying structure as, e.g.,

(17) He says: 'The neighbor's wife is a most beautiful woman'

or

(18) He says: 'Mrs. K. is a most beautiful woman'

There seem to be two answers to this question, the first being that both can be regarded basic to (10). For (17), then, there are no special arrangements to be made, whereas in (18) the constituent 'Mrs. K.' has to be transformed into 'the neighbor's wife' on condition that the speaker considers both expressions full paraphrases, i.e. semantic paraphrases and not merely referential ones (cf. Droste 1974).

The second solution is a simpler one in that it regards only (17) as fundamental to (10), while (18) is a derived structure, secundary in relation to (17). This solution seems the more attractive one, since, otherwise, we are obliged to consider all types of paraphrases uniformly pertaining to one base structure. In that case one has to accept that there exists only one underlying structure for 'John's uncle' as well as for 'the person who is the brother of John's mother or father or the husband of ... etc.' (Chomsky 1971:197) Moreover, Zwicky's examples on reported speech prove that the relation to the original statement has to be nothing but a rough approximation of its content (1971:77).

However, sentences such as (4) and (5) cast shadows of doubt upon even the simple latter solution. As pointed out above, (6), (7), and (8) – and comparable structures also – can be related to (4), but a relation to (5) is explicitly excluded. Moreover, (6) as well as (7) and (8) lack the necessary mechanisms for indicating which indirect speech form it is, that has to be mapped into them. This seems to depend wholly on the situation speaker and hearer are in. In order to sustain this point we once more consider a series of surface structures, this time in their most rudimentary form:

(19) 'You are a lovely creature'
(20) He says: 'You are a lovely creature'

(19) and (20) are related in a direct way and, consequently, allow for only one transformational relation: the underlying structure of a complement S in direct speech is the underlying structure of the S as it has

been uttered in actual conversation. Once more we compare (19) with an indirect form:

(19) 'You are a lovely creature'
(21) He_i says that I/you/Mrs. K./*he_i/*be* a lovely creature

Except for a coreferential NP, almost any subject may appear in (21) in paraphrastic relation to the subject 'you' in (19). The choice between these infinitely many subject constituents cannot be made on independent, i.e. purely competential grounds. Moreover, each of the subject constituents of (21) can be related to the 'you' of (19), but also to NP's such as 'he', 'she', 'that post graduate student of yours', etc., i.e. to an infinite set of constituents also. The conclusion on indirect speech is as irrefutable as the one on direct speech, be it less innocent: the underlying structure of a complement S in indirect speech is explicitly not the same as the underlying structure of the parallel S as it has been uttered in actual conversation, although it may coincide with it for non-fundamental reasons.

The underlying structure of the abstract formula (21), therefore, is a series of base S's, dependent on the subject constituent which has been actualized:

(22) He says (that) I am a lovely creature
(23) He says (that) you are a lovely creature etc.

For the verb *say*, but for other speech reporting verbs as well, it has to be acknowledged that it has different underlying structures for direct and indirect speech respectively. These structures are not immediately related and do not follow the same transformational history. In direct speech *say* refers to the actual conversation and does not depend on the speaker's (= reporter's) attitude. In indirect speech *say* does not refer to the actual conversation in a direct way, but to the attitude of the speaker and to his interpretation of that conversation.

One may try to converge the discerned deep structures for direct and indirect speech by the introduction on a deep level of a variable ranging over NP's that differ in the two complement S's. The scope of the variable would then be determined either by the interpretation of the actual speaker (in direct speech), or by the interpretation of the secundary speaker. For (11), e.g., one could propose something like (11') and for (10) something like (10'):

(11') He says { (neighbor's wife, x) $\wedge$ (*beautiful*, x)}
(10') I say {(n's wife, x) $\wedge$ (he says (*beautiful*, y)) $\wedge$ ($x = y$)}

Apart from problems in presentation and inconsistencies in formal qualities of the strings, this solution seems to appear *ad hoc* in other respects. In (24), e.g.

(24) He says that Mrs. K. is a beautiful woman

it is possible to assume a base S such as (10'), but it is also possible that an underlying string parallel to that of (11') is present. This would imply that in indirect speech forms at least two sentoids must be presupposed, i.c. one with a variable whose scope is determined by the reporter and another where the range of the variable(s) solely depend(s) on the intention of the main clause subject. However, examples such as (21) most definitely prove that the reporter and the reporter only is responsible for the ultimate shape of the complement S.

II. With the above statements on the verb *say* – tentative as they may be – we have entered a domain where small but vehement battles have been fought so far, esp. on the problem of so-called performative verbs. In the Chomskyan approach (let us call it the Classical Theory) the use of typological markers (frame-verbs, performatives, qualifiers) is limited to those sentence types which deviate from the statistically 'normal' ones, viz. from the declarative sentence. In *Aspects* (p. 132), e.g., it is argued that Question transformations must be regarded obligatory and demand a marker in the base string. We could formalize this, in accordance with Jacobs & Rosenbaum (1968:19ff.), as S → Question + S'. The implication of this proposition is clear: only marked sentences, deviating in well-defined aspects from unmarked ones, ask for a typological frame. The unmarked, neutral type, i.e. the declarative sentence, should therefore not be represented as S → Assertion + S'. Contrary to this view, Generative semantics as well as less aggressively semantic theories have argued that the first branching rule of the syntactic rewrite system better be read as S → TYP + S'. The basic rule for generating a sentence can then be schematized as follows:

S → [TYP {NEG (MOD (QUANT (PROPOSITION)))}]

(cf. Droste 1973c:50), in which TYP(ology) should be read either as *I say to you*, or *I ask you*, or *I order you*. In this variant of the Classical Theory the necessity of a general typological frame is indisputable.

Two questions may be raised in connection with this difference in presentation:

(a) is not the Classical presentation simpler and more elegant and, therefore, preferable to the Semantic one, since it operates with a binary opposition in which a true Jakobsonian unmarked case can do without an (otherwise superfluous) operator, whereas the marked case distinguishes itself as such in many ways;

(b) if the Classical presentation has to be refuted – as we hope to prove – must the typological underlying frame then be considered as solely present in underlying structure, or can it also appear in surface structure, viz. as an unmarked main verb (as argued, i.e., by Hetzron 1971)?

Regarding (a) there seem to be arguments in favour of the Chomskyan approach. If we compare

(25) I say to you: 'Hello'
(26) *I say to you that hello
(27) 'Hello'

we could reason as follows: in section I it was proved that (26) but not (25) could be regarded as underlying (27). (26), however, is most distinctly ungrammatical. Therefore, it is unjustified to assume the presence of a typological verb in the underlying structure of non-Questions and non-Commands.

Some necessary conditions, however, fail in this way of reasoning. In the first place it is hardly conceivable to regard (27) as a statement: clearly the above three sentence types should be extended with at least a fourth one, as it has been suggested, i.a. by Seuren (1969:168). Moreover, there is no argument to attribute a function to the verb *say* in relation with the complement S 'Hello', and, worst of all, the surface deviance of (26) could not be regarded an argument for its deviance as an underlying string. So back to normality. We start again with some examples:

(28) He said that Diana was waiting for me

It is clear that this (reported) utterance may very well correspond to a direct speech form such as

(29) 'Beautiful Mrs. K. is waiting for you, Sir'

or even to

(30) 'That woman upstairs seems to be waiting for her companion'

which proves that the ultimate shape of (28) – only inferentially paraphrastic to (29) and (30) – depends on the 'reporter' alone. The following step in this string of arguments attributes a concrete role to this reporter. In utterances such as

(31) He said that I was waiting for the lady

the 'I' can only be explained, syntactically, by presupposing a deep frame to the subject of which it is coreferential. If this argument should not be considered convincing, one should look at

(32) He said that it was my fault

In order to use the possessive pronoun 'my' there must be a personal pronoun it refers to: the referent has to be present, not only pragmatically, i.e. in the 'reporter's situation', but in the linguistic frame-work as well.

As to (b), the surface validity phenomenon, if indeed a TYP verb can appear in surface structure, what consequences does that have for its semantic characteristics? It seems essential, anyway, that the frame verb, in this case *say*, relates to the content of its complement S and not to its form. This is necessary for sentences such as (33) to be valid as an order, and to guarantee the correct transformational history:

(33) *I order you that* (you come upstairs)

It is clear that the complement only obtains its ultimate order form in surface structure by collapsing the typological frame and the complement verb, i.e. the content of the latter with the form of the former verb. Relating the above remarks to *say* we can state the following: only if the complement S's are presented as direct speech forms is it possible to compare them as to their proposition. In (34), e.g., the conjoined constituents do not contradict each other:

(34) I do not say: 'She worships me', I say: 'I am worshipped by her'

while the conjoined constituents in (35) indeed cause a contradiction:

(35) *I do not say that she worships me, I say that I am worshipped by her

This divergence in results corroborates the thesis defended in section I: direct and indirect speech forms cannot be related to the same underlying structure. Moreover, they prove that a typological verb – such as *say* – should be considered as dominating an indirect speech form and not a direct speech form, since only the former pertains only to the content. It is for this very reason that

(36) *She does not worship me, I am worshipped by her

is contradictory in the sense (35) is. Comparisons of this type clarify why an underlying performative verb could never be regarded as a direct speech verb, because (36) in no way paralles (34). It should, by the way, be kept in mind that (35) is a surface structure and that *say* here cannot be considered a deep performative verb: it is generally agreed upon that a typological verb never takes an adverb (quantifier or predicate) such as *not*. Do we have any proof by now that the underlying verb cannot be realized in surface structure? Compare the following dialogue:

(37) 'I think Diana adorable'
('What do you say?')
(38) 'I say that my wife is worth a hell of a lot of attention'

It is clear that (38) parallels (37) in content, and can even count as a paraphrase, be it an inferential one. There is one difference between both, however, connected to the main clause 'I say that'. This functions here as 'I repeat', 'I just said', i.e. it has an explanatory function in relation to the former expression (37). If this is the case, this clause can no longer be regarded neutral; basic to (38), therefore, is a string such as

(39) *I say to you that* (I say that my wife ...)

It has been argued over and over again that a performative frame should be considered neutral in many respects: as to time, aspect, person (*I* ... *you*). We maintain – contrary to views expressed by Austin and Vendler – that such neutral phenomena simply cannot appear in surface structure since here, fundamentally, the sentence is expressed in utterance form and is, as such, attached to context, situation, pragmatics. This implies that I say to you now, or in the past, that I say repeatedly or as a new statement, etc. Conclusion:

(40) Come here!

has an underlying structure representable as

(41) *I order you that* (you come here)

whereas

(42) I order you to come here

has a base Sentence to be characterized as

(43) *I say to you that* (I order you to come here)

III. The above phenomena, examples as well as related statements, suggest that the difference between (*say* (direct speech)$_S$) and (*say* (indirect speech)$_S$) is so manifest, syntactically and semantically, that either two verbs *say* must be distinguished or two possible applications of *say* representing two distinct senses. It is not necessary to consider these possibilities real alternatives: as long as it is acknowledged that say_1 and say_2 (two verbs or two applications of one verb) must be systematically distinguished for semantic as well as syntactical reasons, we are not inclined to waste energy in abasing one of these theses. The distinction, however, seems fundamental to us, and we think it relevant to further theoretical investigations on language structure. It may, e.g., be imperative to acknowledge the difference in order to enter upon the domain of metalinguistics, while considerations relating to meaning and presupposition may also profit by it. We shall thus systematically distinguish between say_1 and say_2, and offer six arguments in support of this distinction; only one argument will obscure a neat division and can, therefore, be counted as favoring the double-application thesis. For reasons of sympathy we call

say_1: *say* + indirect speech
say_2: *say* + direct speech

(a) The complement S's of *say* have to be catalogued either as content objects or as formal objects, as is proved by a comparison of

(44) Did he say: 'I want a banana'
(45) No, he said that he wanted an orange
(46) No, he said: 'I *v*ant a banana'
(47) No, he said: 'I would like a banana'

(45) on the one hand and (46)/(47) on the other serve very different purposes. Of course, (45) could have had a complement S in direct speech, expressing exactly the same message as (45): this, however, is an application we leave aside for the moment. (45), therefore, can be regarded a content answer to (44) which happens to be the normal answer to be expected in non-special language usage. (46) and (47), contrarily, are answers concerning the mode of expression of (44). It is therefore that (46) nor (47) can use the indirect speech form without causing considerable embarrasment to the addressee. And they become near to impossible in this indirect speech form as answers to (44) if the latter has also been expressed indirectly.

It is hardly hazardous to venture as an explanation that in the use of (46)/(47) meta-linguistic aspects are involved (cf. also Verburg 1952:87ff.). The difference between both is comparable to that between

(48) Rome is a proper name
(49) Rome is a four-letter word

in which the former concerns the lexical item 'Rome', i.e. the form-content unity, and the latter the written form only. Whether both expressions fall within the same field of meta-linguistic use or that separate fields have to be distinguished cannot be decided upon here – the (possible) difference seems worth investigating anyway.

The suggested difference between *say*$_1$ and *say*$_2$ is corroborated by the following pair of which only the second is contradictory

(50) He did not say: 'Come here', he only said that I must come
(51) *He did not say that I had to come, he only said that I must come

(It may prove possible to eliminate the contradictory aspects of (51) by adding contrastive accents to, e.g., *had to* and *must*; mechanisms of intonation in its widest sense, however, can often be used to fulfill meta-linguistic functions; we therefore only regard utterances under normal intonation.)

Since the statement ($\neg$ p $\wedge$ p) is contradictory but ($\neg$ p $\wedge$ q) is not, the conclusion is justified that (51) has the former and (50) has the second (underlying) logical structure. The only difference between both utterances relates to the main verbs, since the dependent S's, as regards their contents, do not fundamentally differ. For (50) it stands to reason that the formal aspects of both complement S's are being compared: since they differ indeed, the conjoined statements donot constitute a contradiction. In (51), however, only the contents of the conjoined structures are compared, but this is explicitly due to the sameness of both main verbs *say*.

(b-c) Our second and third arguments in favour of the *say*$_1$-*say*$_2$ distinction concern the sentential structure of the complement S. While

(51) He said: 'Come here'/'Mary'/'Where are you?'/'The next'

demonstrates the syntactic indifference of *say*$_2$ in relation to its object S

(52) He said that *come here/*Mary/*where are you?/*the next

offers a very different pattern, demanding two syntactical characteristics for the complement S of *say*$_1$, viz. (i) the embedded S must be a statement (not, e.g., a question), and (ii) the embedded S must be grammatical in that it shows a NP⁀VP structure.

The latter requirements are not to be neglected. Cf.

(53) *He said that John would come and he said that Mary too

where conjunction reduction is prevented by Ross's coordinate structure constraint (1967:89). Why, then, is (54) fully correct?

(54) He said: 'John will come' and he said: 'Mary too'

The only explanation possible is that in (54) no conjunction reduction has taken place and that both conjoined clauses have the shape they originally had. The implication is clear: although (53) (or rather its correct form), and (54) refer to the same pragmatical phenomena, they cannot be considered paraphrases in the sense that the underlying structures are identical. This observation is not new: Vendler has stated, quite aptly, "the phrase *the thing one says* is ambiguous. It may mean the word, the phrase or the sentence one utters, or the product of the illocutionary act one performs. This duplicity is reflected in the two ways of reproducing what one said, which are commonly known as direct and indirect quotation." (1970:92-3).

In how far is *say*$_2$ indifferent as to its complement, and does this indifference regard formal as well as content aspects? In utterances such as

(55) Superman said: 'Whoo ... ack ... blub'

it appears that anything linguistically expressible can be filled in in the object position of *say*$_2$. In this sense *say*$_2$ strongly deviates from most verbs taking an S complement, while *say*$_1$ falls into the same class as *hope*, *admit*, *believe*, etc. That the latter verbs allow for exceptional structures such as

(56) I believe: John

in reply to the question: 'Who did that?' does not put them in the same category as *say*$_2$: clearly we meet here with so-called elliptic expressions.

Say$_1$, therefore, not only behaves like all other transitive verbs in that its object is dependent on the same grammatical rules that govern the main clause, but the object explicitly demands a statement pattern. *Say*$_2$ on the other hand, does not pose any constraint on the structure of its complement S. It does not only deviate from the *say*$_1$ pattern, but its total absence of subcategorization rules regarding the dependent S puts this verb outside the normal rule governed language use in its non-specific sense.

(d) (57) John said: 'It's cold in here', so we better move at once
(58) John said that it's cold in here, so we better move at once

Although there are situations for which (57) and (58) could be regarded different, is must be stated also that both can refer to the same pragmatical facts, i.e. they do not have to differ in truth value. However, since it has been proved that both do not relate to the same underlying structure, the question arises how to account for the formal ressemblance (with *ad hoc* semantic identity)? In (b-c) above it was suggested that the complement S of *say*₁ is a NP⁀VP statement. Underlying the complement S is the pattern for a full sentence, be it a sentence as it is conceived by the reporter and not the one connected with the main verb. In (58) this embedded S should be derived from 'It *be* cold in here'. Also in

(59) John said that I should visit him tomorrow

where actually John might have said

(60) 'Say, D., come look me up at Friday'

the underlying representation of (59) has no relation to (60) but only to (59), and should be read, approximately, as

(61) ... (*I modal* visit him tomorrow)

Regarding the maximal alikeness of (57) and (58), two aspects should be mentioned: (i) the formal ressemblance is accidental, although there nearly is a one-to-one correspondence of the respective constituents; (ii) the content similarity is fundamental in that there must be a paraphrase relation on the referential level.

As regards (ii), the complement S of (58) refers to the same phenomenon the object S of (57) refers to; both structures intend to represent the same facts, and although there are divergent ways of expressing the same thing, the representations should nonetheless be linked as to their meaning.

Regarding the alikeness of point (i), here the choice of the reporter plays an important role, for while his 'theme' is fixed, his ways of presenting his subject matter is relatively free. This relative freedom goes for the complement in (58), but in (57) there is no freedom at all.

Notwithstanding the referential paraphrastic relation of (57) and (58), there is a difference in presentation which proves to be obligatory for several constituents. Within the complement of a *say*₁ verb deviations from the originally uttered sentence are necessary as soon as and in as far as deictic elements are concerned (pronouns, temporal adverbs, and the like). Sloppily worded, it could be stated that the *say*-object of (57) *is* its underlying structure, whereas the *say*-object of (58) only relates to the content of the (57) complement S, but not to its phrasing – and both for fundamental reasons.

(e) It is hardly astonishing that the difference in scope between both *say*-

variants has certain syntactic implications. Reference could be made to

(62) 'I'll meet him there for the last time', she said
(63) *That she would meet him there for the last time she said

(We refrain from commenting upon the bastardy 'She would meet him there for the last time, she said', in consequence of our attitude in section I.) The deviance of (63) should be explained by relating it to phenomena as described in Kiparsky & Kiparsky (1970), although the $\pm$ factuality criterion seems inadequate as is suggested by the fully correct sentence (62). The explanation, therefore, may prove far simpler: one can state either that the set of transformation rules should comprise a constraint prohibiting the fronting of a (−definite) NP, or that this should be prevented on the level of Discourse. In the latter case it is the so-called perceptual strategy which demands the first place of an utterance to be occupied by a (+definite) constituent (cf. Droste 1973b). Now it cannot be denied that a *that*-phrase is to be considered a (—definite) description, since it comes into existence in dependence of its main verb, the performative. In (63) the proposition 'she ... time' as a proposition, i.e. as a semantic unit, receives its ultimate shape through the illocutionary force of *say*.

Why, then, does the complement of (62) not depend in the same way on its verb? In (62), so it seems, a former utterance it repeated. This utterance has been said and is clearly pre-existent in relation to (62). But this implies that the complement S of (63) can no longer be regarded (-definite). Although the object S 'I'll ... time' syntactically depends on *say*, it is semantically independent in that it contains its own message whose self-consistency has been proved by the preceding statement in the dialogue.

The above reasoning is corroborated by purely formal phenomena of (62) and (63). The first sentence opens in a way that corresponds with the rules of Discourse organisation, its first constituent being (+definite); (63) opens with a subordinating complementizer which implies, at least with a dominating non-factual verb, the (−definiteness) of the complement.

(f) The last argument has already been mentioned, be it casually:

(64) He said: 'You'll receive it tomorrow'
(65) He said that you would receive it yesterday

It is clear that both expressions may refer to an identical situation; (64) may thus relate to the same content as the one represented in (65) and not to a specific manner in which the speaker ('he') expressed himself (cf. Ziff 1971:710). Although (64) and (65) can be used as each other's paraphrases (on referential level) there may nonetheless arise situations in which the choice of one of both is obligatory. Especially (65) proves far more apt for precisely delimiting a series of phenomena, actions, etc. in real life. This can be explained, again, by the possible difference of scope between the deictic mechanismes in both sentences. Even if (64) is a 'content' utterance in the first place its field of application is narrowed by its formal conditions (viz. literal truth of the complement); this is clearly not the case with (65) where there are no formal constraints on referential expressions: 'wednesday' may become 'yesterday' or 'tomorrow' in the same way that pronouns change places. As long as the message in general is not violated, there are no limits to these referential paraphrase actions.

The above six arguments, if not separately then in mutual connection, sustain the distinction *say*$_1$-*say*$_2$. The only counterargument can be read in relations such as (65)-(64) or, more explicitly, in (66):

(66) His mother used to say: 'Do not let them snub you', and we never did

The second half of the sentence, 'we never did', refers to the complement S of the first half, but clearly to the content of this phrase. This embedded S, however, depends upon a *say*$_2$ verb, i.e. a verb governing a direct speech form. This, then, could be considered a paradoxical and even controversial situation since the phrase 'and ... did', refering to a content expression, presupposes a *say*$_1$ verb.

In fact we have met with several of these applications, all of which suggest that the proposed dichotomy is too strict. Indeed, (64), as it has been conceived here can very well assume that *say* is a form verb as to its syntactical application, but a content verb as far as semantics go. The same goes for (57/58) of which pair we stated "that both can refer to the same pragmatical facts",

Our original assumption that a *say*$_1$ and a *say*$_2$ should be discerned, although not incorrect, proves to be too strong in that it disregards the two possible functions of *say*$_2$. The latter, so it seems, although always distinguishing itself from *say*$_1$ in its formal aspects, may parallel its function in that it concentrates on the contents of the complement S. It is on this ground also that we prefer to consider *say*$_1$ and *say*$_2$ variants of the verb *say* and not two distinct verbs. Schematically the relation of both could be expressed as follows

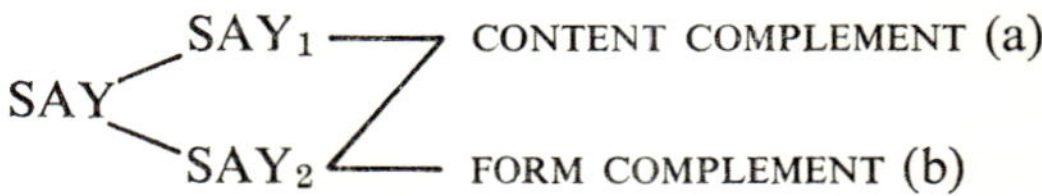

That especially the *say*1 - (a)/*say*2 - (b) distinction has interesting theoretical implications will be argued in the last section.

IV. Several recent papers on the verb and its structural implications for phrase and sentence have concentrated on the complement S; this goes, i.a., for the treatment of presupposition, of fact and of the performative. It could be argued that Austin's search for 'doing by saying' (1962:12) has set this interest rolling, although the revival of the Frege-Russell-Strawson discussion has exerted its influence also (cf. Droste 1974). It is remarkable that in many of the papers on these subjects, apart from those by Austin and Ross, a delimitation of the place of *say* is generally avoided. Neither Garner, Keenan, Langendoen and Savin (all 1971) nor Kiparsky's (1970), Morgan (1969), Vendler (1970) try to locate the verb *say* within the surveys on verbal functions they have sketched, and more studies could be mentioned. Although this should be a clear warning to us, we nonetheless venture upon this dangerous domain, since our interest is related to *say* in its connection with the performatives on the one side and with the (non-)presuppositional verbs on the other.

We start again from an example, viz.

(67) Colorless green ideas sleep furiously

the deviance of which is hardly refutable. Anyway it counts as incorrect if it is regarded a statement about this world; and since no marker for an 'imaginary' or 'different' world is present, it *is* a statement on this world (cf. Lakoff 1968).

Contrarily (68) seems non-deviant, also for our real world:

(68) Chomsky says that colorless green ideas sleep furiously

This fact can be explained in the sense that it is the main clause which is judged as to its correctness, or rather the structure: 'Chomsky says $(\ldots)_S$'; in Chomsky (1957:15) this has indeed been said. The question now arises whether the content of the embedded S clause should be considered deviant or not; we shall not enter upon the discussion of ($\pm$ grammaticality) and simply ask whether in (68) it is well-formed or not. It is commonly agreed to that in

(69) Janine dreamed that her dog had won the Davis cup

the complement S is well-formed since it is true within the world of Janine's dream, or rather (+valid) as we prefer to call it (cf. Droste 1973b). But what about

(70) Janine said that her dog had won the Davis cup

Just like in (69) the content of the S complement is (+valid) within the world delimited by the content of the main clause. In both expressions in the same way we shall have to accept that the assertion of S' does not correspond to the facts of the world in which dogs are even refused admittance to Wimbledon.

As these and many other examples prove there is no fundamental difference to the scope of verbs such as *dream* and *say*: both create a field in which the objects mentioned fit in with the dream- or say-world; such statements are valid by implication. Now *dream* is generally accepted to be a world creating verb. As such it is distinct from factual verbs whose objects are considered (± valid) not by implication but independently. In order to loosely describe the difference between both categories of verbs we can as well follow the Kiparsky distinction (+fact) vs. (−fact), as the logical approach of Keenan (1971), or the so-called time-axis division by Givón. According to Givón presuppositions and implications of complement S's distribute themselves relative to the action time of their governing verb; presuppositions, then, pertain to the time preceding the time-axis, implications to the time following the axis (1973:890ff.). In harmony with the three systems here mentioned the class of world creating verbs comprises *agree*, *allege*, *assert*, *afraid*, *believe*, *conclude*, *doubt*, *dream*, *fear*, *feel*, *imagine*, *suppose*.

The above class of which we only mentioned some examples has to be extended with at least one verb, viz. *say*, or rather, in the above terminology, with say_1. This is not self-evident since all the above verbs in one way or another seem to contain in their semantic structure an element of unreality, phantasy, non-worldliness. On the other hand, there is little reason to incorporate verbs of (special) saying such as *assert*, *state* into the world creating class with the exclusion of the most fundamental verb of saying: *say*.

There are other reasons as well to revise the problem as soon as one agrees with extensions of the verbal category as advocated by McCawley and, after him, by Lakoff. When we consider *not*, auxiliaries, tempus e.t.q. verbs (cf. MacCawley 1972), it is worth considering their behavior as such, esp. in relation with the here treated semantic classes: are they factual, do they have presuppositions related to them, etc. To us it seems justified to consider categories such as *poss*, *nec* – superficially expressed as, e.g., 'possible', 'may' – world creating verbs. Sentences such as

(71) He may have loved her

can be represented as to their underlying structure as

(71′)

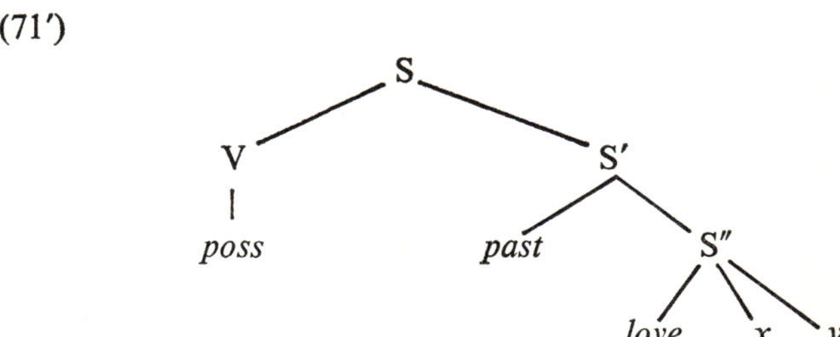

His having loved her can be regarded a correct statement within the reach of *poss*, the 'possible world'in which the proposition of the complement S becomes true.

It is, for that matter, rather tempting to speculate upon the scope of 'verbs' such as *past*: if indeed they prove world creating (together with, e.g., *not*) it would become clear why the 'past tense' in many languages appears apt to express uncertainty, non-reality, in short (-truth) with respect to the real world.

Returning to our own world, the complement S' of *say*, here we have to agree that its well-formedness depends on *say*, as becomes manifest from otherwise 'unreal' propositions:

(72) For Nixon says he is an honorable man

If *say*$_1$ can be classified as a world creating verb, this does not have to imply that *say*$_2$ automatically belongs to the same class, although this is not excluded either. For while *say*$_1$ concerns the proposition of its complement, that is its content, *say*$_2$ – at least its b-form – pertains to formal aspects of its complement. This *say*$_2$ verb can rather be regarded as falling under the same heading as the verb (?) *nonsense*:

(73) It's nonsense to speak of frightening sincerity (Chomsky 1965:157)

and *realize*, as it is mentioned in Chomsky (1971:197) and Lakoff (1972:282 footnote a).

One may wonder whether these and other relations do not oppose to the subclassification of *say*$_2$ into an a- and a b-form. It was Lakoff who correctly stated that *realize* usually regards the content, not the form of its complement. As is proved above this may be the case with *say*$_2$ (cf. (57) and (58)); since this application concerns the V with a direct speech complement, there is reason to classify *say*$_2$ in one group with the content-directed verb *realize*.

However, there is a very different use also, as became apparent from examples such as

(74) He does not say: 'Banana' he says: 'Banan'

As mentioned in section II we here meet with the metalinguistic use of the verb *say*. And it should be noted that this verb on the one hand pertains to the content of its complement and on the other to the formal expression, which again causes a distinct classification. There is no reason to dramatize this phenomenon: the meta-language of which (74) is an example should not be considered as existing outside and apart from the object-language, but as an essential part of natural language. In other words, natural language has as one of its subdomains the field of metalanguage in which statements can be made on the natural language it forms part of. To my mind this statement is not so new as I would like it to be, since Carnap has also defended it, be it in rather ambiguous terms: "If we investigate, analyze, and describe a language L_1, we need a language L_2 for formulating the result of our investigation of L_1 or the rules for the use of L_1. In this case we call L_1 the *object language*, L_2 the *meta-language*. The sum total of what can be known about L_1 and said in L_2 may be called the *metatheory* of L_1 (in L_2)". (1968a:3-4)

This point of view has been formulated more explicitly in the *Logical syntax* where it is said that "die Syntax dieser Sprache in dieser Sprache selbst formuliert werden kann ohne dasz dadurch ein Widerspruch entsteht" (1968b:46). This statement may be read in the sense that meta-language can be considered the syntax of object-language and can be expressed in the object-language itself without producing a contradiction.

The type of meta-language our considerations pertain to can thus be regarded a specific subset of English.

The question now arises whether there are elements in the structure of *say* which explain its use in such widely varying fields as world creation on the one hand and meta-language on the other. Consider, once more, usages such as

(75) He says: 'Louvain is a proper name'

Since it is not correct to state

(76) *Louvain is a proper name and lodges the oldest university of the Low Countries

we must conclude that a complement statement such as in (75), whether or not dependent on *say*$_2$, is not valid for our real world: otherwise the (76) conjunction would have to be considered well-formed. But if the *say* verb in (75) does not evoke a real world, there remains only one conclusion open: *say*$_2$ in (75) is a world creating verb evoking a world which differs from the real one.

And one wonders whether Tarski's statement that the terms 'object-language' and 'meta-language' have only a relative sense (1969:587) should not be read in such a manner that (a) the latter covers a subdomain of the former, and (b) the meta-linguistic use of *say* is a special form of the world creating use of this verb. If both hypotheses prove to be correct, the alleged difference between *say*$_1$ and *say*$_2$ must indeed be considered a mere variation in application and not a phenomenon of homonymy.

This world creating aspect also is less revolutionary than it may seem. According to the Kiparsky's (1970:145) verbs such as *assert, allege, claim* are to be regarded non-factive. In Morgan's (and our) view, therefore, they are world creating, since they "define new sets of presuppositions which hold within their spheres" (1969:170). But it can hardly be denied that all three verbs here mentioned are verbs of saying, or rather: variants of saying. They are, in other words, composite verbs consisting of the semantic prime *say* plus an adverb *x*.

The thin thread of hypothesizing, spanning the cleft between both banks of use, may perhaps be followed into a third domain, that of performative *say* – let us call it, for the moment, *say*$_0$. As Austin has stated (1962:6-7), the term 'performative' "indicates that the issuing of the utterance in the performing of an action – it is not normally thought of as just saying something". And on p. 100ff. he clearly distinguishes the use of *say* from that of, e.g., *advise, order*, in that the first constitutes a 'locution' and only the second an 'illocution'. Both quotations, so it seems, isolate *say* in the sense that it is not a performative verb, although it is also said that "to *say* something is to *do* something".

Do not the above quotations indicate that our former reasoning, esp. that of section II, is not well-founded and should be deserted for less revolutionary hypotheses? In defense of the latter it must first be mentioned that the philosophical approach of Austin in which between 1,000 and 10,000 performative verbs are to be distinguished, differs fundamentally from the linguistic approach we advocated in section II and which has been defended before us by Ross (1970:223ff.). In his theory, followed i.e. by Lakoff, Lakoff, McCawley, Seuren, the underlying structure of a sentence should be read as a typological frame + a proposition, and a declarative sentence, therefore, can be schematized as

(77) *I say to you that* $(\ldots)_S$

There is little reason and less opportunity to enter once more upon the inherent qualities of such a (semantic) presentation. It only should be kept in mind that we tried to prove that the expression *I say that* is a mere underlying representation, not realisable on surface structure level, since the surface verb *say* disposes of connotations which fundamentally fail in deep structure. To underline the importance of this, we once more explain it with an example.

(78) I say to you that I left my beautiful mistress

can only be related to an underlying form such as (79) as is proved by a comparison with (80):

(79) *I say to you that* (I say to you that $(\ldots)_S$)

That (80) indeed differs fundamentally from (78) becomes evident in a dialogue:

(80) I left my beautiful mistress

The latter expression is a natural answer to the question: 'Why do you look so sad?', while (78) could hardly do as an answer (although a difference in truth value between both can not be discovered). I have the impression that McCawley and Ross defend the same thesis, be it with an unclear and incomplete argumentation (Ross 1970:249-50).

Back to our original problem: what in essence is the function of a (deep) performative verb, more specifically, of say_0? If we do accept that an assertion depends on the verb say_0, in the same way a command is dependent on the performative verb *order*, this typological frame verb has a very special function. We do not refer to syntactical arguments (see, again, section II, but also McCawley 1972:508-9), but to deeper, semantic grounds; only semantic arguments can prove the necessity of an underlying performative, which, otherwise, would merely have a formal function (such as distinguishing it from Question).

The speech act, then, presented in whatever form, is in no way a simple mirror image of reality: it is a recreation of this reality – in as far as it is not a pure creation of a language dependent reality – with proper means and in a proper 'language'. Saying something is not doing something in the sense that both actions could ever be collapsed. Saying is doing in a specific material and has to be understood as consisting of this special material. It is therefore that the speech act demands a special operator mechanism, announcing the particular status of the dependent act.

Now it could be argued that the simple assumption of an operator mechanism A – for assertion – (but cf. Langacker's comment on Q for question; 1974) or the symbol say_0 would suffice. But such a proposition is deficient, syntactically as well as semantically. What we need in order to fully recognize the value of the embedded proposition, is a frame not only consisting of the element *say*, but also, and for fundamental reasons, of *I* and *you*. Only if the dependent act has been localized between an LS, a locutionary source, and an LT, a locutionary target, i.e. between *I* and *you* (cf. Garner 1971:24-5), and only if the dependent clause has been recognized as a speech act through the presence of say_0, can we determine the contents of the act. Only then is it expressedly stated that the act does not take place in the real world, but in an autonomous replica world. In this sense we must consider say_0 a world creating verb, or rather *the* world creating verb language fundamentally depends on. (This thesis is corroborated by the highly convincing arguments of Brame; he proves that in Arabic a subset of declarative sentences can only be explained by postulating an underlying performative verb – quoted in Ross 1970:244-5.)

Summarizing the above somewhat disperse remarks, we can state:

(a) direct and indirect speech forms, or rather their surface structures, can never be related to the same underlying string, even if they refer to an identical situation by means of identical lexical formatives. The possibility of deriving an indirect speech form from a base sentence in direct speech is, therefore, excluded for fundamental reasons;

(b) the performative verb *say*, present in the underlying structure of declarative sentences, must be considered very 'verbal' in that it takes two arguments (*I* and *you*), but it is abstract on the other hand, in that it never appears in surface structure. When the main clause in surface structure reads as 'I say to you that', it should be regarded part of the proposition; and in underlying structure this *say* is dominated by a performative *say*;

(c) rather than distinguishing between two verbs *say*, it seems advisable to acknowledge two possible applications of *say*, viz. (*say* (indirect speech)$_S$) and (*say* (direct speech)$_S$). The distinction is due to the overt difference in syntactical structure and the possible difference in semantic scope, while the coherence relates to the also possible sameness of reference;

(d) whereas say_1 can be considered a world creating verb, say_2, delimiting in its purely formal scope a metalinguistic field, can be regarded as subordinated to say_1. The complement S, depending on say_2, expresses a metalinguistic message and in doing so it is valid for a non-existing world, i.e. the formal world created and delimited by the main verb.

The coherence of say_1 and say_2 depends, ultimately, on the semantic function of say_0, the underlying performative verb of every utterance. It is the latter frame especially which qualifies an utterance as a linguistic entity, i.e. a recreation of the real world in an autonomous system.

Department of Linguistics
Leuven University (K. U. L.)

BIBLIOGRAPHY

Austin, J. H.
1962 *How To Do Things With Words*. Oxford.
Bierwisch, M., and Heidolph, K. E. (eds.)
1970 *Progress in Linguistics*. The Hague, Mouton.
Carnap, R.
1968a *Introduction to Semantics and Formalization of Logic*. 3rd ed. Cambridge, Mass.
1968b *Logische Syntax der Sprache*. Wien/New York.
Chomsky, N.
1957 *Syntactic Structures*. The Hague, Mouton.
1965 *Aspects of the Theory of Syntax*. Cambridge, Mass.
1971 "Deep Structure, Surface Structure, and Semantic Interpretation", *Semantics*, ed. by D. D. Steinberg and L. A. Jakobovits. Cambridge.
Cowan, J L. (ed.)
1970 *Studies in Thought and Language*. Tucson.
Davidson, D., and Harman, G. (eds.)
1972 *Semantics of Natural Logic*. Dordrecht, Reidel.
Droste, F. G.
1973a "Model Theory, Logic and Linguistics", *Linguistics*, 105, 5-34
1973b "Presupposition, Truth and Grammaticality", *Communication and Cognition*, 6.
1973c "Qualifying and Relational Terms as Linguistic Universals", *Linguistics*, 118, 43-88.
1974 "A Note on Paraphrasing", *Linguistische Berichte*, 29.
Fillmore, Ch. J., and Langendoen, D. T. (eds.)
1971 *Studies in Linguistic Semantics*. New York, etc.

Garner, R.
1971 "'Presupposition' in Philosophy and Linguistics", *Studies in Linguistic Semantics*, ed. by Ch. J. Fillmore and D. T. Langendoen. New York, etc.
Givón, T.
1973 "The Time-axis Phenomenon", *Language*, 49.
Hetzron, R.
1971 "The Deep Structure of the Statement", *Linguistics*, 65, 25-63
Jacobs, R. A., and Rosenbaum, P. S.
1968 *English Transformational Grammar*. Waltham/Toronto/London.
Jacobs, R. A., and Rosenbaum, P. S. (eds.)
1970 *Readings in English Transformational Grammar*. Waltham/Toronto/London.
Keenan, E. L.
1971a "Two Kinds of Presupposition in Natural Language", *Studies in Linguistic Semantics*, ed. by Ch. J. Fillmore and D. T. Langendoen, New York, etc.
1971b "Quantifier Structures in English", *Foundations of Language*, 7.
Kiefer, F., and Ruwet, N. (eds.)
1973 *Generative Grammar in Europe*. Dordrecht, Reidel.
Kiparsky, P. and C.
1970 "Fact", *Progress in Linguistics*, ed. by M. Bierwisch and K. E. Heidolph, 143-73. The Hague, Mouton.
Lakoff, G.
1968 "Semantics, Logic and Opacity". Paper read at the LSA summer meeting.
1971 "On Generative Semantics", *Semantics*, ed. by D. D. Steinberg and L. A. Jakobovits. Cambridge.
Langacker, R. W.
1974 "The Question of Q", *Foundations of Language*, 11.
Langendoen, D. T., and Savin, H. B.
1971 "The Projection Problem for Presuppositions", *Studies in Linguistic Semantics*, ed. by Ch. J. Fillmore and D. T. Langendoen. New York, etc.
McCawley, J. D.
1971 "Where Do Noun Phrases Come From?", *Semantics*, ed. by D. D. Steinberg and L. A. Jakobovits. Cambridge.
1972 "A Program for Logic", *Semantics of Natural Logic*, ed. by D. Davidson and G. Harman. Dordrecht, Reidel.
Morgan, J. L.
1969 "On the Treatment of Presupposition in Transformational Grammar", *CLS*, 5.
Olshewsky, T. M. (ed.)
1969 *Problems in the Philosophy of Language*. New York, etc.
Quine, W. V. O.
1960 *Words and Objects*. Cambridge, Mass.
Rätsep, H.
1973 "The Verbs of Saying and Action Situations", *Generative Grammar in Europe*, ed. by F. Kiefer and N. Ruwet. Dordrecht, Reidel.
Ross, J. R.
1967 *Constraints on Variables in Syntax*. Dissertation, M.I.T., Cambridge, Mass.
1970 "On Declarative Sentences", *Readings in English Transformational Grammar*, ed. by R. A. Jacobs and P. S. Rosenbaum. Waltham/Toronto/London.
Seuren, P. A. M.
1969 *Operators and Nucleus*. Cambridge.
Steinberg, D. D., and Jakobovits, L. A. (eds.)
1971 *Semantics*. Cambridge.

Tarski, A.
1969 "The Semantic Conception of Truth", *Problems in the Philosophy of Language*, ed. by T. M. Olshewsky. New York, etc.
Vendler, Z.
1970 "Say What You Think", *Studies in Thought and Language*, ed. by J. L. Cowan. Tucson.
Verburg, P.
1952 *Taal en functionaliteit*. Wageningen.
Ziff, P.
1971 "What Is Said", *Semantics of Natural Logic*, ed. by D. Davidson and G. Harman. Dordrecht, Reidel.
Zwicky, A. M.
1971 "On Reported Speech", *Studies in Linguistic Semantics*, ed. by Ch. J. Fillmore and D. T. Langendoen. New York, etc.

THE GOTHIC RUNE NAME *CHOZMA*

ERIC P. HAMP

The name of the *k*-rune in the Salzburg-Wiener Alcuin MS is *chozma*, which must be [kozma]. The account of this word in Feist *Vgl. Wb. der got. Sprache*[3], 1939, p. 112a, while characteristically meticulous, is most unsatisfactory and leaves the question in the midst of unconvincing conflicting speculations.

1. The corresponding rune name in the Norwegian and Icelandic rune poems is *kaun* (neuter) 'ulcer', and the form in the Abecedarium Normannicum is *chaon*. The claimed equation of *chozma* with *kaun* appears to have originated with Bugge. Feist remarks (*loc. cit.*): "Man erwartet als Gegenstück got. **kauns*, runenalphab. **chonz* oder **choz*." Feist does not explain how he reconciles the genders. He continues his patchwork account of the word: "*-ma* vom folgenden *manna*?". Apparently the dismissal of a phonetic feature or two (or are they graphic hastae?) is a minor matter here.

Feist then passes to von Grienberger, who (*Beitr.*, 21, 206) was certainly more careful with the phonetics. He had suggested a comparison with ndl. *kossem* 'Halswamme des Rindes' etc., thus bringing the semantics from the realm of ulcers to that of mumps; it is not at all made clear that this is a semantic transfer which either medical knowledge or contemporary folk tradition would sanction. Marstrander, with his customary prudence and insight, has also spoken out (*NTS*, 1, 151f.) contra Bugge. Yet these healthy reserves against the semantically unclear and phonetically conflicting 'ulcer' do not furnish us with a positive step in the direction of a solution.

Continuing this unprofitable line of reasoning, Feist proposes that the sense 'Geschwür' could be derived from 'Wölbung'. Then Latin *guttur* or Greek γύης and γύαλον are compared, and further mention is made of Latin *uola*' hollow of the hand' This would supposedly lead to a root **g^{u}eu̯-* 'schwellen' Such reasoning is a specimen of the worst sort of etymologizing. First the semantics are allowed to drift without control from a very dim connexion (disease and bodily inflammation linked to supposed physical shape) to the most vague of spatial relations (anything curved). Yet with this the phonetics are abandoned to the most generalized root shapes involving velarity and rounding. No attention whatever is paid to the morphology of the suffixes.

Once again, von Grienberger (*Z.f.d.Ph.*, 32, 312) shows himself at least sensitive to the requirements of phonetic controls by adducing Latvian *guzma* 'Haufe, Höcker'.

E. V. K. Dobbie's verdict (*The Anglo-Saxon Minor Poems*, 154) that *chozma* is of uncertain derivation is surely preferable to the above dim and unprincipled guesses.

2. Apart from the aspects of phonetic, morphological, and semantic laxness criticized above, the real problem in the inadequacy of the above attempts, it seems to me, is a deeper one. The main function of language is to express meaning, to make expressions which are relevant in a situational context – if we may draw on a Malinowskian theme. The above attempts at explanation lose sight totally of this cardinal function. When a Goth said [kozma] or whatever lies behind our word, he was expressing a meaning, a bundle of semantic features; he was also expressing this meaning in a context of cultural background. He was certainly not speaking to carry out a Lautgesetz, nor writing so as to conform or not conform to certain graphic consistencies. Indeed, the last two facets are certainly relevant to our linguistic analysis of the total problem; but they are subsidiary issues that can be considered only after the primary function has been satisfactorily formulated. Let me state immediately, that the foregoing is not a plea for phonological or phonetic looseness; to the contrary, I would underline the continuing need for exact phonetic accounting, the validity of (a modern view of) the Lautgesetz. The question here is rather the priority of consideration in addressing the problem: There is no point in pondering the correctness of a Lautgestz, or formal equation, if no suitable expression has been posited in the first place.

It is essential first to recall the cultural context. We are dealing here with a branch of literacy and learning, perhaps of a somewhat arcane sort, which may even have drawn on old and dimly recalled traditional knowledge. But fundamentally, particularly so far as the letter names were concerned, rune lore is a moderately recent diffusion among the Germanic peoples and not an inheritance i n t h a t f o r m from Proto-Germanic times; this is particularly noticeable and well known in the case of the Gothic rune names. It is therefore a well recognized principle in studying rune names that we must not look for an alphabet of names reconstructible for Proto-Germanic from which observed attestations are to be derived by phonetic rule. In other words, we are in a sphere of investigation where the Lautgesetz cannot be our principal heuristic.

On the other hand, as we have remarked above, the first function of language is to mean; the essential and irreducible characteristic of a rune name must be in some sense a bundle of semantic features. This must be insisted upon even though the name is also required to begin with the correct graph. And this semantic characterization should make sense and find ultimate phonetic fit in some known language of relevance; furthermore the semantics should be appropriate within the special and narrowly circumscribed universe of rune names. This requirement, incidentally, touches upon an interesting and important aspect of the theory of proper names: While it is true that the distinguishing function of a name is to designate an individual (and thereby may often be inappropriate or opaque in its ordinary-language meaning), it is also historically the case that names are normally chosen from within a definable semantic range in their ordinary-language values. Now rune names are not names in the sense that proper names are. They are common nouns denoting the graphs used in that system of writing to represent certain segmental sounds; but these nouns are derived by extension, while preserving identity of initial sound (the acronymic principle), from the ordinary lexicon. Their genesis has something in common with the application of proper names since they are given consciously at a point in time by a person or social group who perform an act which may properly be called naming. Now, surely as a result of the last fact, rune names (though common nouns) share with proper names the characteristic of being chosen from a restricted semantic universe, which we may define without great difficulty. Therefore, it is seen, the task of accounting semantically and historically for rune names is not unrelated to the problem of accounting in general for proper names.

3. Having regard for the diffusional characteristics of the cultural phenomenon called runic alphabets, and for the above stated principles in dealing with runic names and their meanings, it is clear that we must turn in the first place to the semantics of other runic alphabets for clues to the meaning and history of our word. It has already been noted that the Scandinavian correspondent is *kaun* 'ulcer'; we will not henceforth be concerned with the question whether *kaun* is the true phonetic cognate

of other Germanic rune names or whether it was simply a convenient and phonetically similar substitute to carry out the acrophonic principle. The important observation for our present problem is that the matching rune name in Old English is *cēn* (masculine) 'torch' = Old High German *ch(i)en, ken* 'facula'. This, I claim, is the semantic thread that we must seek to trace; this is the meaning that the originator(s) of Gothic *chozma* were reasonably trying to convey.

The problem, then, and simply put, is how to give [kozma] the meaning of OE *cēn* by known and pertinent linguistic forms.

Now we are well aware that Gothic drew liberally by borrowing on the Greek lexicon. It is therefore not unreasonable to look to Greek as a loan-source for a Gothic form, or as a source of conflation particularly if a technical term (as a rune name really was) was involved. When we consider the meaning 'torch' and the phonetic configuration [kozma], the Greek base καίω and its derivatives immediately come to mind. The verb καίω (Attic also κᾴω κᾱ́ω) aor. ἔκαυσα Epic ἔκηα κῆα passive ἐκάην 'kindle, burn' forms the verbal adjective καυτός; the base is of course καϝ-.

As with other verb bases, in the history of Greek alternate forms grew up extended by sigma. Thus we have side by side καυτός and καυστός (poetic) 'kindled, set afire'; καυτήρ ὁ (poetic, Late Greek) 'burner, branding iron' and καύστειρα (Epic) 'hot scorching (μάχη)', καύστρᾱ ἡ (Late Greek) 'burning (fire) place'. The sigmatic formations could also have been aided by the perfectly normal abstract καῦσις ἡ 'das (Ver) Brennen'; pl. 'burning heat'.

When we turn to formations in -μ- we find καύσιμος 'combustible' and καῦμα -ατος 'heat, conflagration, summer heat fever'; in close semantic relation to the last we also find καῦσος and καύσων ὁ (Later Greek) 'heat, fever', built on a sigmatic form of the base. It is clear then that a morphological formation *καῦσμα might equally have existed or have been generated at any time.

I propose therefore that a noun *καῦσμα would have made a perfectly acceptable source, both semantically and culturally, for the Gothic noun that lay behind the graphic shape *chozma*.

4. We must now justify the phonetics. [kozma] cannot be derived directly from *καῦσμα, particularly during the relevant Gothic period. Two avenues are open to us:

a) If a Greek form *καῦσμα had been transmitted via a Latin channel, the source form – surely [kau̯zma] – would have resulted as [kɔzma] or [kozma] under certain circumstances. It is, however, also possible that the sibilant would have remained unvoiced in Latin, or that the diphthong [au] might have been preserved as it was in late forms of *caulis* 'cabbage' etc. Besides, it is analytically less desirable to posit the intervention of a third language, Latin, if we are otherwise able to explain the phenomena in a natural and simple way.

b) There are two ways in which a literate Goth might have arrived at [kozma] from a Greek *καῦσμα, particularly on the basis of written materials. He could of course have interpreted the Greek spelling directly in terms of Gothic graphs; that is, he might have regarded Greek αυ as being the equivalent of his *a* plus *u*, i.e. the digraph which renders Greek omicron in Wulfila's representation of Greek names and loans. This graphic interpretation would then have been transposed into a fresh alphabetic representation.

But there is another way whereby the transfer in vocalism could have been made internally within Gothic. It is well known that there existed in Wulfila's Gothic an automatic alternation of graphic *o* : *au* : *aw*, as in *toja* : *tauja* : *gatawida*; see, for example, James W. Marchand, *The Sounds and Phonemes of Wulfila's Gothic* (The Hague, Mouton, 1973), 71, § 4.21.j. Therefore on the basis of internal Gothic alternations a native speaker could have adjusted a [kauzma] which he heard or read to [kozma] (or [kɔzma]?) by applying the rules of his own grammar.

It is thus seen that there is no phonological obstacle to equating *καῦσμα with *chozma.*

5. In summary, the Gothic rune name *chozma* had nothing to do with the Norwegian and Icelandic *kaun*; it meant 'torch', as did Old English *cēn*, and was a borrowing from Greek *καῦσμα, which was a parallel sigmatic formation to the attested καῦμα.

In this fashion we have not only elucidated an obscure Gothic word; we have also retrieved an additional attestation for the Greek lexicon. Finally, we have recovered one more piece of the mosaic for the history of European grammatical learning; for the full history of the development and diffusion of runic learning remains to be written, and the rôle of Gothic in this unfolding is a particularly dark corner of our knowledge.

University of Chicago

DIMENSIONIERUNG ALS WISSENSCHAFTLICHE TEILAUFGABE IN DER TEXTLINGUISTIK

PETER HARTMANN

0. VORBEMERKUNG

Dieser Beitrag soll eine Jubiläumsgabe sein. Damit er den Adressaten, dem er gewidmet ist, auch interessiert, wurde die oben genannte Thematik gewählt. P. A. Verburg gehört zu den Sprachwissenschaftlern, die immer eine ganz bestimmte Ansicht geäußert und wissenschaftlich verfolgt haben: daß die Aufgabe, die Sprache wissenschaftlich zu erforschen, einen wissenschaftlichen Zugang erfordert, der in Interesse und Analyse den mit der Sprache gegebenen und verbundenen Erscheinungen auch gerecht wird. Er hat in seiner Arbeit schon früh auch philosophische Überzeugungen durchkommen lassen, und er hat im Rahmen seiner Überlegungen zur 'Delotik' zum Teil Tatsachen einbezogen, die heutzutage innerhalb pragmatischer Themenstellungen eine Rolle zu spielen begonnen haben. Dies war bei der bewußt zugrundegelegten integrativen Seh- und Arbeitsweise nicht verwunderlich.

Es gilt also, einem solchen Interesse, das zugleich breit, differenziert und mit einem spezifischen Wissenschaftsimpetus verbunden ist, ein Thema anzubieten, das in der Differenziertheit seines Anspruchs den Ansichten des Jubilars einigermaßen vergleichbar ist.

Hierbei ist allerdings vorweg zu bemerken, daß Themen solcher Art nicht sogleich mit einer 'befriedigenden Theorie' aufwarten und auch nicht einfach von schon bewährten Vor-Erkenntnissen ausgehen können: obgleich auch in ihnen natürlich so etwas wie eine (vor-)theoretische Orientierung zugrundeliegt. Insofern sind die vorgelegten Bemerkungen als Diskussionsbeitrag gemeint und es ist noch hinzuzufügen: falls der Beitrag mit Maßstäben gemessen wird, die schon ein beweisbares, also ein bereits theoriefähiges Wissen voraussetzen, können die vorgelegten Bemerkungen eventuell als ziemlich 'nichts-sagend' erscheinen. Es sollte aber anerkannt werden, daß Fragen der wissenschaftlichen Orientierung durchaus auch zur Wissenschaft selbst gerechnet werden müssen:

zumal dann, wenn man bemerkt hat, daß sich der Wert einer Disziplin auch nach Maßgabe ihrer Rolle richtet, die sie unter den sonstigen gesellschaftlichen und kulturellen Erscheinungen spielt.

1. AUSGANGSPOSITION UND GRUNDANNAHMEN

Es ist üblich und notwendig, daß eine Darstellung, die den Anspruch erhebt, für eine bestimmte Wissenschaft etwas zu erbringen, zuvor darlegt, auf welchen Voraussetzungen sie beruht. Je nach Elaboriertheit des Verfahrenssystems innerhalb einer Wissenschaft kann sich diese Forderung bis dahin steigern lassen, daß an den Beginn eines wissenschaftlichen Aussagenkomplexes bestimmte Axiome gestellt werden, von denen die aus ihnen folgenden Aussagen logisch beweisbar abgeleitet werden.

Im Folgenden handelt es sich aber um Bemerkungen zur eventuellen Weiterentwicklung einer wissenschaftlichen Disziplin, der Sprachwissenschaft, wobei davon ausgegangen wird – und dies ist die erste Grundannahme –, daß eine Disziplin nicht nur ein Erkenntnissystem ist, d.h. nicht mit den in ihr angewendeten Wissenschaftsformen zusammenfällt. Eine Disziplin wird vielmehr – und das ist die zweite Grundannahme – verstanden als eine, wie immer, organisierte Aktivität, in der es qua *Wissenschaftlichkeit* einerseits um den Erwerb verlässlicher und gesicherter Erkenntnis geht, andererseits aber auch um deren Effekt, d.h. um Brauchbarkeit und erfolgreiche Anwendung mit positiver *Auswirkung*. Eine Disziplin ist also eine Aktivität, die eine erkenntnisfordernde Komponente mit einer wirkungspolitischen Zielsetzung verbindet. Aus diesem Grund können hier an dieser prononcierten und anderswo vielleicht mit Axiomen zu besetzenden Stelle, als Ausgangsposition, keine Axiome der üblichen – logisch orientierten – Art stehen. Erst entsprechend durchformalisierte Erkenntnis- bzw. Beschreibungsverfahren können u.U. mit Axiomen beginnen und von ihr ausgehen. Statt dessen wird zunächst bescheidener – insgesamt aber doch anspruchsvoll – eine Ausgangsposition formuliert, und zwar wie folgt:

1. Eine (jede) Wissenschaft legt ihren Interessen-, Gegenstands-, Objekt- und Untersuchungs-*Bereich* fest, ebenso die zu behandelnden Aspekte und die Verfahren der jeweiligen Behandlung.

2. Die Sprachwissenschaft hat hinsichtlich ihrer innerwissenschaftlichen Zwecksetzung die *Aufgabe*, die Sprache zu ihrem Objektbereich zu machen, wobei gilt:

Erkenntnisgegenstand sind die für die Sprache charakteristischen Eigenschaften;
der Hauptaspekt betrifft die Erfassung von Gesetzmäßigkeiten und Regularitäten;
die Behandlungsverfahren bestehen in Methoden, die eine auf Regularitäten und Gesetzmäßigkeiten abstellende systematisierende Erfassung der Eigenschaften der Sprache gestatten, und zwar in ihren einzelsprachlichen Ausprägungen sowie in ihren typisierbaren Grundzügen.

3. Die wissenschaftliche Zwecksetzung erfordert eine Reflexion, Auswahl und Rechtfertigung der zu erforschenden *Aspekte*; die wissenschaftliche Behandlung von Aspekten erfordert in der Theoriebildung und Methode jeweils ein Objekt-, Gegenstands(problem-)spezifisches *Instrumentarium* und dieses besteht z.B. aus Konstrukten, Beschreibungsmitteln, Sondersprachen, etc. Insgesamt also folgt als notwendige Leistung eine jeweils gegenstand-, für die wissenschaftliche Arbeit im einzelnen problemadäquate *Dimensionierung*, die mit dem jeweiligen Erkenntnisinteresse in Korrelation steht; diese Dimensionierung hat sich in der *Theoriebildung* niederzuschlagen, die für wissenschaftliche Arbeit notwendig ist, bzw. aus ihr resultiert.

4. Die wirkungsspezifische ('politische') Zielsetzung erfordert eine Relationierung der innerwissenschaftlichen Effekte (Ergebnisse) mit der Möglichkeit zu Anwendung und Auswirkung, woraus sich ein Reflex in der gesellschaftlichen Umwelt ergibt. Hieraus folgt die Notwendigkeit und Forderung einer ständigen 'Fortschreibung', d.h. eine *Modifikation* des wissenschaftlichen Arbeitsinteresses der Disziplin anhand von sich abzeichnenden Tendenzen (Leistungen) in der Wissenschaft sowie anhand der sich abzeichnenden Trends (Anforderungen) in der Gesamtsituation.

Somit ergibt sich als Fazit: Für die Sprachwissenschaft insgesamt und im Falle einzelner wissenschaftlicher Aktivitäten in Forschung, Lehre und Anwendung ist eine *Dimensionierung vorzunehmen* nach gewähltem Problem (Erkenntnisinteresse), Bezugsbereich (Untersuchungsgegenstand), und Weise der Verbindung zwischen der ergebnisbringenden wissenschaftlichen Arbeit mit der Umwelt (gesellschaftlicher Entwicklung, Adressaten).

Diese Kennzeichnung der jetzigen Ausgangsposition läßt eine dritte zugrundeliegende Grundannahme erkennen: die Sprachwissenschaft ist als in mehreren und unterschiedlichen *Bezugssystemen* stehend anzusehen, innerhalb derer sie Funktionen zu erfüllen hat und Wirkungen erbringt. Diese Bezugssysteme reichen von den sogenannten Randbedingungen bis in die Wissenschaft selbst. Man kann sie kurz bezeichnen als

- Sprachwissenschaft in der Welt ('Welche Funktionen hat sie?')
- Sprachwissenschaft in spezifischen Anforderungssystemen ('Wofür erbringt sie Leistungen?')
- Sprachwissenschaft als wissenschaftliche Leistung ('Was hat sie erarbeitet?')

Hierdurch wird einmal eine Funktionalisierung der innerwissenschaftlichen Arbeit nach außen möglich, zum anderen eine Beurteilung dieser Arbeit in Relation zu den verschiedenen Außen- und Auswirkungsbereichen.

Die erwähnte Dimensionierung der einzelnen Problemlösungen (Forschungen) erfolgt aufgrund bewußter *Relationierung* zu Bereichen oder Möglichkeiten der Weiterverwendung der erstrebten wissenschaftlichen Ergebnisse und führt dazu, daß auch einzelne, nur innerwissenschaftliche Fragestellungen einen integrativen Charakter bekommen. Damit gilt es, in einer bewußt am Wert (Funktion und Leistung) der eigenen Wissenschaft orientierten Überlegung auch eine bewußte *Dimensionierungstypik* auszuarbeiten. In ihr ist festzuhalten, welche Fragestellungen (Probleme, Aspekte) anzugehen sind und welche Dimensionen (Begriffsebenen) also bei entsprechenden Problemlösungsverfahren (Forschungsverfahren) zu berücksichtigen bzw. miteinander zu verbinden sind. Die Aufgabe der sprachwissenschaftlichen *Heuristik*, die einen problemspezifischen Bereich durchzumustern und die dafür infragekommenden Arbeitsformen (Theorien, Methoden) festzustellen hat, kann damit allgemeiner bezeichnet werden: als die Feststellung der zur Lösung eines wissenschaftlichen Problems infragekommenden Dimensionen und der infolgedessen anzuvisierenden Bearbeitungsweisen (Theoriebildungen, Methoden).

Beispiele für derartige Vorgänge, die zum Teil eine Veränderung im wissenschaftlichen Zugang bedeuten, bieten insgesamt gesehen wohl alle Fortschrittsetappen in der Wissenschaftsentwicklung, besonders deutlich aber der jüngste Entwicklungsschritt in der Sprachwissenschaft: die Hinwendung zur Pragmatik: hier sollen integrativ Syntax, Semantik und sprachliche Wirkungen bis hin zur Soziolinguistik miteinander verbunden werden.

Als Nebenbemerkung darf angefügt werden, daß dem zuvor Gesagten als eine der (vor-)theoretischen Orientierungen natürlich ein bestimmter Begriff von der *Wissenschaft*, genauer: von der Forschung zugrundeliegt. Es wird nämlich davon ausgegangen, daß mit wissenschaftlichen Mitteln betriebene *Forschung* immer auch die Verwendbarkeit der erarbeiteten Ergebnisse einschließt, wobei Anwendungen sowohl innerhalb weiterer wissenschaftlicher Arbeit erfolgen können (sog. Grundlagenforschung) wie auch außerhalb wissenschaftlicher Zusammenhänge in technologischen Bereichen (sog. Angewandte Forschung, Entwicklung). Die grundsätzliche Verwendbarkeit resultiert daraus, daß Forschungserkenntnisse, um als *Ergebnisse* gelten zu können, so formuliert worden sein müssen, daß die Teilaussagen untereinander in einem begründbaren ('logischen') Zusammenhang stehen müssen. Dies wird bei Befolgung von wissenschaftlich anerkannten ('bewährten') Methoden durch deren Folgezusammenhang zwischen Ziel (Absicht) und Erfolg (Effekt) sichergestellt. Es ist damit in jedem Fall von Forschungsergebnissen möglich, von deren Auswirkungen aufgrund von weiterer *Verwendung* (Ausnutzung) zu sprechen. Insofern ist es auch angemessen und notwendig, Gesichtspunkte der Verwendbarkeit und der Auswirkung (des Nutzens für andere) bereits in das Forschungskonzept einzubeziehen, also in die Anlage der Strategie und der Theoriebildung.

2. DIMENSIONIERUNG ZWECKS BESTIMMUNG TEXTIMMANENTER SINNGEHALTE UND BEDEUTUNGEN

Der vorliegende Beitrag soll die These erhärten, daß die Frage 'Wie kommt das Verständnis von Texten zustande?' auch für den Bereich der Textlinguistik relevant ist und also dort soweit anzusprechen ist, wie dies die textlinguistischen Mittel erlauben.

Die genannte Frage rückt unmittelbar und direkt in den Interessenbereich der Textlinguisten, sobald diese sich beim textanalytischen Geschäft nicht nur auf 'äußere' oder 'objektive' Merkmale gegebener Äußerungsprodukte (Sprachmanifestationen, Text-'Gestalten', Texte im materiellen Sinn) beziehen, sondern auch das einbeziehen, was derartige Produkte ('Gebilde') in ihren Funktionen erfahrbar und verstehbar, d.h. analysierbar macht. Dabei wird nicht abgestritten, daß es mit einer gewissen Einschränkung des Begriffs 'objektiv', 'rein objektive' Analysen anhand und anläßlich von gegebenen Textmaterien geben kann: etwa, wenn dort vorkommende und zuvor festgelegte Einzelerscheinungen aus Grammatiksektoren wie Phonologie, Morphologie, Syntax z.B. statistisch festgestellt oder systematisierend untersucht werden. Weiterhin wird anerkannt, daß solche Beobachtungen ihre Funktion im wissenschaftlichen Erkenntnisprozess haben. Es wird aber behauptet, daß bei solchen Untersuchungen die vorangestellte Frage –

'Wie kommt das Verständnis von Texten zustande?' – entweder (noch) keine Rolle spielt oder als zuvor gelöst angesehen wird. Letzteres würde bedeuten, daß der Analysator diese Frage nicht als illegitim einfach abgewiesen hat, sondern daß er sie in seinem Fall nicht zu thematisieren braucht.

Anders wird das, wenn bezüglich irgendwelcher Elemente, Momente oder Eigenschaften eines Textes Gesichtspunkte oder Fragen funktionaler Orientierung ins Spiel kommen. Dies ist immer dann der Fall, wenn im Sinne einer Zuordnung von Produkt und Zweck ('Gestalt' und 'Sinn') der Text als ganzes oder einzelne seiner Eigenschaften *funktional erklärt* werden sollen. Dies wird auch dort notwendig, wo man sich zwar auch noch auf eine materialinterne Systematisierung beschränken könnte (z.B. bei der Feststellung/Aufzählung vorkommender Lexikonelemente), wo aber textfunktionale (Textzweck-)Zusammenhänge bereits deutlich sichtbar werden (Wortbedeutungen): Die bekannte Feststellung, daß sich die Bedeutung von Einzelwörtern bei aktueller Verwendung – d.h. in Texten – nach dem Kotext (gelegentlich noch 'Kontext' genannt) richtet, deutet diese Lage schon an, obgleich noch nicht in ihrer tatsächlichen Reichweite. Immerhin können auch die Bedeutungen einzelner Textelemente nicht ganz von der Funktion des Gesamttextes isoliert gesehen werden. Erst der spezifisch textlinguistische Zugang jedoch ist es, der die *Textfunktionalität* selbst und als solche zum Ausgangspunkt für Text- und Textelementanalysen macht und machen muß: ausgehend von der *Rolle* des betreffenden Textes im Kommunikations- und Sprechhandlungsgeschehen werden die Gesamtfunktion und die Teilfunktionen der anteilig wirksamen Textbestandteile bzw. aller Texteigenschaften zum Analyse-Gegenstand.

Somit kann man hier eine erste *Form der Dimensionierung* in der sprachwissenschaftlichen Arbeit feststellen, d.h. eine Mehrfach-Methodik nach 'Gestalt' und 'Sinn'. Sie erfolgt dadurch, daß der Analysator *mehr als eine* Gesichtspunkt-, Problem-, Methoden- und Ergebnis-Ebene anerkennt und durchverfolgt, wobei er von der grundsätzlichen Freiheit Gebrauch macht, diejenigen und soviele analytische Ebenen (Dimensionen) zu wählen, wie er angesichts des untersuchten Gegenstandes (hier: eines Textes) für angemessen hält. Eine jede Dimension ist dabei durch dasjenige Ensemble von Gesichtspunkten, Kategorien, Begriffen, Konstrukten und Kriterien gekennzeichnet, das für sie zur Verfügung steht bzw. für sie eingesetzt wird.

So gesehen gibt es in der textlinguistischen Arbeit verschiedene Dimensionierungen, denen auch unterschiedliche Forscher- oder Erkenntnisinteressen entsprechen:

> produktorientierte Dimensionierung – Bezugsobjekt:
> die manifestierte Textsubstanz (Textzeichen);
> produktionsorientierte Dimensionierung – Bezugsobjekt:
> die Herstellung von texthaften Zeichen (-mengen) in Bezug auf beabsichtigte Wirkungen;
> funktionsorientierte Dimensionierung – Bezugsobjekt:
> Zusammengehören von Textmaterie und Textinhalt;
> partnerorientierte Dimensionierung – Bezugsobjekt:
> Sender- Text- Empfänger-Verhältnisse.

Man hat somit davon auszugehen – und dies ist in der Ausgangsposition begründet –, daß jeder Sprachwissenschaftler, wie jeder Wissenschaftler aus einer beliebigen Disziplin und überhaupt jeder Mensch auch bei unwissenschaftlichem Zugriff, seine Absicht immer im Rahmen einer von ihm selbst abhängenden und also steuerbaren *Verfahrensweise* verfolgt und im Falle des Erfolges erreicht. Dies ist eine so selbstverständliche und vorwissenschaftliche Feststellung, daß sie hier ohne weitere Bezugsreferenzen stehen bleiben kann. Sie kann natürlich auch schon als meta-wissenschaftlich gelten.

Hiernach kann festgestellt werden: Befaßt man sich mit einer Dimensionierung in Bezug auf Textmaterie *und* Verständnis, so sind hier zwei Begriffsinstrumentarien zu verbinden: eines für die Textmaterie und eines für das Textverständnis, beide jeweils für die Heuristik und für die wissenschaftliche Beschreibung.

Es könnte der Eindruck entstehen, und auch dahingehend Kritik geäußert werden, daß das Gesagte nun wahrlich keine linguistisch interessanten und schon gar nicht linguistisch relevante Bemerkungen seien: all das läge noch vor aller wirklichen wissenschaftlichen Arbeit und Leistung und sei überdies in hohem Maße trivial. Aber, es gehört gerade zum Ziel des vorliegenden Beitrages, darauf hinzuweisen und davon auszugehen, daß eine, wo immer, sich zeigende wissenschaftliche Verläßlichkeit, Erkenntnissicherung oder Befriedigung eine *Folgeerscheinung* ist: sie kommt erst innerhalb eines Systems mit Folgerungscharakter (einer Theorie) zustande, beruht also in ihrer system- und theoriegesicherten Verläßlichkeit auf *Vorstufen*, die die Folgerungsrichtung festlegen, und setzt solche durchaus voraus. Die Theorie, welche die Sicherheit des Wissens ('Wissenschaftlichkeit') ergibt, beruht also selbst auf Vor-Einstellungen – nämlich solchen, die die Dimensionierung festlegen. Dimensionierungsoperationen bestimmen somit den *Rahmen* für eine Theorie, die – sofern sie 'einwandfrei' ist – wissenschaftliches Wissen sichert und insofern einen Teil einer bestimmten Wissenschaft ausmacht.

Zudem ist die Tatsache der Dimensionierung selbst weder neu noch ungewöhnlich. Sie tritt als Aufgabe z.B. immer dann auf, auch wenn man dies nicht eigens reflektiert, wenn sogenannte interdisziplinäre Vorhaben in Angriff genommen werden. Deren Kennzeichen ist – sofern sich nicht nur Nachbardisziplinen additiv an ein und demselben Gegenstand versuchen – daß mehr als eine Methode (Instrumentarium, Theorie) herangezogen werden muß und daß nur so eine befriedigende Behandlung zustandekommt. Die Aufgabe besteht hier in der Entwicklung einer *Mehrfach-Dimensionierung*. Ausgangspunkt derartiger Vorhaben sind denn auch Fragestellungen, die die Mehrfach-Dimensionierung eines Themas (Gegenstandes) erfordern oder erzwingen. Würde man eine Zweifach-Dimensionierung in Bezug auf Textmaterie und Textverständnis hinsichtlich der Instrumentarien auf mehrere Disziplinen verteilen (Textmaterie: Sprachwissenschaft; Textverständnis: Psychologie usw.), so würde das hier gewählte Thema als Fall einer interdisziplinären Themenstellung erscheinen.

Abschließend läßt sich feststellen: da ein als Sprachverwendungsprodukt vorliegender (geäußerter) Text nur nachdem bzw. indem er verstanden wird analysierbar wird, darf die *Verbindung von Textmaterie und Textverständnis* als Untersuchungsgegenstand linguistisch für interessant gelten und die Themafrage nach der textkonformen Sinnbestimmung als eine für die Linguistik relevante Fragestellung. Die Grundlage im Sinne einer operativen Basis hierfür ist jedoch eine Dimensionierungsoperation, die simultane Verbindung von zwei Erkenntnis- und Analyse-Absichten, die jede für sich betrachtet eine eigene Dimension darstellen: einen Bereich, der durch die Besonderheit eines bestimmten Instrumentariums ausgezeichnet ist.

3. FUNKTIONSORIENTIERTE DIMENSIONIERUNG

Im Vorstehenden wurde die These vertreten, daß auch eine Mehrfach-Analyse von linguistischer Relevanz ist, und es wurde versucht, diese These zu rechtfertigen. Dabei wurden unterschieden: Instrumentarien zur Analyse von Textmaterie neben Instrumentarien zur Analyse von Textverständnis. Man kann davon ausgehen, daß für die Analyse und Beschreibung von Textmaterie, d.i. von textförmigen Sprachsymbolkomplexen, verschiedene Angebote aus der bestehenden Linguistik bereitstehen. Sie reichen von traditionellen über strukturalistische bis hin zu generativen Methoden (Grammatiken) und sollen hier nicht besprochen oder in ihrer Anwendung verfolgt werden.

Es geht im Rahmen dieses Beitrags vielmehr um Vorschläge für die Entwicklung der dazu komplementären *Dimension der Textfunktionalität.* Dies scheint darum wichtig, weil Texte als sprachsymbolförmige Produkte anzusehen sind, die im Zuge von Sprechen, d.h. von Sprach(system)-verwendung im weitesten Sinne zustandegebracht werden, und weil Sprache nicht anders vorkommt bzw. manifest wird als im Rahmen von Zusammenhängen, die allgemein als Handeln mit/unter Einbeziehung von Sprache angesehen werden können. Man kann sagen, Texte allein oder 'als solche' kommen nicht vor, weil sie ihrerseits gar keinen (Situations-)Kontext hätten, in dem und auf den sie Wirkung oder Funktion haben könnten. Was also linguistischerseits zu leisten ist, besteht einmal in der Anerkennung dieses notwendig weiteren Horizontes aller Spracherscheinungen, sofern sie in actu und in concreto vorliegen, zum anderen in der Lösung der Aufgabe, den damit notwendigen Beitrag der Linguistik zur Gewinnung/Erarbeitung wissenschaftlichen Wissens festzustellen und zu erbringen.

Nimmt man das zuvor Gesagte hinzu, so ist damit auch die Frage verbunden, wie weit und unter welchen Voraussetzungen die bisherigen 'gestalt'bezogenen linguistischen Instrumentarien ('Grammatiken') zu einer solchen Aufgabe beitragen können. Eine Weiterentwicklung oder Modifikation dieser Instrumentarien wird damit also nicht von vornherein ausgeschlossen.

3.1 *Textfunktionale Gesichtspunkte*

Von 'textfunktionalen Gesichtspunkten' wird hier gesprochen, weil in dieser – dezidiert heuristischen – Phase der Überlegungen zunächst nur Feststellungen getroffen werden sollen bezüglich solcher mit Textvorkommen verbundenen Erscheinungen (Text-'Eigenschaften'), die als Hinweise auf die Funktionsspezifität gewertet werden können. Es ist dabei klar, daß einige der zu vermerkenden *Texteigenschaften* kaum noch als Eigenschaften dieser betreffenden Texte angesehen werden können, sondern vielmehr eher als Eigenschaften ihrer Umgebung, ihres Vorkommenskontextes bzw. der 'Situation', in der die eine Rolle spielen. Dennoch wird dieser Unterschied im Moment nicht besonders betont, weil es Sache einer späteren Unterscheidungsoperation ist, festzulegen, wer sich mit welchen dieser Eigenschaften wissenschaftlich zu befassen hat. Bewußt wird also gegenwärtig nicht eine *Grenze der Linguistik* – des linguistischen Erkenntnis- und Fachinteresses – angesetzt und dominant gemacht, sondern die Aufnahme von Texteigenschaften auch bis auf die Kontexte ausgedehnt, in denen diese Texte vorkommen. Dies scheint nicht a limine unzulässig angesichts der Tatsache, daß ja auch etwas wie Bedeutungen, Funktionen, Effekte, Wirkungen usw. zwar wie Eigenschaften der betreffenden Sprachelemente und Texte behandelt werden, es aber – genau besehen – nicht sind, weil es sich eigentlich um *Konstitutionsphänomene* bei Rezipienten anhand dargebotener Sprachsymbolmengen handelt.

Man kann hinter diesen Worten als These ansetzen: In dem Maße, wie es unmöglich und somit unsinnig ist, Textvorkommen und Textbildung ohne Blick auf Textfunktion zu erklären, ist es angebracht, zwecks Funktionsanalysen über textinterne Eigenschaften hinauszugehen. Wie bereits gesagt, bleibt es dabei hier noch offen, wie weit damit die 'eigentliche Linguistik' überschritten wird, was aber auch bedeutet, in welchem Ausmaß die bisherige Linguistik in der Lage ist, diesbezügliche Arbeit zu leisten.

3.2 *Funktionale Textspezifikatoren*

Von 'Spezifikatoren' wird gesprochen, um für die angedeutete Unterscheidung von textinternen (Text-)Eigenschaften und textexternen (Kontext-)Eigenschaften eine zusammenfassende Bezeichnung zu haben. Es wird somit davon ausgegangen, daß sowohl *textinterne Eigenschaften* als auch *textexterne Gegebenheiten* einen Text hinsichtlich seiner Funktionalität spezifizieren. Man kann dann einfach von textinternen und textexternen Spezifikatoren sprechen, indem die Funktion das ist, was thematisiert wird, und die Sachlage, wo bestimmte Funktionsspezifikatoren auffindbar sind – im Text selbst oder außerhalb der Textmaterie – von sekundärem Belang ist. Es wird damit möglich, unterschiedliche Weisen der Kennzeichnung von Textfunktionen, auch ein und derselben Textfunktion anzuerkennen. Die für Textproduzenten typischen Fragen 'Was soll dieser Text erreichen?', 'Was kann man tun und welche Wege gibt es, den bestimmten Zweck zu erreichen, einem Text eine bestimmte Funktion zu geben?' zeigen an, daß man sich hier ziemlich nahe an der sogenannten Praxis befindet, etwa von Redakteuren, Werbefachleuten, usw., für die eine funktionsorientierte Wahl zwischen textformulierenden und textanordnenden Praktiken zum Alltagsgeschäft gehört. Man kann sich hier der Deutlichkeit halber am besten auf ein solches bestimmtes Textgebiet beschränken.

Das Verstehen eines Textes – allgemeiner: einer kommunikativ wirksamen sprachlichen Einheit ('Kommunikativer Einheiten') – ist in einer ersten Näherung als ein kombiniertes Ergebnis ('Syndrom') zu kennzeichnen, d.h. als Folge von mehreren – individuell verschiedenen — Erfahrungs- und Analyseprozeduren (Operationen). Sie sind im Wege einer Heuristik zunächst festzustellen, später ist zu untersuchen, wie man sie 'wissenschaftlich in den Griff bekommt'. Es ist davon auszugehen, daß sich ein Verstehen von Texten insofern auch durch die Texte selbst ergibt, als dieses Verstehen anhand eines bestimmten Textes gesteuert wird, sich also mittels weitgehend textgesteuerter Bestimmungsschritte einrangiert. Das Geschehen eines sich auf diese Weise aufbauenden (konstituierten) Textverständnisses kann dann bezeichnet werden als sukzessive Festlegung ('Determination') von Werten der Bedeutung, des Sinnes, der Funktion, kurz von Verstehenswerten. Diese Verstehenswerte werden oft als an die betreffenden Textpassagen oder Textelementen 'gebunden' aufgefaßt. Wie weit diese als lediglich 'intensional' anzusehen sind, soll hier nicht diskutiert werden.

3.3 *Liste von Funktionsdeterminanten*

Faßt man eine solche Prozedur des Gesamtverständnisses – für deren Beschreibung mittels einer wissenschaftsgerechten Theorie später Verfahren und Konstrukte usw. entwickelt werden müssen – als eine bestimmte Art von text'interner' Definitorik, nämlich als eine durch den Textverlauf *gesteuerte Sinndetermination,* so wird es plausibel und notwendig, für die Sinnfestlegung von Texten Funktionsdeterminanten anzusetzen. Für sie sind bezüglich der konkreten Fälle von Texten in Funktionszusammenhängen die unterschiedlichen *Indikatoren* aufzusuchen, zunächst wieder in heuristisch-phänomenologischer Weise. Die Funktionsdeterminanten werden hier aus den zuvor erwähnten Gründen (einheitliche Bezeichnung für textinternes und textexternes Vorkommen) als funktionale Textspezifikatoren bezeichnet. Maßgeblich ist dabei, daß sie anhand von Beobachtungen feststellbar sind, wie sie ja auch – wie das allgemeine Sprachgeschehen zeigt – von den Kommunikationspartnern verstanden bzw. richtig eingeschätzt und erfolgreich eingesetzt werden.

Folgende funktionsdeterminierende Spezifikatoren sind ohne große Mühe erkennbar:

Außertextlich

KONTEXTSTELLE	Zusammenhang, in dem der Text vorkommt und Funktion/Erfolg hat; Vorkommensort im 'Erwartungshorizont'. Determiniert das Verhältnis von Text-'rolle' und Situationalität.
PARTNERBEZUG	Art, Zustand, Sozialstatus, Festgelegtheit usw. von Sprecher(n) und Hörer(n), wobei beliebig genaue Spezifikationen nach soziokulturellen Bedingungen möglich sind. Determiniert das Verhältnis von Text-Intention-Interpretation.

Textart

KOMMUNIKATIONSFORM	Vorkommensart, in der ein Text als sprachlicher geäußert wird: als Dialog/Gespräch, Buch, Zeitung, usw. Determiniert die Funktion einer bestimmten kommunikativen Einheit.
LOKALISIERUNG	Einordnung, Vorkommensort innerhalb einer Textmenge, Rubrik, als Teiltext innerhalb eines Gesprächs usw. Determiniert die Funktion des betreffenden Textes in seiner Rolle als bestimmte kommunikative Einheit, z.B. als Nachricht, Kommentar, Leitartikel usw. ('Textsorte').

Vertextungsart

SIGNALEMENT	Besonderheiten in der Äußerungsweise wie z.B. laut, leise, schnell, langsam usw., Schriftart, 'Aufmachung', mit/ohne Überschrift. Determiniert die Textdarbietung.

DURCHFÜHRUNG	Verlauf der Thematik passagenweise, 'Satzgruppenwerte'. Determiniert den thematischen Verlauf ("Isotopie(n)").
Vertextungsweise	
GESAMTAUSSAGE	Was ist mit dem Text gesagt/gemeint/gewollt? Determiniert die sinngebende Funktion aufgrund von einzelnen Aussageinhalten, Aussageformen.
AUSSAGEINHALTE	Das im Text Angesprochene, direkt/indirekt, Inhalte der linearen Verlaufssukzession. Determiniert Bezugsgegenstände, Bezugswelten.
AUSSAGEMODUS	Wie das Gesagte im einzelnen formuliert wird, unterschieden nach Spezifica in Wortwahl, Wortschatz (Bezugs-Charakterisierung); Spezifica in der Kombinatorik, Kotextbildung, Bedeutungsmodifikation und Bedeutungsfestlegung mittels Wortwertkombination (syntaktisch bedingte Bedeutungseffekte); Spezifica der 'Grammatik', Satzbau, Einsatz und Wahl der grammatischen Levels (Morphologie der Teilausdrücke). Determiniert die jeweilige individuelle Aussageweise des vorliegenden Textes.

Die angeführten Funktionsdeterminanten können im einzelnen weiter spezifiziert werden, etwa indem man unter PARTNERBEZUG auch die Sprachfunktionen P. A. Verburgs (kurativ, clarity, usw.) einbezieht. Überhaupt wird in dieser Phase der Heuristik keine Funktionsbestimmungskomponente prinzipiell ausgeschlossen. Die Auswahl der signifikanten und der systematisch behandelbaren Determinanten muß später erfolgen. Insgesamt aber darf gelten, daß es derartige Determinanten sind, anhand deren ein Textanalysator – Partner, Hörer, Leser, Linguist – je nach Aufnahmefähigkeit und Bereitschaft einen speziellen Text als in einem bestimmten Zweck- und Wirkungsbezug stehend erfaßt und bewertet. Je nach seiner Einstellung reagiert er dann darauf.

Es ist, allgemein gesprochen, die Rolle dieser Determinanten, den mit einem Text verbundenen (beabsichtigten) Situationsbezug, seine Wirkung in einer bestimmten kommunikativen Lage, deutlich zu machen. Ein Sprecher bezieht alle derartigen 'Gesichtspunkte' mehr oder weniger 'automatisch' mit ein. Die Feststellung und das Verstehen dieses die Textproduktion motivierenden Wirkungsbezugs ist somit aufzufassen als eine anhand des gegebenen Textes vorgenommene *Interpretation* hinsichtlich seiner funtionalen Rolle als Bestandteil einer sprachlich beeinflußten Kommunikationssituation. Da Texte im allgemeinen hinsichtlich dieses (ihres 'eigentlichen') Bezugs tatsächlich verstanden und – eventuell aufgrund von Nachfragen – richtig bewertet werden, ist anzunehmen, daß sie entsprechende Funktionsdeterminanten in Form von Indikatoren in zureichendem Ausmaß 'enthalten' in dem Sinne, daß diese *zusammen mit sonstigen* vorgegebenen (auch außertextlichen) Textwertdetermininanten eine zureichende textbewertende Interpretation ergeben. Die beabsichtigte Textwirkung tritt ein, wenn die vollzogene Interpretation (Textbewertung) *bejaht* bzw. geglaubt wird, sonst nicht.

Eine genauere Analyse wird davon ausgehen, daß dieses 'zusammen mit' derart zustandekommt, daß textinterne Erscheinungen der Textbildung nach Maßgabe einer *Bezugnahme* auf textexterne Vorgegebenheiten zustande gebracht werden: die betreffenden Textelemente haben dann die 'Bedeutung', den Text auf seinen Vorkommens- und Wirkungskontext abzustimmen, ihn einzupassen, ihn erfolgreich zu machen usw. Wobei zugleich deutlich wird, daß mit einem Wort wie 'Bedeutung' auch hier nicht mehr überzeugend gearbeitet werden kann.

Es mag überraschen, daß diejenigen Analyse-Ebenen, auf denen die bisherige Linguistik die meisten Beiträge zu Instrumentarien (Methoden) entwickelt hat, erst an letzter Stelle auftauchen (vgl. AUSSAGE, AUSSAGEINHALT, AUSSAGEMODUS). Dies hat seinen Grund darin, daß die hierher gehörenden textinternen Indikatoren erst bei Hinzunahme der davor genannten Spezifikatoren einen Wert als *funktionale* Determinanten bekommen. Man kann dies an solchen Fällen erkennen, wo Texte isoliert von ihren ursprünglichen Situationen (Kontextstellen) gegeben sind – z.B. als Zeugnisse aus früheren Zeiten – und nur soweit verstanden werden, wie es gelingt, die kommunikativen Originärsituationen (Partner-, Wirkungsbezüge) zu erschließen, so daß die partner- und situationsspezifische Bewertungsinterpretation – also der Wirkungsbezug – erkennbar wird.

4. KONSEQUENZEN

Bevor man zu weiteren Schritten übergeht, z.B. zur Bildung einer mehrdimensionalintegrativen Theorie, sind die Konsequenzen eines derartigen Ansatzes klarzustellen und in der Disziplin zu diskutieren. Aus diesem Grunde soll der vorliegende Beitrag zunächst ein Diskussionsbeitrag sein und noch nicht bis zu irgendeinem Theoriebildungsversuch vorschreiten, obgleich natürlich erst eine gelungene Theoriebildung innerhalb der Wissenschaft Überzeugungswert besitzen kann. Es wird aber, im Moment, für primär wichtig gehalten, die *Richtung* des zuvor angedeuteten Erkenntnisinteresses vorzustellen: nicht zuletzt, weil dies unter Umständen auch die Frage einer Grenzziehung für die linguistische Disziplin betrifft, und weil auch mit Argumenten zu rechnen ist wie 'Das überschreitet die Linguistik!' oder 'Dies kann die Linguistik nicht leisten!' usw.

Nachfolgend werden daher noch einige Konsequenzen aufgeführt. Sie sind dahingehend zu beurteilen: ob, wie und von wem die mit ihnen gegebenen Anforderungen erfüllt werden können. Danach läßt sich sagen, ein wie beschaffener Arbeitsbereich dem genannten Erkenntnisinteresse, wenn es anerkannt ist, entsprechen müßte.

4.1 *Textanalyse*

Die bisherigen Bemerkungen liegen alle, wie gesagt, nur auf der Ebene der Heuristik. Das hat seinen Grund darin, daß vor einem wissenschaftlich orientierten Einstieg in Problemlösungsverfahren – also vor Beginn einer Forschung – die *Phänomenologie* des anzugehenden Objekt- und Gegenstandsbereichs in Betracht gezogen werden muß hinsichtlich der dort vorfindlichen Realfaktoren und Abhängigkeiten. Aus einer Festlegung der untersuchenswerten Signifikanzen im Objekt- und Gegenstandsbereich ergeben sich dann, in einem zweiten Schritt, die *Rahmenanforderungen* an zu wählende Methoden und an zu erstrebende Theoriebildungen.

Für die linguistische Textanalyse ergibt sich aus der vorgeführten Perspektive die Notwendigkeit einer Abschätzung der *Leistungsfähigkeit* bisheriger Theorien und Methoden ('Textgrammatiken'), d.h. ihrer Reichweite und ihres Verwendungswertes. Ein Verwendungswert kann z.B. darin liegen, daß sie den Einsatz von Datenverarbeitungsverfahren ermöglichen, für Dokumentationsfragen brauchbar sind (Abstrakt-, Extrakt-, Kondensatbildung; Indexierung), usw. Eine wichtige Frage wird die sein: ob und wie weit auch funktionale Indikatoren in die bisherigen Textgrammatiken Aufnahme finden können (etwa in deren Lexikon, Thesaurus), oder ob in eine Textgrammatik noch die – für Einzelsätze nicht gleicherweise relevanten – Kombinations('Syntax')-werte aufzunehmen sind.

4.2 *Textlinguistik*

Hier werden die Konsequenzen am deutlichsten sein. Es resultiert zunächst die Aufgabe zu klären, was *Gegenstand* der textlinguistischen Arbeit sein bzw. werden soll und kann. Wenn nur Textgrammatik betrieben wird, ist zu klären, wie weit diese gehen, d.h. in ihren Aussagen reichen soll, ob sie beschränkt bleibt, indem sie von Textfunktionen absieht. Wenn die Pragmatik mit einbezogen werden soll, ist zu klären, wie weit sich die vorliegenden Vorschläge hierzu als Beitrag oder Ergänzung eignen. Wenn die Handlungstheorie einbezogen werden soll, so ist zu klären, ob die Funktionsdeterminanten auch handlungs- und erfolgsspezifische Aussagenstrukturierung erlauben. Wenn auch die Soziolinguistik einbezogen werden soll, ist zu klären, wie weit 'Rolle', 'Status', u.a.m. weiter differenziert werden müssen.

4.3 *Experimentelle Verfahren*

Es liegt auf der Hand, daß die notwendige *Tatsachen-Feststellung* im hier angesprochenen Themenbereich eine experimentelle Grundlegung nahelegt. Sie wird nötig, um von den zahlreichen intuitiven Annahmen eines Analysators wegzukommen, die dieser – etwa, wenn er Linguist ist – bezüglich der Textfunktionalität macht, weil er selbst permanent als Ausgangs- und Bezugsperson für Sprachgeschehen (Textbildung) betroffen ist. An dieser Stelle kann noch nicht auf die zu entwickelnden Experimentstrategien eingegangen werden, da zunächst zu klären ist, ob sich hierzu bereits mögliche Beiträge aus experimentierenden Disziplinen wie (Sprach-)Psychologie und (Sprach-)Soziologie ergeben.

4.4 *Kommunikationsmodell*

Man kann davon ausgehen, daß für bestehende Kommunikationsmodelle weitergehende Differenzierungen zugelassen und vorgesehen sind, zumal dann, wenn bereits Gesichtspunkte der Soziolinguistik und der Sprechhandlungstheorie anvisiert wurden. So werden die Funktionsdeterminanten 'Kontext', 'Kommunikationsform/Kommunikative Einheit', 'Partnerbezug/Sozialstatus', ebenso auch die Art der Vertextung (SIGNALEMENT und DURCHFÜHRUNG) mit entsprechenden Forderungen oder Erweiterungsabsichten wahrscheinlich ziemlich direkt-kohärent sein.

Wenn es gelingt, nachfolgend auch noch die besprochenen Zuordnungen von textinternen Inhaltsansprachen und Aussageformen zu den textspezifischen Funktionsdeterminanten vorzunehmen, dann wird sich hieraus auch für kommunikationsorientierte Arbeiten eine zusätzliche Bereicherung sozusagen 'nach unten' ergeben, d.h. eine *kommunikative Analyse* bis in den Text selbst hinein. Wie weit es hierzu außerdem des Einsatzes von experimentellen Methoden bedarf, ist gesondert zu klären.

Zusammenfassend ist festzuhalten, daß die angeführten Konsequenzen exemplarisch zeigen sollen, wie sich eine differenzierte Dimensionierung auswirken kann. Nachdem hierbei anerkannt ist, daß man in dieser Richtung arbeiten sollte, wären in einem nächsten Schritt die geeigneten Konstrukte, Methoden und Theorien zu erarbeiten. Die Absicht des vorliegenden Beitrags war lediglich, ein Konzept für die Objekt- und Themenwahl der Textlinguistik zur Diskussion zu stellen, das mit seinem Spektrum an textfunktional relevanten Gesichtspunkten eine Reaktion und Resonanz bildet auf die von P.A. Verburg angezielte Bereicherung der allgemein-sprachwissenschaftlichen Sehweise.

SCHLEICHER'S TREE AND ITS TRUNK

HENRY M. HOENIGSWALD

1. In any discussion of the merits and weaknesses of the language family tree there are at least three issues: (a) under what circumstances and by whom the schema of the tree is chosen; (b) what relations and inferences the tree is called upon to depict; and (c) what trees are like. Involved are, in other words, (a) the history of scholarship; (b) views of linguistic change; and (c), to however elementary an extent, graph theory.

2. The tree is often associated with August Schleicher, though Schleicher was not the first to use it, even in connection with language, let alone with other phenomena that occur and differentiate over time. The tree schema fits language descent (that is, a particular conception of language descent) better than it fits, say, human genealogy, where, for the purposes of the graphic array as such, *la recherche de la paternité*[1] *est interdite* by the exigencies of the two-dimensional page. Whatever a line of language descent (e.g. from Old French to Modern French, or from proto-Iroquois to Tuscarora) may be – not a particularly simple thing to state, for that matter – such descent is, despite occasional ingenious disclaimers, thought of as parthenogenetic, if it is recognized at all. And if it is not recognized, there is no tree to discuss.

3. What makes the rooted tree useful is the ease with which it symbolizes successive bifurcations (or multifurcations) of speech communities. It has a root point (representing the ancestor),[2] non-terminal vertices (subancestors) and terminal vertices (languages later stages of which do not exist, are not known, or not considered[3]). It has edges and paths (lines of descent) which may or may not be endowed with meaningful metric length (to measure time elapsed, or the extent of change undergone, or both in correlation)[4] but which in any case have meaningful direction away from the root (downward in time). This is enough. In particular, the family tree needs no stem.[5]

4. But Schleicher's tree did have a stem. To Schleicher, as to some others past and present, the bifurcation of a speech community A is not so much a splitting apart (A → B, C) as a splitting-off (A → A', B). For he not only sets up two initial successive bifurcations – first of Indo-European into Slavo-Germanic and Ario-Greco-Italo-Celtic, and then of the latter into Greco-Italo-Celtic and Indo-Iranian – but he is also sure that Slavo-Germanic separated 'from' Ario-Greco-Italo-Celtic rather than either the reverse or than (as we would say) that the two separated from each other. Likewise he says that Greco-Italo-Celtic split off 'from' Indo-Iranian. He uses the same terminology for subsequent separations. His family tree has a trunk, or stem, up to the point where the Indians, as the most recent prehistoric migrants along that particular line, 'left the ancestral seat'.[6]

5. So far the distinction between trunk and branches is clear: it has, in large part, to do with the geographic location of the speakers. Knowledge of such matters can have divers sources: it may be direct, or at least explicit (e.g. the location of the speakers of proto-Romance); it may be inferred, in the well-known manner, from some of the semantic content of the reconstructed vocabulary (as in the case of the beech-tree); it might also be based on a specific migration theory.[7] In a sense, Schleicher had such a theory, since he presents it as a finding that the farther east an Indo-European descendant language is found, the more old material it retains, while the southern and, especially, the northern languages have innovated more. This is, in part, how he obtains his tree.

6. We still believe, like Schleicher, that it is to a statable extent possible to distinguish, in a collection of related languages, between retention (of ancestral traits) and innovation. But Schleicher also thought that some descendant languages are significantly more innovating than others and that the degree of innovation is an index of the geographic dislocation of the speakers. Quite aside from such specific issues as those connected with the Indo-European vocalism which he judged differently from his later colleagues, he was apparently not troubled by the fact that the old Sanskrit and Iranian texts are simply older than the Greek and Latin ones, and these, in turn, older than those in Germanic, Baltic, and Slavic. It remained for Delbrück and Brugmann to make clear that the degree of innovation does not have to be estimated for a tree to be constructed since, in principle, the simple presence or absence of exclusively shared innovation determines the proper subgrouping.[8] And the matching

procedure quaintly known as the 'comparative' method (in the narrow sense of the term) suffices in itself to tell innovation from retention under certain conditions.[9] Trees so constructed, to be sure, have no stems. Their validity is consistent with any assumption one wishes to make about the degree to which innovation has occurred – including the possibility that innovation is not clearly measurable or that its rate is in some statistically valid sense constant from language to language, stationary as well as migratory.

7. One wonders, however, if those who have fallen back on the schema of the stemmed tree or who suggest at least implicitly that it has merit, necessarily share Schleicher's bias with regard to migration and its effects. Occasionally one suspects an even simpler temptation to have been at work. Filiation can be wildly uneven; some lines of descent may survive and proliferate while others stop producing offshoots and terminate. Indo-Europeanists have often reflected that there must have been many extinct Indo-European languages which never came to anyone's notice. There are now many Iranian languages in existence while, say, Albanian survives only in one, relatively undifferentiated, shape. It is not quite easy to disregard the possibility that this state of affairs has sometimes led to the belief that a branching the descendancy of which ends up in a state of extensive diversification already possesses privileged status at the time of filiation. While nobody will seriously maintain that the future vigor of particular descendants can be predicted from the nature of the separate change processes that characterize the branching, a tree with a trunk representing the more prolific, and with side branches representing the relatively less prolific, lines of descent may still be drawn.[10] To be sure, the distinction between trunk and branches does not provide any information beyond that which is already contained in the unstemmed schema.

8. In short, the family trees which are sometimes used to represent certain relations obtaining among related languages are of the following types. They may be non-metric and unstemmed, in which case each edge simply stands for the presence of innovation (for instance, phonemic merger, the incorporation of given loanwords, etc.). They may be metric, with edges and paths measuring either known time, or extent of innovation (and hence, under some suitable hypothesis, inferred time). Finally, stemmed trees have also been used, but there is no agreement on how to interpret the stem in an interesting way. Schleicher apparently thought

of it as a device to indicate descent within the stationary portion of the population, recognizable as such by the fact that there is less innovation than in the other lines of descent. Thus, degree of change, measured in whatever fashion, has sometimes been associated with the lapse of time, and sometimes with mobility. The former association, while not generally accepted, seems more reasonable now than the latter.[11] The unadorned non-metric, unstemmed tree at least allows us to bypass these unnecessary problems and perhaps saves us from other consequences involved in letting a model with too many special geometric properties take over. "Bilder," said Johannes Schmidt (himself the creator of the wave image to depict language relationship), "haben in der Wissenschaft nur sehr geringen Wert."[12]

University of Pennsylvania

NOTES

1 Or of the maternity, according to choice and tradition. A reference to the other parent is usually adscribed to the node.
2 The 'root' is of course ordinarily put at the top.
3 Except where the terminal vertex is the root point – a proviso which should be added also to H. M. Hoenigswald, *Studies in Formal Historical Linguistics* (Dordrecht, 1973), 26.
4 Strictly, it is the length of the projections of these paths on the vertical scale which is commonly used in this way.
5 On stemmed trees see O. Ore, *Theory of Graphs* (Providence, 1962), 59.
6 *Compendium der vergleichenden Grammatik der indogermanischen Sprachen*[2] (Weimar, 1866), 8.
7 See, e.g., I. Dyen, *Language*, 32 (1956), 611-26.
8 See I. Dyen, *Language*, 29 (1953), 577-90; C. D. Chrétien, *International Journal of American Linguistics*, 29 (1963), 66-8. Scholars holding the view here alluded to usually add that these shared innovations must be 'significant' and that 'accidental' duplication, or duplication of 'trivial' changes that are easily duplicated, will not do.
9 H. M. Hoenigswald in T. A. Sebeok et al. (ed.), *Current Trends in Linguistics*, 11 (The Hague and Paris, 1973), 57.
10 An example may be found in G. L. Trager and H. L. Smith, Jr., *Studies in Linguistics*, 8 (1950), 64; but see now Trager, *Language and Languages* (San Francisco, etc., 1972), 169-74.
11 It may be that in Schleicher's conception there lingers a reluctance to recognize to the full the possibility that the 'common source', in Sir William Jones' words, 'no longer exists'. If it no longer 'exists', then at least something approaching it ought to exist.
12 *Die Verwandtschaftsverhältnisse der indogermanischen Sprachen* (Weimar, 1872), 28.

SOME OBSERVATIONS ABOUT SEMITICS AND GENERAL LINGUISTICS

J. H. HOSPERS

G. Cragg, Sumerian scholar from Chicago, in 1973 introduced his very interesting article entitled, "Linguistics, Method and Extinct Languages: The Case of Sumerian", with the following words: "At present researchers in areas which until recently had gotten along quite well, it seemed, in happy innocence of linguistics are increasingly confronted with articles of the genre 'Linguistics and...' or 'Linguistic approach to' their own field [...] the various language disciplines."[1] However, contributing as I am doing to an anniversary volume which will be presented to my friend and colleague Prof. Dr. P. A. Verburg on the occasion of his seventieth birthday, it seems to me very fitting all the same to add one more article to those mentioned by G. Cragg, and not to publish something about a detailed subject from my own special field, that of Semitics. For P. A. Verburg, the first to become Professor of General Linguistics in our University, is the very man who during concerted action in our faculty and subfaculty, an action lasting for many years, has been so instrumental in enlarging my understanding of the relationship between general linguistics and Semitics. It is true that already before this relationship had been of great interest to me, but it was due to the activities of P. A. Verburg – who also on account of his world-wide relations in the science of general linguistics knew how to recognise its really important trends (whether he could be in agreement with them or not) – that I was guided through the vast field of general linguistics. There will be no need for a detailed account of how important and inspiring all this has always been for the linguist whose field of studies for a long time formed part of the "areas which until recently had gotten along quite well, it seemed, in happy innocence of linguistics".[2]

In fact as late as 1966 I felt obliged to state in an article about the relationship between Semitics and general linguistics: "Of recent years developments within general linguistics have proceeded at a somewhat tempestuous pace, and it proved unavoidable that many theories should be launched which afterwards had to be abandoned completely or in part. Semitics took little part in all this",[3] even if the same article already contained my references to various scholars of Semitic, such as H. Birkeland, Z. S. Harris, J. Cantineau, H. B. Rosén, and others who by their publications had, at the time already, given proof of their unmistakeable interest in the developments appearing in the field of general linguistics.[4]

Fortunately, this last mentioned trend has been continuing since 1966, so that in this article I should like to mention briefly a few recent publications bearing witness of it. In doing so I shall confine myself to the classical Semitic languages. Present-day spoken Hebrew and the modern Arabic colloquials, the linguistic areas of which have been the subject of linguistically well-founded publications in this past decade, I shall leave out of account. Because of the space permitted to me I shall of necessity be very selective – a necessity which is gratifying in itself – and be in a position to mention only those publications which, in my opinion, are the best illustration of this changing attitude. Naturally I am very much aware of the subjective element in choosing these publications.

It is true that, as G. Cragg aforementioned did, it can be concluded "that there is, even in Ancient Near Eastern Circles, an awareness of and curiosity about recent developments in linguistics".[5] I even consider this putting it rather mildly, for in my opinion Semitics are generally speaking on the right road.[6] Hence the appearance, in the year 1966, in the field of Akkadian, of a description of this language from the pen of Erica Reiner,[7] an essentially distributional work, but also already based on a few elements of transformational generative grammar in its earliest phase of development. Later she wrote various interesting studies in the grammatological field,[8] in which also the present position of this science, and in particular as regards its relations to linguistics, have been wholly taken into account. In 1969 I. J. Gelb, founder of grammatology as a discipline in its own right, published a most important work about Proto-Akkadian,[9] which is, like Erica Reiner's, a distributional synchronic study based on a distributional 'item and arrangement' analysis, involving the use of a computer.

In the field of Classical Hebrew, the following are recent publications well-founded from the point of view of general linguistics. First and foremost should be mentioned the works of J. Barr,[10] who is a powerful advocate of the integration of general linguistics into Semitics. Further the publications by J. F. A. Sawyer,[11] who takes the same line as Barr but is sometimes found to be ably defending his own views against those of Barr. He moves in the field of semantics, thereby aptly applying the notion of 'semantic field' (launched by J. Trier in 1931) to Hebrew. In his latest publication a great deal of his attention has been given to the ideas of Hoenigswald and Labov. In the field of semantics mention, too, may be made of studies such as those by H. J. van Dijk[12] and G. Schmuttermayr.[13] In the phonological field there are studies by K. Aartun,[14] J. W. Wevers,[15] T. Muraoka,[16] and J. O. Lehman.[17] These, with various others of the same nature, may be quoted as works in which the developments in general linguistics have been duly taken into account by their respective authors. In the morphological field I should like to mention the studies by M. Azar,[18] J. Blau,[19] and M. M. Bravmann[20] as good examples of what I mean here; and in the syntactical field the same applies to the works by S. H. Siedl,[21] H. Bobzin,[22] E. Jenni,[23] and F. J. Andersen.[24]

As regards Classical and Literary Arabic some material may be found in the survey written by D. Cohen.[25] However, besides the little manual of M. C. Bateson briefly discussed by D. Cohen in his survey, the works by A. F. L. Beeston,[26] J. Stetkevych, [27] and W. Fischer[28] should certainly not be forgotten as good examples of modern descriptions of language.

In the fields of Phoenician, Ugaritic, Aramaic/Syrian, and Ethiopean the trend to profit to a greater extent from the developments in general linguistics has not been so spectacular, although it has to be granted that during the period under discussion many useful detailed studies have seen the light.

The situation is different as regards General Semitics and Comparative-Historical (Chamito-)Semitic Philology. First of all mention should be made of an article by J. Barr,[29] in which principle is an essential element. In the article the writer represents the methods and views of linguistics as indispensable to students of Semitics. The collective work of Th. A. Sebeok[30] in general clearly shows the lasting influence of such views. An article written by the Italian Semitic scholar P. Fronzaroli,[31] which was very recently published, treats the typological classification on a quantitative basis and is also concerned with the problems of lexicostatistics and glottochronology. R. Hetzron has given a good introduction to the problem of the formation of rules and diachronics, as regards the Semitic languages.[32] From the pen of G. Garbini appeared two successive articles forming an excellent survey of Semitics for the period 1969-1971,[33] and also a book which is a collection of articles already published before, together with various recent observations. These have been arranged to chapters in such a way that virtually all the Semitic languages are discussed in the work.[34] Further, there are the first two issues of the periodical *Orientalia*[35] to be considered. These issues form a true 'Fundgrube' of articles, and their respective authors have succeeded in illustrating the present-day integration of general linguistics into Semitics. In fact this should not cause any surprise, for these issues of *Orientalia* are meant as a commemorative volume to be presented to I. J. Gelb, of whom G. Buccellati, in a fine survey introducing this collection,[36] says that he "... too has broken ground in a most innovative and authoritative way, by keeping abreast of general linguistic theory and utilizing it for a more insightful and accurate presentation of the data".[37] But also outside the collection mentioned attention should be directed to various publications bearing witness of fresh ideas blown over from general linguistics into Semitics.

In this connection the following studies are worthy of mention in the phonological and morphological fields: by J. Blau about the phenomenon of pseudo-corrections;[38] by M. M. Bravmann about the Semitic causative praeformativum;[39] by R. Hetzron (two articles) about proto-Semitic forms;[40] by J. M. Diakonoff about 'root structure';[41] by G. Janssens about the Present-Preterite;[42] by J. Kuryłowicz about Semitic grammar and prosody.[43] In this last-mentioned work, a book, the writer has elaborated his theories laid down in an earlier work called *L'Apophonie en Sémitique* (The Hague, 1962), notably as regards the verbal aspect and the prosody. Among some of his writings there is A. Zaborski's observation: "Kuryłowicz' great works on comparative-historical problems of Semitic languages are simply not understood by most Semitists since the gap is too wide",[44] but in my opinion it is caused by the fact that Kuryłowicz arrived at Semitics from the study of Indo-Germanic, and during this study he had already occupied himself with apophonics which has resulted in his laryngeal theory. However, it seems to me that by now his theory on general linguistics has been understood by most Semitists, even if there are still some among them who are opposed to his conception of apophonics in Semitic, as recently demonstrated by A. Hamori.[45]

In the semantic and lexicographical fields mention may be made of a first issue of a Semitic dictionary of roots by D. Cohen and J. Cantineau.[46] This enterprise shows its weak sides undoubtedly, and these were mercilessly exposed by W. von Soden in an article appearing in the issue under discussion – the festive collection for I. J. Gelb – of the periodical *Orientalia*.[47] Von Soden is of the opinion that in this field Semitic scholars might profit, as regards the methods applied, by the effort of scholars of Indo-Germanic, as for example the work of J. Pokorny.[48] At the same time he would prefer the application of a greater differentiation between the 'Hauptwortklassen'. Also there is, in the same issues of *Orientalia*, an excellently founded article from the pen of S. Segert and J. R. Hall, Jr., about the use of the computer in Semitic comparative lexicography.[49] Already before, Segert had published an article on the subject.[50]

In the field of syntax mention should be made here of an article by J. Kuryłowicz – likewise in the collection destined for I. J. Gelb – in which the author, with reference to the Semitic verbal aspect, discusses the contrast between the structural components of a system.[51]

In the field of Chamito-Semitics I want to restrict myself here to mentioning two publications only. For the first of these, from the pen of D. Cohen,[52] contains a very good survey, written primarily with reference to the publication, in 1965, of I. M. Diakonoff.[53] It is praised by Cohen as a "travail intéressant où se deploie une compétence multiple dans les langues envisagées, dans la théorie linguistique en général et dans la technique comparative".[54] The second publication is by K. Petráček and is concerned with the limits of Chamito-Semitics in phonological respect.[55] As is the case with virtually all the works from the Czech school of Semitists – their periodical *Archiv Orientálni* is also meant for other scholars, non-Semitic Orientalists – its writer shows to have kept abreast of the present-day developments in general linguistics.

In conclusion I think I may state that especially during the previous decade rapid and good progress could be observed to have been made in Semitic studies in relation to the assimilation of general linguistic ideas. As late as 1956 H. Birkeland wrote:

"In conclusion it must be repeated that Semitic linguistics are in need of a supply of ideas from general linguistics, above all in its structural form. That means that it is in need of scholars trained in pure linguistic science as distinct from philology."[56] He, too, blamed this neglect of general linguistics on the special nature of the sources of the Semitic languages, and because of the leading role of Hebrew it was especially the occupation of theologians who had not received a training in general linguistics. For the rest it is natural that to him – in 1956! – general linguistics and structural linguistics were the same thing. In 1966 I myself wrote:

"Semitics took little part in all this (i.e. the developments within general linguistics), but it is now all the more able to reflect upon the choice to be made of all the novelties advanced, to combine and if necessary to reject."[57] Semitics have come up to these expectations and scholars are now also occupied in applying, in a way that is on the whole thoughtful, the various more recent theories based on transformational generative grammar to their linguistic researches. This development might in itself be called a gratifying one because both Z. S. Harris and his alumnus, N. Chomsky, began their work as Semitists. The fact that general linguistics have come to engage the attention of Semitic scholars at such a late date, whereas Indo-Germanic scholars took up the subject much earlier, may actually result in the advantage of a measured judgment as regards the stormy developments in a field of which scholars had been ignorant for such a long time.

But now matters have been set in motion and it should be borne in mind that the authors mentioned by me in this article, besides others, have all their alumni to whom these more modern views may be passed on.

In one field Semitics are rather lagging behind even now, namely that of applied linguistics. A. Zaborski, already quoted by me, writes: "The Semitists' neglect of the developments and achievements in general linguistics is especially apparent in the outdated and very unproductive methodology of language teaching and of teaching in general as it does not prepare the new adepts for the application of new methods. This is still the case to a considerable extent even with literary Arabic."[58] But this matter, too, has been recently set in motion, if unfortunately mostly through theologians who, from a justified desire to arrive at improved didactic methods for Classical Hebrew, are advocates of the very principles of applied linguistics which, for the greater part, have meanwhile been abandoned again.[59] Therefore it is especially here that the ties with general linguistics and applied linguistics derived from them will have to be drawn a little closer.

University of Groningen

NOTES

1 G. Cragg, "Linguistics, Method, and Extinct Languages: The Case of Sumerian", *Orientalia*, 42, 1973, 75-96, 78.
2 G. Cragg, *op. cit.*, p. 78.
3 J. H. Hospers, "A Hundred Years of Semitic Comparatic Linguistics", *Studia Biblica et Semitica Th. C. Vriezen Dedicata*, Wageningen, 1966, 137-51, 150.
4 J. H. Hospers, *op. cit.*, 149. Already at the time a few more names could have been added to this list, e.g. those of J. Barr, G. M. Schramm, and J. H. Greenberg.
5 G. Cragg, *op. cit.*, 78.

[6] In my opinion the fact that in relation to general linguistics Semitic studies were lagging behind is essentially due to the fact that these studies – and especially Hebrew – are almost exclusively the occupation of theologians who, notwithstanding their mostly excellent knowledge of one or more Semitic languages, were not real linguists, and who had not received any training in the principles of general linguistics. A scholar such as J. Kuryłowicz, who had approached Semitics from his Indo-Germanic studies, did receive such training, as is clearly borne out by his publications.

[7] Erica Reiner, *A Linguistic Analysis of Akkadian*, The Hague, 1966.

[8] Erica Reiner, "New Cases of Morphophonemic Spellings", *Orientalia*, 42, 1973, 35-38; and "How we Read Cuneiform Texts", *Journal of Cuneiform Studies*, 25, 1973, 3-58.

[9] I. J. Gelb, *Sequential Reconstruction of Proto-Akkadian*, Chicago, 1969.

[10] J. Barr, "St. Jerome and the Sounds of Hebrew", *Journal of Semitic Studies*, 12, 1967, 1-36; *Comparative Philology and the Text of the Old Testament*, Oxford, 1968.

[11] J. F. A. Sawyer, "Root-meanings in Hebrew", *Journal of Semitic Studies*, 12, 1967, 37-50; *Semantics in Biblical Research: New Methods of Defining Hebrew Words for Salvation*, London, 1972; "Hebrew Words for the Resurrection of the Dead", *Vetus Testamentum*, 23, 1973, 218-234; "The Place of Folk-linguistics in Biblical Interpretation", *The Fifth World Congress of Jewish Studies*, IV, Jerusalem, 1973, 109-113.

[12] H. J. van Dijk, "A Neglected Connotation of Three Hebrew Verbs (nātan, šîm, šît)", *Vetus Testamentum*, 18, 1968, 16-30.

[13] G. Schmuttermayr, "Ambivalenz und Aspektdifferenz: Bemerkungen zu den hebräischen Präpositionen כ, ל und מן", *Biblische Zeitschrift*, 15, 1971, 29-51.

[14] K. Aartun, "Althebräische Nomina mit konserviertem kurzem Vokal in der Hauptdrucksilbe", *Zeitschrift der Deutschen Morgenländischen Gesellschaft*, 117, 1967, 247-265.

[15] J. W. Wevers, "Ḥeth in Classical Hebrew", *Essays on the Ancient Semitic World*, ed. by J. W. Wevers and B. C. Redford, 101-112, Toronto, 1970.

[16] T. Muraoka, *Emphasis in Biblical Hebrew*, Oxford, 1969.

[17] J. O. Lehman, "A Forgotten Principle of Biblical Textual Tradition Rediscovered", *Journal of Near Eastern Studies*, 24, 1967, 93-101. To this a complementary article by W. Watson, "Shared Consonants in Northwest Semitic", *Biblica*, 50, 1969, 525-533; "More on shared Consonants", *Biblica*, 52, 1971, 44-50. However, these complementary writings by Watson, as regards the explanation offered from a generally linguistic point of view, are much less up-to-date than Lehman's explanation (speechsound as continuum).

[18] M. Azar, *Analyse morphologique du texte hébreu de la Bible*, 2 vols., Nancy, 1970.

[19] J. Blau, "Studies in Hebrew Verb Formation", *Hebrew Union College Annual*, 42, 1971, 133-158.

[20] M. M. Bravmann, "The Hebrew Perfect Forms: qat^{e}lā, qat^{e}lū", *Journal of the American Oriental Society*, 91, 1971, 429-430.

[21] S. H. Siedl, *Gedanken zum Tempussystem im Hebräischen und Akkadischen*, Wiesbaden, 1971.

[22] H. Bobzin, "Uberlegungen zum althebräischen "Tempus" system", *Die Welt des Orients*, 7, 1973, 141-153.

[23] E. Jenni, *Das Hebräische Piʿel: Syntaktisch semasiologische Untersuchung einer Verbalform im Alten Testament*, Zurich, 1968.

[24] F. J. Andersen, *The Hebrew Verbless Clause in the Pentateuch*, Nashville-New York, 1970

[25] D. Cohen, "Les études linguistiques arabes: A propos de quelques ouvrages récents", *Revue des Etude Islamiques*, 39, 1971, 177-183.

[26] A. F. L. Beeston, *The Arabic Language Today*, London, 1970.

[27] J. Stetkevych, *The Modern Arabic Literary Language: Lexical and Stylistic Developments*, Chicago and London, 1970.
[28] W. Fisher, *Grammatik des klassischen Arabisch*, Wiesbaden, 1972.
[29] J. Barr, "The Ancient Languages – the Conflict between Philology and Linguistics", *Transactions of the Philological Society*, 1968, 37-55.
[30] Th. A. Sebeok (ed.), *Current Trends in Linguistics*, 6: *Linguistics in South West Asia and North Africa*, The Hague-Paris, 1970 (especially Part Three: "Afroasiatic Languages", 237-661).
[31] P. Fronzaroli, "Statistical Methods in the Study of Ancient Near Eastern Languages", *Orientalia*, 42, 1973, 97-113.
[32] R. Hetzron, "The Shape of a Rule and Diachrony", *Bulletin of the School of Oriental and African Studies*, 35, 1972, 451-75.
[33] G. Garbini, "Linguistica Semitica 1969-1971", *Annali dell'Instituto Orientale di Napoli*, 33, 1973, 81-92 and 263-76.
[34] G. Garbini, "Le lingue semitiche", *Studi di storia linguistica*, Napoli, 1972.
[35] *Orientalia*, 42, 1-2; "Approaches to the Study of the Ancient Near East: A Volume of Studies Offered to Ignace Jay Gelb on the Occasion of his Sixtieth Birthday, October 14, 1972", Roma, 1973.
[36] G. Buccellati, "Methodological Concerns and the Progress of Ancient Near Eastern Studies", *Orientalia*, 42, 1973, 9-20.
[37] G. Buccellati, *op. cit.*, 10.
[38] J. Blau, *On Pseudo-Corrections in Some Semitic Languages*, Jerusalem, 1970.
[39] M. M. Bravmann, "The Semitic Causative Prefix Š/S A", *Le Muséon*, 82, 1969, 517-22.
[40] R. Hetzron, "Third Person Singular Pronoun Suffixes in Proto-Semitic", *Orientalia Suecana*, 18, 1969, 101-127, and "The Evidence for Perfect *yáqtul and Jussive *yaqtúl in Proto-Semitic", *Journal of Semitic Studies*, 14, 1969, 1-21.
[41] J. M. Diakonoff, "Problems of Root Structure in Proto-Semitic", *Archiv Orientální*, 38, 1970, 453-80.
[42] G. Janssens, "The Present-Imperfect in Semitic", *Bibliotheca Orientalis*, 29, 1972, 3-7.
[43] J. Kuryłowicz, *Studies in Semitic Grammar and Metrics*, Wrocław-London, 1972-1973.
[44] A. Zaborski, "Teaching the Language of the Bible", *Folia Orientalia*, 14, 1973, 65, fn. 1.
[45] A. Hamori, "A Note on yaqtulu in East and West Semitic", *Archiv Orientální* 41, 1973, 319-24.
[46] D. Cohen, *Dictionnaire de racines sémitiques ou attestées dans les langues sémitiques*, I: '/H-'TN, The Hague-Paris, 1970.
[47] W. von Soden, "Ein semitisches Wurzelwörterbuch: Probleme und Möglichkeiten", *Orientalia*, 42, 1973, 142-48.
[48] J. Pokorny, *Indogermanisches etymologisches Wörterbuch*, Bern-München, 1959-1969.
[49] S. Segert and J. R. Hall, Jr., "A Computer Program for Analysis of Words According to their Meaning: Conceptual Analysis of Latin Equivalents for the Comparative Dictionary of Semitic Languages", *Orientalia*, 42, 1973, 149-57.
[50] S. Segert, "Die Arbeit am Vergleichenden Wörterbuch der Semitischen Sprachen mit Hilfe des Computer IBM 1410", *Zeitschrift der Deutschen Morgenländischen Gesellschaft*, Supplemental, 2, Wiesbaden, 1969, 714-17.
[51] J. Kuryłowicz, "Verbal Aspect in Semitic", *Orientalia*, 42, 1973, 114-20.
[52] D. Cohen, "Problèmes de linguistique chamito-sémitique", *Revue des Études Islamiques*, 40, 1972, 43-68.
[53] J. M. Diakonoff, *Semito-Hamitic Languages*, Moscou, 1965.

54 D. Cohen, *op. cit.*, 44.
55 K. Petráček, "Die Grenzen des Semitohamitischen": Zentralsaharanische und semitohamitische Sprachen in phonologischer Hinsicht", *Archiv Orientální*, 40, 1972, 6-50.
56 H. Birkeland, "Some Reflexions on Semitic and Structural Linguistics", *For Roman Jakobson*, ed. by M. Halle, H. G. Lunt, H. McLean, and C. H. van Schooneveld, The Hague, 1956, 44-51, 51.
57 J. H. Hospers, *op. cit.*, 150.
58 Z. Zaborski, *op. cit.*, 66.
59 Cf. J. H. Hospers, "Some Observations about the Teaching of Old Testament Hebrew", *Symbolae Biblicae at Mesopotamicae, F. M. Th. de Liagre Böhl Dedicatae*, ed. by M. A. Beek, A. A. Kampman, C. Nijland, J. Rijckmans, 188-198, Leiden, 1972, and "The Teaching of the Old Testament Hebrew and Applied Linguistics", *Travels in the World of the Old Testament: Studies presented to Professor M. A. Beek*, ed. by M. S. H. G. Heerma van Voss, Ph. H. J. Houwink ten Cate, N. A. van Uchelen, Assen/Amsterdam, 1974, 94-101.

WHAT BECAME OF LAD?

W. J. M. LEVELT

Since about 1960 the interest of linguists and psycholinguists in the study of child language has been rapidly expanding. The new impetus derived especially from Chomsky's formal approach to the genesis of language, the so-called Language Acquisition Device, or LAD. This article is intended to be a short historical and critical note on what happened to LAD. It will be historical in that a description will be given of the early conception and impact of the model, as well as of its falling back into obsolescence; it will be critical in the sense that some major causes will be analyzed which can explain this latter fate. These causes are partly to be found in the structure of communication between formal and empirical disciplines, but mostly in the untenability of the empirical assumptions on which the theory was based. In a final paragraph a summary review will be presented of the main theoretical changes that were made to replace these empirical assumptions, and with them the whole LAD-model.

1. THE CONCEPTION OF LAD

The first steps towards a formal characterization of human language acquisition went somewhat as follows. Within the framework of his discussions about the goals of a linguistic theory, Chomsky (1955, 1957) presented the idea of formalizing linguistic discovery procedures as mechanisms which take a corpus as input, yielding a grammar as output. The first actual proposals with respect to the construction of such machines seem to have been made in a conference paper by Miller & Chomsky (1957). That paper was never published, and meanwhile Miller lost all his copies (see Miller, 1967). But the problem posed in that paper was roughly as follows: Given a language (natural or artificial) for which a (finite) grammar exists, could one conceive of a procedure for inferring the grammar from a finite set of (linguistic) observations? It was clear from the outset that, without further qualifications, this question could not be answered. Both in the paper, and also subsequently many qualifications were indeed made, as we shall discuss in a moment. It seems also to have been immediately obvious that an answer to the question could be highly relevant for the understanding of the child's acquisition of language. At a conference in 1960, Chomsky (1962) stated that relation as follows:

> ..., we might attempt to construct a device of the kind
>
> (1) utterances of L → ☐ → formalized grammar of L
>
> This represents a function that maps a set of observed utterances into the formalized grammar of the language of which they are a sample. Given as input a sufficiently large and representative set of utterances of any language (English, Chinese, or whatever), the device (1) would provide as output a formalized grammar of this language. A description of this device would therefore represent a hypothesis about the innate intellectual equipment that a child brings to bear in language learning.

If such a 'Language Learning Device', later rebaptized as 'Language Acquisition Device', could be conceived of, it could function as an ideal model for human language acquisition. As for any ideal model, the subsequent step should be to compare the model with the actual situation, i.e. the child's language acquisition, and to see how the model has to be adapted in order to work in real time and to display the typical characteristics of the child's growing linguistic competence. Chomsky (1965) denotes these two aspects of the problem by 'adequacy-in-principle' and 'feasibility' of LAD, respectively.

For an adequate understanding of the further developments since the conception of LAD, one should be reminded of the fact that Chomsky's formal approach to language was the main impetus to the rise of two rather independent disciplines. The first was transformational grammar, the second was the theory of formal grammars, a branch of mathematics and computer science. Both disciplines took up the notion of a language learning device and developed it according to their own needs. In linguistics and psycholinguistics the main interest was in the explanation of human language acquisition, and the term LAD became generally used for formal theories in this area. (In reaction to structuralism Chomsky (1957) ruled out as 'unreasonable' and 'very questionable' the formalization of linguistic discovery procedures, and consequently very little, if any, attention was given to the development of LAD for that purpose.) In computer science, on the other hand, one preferred to speak about theories of 'grammatical inference'. They were designed to show the existence of effective procedures for inferring grammars from finite presentations of various formal languages (or their complements). Communication between the two developments, however, was minimal to the detriment of both as we will argue.

2. DEVELOPMENTS IN GRAMMATICAL INFERENCE

The challenge in the Miller & Chomsky (1957) paper was first taken up by Solomonoff (1959, 1964), whose work was subsequently greatly expanded by Gold (1967) and by Feldman (1967) and his coworkers at Stanford University. It is unnecessary to give anything but a very incomplete survey of the inference work in the present context. A good review is available in the literature (Bierman & Feldman, 1972), and we only need an indication of results that are directly relevant for LAD. For this we best start from Gold's formulation of grammatical inference.

Gold (1967) studied the question of adequacy-in-principle, or 'learnability' as he calls is, for various classes of formal languages. More specifically, he proved the existence or nonexistence of procedures for inferring ('learning') an adequate grammar for L from finite sets of observations from the language or its complement. 'Learnability' appeared to depend on what was called (a) the *hypothesis space*, and (b) the *observation space*. The hypothesis space is the a priori knowledge, available to the inference procedure. In Gold's paper it is defined as the class of languages to which L belongs. Gold studied the 'learnability' of L in case it is known beforehand that L is either finite, regular, context-free, etc., up to merely recursively enumerable. The observation space is defined by the observations available to the inference procedure. Gold assumes that observations are made one by one. They are either of the type 'string x is in L', or of the type 'string x is not in L'. The former is called a *positive instance*, the latter a *negative instance*. A string of instances is called an *information sequence*. If all of the instances in the sequence are positive, one has a *positive information sequence*; if negatives also occur, one has a *mixed information sequence*. A *complete information sequence* is a mixed information sequence in which all positive and negative instances are enumerated; such sequences are generally infinite in length. They are also called *informant presentations*, since it is as if each possible string of words is presented to an informant who provides the information 'grammatical' or 'ungrammatical'. A complete positive information sequence is an enumeration of all positive instances. It is also called a *text presentation*, since it is as if one is reading a text containing all and only the grammatical strings of L.

A language L is called 'learnable' by text, respectively informant presentation, if an algorithm exists which for every complete information sequence performs as follows: (i) each time a new instance is presented, a grammar is produced of the predetermined class (context-free, etc) which is consistent with the information received up to that point; (ii) after a finite number of instances, the output remains constant: the grammar produced is the same or equivalent after each instance, and is a grammar of L. A class of languages is called 'learnable' if every language in it is learnable.

Gold could prove that under these definitions only finite languages are learnable by text presentation. Chomsky's question of adequacy-in-principle had to be answered in the negative for all classes of infinite languages considered. For informant presentation, however, 'learnability' proved to exist for a wide range of language classes (up to primitive-recursive).

Though one has to be quite careful in generalizing these results to natural languages, it seems safe to conclude that under reasonable assumptions natural languages are 'learnable' by informant presentation, but not by text presentation (see Levelt 1974 for a detailed discussion).

Further work in grammatical inference has added to Gold's findings in several respects. Stochastic models for learning by text presentation were developed (Horning, 1969) in order to find ways for inferring a least complex grammar for L (not just any grammar). One started experimenting with weaker definitions of learnability, such as the requirement that each non-adequate grammar in the hypothesis space should be rejected within finite time (Horning 1969, Feldman, 1970). And for cases where 'learnability' could be proven, one began studying the efficiency of different inference procedures (akin to Chomsky's real-time issue), often noticing that even very clever heuristics could not prevent astronomical learning times for languages of context-free and higher classes. It is also true for these later developments that generalizations to natural language is somewhat premature. It seems rather safe, however, to say that for text presentation there is either no 'learnability', or inference makes very unrealistic demands on computing time and tape space. Informant presentation certainly gives better prospects (see Levelt, 1974).

From the point of view of LAD three things are notoriously absent in the literature on grammatical inference:

(1) Very little attention has been given to other varieties of presenting the language than text or informant presentation. Both are so little restrained forms of input that they are quite unnatural with respect to the linguistic environment of the child, as we will discuss shortly. What is much needed, in our view, is the study of what we will call *intelligent text presentation.*

(2) The whole inference literature is purely syntactic. There is no formal work on inference where there is a *semantic* component to the grammar. One could imagine several varieties of such work. One might allow for input of the sort 'strings x and y are paraphrases', or 'if x is true, then y is also true', etc. One could choose among different semantic formulations, such as model theoretic approaches (cf. Suppes, 1971), propositional languages (cf. Cresswell, 1973), etc.

(3) The inference literature is exclusively linguistic. I know of no work where the inference of a language is studied in the wider context of inferring a representation of a world-to-be-talked-about, i.e. a model of *cognitive inference.* Appealing 'language plus world'-models have been developed in the artificial intelligence literature (cf. Winograd 1972, Schank 1972), but no inference work seems to be available as yet.

We shall now turn to the fate of LAD in the (psycho-) linguistic literature, and show that the empirical assumptions on which a formal approach to language acquisition was initially based could not be maintained. No formal models, however, were available for the description of new empirical challenges, since these implied precisely the existence of intelligent presentation of language, as well as roles for semantic and general cognitive factors in language acquisition.

3. DEVELOPMENTS IN LAD

The initial impact of Chomsky & Miller's LAD-model on the (psycho-) linguistic approach to language acquisition was enormous. Numerous researchers in the early sixties turned toward studying very early language development (Braine 1963, Brown & Fraser 1963, Ervin-Tripp 1964, McNeill 1966, and many others). For the first time in history grammars were written for the two- and three-word sentence stage in language development. A rather influential formalization was Braine's 'pivot-grammar'. Methods for the systematic sampling and analysis of early child language were developed and yielded a wealth of new insights. Cross-linguistic studies were being initiated (Slobin 1966), and experiments on the effects of imitation, expansion and training on language learning were started (Brown & Bellugi 1964, Cazden 1965).

The theoretical framework in most of these studies was implicitly or explicitly the LAD-schema: the empirical work was often designed to substantiate the empirical assumptions underlying Chomsky's version of LAD.

It seems to me that the lion's share of these empirical assumptions fall into three categories: (1) the relative unimportance of input, (2) the marginal role of semantics, and (3) the cognitive independence of language. I will discuss these in turn.

3.1 *The Relative Unimportance of Input*

Most researchers were inclined to assume that the linguistic environment of the child is very little restricted. A typical and not at all far-fetched statement along these lines can be found in Fodor (1966):

> (...) the child gets a *corpus*. That is, he gets a sample of the kind of utterances fluent speakers of his language typically produce. It is conceivable that this sample is biased in certain respects in comparison to a purely random sample.

It is then added that the language addressed to children could be simplified and that research on this matter is going on.

> Until the results of this research are known, however, it would be methodologically sound to assume that the child's increasing linguistic proficiency is not to be attributed to any significant extent to the special character of the utterances he hears.

In fact, the corpus is assumed to extend far into the ungrammatical domain:

> If it is anything like a randomly selected corpus of adult utterances, it must contain a very substantial number of false starts, slips, grammatical mistakes, and so forth.

Since "much of what children hear is overheard and (...) all normal children learn to speak", language should be learnable under a very wide variety of input conditions. No wonder that, as Eve Clark (1973a) remarks,

From this, it has been concluded that the child could not possibly learn the syntax of his language unless he was endowed with some innate, language-specific, mechanism for just that purpose.

These nativist assumptions led to intensive search for early language universals. Since the pet idea of transformational linguists at the time was that the base grammar of different languages would be very similar or universal, whereas the transformational component would be more language-specific, it is not surprising to read:

Accordingly we should expect to find that the earliest grammatical production of children will contain the abstract features of the deep structure but few of the locally appropriate transformations. Young children should 'talk' deep structures directly. And that is precisely what an examination of children's early speech shows (Miller & McNeill, 1968).

Such dogmatic and empirically untenable positions had to be taken to protect the idea of spontaneous emergence of language. This tabu did not hold for transformational development. Transformations had to be acquired specifically through scrutinizing the linguistic input. The initial studies in early transformational development (cf. Bellugi 1967, Menyuk 1963, 1964, C. Chomsky 1969) were therefore much less prejudiced and still have not lost their significance.

Within the LAD-model, the nativist position could be very easily formalized. Learnability can either be increased by narrowing LAD's hypothesis space, or by making the inference procedures very powerful or 'clever'. Chomsky & Miller (1963:276-277) do not hesitate to make the nativist choice:

The proper division of labor between heuristic methods and specification of form remains to be decided, of course, but too much faith should not be put in the powers of induction, even when aided by intelligent heuristics, to discover the right grammar. After all, stupid people learn to talk, but even the brightest apes do not.

And in Chomsky (1965) we read:

This requires a precise and narrow delimitation of the notion 'generative grammar' – a restrictive and rich hypothesis concerning the universal properties that determine the form of the language.

In terms of LAD the rationalist position means: relative unimportance of the observation space plus very restrictive hypothesis space, whereas the empiricist position would be formalized as: a very wide or unspecific hypothesis space plus an important role for the observations which are analyzed by powerful inductive heuristics. Chomsky (1965) tries to give his choice the appearance of a logical necessity. Discussing the earlier mentioned questions of 'adequacy-in-principle' and 'feasibility' of LAD as a model for human language acquisition, he remarks:

In fact, the second question has rarely been raised in any serious way in connection with empiricist views (...) since study of the first question has been sufficient to rule out whatever explicit proposals of an essentially empiricist character have emerged in modern discussions of language acquisition.

Here, Chomsky is using the shield of non-existing results in computer science. As we have noticed above, the first definite results in learnability were obtained two years later by Gold (1967). These results moreover, if generalizable to natural language would indicate that no adequate procedure exists for inferring a natural language by text presentation, irrespective of computational power, i.e. both a rationalist and an empiricist version of LAD would be inadequate-in-principle for text presentation (see Levelt 1974). Braine (1971) makes it rather likely that, from the point of view of syntax the child is very much in a situation of text presentation since speech to children is highly grammatical (we will return to this), syntactic corrections are seldom made, and marked negative instances are hardly ever presented. (Braine uses these observations as an argument against the rationalist version of LAD, but it applies to the empiricist version as well. See Levelt 1974 for a more detailed discussion.)

The applicability of results in computer science to natural language is still very much an open issue, as we have seen. But it should be clear that already as early as 1965, Chomsky had lost contact with relevant developments in computer science, a situation which remained also characteristic for all (psycho-)linguists working in the field of language acquisition. (A notable instance is Peters' (1972) article on inferring grammars. The paper, though quite interesting in itself, lacks any reference to the post-chomskian literature on grammatical inference. The inference problem is introduced from scratch, so to say.)

In a later section it will be discussed how the empirical assumption of a rather unrestricted linguistic environment for early language development became challenged, but we first turn to the second empirical assumption on which the early LAD-studies were based.

3.2 *The Marginal Role of Semantics*

LAD had been conceived as a device for learning a grammar. In 1957 Chomsky's study of grammar was independent of semantic considerations, and he tried to realize the same for the study of language acquisition. The role of semantic input in the learning of language was minimized:

> For example, it might be maintained, not without plausibility, that semantic information of some sort is essential even if the formalized grammar that is the output of the device does not contain statements of direct semantic nature. Here, care is necessary. It may well be that a child given only the input of (1) [LAD] as nonsense elements would not come to learn the principles of sentence formation. This is not necessarily a relevant observation, however, even if true. It may only indicate that meaningfulness and semantic function provide the motivation for language learning, while playing no necessary part in its mechanism, which is what concerns us here (Chomsky, 1962).

And in *Aspects* (1965) Chomsky repeats essentially the same arguments.

Consequently, most work in early grammars was purely syntactic in nature, and one tried to argue for the correctness of this approach in several ways. We find methodological arguments, such as Fodor's (1966):

> The difficulty with relying upon 'semantic' considerations in explaining language learning is not, then, that such considerations are known to be irrelevant but simply that we do not know how to describe them in any revealing way.

And we find empirical arguments. As Eve Clark (1973a) notes, an experiment on the learning of an artificial language by Miller & Norman (1964) seemed to have reinforced Chomsky in his claim, since "subjects learning the language with semantic reference appeared to learn in exactly the same way as subjects not given any semantic information". In her paper, Eve Clark then shows by reference to the work of Moeser & Bregman (1972) how much these early results were determined by the experimental procedure used, and how important the role of semantic input turned out to be in Moeser & Bregman's study.

3.3 *The Cognitive Independence of Language*

The LAD-model was not only purely syntactic: it also implied the tacit assumption that language development could be satisfactorily explained *in vitro*. LAD would only need linguistic input, and the procedures would be sufficient to derive a grammar. Neither non-linguistic (i.e. visual, kinesthetic, etc) input, nor non-linguistic foreknowledge would be essential in a model of language acquisition. Notably missing in the early LAD-studies are discussions of the knolwedge structure that the child has acquired before the first grammatical structures arise. This language-*in-vitro* approach was closely related to dominant opinions on the status of linguistic competence in the adult. Competence was considered to be an autonomous faculty of mind, which might interact with other psychological factors in the causation of linguistic performance, but which could never be confused with these factors (see Levelt 1972 for an analysis of the psychological status of competence).

Syntactic development is a respectable field of study, but negating the importance of cognitive factors for its explanation is less respectable:

> It is tragic to cutt off from the domain of research the large field of cognitive relations which are found in early sentences (...) by assuming *a priori* that there are no interesting problems in their acquisition. Dogmatism without evidence is to say the least presumptuous (Ervin-Tripp, 1971).

So it appears that the early work on LAD showed the same limitations as those we observed for grammatical inference theory: little attention to varieties of language presentation, ignorance of semantics, and ignorance of non-linguistic variables.

During the second half of the sixties linguistic attention turned to these much neglected areas, leading to the obsolescence of LAD, and to the rediscovery of older European and American traditions in the study of language acquisition. In a last paragraph we will touch on each of these three areas in a very summary fashion.

4. LATER DEVELOPMENTS

All three characteristic empirical assumptions on which LAD was based were challenged by later developments as we shall now discuss.

4.1 *The Linguistic Environment*

The assumption that the child has to acquire his language in a virtually unlimited linguistic environment, mainly consisting of overheard material full of lapses, false starts and errors became rejected on good empirical grounds. Brown & Bellugi (1964) had already noticed that the speech of adults to children is mostly very simple and grammatical. However, it was only around 1970 that a real boom of studies appeared about how adults speak to children. Eve Clark (1973a) gives a summary, but additional work is appearing fast. We mention studies by Berko Gleason (1973), Bowerman (1973), Broen (1972), Brown & Henlon (1970),

Clark (in press), Ervin-Tripp (1970, 1971), Farwell (1973), Friedlander et al. (1972), Holtzman (1972), Moerk (1972), Phillips (1973), Remick (1972), Sachs et al. (1972), Shatz & Gelman (1974), Shipley et al. (1969), Snow (1972a, b), and Van der Geest et al. (1973).

From these studies it appears that adults in addressing children use short, simple sentences with little embedding and inflection (Sachs et al., Snow). Sentence boundaries are well marked in speech to young children (Broen). More generally, intonation is high and 'exaggerated', clearly marking for the child what he should attend to. Overheard speech is therefore not to be considered as important imput. (Labov (1970) moreover showed that such adult-to-adult speech is not as ungrammatical as had been generally supposed.) The syntactic complexity of adult's speech grows with the child's syntactic competence. More specifically, it seems that new semantic features are introduced by the child, to which the adult reacts with the more advanced syntactic construction by which they can be expressed (Van der Geest et al.). Much adult effort goes into elicitation of specific reactions. Eve Clark (in press) shows that conversational patterns are trained (*Where's the ball? Here's the ball.*), by means of slow and explicit routines. There is a high incidence of questions in adults' speech to children (Ervin-Tripp), apparently to check whether the child is still following.

From the point of view of the syntactic structure of the child's 'observation space', all this amounts to what I called earlier 'intelligent text presentation': the child is presented with grammatical strings from a miniature language, which is systematically expanded as the child's competence grows. As we have seen, the literature on grammatical inference gives little attention to intelligent information presentation, but it is noteworthy to cite a remark by Horning (1969), which was made before these studies became available. After having discussed the real time problems into which even succesful procedures for grammatical inference are running, he writes:

> does language acquisition by children suggest means for improving our grammatical inference procedures? We believe that it does, and we conjecture that an important distinction between the child's experience and that we have assumed for our procedures is this: The child is not initially presented the full adult language he is ultimately expected to learn. Rather, he is confronted with a very limited subset, both in syntax and vocabulary, which is gradually expanded as his competence grows.

The conclusion, then, is

> We should not expect our inference procedures to perform well when confronted directly with complex languages,

and it is suggested that the procedure should first be exposed to small sublanguages, which are later combined and expanded.

These perceptive remarks have not been followed up in computer science, though work on interactive programming (cf. Klein & Kuppin, 1970) seems to go in the right direction. The result is that at present no formal models of the LAD variety are available to psycholinguists for the analysis of their new empirical findings on adults' speech to children. It should, however, be obvious that from the purely syntactic point of view the urge for strongly nativist assumptions has been diminished by these findings. Nativist assumptions now enter at other places as we shall see.

4.2 *The Role of Semantics*

Chomsky's assumption that semantic information is non-essential for the manner in which syntax is learned, has not only been challenged by work on the learning of artificial languages (such as Moeser & Bregman's), but especially by careful study of language development in children. Examples of such studies are Slobin (1970), Bloom (1970), and Schaerlaekens (1973). In these studies one derived the *intention* or *semantic function* expressed by an utterance from the context in which it was spoken. It is obvious that the child masters such semantic functions long before the two-word stage, i.e. he may already know that something is typically *located* at a certain place, that something *belongs* to somebody, etc. At learning a language, the child tries to cast such semantic relations in grammatical form by choosing a particular word order, inflexion, etc. One could of course still think of the existence of a priori and universal grammatical means to express such intentions. But Schaerlaekens (1973) shows rather convincingly that this cannot be maintained: the child tends to use a particular word order to express a certain semantic function, and more often than not the order chosen is the dominant word order in the native language, or better: the dominant order of concepts, since categorial knowledge is notably missing in early child language. *Airplane by* can stand for an actor/action relation, though *by* is a preposition, not a verb. This latter example is taken from Schlesinger (1971), who gave a first formal exposition of this intentional approach to language learning (see Levelt 1974 for a more detailed discussion).

With respect to universality the obvious new insight is that the *intentions* expressed in early language are universal, there is no need to assume a priori knowledge about syntactic categories or word order. Slobin (1970) compared two-word sentences which he collected from children (aged 1;6-2;0) in six different language communities. He remarks the following about their striking correspondence:

> If you ignore word order, and read through transcriptions of two-word utterances in the various languages we have studied, the utterances read like direct translations of one another (...). There is a great similarity of basic vocabulary and basic meanings conveyed by the word combinations. There is a small class of frequently-occurring operators performing basic functions, and a large number of content words.

As examples of basic functions Slobin mentions ostension, request, negation, question. Typical semantic relations are conjunction, attribution, genetive, locative, subject-action, etc.

It was noted earlier that no inference models for this sort of data are available in computer science. Interesting is to observe that though there is a near absence of syntactic corrections in mothers' speech to children, frequent corrections are made with respect to the truth value of the child's utterances (cf. Brown & Henlon, 1970). This could be conceived of as a semantic form of informant presentation, as Eve Clark (1973a) remarks.

4.3 *Language Development as Part of Cognitive Development*

Closely related to the recognition of semantic factors in the causation of grammar is the rejection of the third assumption underlying the original LAD-approach: the cognitive independence of language. In retrospect it is impossible to indicate which publication was first to challenge this assumption. One can find early suggestions along these lines even in the most orthodox LAD-literature. An example is McNeill's (1970) proposal to distinguish between strong and weak linguistic universals. The first would be the reflection of a specific *linguistic* ability "and may not be a reflection of a cognitive ability at all" (*nota bene* the contrast). The second reflects a universal *cognitive* ability. Cognitive abilities can, therefore, cause specific linguistic structures. This latter point is rather more strongly made in two influential papers by Bever (1970a, b). He argues that certain grammatical rules themselves may be shown to be structural accomodations to behavioral constraints. Thus certain universal structural properties of language may express general cognitive constraints rather than particular innate linguistic structures (1970 b).

These constraints are to be found especially in features of perceptual processing, as Bever demonstrates by means of various examples.

Slobin (1971), after noticing that

the first and most obvious point that comes to mind is that language is used to express the child's cognitions of his environment — physical or social — and so a child cannot begin to use a given linguistic form meaningfully until he is able to understand what it means,

puts the critical question without restrictions:

Is it possible, then, to trace out a universal course of linguistic development on the basis of what we know about the universal course of cognitive development? (Can one take Piaget as a handbook of psycholinguistic development?)

The latter addition puts the new concern in due historical context. Not only Piaget's work, but most of the pre-chomskian tradition in language acquisition research had been based on the assumption that the development of language proceeds from and is part of the general cognitive development of the child. Such was also the position taken by the pioneers like Preyer (1882), Wundt (1885), C. & W. Stern (1907), Bühler (1918), and many others. The special mention of Piaget, however, is not without significance. Firstly, Slobin acknowledges the importance of the Genevian studies on language acquisition by Sinclair-de Zwart (1967, 1969), which form the *trait-d'union* between the Piagetian and Chomskyan traditions in language acquisition (see also Sinclair-de Zwart, 1973). Secondly, Piaget is apparently referred to as an encyclopedia. And indeed, if one wants to know how the child builds a knowledge structure through interaction with his environment, the most sensible step to take is to start from Piaget's epistemological theory, since it is the most elaborate and best founded today.

Cognitive studies of language development are so numerous these days, that even a very summary review is unfeasible in the present context. Several conferences have been devoted to the relation between cognition and language development, and we better refer the reader to the following proceedings: Hayes (1970), Flores d'Arcais & Levelt (1970), Moore (1973), Ferguson & Slobin (1973), Connolly & Bruner (1974).

Essential in the present context, however, is the question what sort of experimental paradigm is required to demonstrate the correctness of the new (and old!) empirical assumption. One should be able to show that a certain knowledge structure and certain information processing strategies are available before a particular linguistic form emerges, and that initially linguistic information is analyzed in terms of that non-linguistic knowledge structure by means of these non-linguistic processing strategies. This is not easy to accomplish. One mostly relies on a weaker paradigm: the demonstration that a particular way of processing linguistic material by the child is accompanied (and preceded) by the same way of processing certain non-linguistic material. This paradigm requires therefore a linguistic plus a non-linguistic experiment. The latter, however, is often omitted. Slobin's (1971) paper, which was especially written to comment upon the link between early non-linguistic processing and language acquisition does not give a single example of an independent non-linguistic experiment. In this way one goes around a vicious circle: in order to proof the cognitive basis for a particular fact of language behavior one 'translates' a particular linguistic processing strategy in general cognitive terms, and the latter is then taken to be the basis of the former. Fortunately, examples of correct application of the paradigm are available. A beautiful case with very positive results is presented by Eve Clark (1973b).

Returning to LAD, and after rejection of all three empirical assumptions on which it was based, one should ask what remains of a nativist approach to language acquisition. We have already noticed the existence of a remarkable universality in the semantic functions that are expressed in early language. The cognitive approach might provide an explanation for such universals, and the explanation is nativist to a certain extent though most empiricists would have no problems with it. We close with a citation from Herbert Clark (1973) in which the idea is clearly expressed:

> the child acquires English expressions of space and time by learning how to apply these expressions to the a priori knowledge he has about space and time. This a priori knowledge is separate from language itself and is not so mysterious. The knowledge, it will be argued, is simply what the child knows about space given that he lives on a planet, has a particular perceptual apparatus, and moves around in a characteristic manner. The exact form of this knowledge, then, is dependent on man's biological endowment – that he has two eyes, ears, etc., that he stands upright, and so on – and in this sense it is innate.

Nijmegen University

REFERENCES

Bellugi, U.
1967 *The Acquisition of Negation.* Ph.D. Thesis, Harvard University.

Berko Gleason, J.
1973 "Code Switching in Children's Language", *Cognitive Development and the Acquisition of Language*, ed. by T. E. Moore. New York, Academic Press.

Bever, T. G.
1970a "The Cognitive Basis for Linguistic Structures", *Cognition and the Development of Language*, ed. by J. R. Hayes. New York, Wiley.
1970b "The Influence of Speech Performance on Linguistic Structures", *Advances in Psycholinguistics*, ed. by G. B. Flores d'Arcais and W. J. M. Levelt. Amsterdam, North-Holland.

Bierman, A. W., & Feldman, J. A.
1972 "A Survey of Results in Grammatical Inference", *Frontiers of Pattern Recognition*, ed. by S. Watanabe. New York, Academic Press.

Bloom, L. M.
1970 *Language Development: Form and Function in Emerging Grammars.* Cambridge, Mass., MIT Press.

Bowerman, M. F.
1973 *Early Syntactic Development: A Cross-linguistic Study with Special Reference to Finnish.* Cambridge, University Press.

Braine, M. D. S.
1963 "The Ontogeny of English Phrase Structure: The First Phase", *Language*, 39, 1-13.
1971 "On Two Models of the Internalization of Grammars", *The Ontogenesis of Grammar*, ed. by D. I. Slobin. New York, Academic Press.

Broen, P.
1972 "The Verbal Environment of the Language-learning Child", *Monographs of the American Speech and Hearing Association*, 17.

Brown, R., & Bellugi, U.
1964 "Three Processes in the Acquisition of Syntax" *Harvard Educational Review* 34, 133-51.

Brown, R., & Fraser, C.
1963 "The Acquisition of Syntax", *Verbal Behavior and Learning: Problems and Processes*, ed. by C. N. Cofer and B. S. Musgrave. New York, McGraw-Hill.

Brown, R., & Henlon, C.
1970 "Derivational Complexity and Order of Acquisition in Child Speech", *Cognition and the Development of Language*, ed. by J. R. Hayes. New York, Wiley.

Bühler, K.
1918 *Die geistige Entwicklung des Kindes.* Jena.

Cazden, C. B.
1965 *Environmental Assistance to the Child's Acquisition of Grammar.* Ph. D. Thesis, Harvard University.

Chomsky, C.
1969 *The Acquisition of Language from Five to Ten.* Cambridge, Mass., MIT Press.

Chomsky, N.
1955 *The Logical Structure of Linguistic Theory.* Microfilm.
1957 *Syntactic Structures.* The Hague, Mouton.

1962 "Explanatory Models in Linguistics", *Logic, Methodology, and Philosophy of Science: Proceedings of the* 1960 *International Congress*, ed. by E. Nagel, P. Suppes, and A. Tarski. Stanford, University Press.
1965 *Aspects of the Theory of Syntax*. Cambridge, Mass., MIT Press.

Clark, E.
1973a "What Should LAD Look Like? Some Comments on Levelt" [reference to Levelt 1973]. Discussion paper for colloquium on "The Role of Grammar in Interdisciplinary Linguistic Research", Bielefeld, December 1973.
1973b "Non-linguistic strategies and the Acquisition of Word Meanings", *Cognition*, 2, 161-82.
in press "First Language Acquisition", *Psycholinguistic Series*, ed. by J. Morton and J. R. Marshall. London, Paul Elek.

Clark, H.
1973 "Space, Time, Semantics, and the Child", *Cognitive Development and the Acquisition of Language*, ed. by T. E. Moore. New York, Academic Press.

Connolly, K. J., & Bruner, J. (eds.)
1974 *The Growth of Competence*. London, Academic Press.

Cresswell, M. J.
1973 *Logics and Languages*. London, Methuen.

Ervin-Tripp, S.
1964 "Imitation and Structural Change in Children's Language", *New Directions in the Study of Language*, ed. by E. Lenneberg. Cambridge, Mass., MIT Press.
1970 "Discourse Agreement: How Children Answer Questions", *Cognition and the Development of Language*, ed. by J. R. Hayes. New York, Wiley.
1971 "An Overview of Theories of Grammatical Development", *The Ontogenesis of Grammar*, ed. by D. I. Slobin. New York, Academic Press.

Farwell, C. B.
1973 *Papers and Reprints in Child Language Development* (= *Stanford University Working Paper Series*), 15, 30-60.

Feldman, J. A.
1967 "First Thoughts on Grammatical Inference", *A. I. Memo* Nr. 55, Computer Science Department, Stanford University.
1970 "Some Decidibility Results on Grammatical Inference and Complexity", *A. I. Memo* Nr. 93. 1, Computer Science Department, Stanford University.

Ferguson, C. A., & Slobin, D. I. (eds.)
1973 *Studies of Child Language Development*. New York, Holt, Rinehart, and Winston.

Flores d'Arcais, G. B., & Levelt, W. J. M. (eds.)
1970 *Advances in Psycholinguistics*. Amsterdam, North-Holland.

Friedlander, B. Z., Jacobs, A. C., Davis, B. B., & Webstone, H. S.
1972 "Time-sampling Analysis of Infants' Natural Language Environments in the Home", *Child Development*, 43, 730-40.

Gold, E. M.
1967 "Language Identification in the Limit", *Information and Control*, 10, 447-74.

Hayes, J. R. (ed.)
1970 *Cognition and the Development of Language*. New York, Wiley.

Holtzman, M.
1972 "The Use of Interrogative Forms in the Verbal Interaction of Three Mothers and Their Children", *J. Psycholinguistic Research*, 1, 311-56.

Horning, J. J.
1969 "A Study of Grammatical Inference", *Technical Report CS* 139, Stanford

Artificial Intelligence Project, Computer Science Department, Stanford University.

Klein, S., & Kuppin, M. A.
1970 "An Interactive Heuristic Program for Learning Transformational Grammars", *Technical Report*, Computer Science Department, University of Wisconsin.

Labov, W.
1970 "The Study of Language in Its Social Context", *Studium Generale*, 23, 30-87.

Levelt, W. J. M.
1972 "Some Psychological Aspects of Linguistic Data", *Linguistische Berichte*, 17, 18-30.
1973 "Grammatical Inference and Theories of Language Acquisition". Discussion paper for colloquium on "The Role of Grammar in Interdisciplinary Linguistic Research", Bielefeld, December 1973. [Available as Report FU 73-1, Department of Psychology, Nijmegen University.]
1974 *Formal Grammars in Linguistics and Psycholinguistics*, I: *An Introduction to the Theory of Formal Languages and Automata*; II: *Applications in Linguistic Theory*; III: *Applications in Psycholinguistics*. The Hague, Mouton.

McNeill, D.
1966 "Developmental Psycholinguistics", *The Genesis of Language*, ed. by F. Smith and G. A. Miller. Cambridge, Mass., MIT Press.
1970 *The Acquisition of Language: The Study of Developmental Psycholinguistics*. New York, Harper and Row.

Menyuk, P.
1963 "A Preliminary Evaluation of Grammatical Capacity in Children", *J. Verb. Learn. Verb. Beh.*, 2, 429-39.
1964 "Syntactic Rules Used by Children from Preschool through First Grade", *Child Development*, 35, 480-88.

Miller, G. A.
1967 *The Psychology of Communication: Seven Essays*. New York, Basic Books.

Miller, G. A., & Chomsky, N.
1957 "Pattern Conception". Paper for Conference on Pattern Detection, University of Michigan.
1963 "Finitary Models of Language Users", *Handbook of Mathematical Psychology*, ed. by R. D. Luce, R. R. Bush, & E. Galanter, Vol. 3. New York, Wiley.

Miller, G. A., & McNeill, D.
1968 "Psycholinguistics", *Handbook of Social Psychology*, ed. by G. Lindzey and E. Aaronson. Reading, Mass., Addison Wesley.

Miller, G. A., & Norman, D. A.
1964 "Research on the Use of Formal Languages in the Behavioral Sciences", *Semi-annual Technical Report*, Department of Defense, Advanced Research Projects Agency.

Moerk, E.
1972 "Principles of Interaction in Language Learning", *Merrill Palmer Quarterly*, 18, 229-58.

Moeser, S. D., & Bregman, A. S.
1972 "The Role of Reference in the Acquisition of a Miniature Artificial Language" *J. Verb. Learn. Verb. Beh.*, 11, 759-69.

Moore, T. E. (ed.)
1973 *Cognitive Development and the Acquisition of Language*. New York, Academic Press.

Peters, S.
1972 "The Projection Problem: How is a Grammar to be Selected?", *Goals of Linguistic Theory*, ed. by S. Peters. Englewood Cliffs, Prentice-Hall.
Phillips, J.
1973 "Syntax and Vocabulary of Mothers' Speech to Young Children: Age and Sex Comparisons", *Child Development*, 44, 182-85.
Preyer, W.
1882 *Die Seele des Kindes*. Leipzig.
Remick, H.
1972 "Material Speech to Children during Language Acquisition". Paper presented at International Symposium on First Language Acquisition, Florence.
Sachs, J., Brown, R., & Salerno, R.
1972 "Adults' Speech to Children". Paper presented at International Symposium on First Language Acquisition, Florence.
Schaerlaekens, A. M.
1973 *The Two-word Sentence in Child Development*. The Hague, Mouton.
Schank, R.
1972 "Conceptual Dependency: A Theory of Natural Language Understanding", *J. Cognitive Psychology*, 3, 552-631.
Schlesinger, I. M.
1971 "Produktion of Utterances and Language Acquisition", *The Ontogenesis of Grammar*, ed. by D. I. Slobin. New York, Academic Press.
Shatz, M., & Gelman, R.
1974 "The Development of Communicative Skills: Modifications in the Speech of Young Children as a Function of Listener", *SRCD Monographs*.
Shipley, E. F., Smith, C. S., & Gleitman, L. R.
1969 "A Study in the Acquisition of Language: Free Responses to Commands", *Language*, 45, 322-42.
Sinclair-de Zwart, H.
1967 *Langage et opérations: Sous-systèmes linguistiques et opérations concrètes*. Paris, Dunod.
1969 "Developmental Psycholinguistics", *Studies in Cognitive Development: Essays in Honour of Jean Piaget*, ed. by D. Elkind and J. H. Flavell. New York, Oxford University Press.
1973 "Language Acquisition and Cognitive Development", *Cognitive Development and the Acquisition of Language*, ed. by T. E. Moore. New York, Academic Press.
Slobin, D.
1966 "The Acquisition of Russian as a Native Language", *The Genesis of Language*, ed. by F. Smith and G. A. Miller. Cambridge, Mass., MIT Press.
1970 "Universals of Grammatical Development in Children", *Advances in Psycholinguistics*, ed. by G. B. Flores d'Arcais and W. J. M. Levelt. Amsterdam, North-Holland.
1971 "Developmental Psycholinguistics", *A Survey of Linguistic Science*, ed. by W. O. Dingwall. University of Maryland, Linguistics Program.
Slobin, D. (ed.)
1971 *The Ontogenesis of Grammar*. New York, Academic Press.
Snow, C. E.
1972a "Mothers' Speech to Children Learning Language", *Child Development*, 43.
1972b "Young Children's Responses to Adult Sentences of Varying Complexity". Paper presented at Third Annual Congress of Applied Linguistics, Copenhagen.

Solomonoff, R. J.
1958 "The Mechanization of Linguistic Learning", *Proceedings of the Second International Congress of Cybernetics*. Namur.
1964 "A Formal Theory of Inductive Inference", *Information and Control*, 7, 1-22, 224-54.
Stern, C. & W.
1907 *Die Kindersprache*. Leipzig.
Suppes, P.
1971 "Semantics of Context-free Fragments of Natural Languages", *Technical Report* 171, Inst. Math. Stud. Soc. Sc., Stanford University.
Van der Geest, T., Snow, C., & Drewes-Drubbel, A.
1973 "Developmental Aspects of Mother-Child Conversation", *Report*, Department of Linguistics, Amsterdam University.
Winograd, T.
1972 "Understanding Natural Language", *Cognitive Psychology*, 3, 1-191.
Wundt, W.
1885 *Die Sprache und das Denken*: *Essays*. Leipzig.

ON THE SEMANTICS OF PROPER NAMES

BENSON MATES

1. INTRODUCTION

Recent philosophical discussion of the semantics of proper names makes essential use of a number of terms or expressions – 'concepts' is the fancy word – that are themselves greatly in need of explication. This, of course, is hardly surprising; perhaps it is even inevitable, as Aristotle remarked when considering similar matters. But in any such inquiry the time comes when further progress requires a reexamination of the foundations upon which one is attempting to build. To this end the present paper offers a few distinctions and (I hope) clarifications.

Much of the discussion to which I have reference was triggered by the question 'Do proper names have sense?' (here the term 'sense' is used technically for Frege's 'Sinn'). This question has sometimes been run together with a similar one, 'Do proper names have connotation?'. In either case, some authors have answered 'yes', some 'no', some 'yes and no', and some have tried to recast the issue as one of getting clear on 'how the reference of a proper name is fixed'.

The metaphysical framework within which the arguments proceed is, it seems to me, something like the following. The extralinguistic world, which we attempt to describe and otherwise cope with by means of language, consists of individuals that have attributes (properties) and stand in relations to one another. Proper names, with a few exceptions, are associated with – let us say 'denote' – these individuals, either by virtue of some sort of 'dubbing' or 'labelling', or perhaps by virtue of connoting certain attributes that the respective individuals have or are thought to have. In the latter case, the question inevitably arises as to whether the individual denoted by a proper name *necessarily* has the attributes by virtue of which the name denotes him or by means of which the users of the name recognize him as what the name denotes. Hence, *necessity* enters the picture, in both its *de dicto* and *de re* forms. And, of course, *essence* and *accident* are not far behind. For, e.g., if the attribute of Manhood is one of the very criteria by consideration of which the users of the name 'Julius Caesar' decide whether that name does or does not apply to a given individual, is that attribute not *essential* to Caesar?[1]

Thus the discussion has involved, besides the concepts of sense, connotation, individual, and attribute, those of necessity and essence, as well as that of an attribute's being used as a criterion for the application of a name to an individual, and that of an attribute's being ascribed to an individual or being thought to belong to the individual denoted by a given name. These, and their various near relatives that always accompany them, constitute a collection of 'disorderly elements',[2] if there ever was one. Though they are disorderly, however, they nevertheless manage to stick together remarkably well, so that attempts to explicate any one of them without invoking the others seem never to succeed.

In what follows I seek to investigate some of the interconnections among these bad actors. The relationships are rather more clear than the relata, fortunately, so that the obscurity of the latter does not render the project wholly unfeasible. At any rate, I hope that my efforts will at least expose some of the complexities of the subject before us.

2. CONNOTATION

Connotation is introduced by Mill[3] in connection with what he calls 'names' or 'terms'; these are classified as general and singular, with the proper names considered as a subclass of the singular. 'Man' and 'stone' are offered as examples of general terms; 'William the Conqueror' is a proper name; 'the king who succeeded William the Conqueror' and 'the place which the wisdom or policy of antiquity had destined for the residence of the Abyssinian princes' are examples of singular terms that are not proper names.

"A connotative term," says Mill, "is one which denotes a subject and implies an attribute", where "by a subject is here meant anything which possesses attributes." A term is said to denote the subjects that fall under it, and to connote the attributes it implies. Thus the connotation of a term seems in effect to be the set of all attributes a thing must have in order to fall under (be denoted by) it. (Clearly, 'denotation' is here used in the sense of 'multiple denotation'.) As an example Mill gives the attributes of corporeity, animal life, rationality, and a certain external form, as the connotation of the general term 'man'. "Every existing thing which possessed all these attributes," he tells us, "would be called a man, and anything which possessed none of them, or only one, or two, or even three of them without the fourth, would not be so called."

In order to facilitate the comparison of connotation with other notions, let us attempt to formulate a criterion for it in a somewhat sharper way (so as to take account, for example, of the distinction between being *called* 'a man' and *being* a man). Accordingly, for any general or singular term N consider the schema

(1) $\Box$ (x) (If x is (a) N, then ... x ...)

When an open sentence with 'x' as its only free variable is substituted for '... x ...' in (1), the result is a sentence. If and only if this resulting sentence is true, the attribute (if any) expressed by the substituted open sentence belongs to the connotation of N.[4]

It is certain, I think, that Mill would not regard every open sentence with one free variable as expressing an attribute, but I have no idea how he or other philosophers who use the term 'attribute' would specify the appropriate subclass. Sometimes the criterion seems to be nothing more sophisticated than the presence in the natural language of a corresponding abstract term. Thus there is the attribute Whiteness corresponding to the open formula 'x is white', and the attribute Corporeity corresponding to 'x has a body', but presumably no attributes correspond to 'x is white and x has a body' or 'x is a philosopher or x is Julius Caesar', though we would have Parenthood for 'x is a mother or x is a father'. At any rate, the decision as to which open formulas determine attributes and which do not introduces a variable parameter into much of the following analysis.

Singular terms that are not proper names will in general have connotation, according to Mill. Thus, 'the king who succeeded William the Conqueror' connotes the attribute of Kingship, for the sentence

$\Box$ (x) (If x is the king who succeeded William the Conqueror, then x is a king)

is true. "Proper names," on the other hand, "are not connotative: they denote the individuals who are called by them; but they do not indicate or imply any attributes as belonging to those individuals." Hence, although the singular term 'the Roman general who wrote *The Gallic War*' would connote authorship, the proper name 'Julius Caesar', which denotes the same individual, would not. Indeed, the latter term would not even connote the attribute of humanity; i.e., the sentence

$\Box$ (*x*) (If *x* is Julius Caesar, then x is human)

would not, I think, be regarded by Mill as true.

3. ESSENCE

Let us now try to compare the conditions under which an attribute would belong to the connotation of a given term, with those under which it would be essential (as contrasted with accidental) to all the individuals actually or possibly falling under the term.[5] These conditions must be distinct, for there appear to be many examples of attributes that are connoted by a term without being considered essential to any of the individuals falling under the term. The term 'bachelor' connotes the attribute of being unmarried, but this attribute is not supposed to be essential to any individual falling under (i.e., denoted by) the term. The term 'bachelor' also connotes the attribute of being an animal, and this attribute, unlike the other, *is* considered essential to all individuals to which the given term applies. Apparently every attribute essential to the bachelors is part of the connotation of 'bachelor', but the converse does not hold. For the term 'man', on the other hand, the connotation and the set of attributes essential to the denotata coincide; such terms determine what are sometimes called 'natural classes'.

To formulate a criterion analogous to what was given above for connotation, we proceed as follows. For any general or singular term *N*, consider the schema

(2) $\Box$ (*x*) (If *x is* (a) *N*, then $\Box$ (if (E*y*) *y* is x, then ... *x* ...))

When an open sentence with '*x*' as its only free variable is substituted for '... *x* ...' in (2), the result is a sentence. If and only if this resulting sentence is true, the attribute (if any) expressed by the substituted open sentence belongs essentially to all individuals actually or possibly falling under *N*.[6]

Applying this to the case of 'bachelor', we have the result that rationality is an essential attribute of every individual actually or possibly falling under that term, because allegedly it is not possible that anything should be a bachelor and yet be capable of existing without being rational. The attribute of being unwed, on the other hand, evidently fails the test, for there seems to be no reason in logic why persons who are in fact bachelors could not have been married.

Returning to the question whether the attributes connoted by a given name N coincide with the attributes that belong essentially to all individuals actually or possibly falling under N, we see, on the basis of the criteria stated above, that the answer to this question is affirmative, provided that

(3) $\square$ (x) (If x is (a) N, then $\square$ (if $(\mathrm{E}y)$ y is x, then x is (a) N))

is true for N.

Now Mill, if I understand him correctly, while asserting that the general term 'man' connotes the attribute of rationality, would deny that rationality is essential in our sense to all individuals that fall under the term; he thinks that the same individuals ('things') that are in fact men could have existed without being rational (and, indeed, without being men). Thus, he would not accept (3) as holding for the general name 'man'. He does say, however, that if the same individual that is in fact a man had lacked rationality, he would not be denominated 'man'. But this is a fact about "the conventions of language, which will not allow the thing, even if it exists, to be called by the name which is reserved for rational beings"; it is thus not relevant to the question whether rationality is essential to men.[7]

As mentioned above, Mill stated that proper names do not connote; hence, if the foregoing explications are right, he ought also to hold that no attribute is essential to any individual. And this, I believe, is exactly what he does hold. Again, the question of which open sentences with one free variable are taken to express attributes is crucial. If the proper name 'Julius Caesar' is to have no connotation, in the sense of 'connotation' we have been trying to characterize precisely, then 'x is Julius Caesar' must not express an attribute. Otherwise the corresponding instance of (1) would be true. The same verdict about 'x is Julius Caesar' would allow Mill to accept the corresponding instance of (3) without agreeing that Julius Caesar had an essential attribute. And this is just as well, for rejection of (3) for a proper name N would be extremely counter-intuitive; one would have to suppose it possible, for example, for something to be Julius Caesar and yet be capable of existing without being Julius Caesar, i.e., one would have to suppose it possible for Julius Caesar to have been some individual other than Julius Caesar.

Besides Mill's position, that the same individual that is in fact a man could have existed without being a man, and the (perhaps more common) view to the contrary, there is also a third position that in a sense is intermediate between these two. It is based on the idea that 'same', used *simpliciter*, is devoid of sense; if asked whether x and y are the same, we ought to reply: same *what*? When the scribe erases the text of Homer's *Iliad* from a parchment manuscript and copies out instead a version of Aristotle's *Categories* on it, what is left is the same parchment but not the same manuscript. From this point of view one could argue that, given a particular man, e.g., Julius Caesar, it is the case that no individual lacking the attribute of rationality could be that *same man*, though such an individual could perhaps be that *same animal*. The question whether such an individual would be the *same individual* would presumably be rejected; the general terms that can meaningfully complement 'same' must not be so general as 'individual' or 'thing'. I shall not attempt to evaluate this well-known approach; suffice it to say that tampering with so fundamental a notion as identity has very far-reaching effects, which are difficult to comprehend.

4. SENSE

The notion of sense, as employed in recent philosophical discourse, derives of course from Frege.[8] He tells us that for any name there is, in addition to that which the name designates, which may be called its 'denotation', also that which he proposes to call its 'sense', "wherein is contained the way in which the denotation is given". For example, if a, b, and c are the medians of a triangle, then their common point of intersection may be described as 'the intersection of a and b' or 'the intersection of b and c'; both descriptions have the same denotation, but this denotation is 'given' differently in the two cases, and hence the senses are not the same. Beyond the information that the sense of a name in some way reflects the manner in which the denotation is 'given', we have also the explanation that "the sense of a name is grasped by everybody who is sufficiently familiar with the language or totality of designations to which it belongs", but that "the denotation, if any, is illuminated thereby from one side only". The metaphor of *grasping* is reminiscent of the ancient Stoic description of the sense (of Greek discourse) as what the Greeks grasp, but the barbarians do not, when they hear Greek spoken.

Much more instructive than these vague hints and metaphors, however, are five conditions laid down by Frege as characterizing sense and denotation. They are:

i) The sense of a complex expression is a function of the senses of its parts;

ii) The denotation of a complex expression is a function of the denotations of its parts;

iii) The sense of an expression uniquely determines its denotation;

iv) The ordinary denotation of a declarative sentence is its truth-value;

v) The denotation of an expression occurring in an oblique context (e.g., following "believes that ...", "wonders whether ...", and the like) is the same as its ordinary sense.

From these it follows that if two names have the same sense, they will be interchangeable *salva veritate* in all declarative sentences, including those in which they occur obliquely. Further, the converse of this seems intended to hold, too: if two names N and N' have different sense, then there will be at least one declarative sentence, e.g.,

> It is possible to wonder whether something is (an) N without wondering whether it is (an) N'.

in which replacement of N' by N will reverse truth-value. Thus, we have the following generalization: the names N and N' have the same sense if and only if they are interchangeable in all declarative sentences *salva veritate*.[9]

It follows from the foregoing that if two names have the same sense, they have the same connotation. For they would be interchangeable in the criterion-sentences (1). Similarly, their interchangeability in the criterion-sentences (2) would guarantee that the set of attributes essential to all individuals actually or possibly falling under either of them was identical with that for the other. In neither case, however, does the converse appear true. The sense of 'least even number' is different from that of 'only even prime' although they have the same connotation; and 'man' and 'short man' have different sense although the attributes essential to all individuals falling under one are the same as those essential to all individuals falling under the other.

Frege assumes that all names, including proper names, have sense. Others have argued that proper names have denotation but no sense. In support of this view they point out that we never ask for the *meaning* of a proper name; we do not ask 'What does the name 'Pausanias' mean?', but rather, 'Who was Pausanias?'. They remind us further that the descriptions we receive in answer to the latter sort of question are clearly not intended as synonyms for the names concerned. Thus, even if in answer to our question about Pausanias we are told that 'Pausanias was a 2nd century Greek traveller and geographer who wrote an important work called 'A Tour of Greece'', it is accepted on all sides that e.g. the sentence

Pausanias existed but did not travel

expresses a logically possible state of affairs, which it would not if 'Pausanias' had the sense of the description given.[10]

But clearly these considerations do not suffice to show that proper names have no sense. First of all, it is not obvious or even plausible that if a proper name is to have sense at all, it must have the same sense as some description that is itself free of proper names. And, secondly, our disinclination to ask questions like 'What does 'Pausanias' mean?' can perhaps be explained by reference to the pragmatics of questions of that form: ideally, an appropriate answer to 'What does *N* mean?' would be a synonym of *N* that is composed of terms the questioner already understands, so that if it is clear in advance that no such synonym is available, the question will be felt as odd. Thus if, for example, the only expressions that are completely interchangeable *salva veritate* with 'Julius Caesar' are expressions like 'Caesar', 'The man Julius Caesar', 'The individual who is Julius Caesar', which contain the name itself, then there would be no point in anyone's asking 'What does 'Julius Caesar' mean?' even if 'Julius Caesar' had a sense.

Another type of consideration that has led people to doubt that proper names have sense is the following. From a certain philosophical point of view it seems natural to think of necessary truths as sentences that are 'true by virtue of the meanings of their terms', whereas contingent truths are 'true by virtue of facts in the extra-linguistic world'. Contingent truths, it is said, give us information about the world, but necessary truths do not; they are only sentences that automatically 'come out true' once the meanings of their components are fixed. Associated with this same point of view is the idea that necessary truths can be divided into two categories: (*a*) those that are true simply by virtue of the meanings of their 'logical' words (e.g., 'and', 'not', 'or', 'all', 'some', 'same'), and (*b*) the remainder. Now it may be argued that if a proper name has sense, it must occur in some necessary truth that is true 'by virtue of' that sense and hence will be in category (*b*). Note that the fact that the general name 'bachelor' has a sense manifests itself in the necessary truth 'all bachelors are male', which belongs in category (*b*). But proper names, unlike general names, seem only to occur vacuously in the necessary truths in which they do occur; i.e., in such contexts they can be replaced *salva veritate* by any other proper names. Thus, 'Socrates is a Greek or it is not the case that Socrates is a Greek' is a necessary truth, but it is not true by virtue of any sense that the name 'Socrates' might have, for any other name could be substituted for 'Socrates' without changing the truth-value. Consequently, it is argued, since we can find no necessary truth that is true by virtue of the meaning of some proper name, proper names do not have sense.

This argument has at least two weak premises, (1) that if a proper name has sense there must be a necessary truth that is true by virtue of that sense, and (2) that proper names occur vacuously in all necessary truths in which they occur. The first of these needs substantiation, and various apparent counterexamples to the second readily occur. Thus,

(4) Julius Caesar is not Pompey

(in the sense of 'It is not the case that Julius Caesar is Pompey') would seem to be true of all possible worlds although it is not formally valid. Therefore, if necessary truths are true by virtue of the meanings of their terms, as alleged, we ought to conclude in this case that the name 'Julius Caesar' or the name 'Pompey' has a sense, and, since they are obviously on a par, that both have sense.

The doctrine outlined in the penultimate paragraph above is often supplemented by the further thesis that the necessary truths of category (*b*) are reducible to those of category (*a*) by substituting synonyms for synonyms. To cite the classical example again, 'No bachelor is married' is reducible to 'No unmarried man is married' by replacing 'bachelor' by its synonym 'unmarried man'. Now it must be confessed that no synonyms for 'Julius Caesar' and 'Pompey' spring to mind that would allow reduction of (4) to a necessary truth of category (*a*), and this may be considered a further indication that proper names do not have sense. A better conclusion, I should think, would be simply that the cited thesis is false.

We have examined some of the arguments against the view that proper names have sense. Among the arguments *pro*, the following is to me one of the more persuasive. Consider the two sentences

(5) Caesar was the victor at Pharsalus.
(6) Pompey was the victor at Pharsalus.

These two sentences have opposite truth-values; since sense uniquely determines denotation, they therefore differ also in sense (which is completely obvious, anyway). Now the reason why, e.g.,

(7) The author of *The Gallic War* was the victor at Pharsalus

and

(8) The victor at Pharsalus was the victor at Pharsalus

have different senses must be, as Frege would say, that their subject terms have different senses, for their predicates are identical; similarly, it would seem, the difference in sense between (5) and (6) must be due to a difference in sense between 'Pompey' and 'Caesar'.

Although this argument is persuasive, to me at least, it obviously is not logically sound. To tighten it up we would need to assume, unfortunately, just the point at issue, namely that the proper names 'Caesar' and 'Pompey' have sense. It is clear enough that if they have sense at all, their senses must be different (since their denotations differ), but what is not clear is that in general if two expressions with different sense are alike except that one contains a word *W* where the other contains another word *W'*, then *W* and *W'* must have different sense. Compare, e.g., the words 'in' and 'on', which, as so-called syncategorematic words, may be considered to have no independent meaning, i.e., no sense, and which yet can make a great difference to the sense of compounds in which they occur.

5. CRITERIA

The notions of connotation and sense belong to the semantics of language, while that of essence seems to belong primarily to metaphysics. The next notion to be considered, namely, *that the attributes expressed by sentence-forms* Γ *are used as criteria for the application of the general or singular term N*, belongs to the pragmatics of language. We shall want to distinguish sharply between, on the one hand, those attributes we in fact use as criteria for application of a given name, and, on the other hand, both the connotation of the name and the set of attributes essential to all individuals actually or possibly falling under the name.

Take, for instance, the general names

(9) tiger

and

(10) a large Asiatic carnivorous mammal of the cat family, of a tauny color transversally striped with black.

Although the second of these connotes the attribute expressed by 'x has stripes', the first does not, for presumably it is logically possible that there should exist a tiger that had no stripes. The sentence form 'x is an animal', on the other hand, seems to express an attribute that is essential to all individuals actually or possibly falling under either of the two names; the attribute expressed by 'x has stripes' would be an accidental attribute of these same individuals. Now consider the attributes actually used as criteria for the application of these two names, especially the first of them. I venture to say that for most speakers of English one such attribute would indeed be that of stripedness. But while we recognize that we do in fact use stripedness as part of the basis for applying the term 'tiger' to a given individual, we agree at the same time that although it is necessary that whatever is a large striped cat is striped, it is by no means essential to the objects falling under the names (9) or (10) that they be striped. Thus, the question 'Is a an essential attribute of tigers?' is not to be confused with the question 'Would we call an animal that lacked a 'a tiger'?'. For it would be silly to deny that if an object resembles a tiger closely enough we shall be willing to call it 'a tiger', whether it is a tiger or not, and, conversely, if a tiger is disguised sufficiently we shall not apply the term 'tiger' to it even though such application would be correct.

The same sort of distinction needs to be made in the case of singular descriptions and proper names. Let us consider some names of an individual who has been much discussed of late,

(11) Richard M. Nixon

and

(12) The man who was President of the U. S. A. in 1973.

As we have seen, (12) connotes certain attributes that are not connoted by (11), and it may well be that various attributes essential to all individuals actually or possibly falling under (11), i.e., to Richard M. Nixon, are not essential to all individuals actually or possibly falling under (12). But in any case, most of the attributes that we actually employ as criteria for the application of the name 'Richard M. Nixon' are neither connoted by (11) or (12) nor belong essentially to Mr. Nixon. They are instead such attributes as a certain posture resembling that of Ed Sullivan, a characteristic physiognomy that we have all come to know, certain behavior patterns such as a tendency to blink the eyes rapidly while looking pleased, and so on; and none of these are regarded as attributes that Mr. Nixon could not have been without. Indeed, it seems possible, maybe even likely, that one or more of the actual criteria for the application of the name 'Richard M. Nixon' are attributes that the man in question does not have at all but is only *thought* to have.

Now it will be objected at once that we are using far too naive and superficial a notion of criterion when we suggest that our criterion for application of the name (11) is merely that the individual concerned look so much like Richard M. Nixon that we cannot easily tell the difference. Certainly this sort of criterion will not work for names like 'Julius Caesar' or 'Pompey', where we have only the haziest idea of how the individuals in question looked. It is not even clear what 'to apply a proper name' means when the individual named is not available to be indicated with a 'That's Nixon' or 'That's Brandt'.

A clarification of this would probably proceed along the following lines. John Smith uses the (set of) attributes expressed for him by the sentence-forms $A_1, \ldots, A_n$ as a criterion for applying the name 'Julius Caesar' if, whenever he hears someone described by $A_1, \ldots, A_n$ he is disposed to think or say (if the question is raised) something like 'That's Julius Caesar (you're talking about)'. Whether the attributes do in fact belong to Caesar or anyone else is irrelevant; the crux is whether John *thinks* that they do; whether the sentence-forms do express the attributes in question is again irrelevant; what is relevant is whether for John they do. Admittedly this is all pretty woolly, involving, as it does, oblique contexts within oblique contexts, but it is at least a start toward giving some empirical content to the notion that a person P uses the attributes expressed for him by the sentence forms $A_1, \ldots, A_n$ as criteria for application of the name N.[11]

Even at so low a level of preciseness, however, it is clear enough that the attributes used as criteria for application of a name like 'Julius Caesar' will vary from person to person and from time to time. One might suppose that in this regard the situation is no worse than it is with sense and denotation generally, for different individuals speaking the same language can and do attach different senses and even different denotations to the same expression. But the cases are not really parallel. We can define, whether statistically or in some other way, a useful 'public' sense of 'the sense of the expression E in English', which would be such that, e.g., the sense of 'flotilla' in English is that of 'small fleet', even if Smith, who is a native speaker of English, occasionally uses 'flotilla' in another sense. And similarly for denotation. The criteria for application of a name, on the other hand, vary so much with other properties of individual speakers that there is no obvious way of specifying a 'standard' set; and even when the attributes used by the speakers of a language for application of a given name do converge on a fixed set, as may happen in the case of a name like 'Diocles Magnes' (where almost nothing is known of the individual concerned), these attributes need not even belong to the individual, let alone be essential to him or connoted by his proper name.

The distinction between the attributes an individual must have in order to be x, and those which any speaker or group of speakers actually use as criteria for application of the proper name of x, is frequently obfuscated by means of a certain phrase that figures prominently in philosophical discussions of language. This is the phrase 'to identify a as b', as in 'I identify the author of *The Gallic War* as Julius Caesar'. Now it is one thing for me to find that the author of *The Gallic War* has the attributes I use as criteria for application of the name 'Julius Caesar', and something quite different to find that he has the attributes essential to being Julius Caesar, i.e., that he *is* Julius Caesar. The phrase 'to identify, etc.' seems ambiguous as between these and other senses. In some of them I might identify someone as Julius Caesar who was actually somebody else, but in others this would be absolutely impossible. Note also that both arguments of the phrase 'to identify a as b' occur obliquely and hence are not accessible to the logical operations of quantification, class abstraction, or substitution in accord with Leibniz's Law; this crippling fact seems unfortunately to be overlooked by nearly every author who makes use of the phrase.

6. ASCRIPTION

What does it mean to say that an attribute is 'commonly ascribed to Aristotle by users of the name 'Aristotle'? Evidently, something like this: an attribute expressed by a sentence-form '... x ...' is commonly ascribed to Aristotle by users of 'Aristotle' if such users either commonly *do* assert or, if asked, *would* assert the corresponding sentence '... Aristotle ...'.[12] Here we have again all the problems reviewed in the previous section, but even through the haze it can be seen that, e.g., the attributes commonly ascribed to Aristotle need not be the same as the attributes we use as criteria for the application of the name 'Aristotle', and that neither group need coincide with the attributes essential to the man or connoted by his name.

It is sometimes said that an individual *must* have at least some of the attributes commonly ascribed to him. This is probably trivially true, for often contradictory attributes are ascribed (some people think that Aristotle wrote the whole of the *Categories*, and some people think that he did not; some people think that Nixon knew in advance about Watergate, and some people think that he did not; and, for each one of us, I suppose, some of those who use our names are willing to say that we shall exist after death and pay for our sins, etc., and others will deny that this is so). In general, though, the truth of the claim that an individual must have some of the attributes commonly ascribed to him will depend purely and simply upon whether or not any of his essential attributes happen to be commonly ascribed to him. Essential attributes may be ascribed, of course, but an attribute does not become essential by being ascribed, no matter how often and by how many speakers such ascription is made.

7. FIXING THE REFERENCE

Another theme of recent philosophizing about proper names centers around the question of how the reference (i.e., the denotation) of a proper name is 'fixed' or 'determined'. There is a bothersome ambiguity about this question. Sometimes it seems to mean: how does a user of language come to find out what a given proper name denotes? Taken in this way it is answered by describing various circumstances that (presumably) actually occur. E.g., one may be present at an initial christening, where in a kind of ostensive definition the name is associated with whatever it denotes.[13] Or, one may be told something like 'Nixon is the man you heard speak on the television earlier this evening' or 'Aristotle was the pupil of Plato and teacher of Alexander the Great'. In these latter cases it is clear that the descriptions are furnished, not as purported synonyms of the proper name, but just to 'fix' or 'determine' its denotation.

Sometimes, on the other hand, the question about "fixing the reference" seems to mean: under what conditions is a sentence of the form

N denotes x

true? On this interpretation it seems to be a semantic question, having no simple connection with such pragmatic matters as how the individual speaker S comes to discover what N denotes or how S acquires the use of N or what N denotes for S.

Two principal theories or 'pictures' are presented in answer to the question, which I shall henceforward interpret in the second of the two ways mentioned. What is sometimes called 'The Cluster Theory' was put forward by John Searle as follows:

Suppose we ask the users of the name 'Aristotle' to state what they regard as certain essential and established facts about him. Their answers would constitute a set of identifying descriptions, and I wish to argue that though no single one of them is analytically true of Aristotle, their disjunction is. Put it this way: suppose we have independent means of identifying an object, what then are the conditions under which I could say of the object, 'This is Aristotle'? I wish to claim that the conditions, the descriptive power of the statement, is that a sufficient but so far unspecified number of these statements (or descriptions) are true of the object.[14]

In other words, if a 'sufficient' subset (sometimes 'most, or a weighted most') of the set of properties commonly attributed to Aristotle by users of the name 'Aristotle' uniquely determines an individual x, then x is the denotation of the name; otherwise the name has no denotation.

Against this there is arrayed the 'Chain of Communication' theory or picture. As presented by Saul Kripke:

... Someone, let's say, a baby, is born; his parents call him by a certain name. They talk about him to their friends. Other people meet him. Through various sorts of talk the name is spread from link to link as if by a chain. A speaker who is on the far end of this chain, who has heard about, say Richard Feynman, in the market place or elsewhere, may be referring to Richard Feynman even though he can't remember from whom he first heard of Feynman or from whom he ever heard of Feynman. ... Not only that: he'd have trouble distinguishing between Gell-Mann and Feynman. So he doesn't have to know these things, but, instead, a chain of communication going back to Feynman himself has been established, by virtue of his membership in a community which passed the name on from link to link, not by a ceremony that he makes in private in his study: 'By "Feynman" I shall mean the man who did such and such and such.'[15]

The idea here, as I understand it, is that in using a name N a speaker S refers to x if there is a causal chain of the requisite kind leading from an initial baptism of x, "which is explained in terms either of fixing a reference by description or by ostension", to the acquisition of the use of N by S. Since ordinarily S acquires this use from a number of members of his language community, it is possible that the community should be an additional parameter here. At any rate, Kripke is very circumspect in the way in which he puts his theory forward, acknowledging that it is imprecise and that there may be some cases of which the Cluster Theory is true, but in the end he considers it "a better picture than that given by description theorists". (The locution '*N* denotes *x*' is presumably to be explicated in terms of '*S*, in using *N*, refers to *x*' by some sort of quantification over speakers *S*.)

As a prod to our intuitions in assessing these two theories, it is useful to keep in mind the collection of seemingly trivial truths of the form

'Vergil' denotes Vergil,

and, in considering them, to endeavor to look both *through* and *at* language, as it were. We are saying that the name 'Vergil' denotes an individual. Which individual? Why, Vergil, of course, and nobody else.

Now, as concerns the Cluster Theory, let us ask: could it turn out that either no individual or some individual other than Vergil had most or a weighted most of the properties commonly ascribed to Vergil? The answer would seem to be a clear 'yes'. For instance, it is abstractly possible for somebody, or even a whole community of people, to ascribe to Vergil any number of the properties of Ovid. But in that case the Cluster Theory could give the odd result that the ascriptions were *true*, because actually Ovid was the individual referred to although he was being called 'Vergil'. Surely, this is not acceptable.

On the other hand, applying this same approach to the Chain of Communication Theory, we ask: could it be that at the far end of the chain leading back from our acquisition of the name 'Vergil' there is either nobody at all or else some individual other than Vergil? Again, the answer seems to be a clear 'yes'. It is not hard to imagine circumstances other than an initial baptism of Vergil that could have started a 'chain of communication' leading to our use of the name. E.g., it could have been the case that somebody else – call him 'Fabius' – was baptized 'Vergil', and yet the effect of this was offset by an error made by somebody who was located at a crucial point later in the chain and who thought that Fabius (whom he was calling 'Vergil') wrote the *Aeneid*, etc., etc. Therefore it could be the case that 'Vergil' does not denote the person whose baptism initiated the chain leading to our use of the name. In short, unless Vergil is at the far end of the chain, the name will not denote the person who is at the far end of the chain.

Now we are not denying that, as a matter of fact, Vergil probably has most, or a weighted most, of the properties commonly ascribed to him – that would be no great surprise – nor are we denying that, as another matter of fact, Vergil is probably located at the far end of some sort of causal chain leading to our use of his name. And it is plausible to suppose that the corresponding facts are true for most other proper names if they denote anything at all. What we are denying is that it is anything more than contingently true that the individual we refer to by using the name 'Vergil' is that unique individual, if any, who has a 'sufficient number' of the properties commonly ascribed to Vergil, or that he is the unique individual, if any, whose baptism is located at the beginning of a certain kind of causal chain reaching down to our use of the name. One wants to say instead, 'When I use the name "Vergil" I am referring to *Vergil*, regardless of whether there is an unbroken line of transmission (with all of the transmitters having the right intentions) reaching back to him and to nobody else, and regardless of whether most or even some of what people have said about him is true.'

In sum, the proper locale of these two theories is in the field of pragmatics. Both make useful observations, but, considered in relation to the question whether proper names have sense, both are equally off the target. One gives a plausible account of the mechanism by which we acquire the use of a proper name, emphasizing our intention to denote by it what the other members of our linguistic community are denoting by it. The other in effect draws attention to another feature of our use of a proper name, viz., that if it turns out that no sufficiently large or important group of the properties we have been ascribing to the bearer of a given name belong in fact to any one individual, then we drop the name from use. This will happen, I am convinced, even if we discover also that we have derived the name by an acceptable chain from a surprising source. E.g., if it should turn out that nobody wrote the *Aeneid* or the *Bucolics* or the *Georgics*, and that no important Latin poet lived before Lucan, and so on, we would give up use of the name 'Vergil', even if it also turned out that there *was* an obscure man who was called 'Vergil' and to whose baptism our use was ultimately traceable. So the reason why we would never assert such a sentence as 'Vergil wrote neither the *Aeneid*, the *Bucolics*, nor the *Georgics*', is not that the statement expresses a logical impossibility, but rather that our belief in the circumstances that would make it true would lead us to drop the use of the name "Vergil" altogether.[16]

University of California,
Berkeley

NOTES

1 The only proper names I consider in this paper are those of human beings. This is done as part of an effort to sidestep, so far as possible, the very difficult question of how to decide in general whether a given expression is or is not a proper name.

2 To use an apt phrase of Quine's. See "On What There Is", *Review of Metaphysics*, 2 (1948), 23.

3 J. S. Mill, *A System of Logic*, I, ii, 3ff.

4 In schema (1) the substituends for the variable 'x' are to be individual names, e.g., 'Julius Caesar', 'Hamlet'; the symbol '$\Box$' is a sentential operator carrying the sense of 'necessarily', so that a sentence $\Box S$ is true of a possible world W if and only if S is true of all possible worlds; the universal quantifier is given the so-called 'substitution' interpretation, so that a sentence $(v)S$ is true of a possible world W if and only if S v/n is true of W for every individual name n denoting in W.

Of course I realize the hazards of employing such combinations of logical notation and ordinary phraseology.

5 When it is said, e.g., that rationality is essential to men, it is meant, I take it, that not only is it true of the individuals actually falling under the name 'man' that they could not exist without being rational, but also it is impossible that there should be a man of whom this was not the case. In other words, substituends for the quantified variables in schema (2) below should include names like 'Hamlet' as well as those like 'Julius Caesar'. This is what I am trying to indicate by the unsatisfactory phrase 'individuals possibly falling under the term'.

6 See footnote 4 above. We do not suppose that sentences of the form 'x is x' are necessary truths; the component '(Ey) y is x' may be read 'x exists'. Note also that an attribute's not belonging essentially to all individuals falling under a name N does not preclude its being essential to some; e.g., rationality is not essential to all individuals falling under 'animal' but only to those which also fall under 'man'.

7 J. S. Mill, *op. cit.*, I, vi, 2.

8 G. Frege, "Über Sinn und Bedeutung", *Zeitschrift für Philosophie und philosophische Kritik*, 100 (1892), 25-50.

9 Obviously, this notion of synonymy applies only to names belonging to a single language.

Of course here, as in all other discussions of language, whether conducted by philosophers, psychologists, or linguists, a great deal of abstraction from the full complexity of the actual facts is going on. Probably no two expressions are fully interchangeable *salva veritate* throughout the discourse of any one person, let alone that of a whole community of speakers; we are ignoring the phenomena of ambiguity and vagueness, as well as all those phenomena that have led some philosophers to insist that so-called statements, and not sentences, are the bearers of truth and falsehood; and we are abstracting from many other features of language as actually used. At a different level of abstraction one might wish to introduce a notion of similarity of sense, that would admit of degrees, or one might relativize sense to linguistic context, or to a given speaker, or to time, place, and other circumstances, or to any combination of these and many other variables that would need to be mentioned in a full account of things as they really are.

10 The existence clause is frequently omitted in arguments of this type, to their considerable detriment.

11 No doubt it is only a start. But as we refine the account, until we get to the point of making the attribute of *being Julius Caesar* the criterion for application of the name 'Julius Caesar', at which point all empirical content disappears, it will always be possible that some individual other than Julius Caesar should have all the criteria-attributes of the name.

[12] Or, if 'Aristotle' is felt to occur directly, i.e., not obliquely, in 'commonly ascribed to Aristotle', then the last clause should read '*would* assert a corresponding sentence "... *N* ..." for some name *N* denoting Aristotle'.

[13] Throughout this section, 'christening' and 'baptism' are used without religious connotations simply to denote an original act of giving a name to a human being. In this sense, lots of heathens have been baptized.

[14] J. Searle, *Speech Acts*, Cambridge, Cambridge University Press, 1969, p. 169.

[15] S. Kripke, "Naming and Necessity", *Semantics of Natural Language*, edited by D. Davidson and G. Harmon, Dordrecht-Holland, D. Reidel, 1972, pp. 298-9.

[16] I wish to express my indebtedness to Mr. Charles Silver for many stimulating conversations on the topics discussed in this chapter.

ON REFERENCE

J. J. A. MOOIJ

Philosophical literature is rich in the terms 'reference', 'referential', and 'to refer'. These terms are mostly USED, not MENTIONED, but occasionally they are themselves taken into consideration, for instance when an author attempts to define them. As to their use, the three terms and their further derivatives reveal a broad spectrum of meaning. Although the definitions of the terms in philosophical literature (and in the theory of language, for that matter) pertain to their central meanings, the original spectrum is to some extent reflected in the attempts at a definition. Consequently, the resulting definitions also show a certain divergence.

There are at least three types of definitions, corresponding to what could be regarded as three different notions of what it is for an expression to refer.

Firstly, reference is seen as something belonging to the members of a wide class of words, apart from any special context. Members of this class are many nouns (e.g. 'book', 'mountain', 'snow'), many adjectives (e.g. 'black', 'big', 'easy-going'), and many verbs (e.g. 'to walk', 'to teach', 'to snow'). This notion of 'reference' is circumscribed by John Lyons when he says that the term 'reference' indicates "the relationship which holds between words and the things, events, actions and qualities they 'stand for' ".[1]

As a matter of fact, it is far from clear which members this class of words precisely contains. Have words such as 'opportunity', 'exception', 'general', 'fine', 'to become' or 'to refer' a reference in the sense now under discussion? To be sure, it is often preferred to use 'to denote' instead of 'to refer' in this connection. And, accordingly, the class of things, events, etc. referred to is called the 'denotation' of the word. Mostly, however, yet another term is used to indicate the class of referents, viz. 'extension'.[2] One further complication is that many authors consider only classes of THINGS, as opposed to events, qualities, etc., as denotations or extensions (the extension of 'to walk', e.g., being the class of walking beings, not of instances of walking). All these terminological and substantial complications notwithstanding, we have to do here with one notion of reference. I shall call this first notion the DENOTATION USE of 'reference', or D-REFERENCE for short. The distinction between divided and undivided reference pertains to it.

Secondly, there is the use of the term 'reference' which is especially connected with so-called referring expressions. These are generally defined as expressions used in a certain context to identify, or pick out, an individual or group of individuals that one wants to speak about (either in the mode of asserting or in that of questioning, or otherwise). Consequently, referring expressions are contrasted with predications, among other things; according to this use of 'reference', predicative expressions would not refer at all. More often than not, I think, the identification of exactly one individual is considered to be the paradigm case of reference in this sense. Proper names, certain pronouns, and certain definite descriptions[3] together would constitute the paradigmatic case of referring. Witness J. R. Searle, who is one of the propounders of this notion of reference. He says that "the utterance of a referring expression CHARACTERISTICALLY serves to pick out or identify a PARTICULAR object apart from other objects".[4] And according to him there even is "a case for refusing to call singular INdefinite referring expressions instances of reference at all".[5]

This second notion of reference is probably the main one in recent philosophical and linguistic literature. It has been extensively discussed, e.g. by P. F. Strawson, W. V. O. Quine, L. Linsky and Keith Donnellan, and some important distinctions have been made in connection with it, e.g., between opaque and transparent contexts[6] and between 'to refer correctly' and 'to refer incorrectly'.[7] For obvious reasons it has sometimes been called 'identifying reference'.[8] I shall speak of the IDENTIFICATION USE of 'reference', or I-REFERENCE for short.

There are, of course, essential differences between D-reference and I-reference. D-reference is a property of words in the abstract, while I-reference is often dependent on the context. Moreover, while D-reference is completely within the sphere of semantics as defined by C. W. Morris (semantics being the study of the relations of signs to the objects which they may or do denote), I-reference is at least partly within the sphere of pragmatics (i.e. the study of the relations between signs and their interpreters). For it can be argued that it is the speaker who ultimately does the I-referring (though by means of the relevant expression), and in very many cases he I-refers on behalf of his readers or listeners.

Next to the denotation-use and the identification-use of 'reference' there is at least one more use of 'reference' current in the literature on the subject. It is the one applied, for instance, in the broad opposition between the referential and the emotive (or expressive) use of language, and in such locutions as 'the referential dimension of lingiustic expressions'. Of course, this third notion of 'reference' is used in many contexts more or less inadvertently, for instance, when a report is said to refer to the event reported.[9] But it is also present in many discussions on reference itself, even apart from the fundamental distinctions and locutions referred to above (which are often introduced by means of a definition). An article by Jan Srzednicki on "Reference and Description" uses the term 'reference' mainly in its identification-use (one of the author's provisional definitions being "To refer is to indicate an object"), so in contrast with description ("To describe is to say something about an object").[10] However, in the course of his argument Srzednicki casually characterizes description as "reference to a feature". This seems to amount to the introduction of a generic notion of reference of which reference to an object *and* reference to a feature are special variants.[11]

I think that 'to mention' is sometimes used rather synonymously with 'to refer' in its third meaning. For this reason, I shall call this last concept the MENTIONING USE of 'reference', or M-REFERENCE for short.

M-reference, though different from the other two, shows certain similarities to the identification-use as well as to the denotation-use of 'reference'. Its similarity to I-reference is due to the fact that either of them concerns the *use* of language rather than language in the abstract. Actually, M-reference includes I-reference. On the other hand, its similarity to D-reference is due to the fact that reference is here taken rather broadly and covers the relations between many different types of expressions on the one hand, and many different aspects of what it is that language is, or can be, about, on the other. Moreover, the D-reference of a word delimits (up to a point at least) what it can M-refer to.

Along with I-reference, also that which P. F. Strawson has called "THE INTRODUCTION OF A TERM into a remark" is part of M-reference. Discussing the two assertions 'Raleigh smokes' and 'Socrates is wise', Strawson proposes to say "that the expression 'Socrates' ('Raleigh') serves to INTRODUCE the particular person, Socrates (Raleigh), into the remark, and that the expression 'is wise' ('smokes') serves to INTRODUCE the quality, wisdom (the habit, smoking), into the remark". Strawson also suggests "that anything which is introduced, or can be introduced, into a remark by an expression is a TERM".[12]

However, identifying reference and the reference to (Strawsonian) terms are not the only forms of M-reference. M-reference also covers the reference of a report to the states or events which are reported. Accordingly, M-reference shows a certain internal hierarchy since the reference of a complex expression (e.g. a report) depends upon the subordinate references made by parts of it. Of course, the same is true for D-reference and I-reference as well.

But let us consider this hierarchical structure of M-reference somewhat more closely, restricting ourselves to reporting discourse. Even in such a simple case as 'Raleigh smokes' the terms cannot be completely determined before the total statement has been taken into consideration. Compare, e.g., 'Raleigh smokes' with 'the fire smokes'. The terms corresponding to the expression 'smokes' in these statements are certainly not identical. Generally speaking: Although a reader, in order to understand a statement, has to know beforehand something about what its words can M-refer to, i.e. something about their D-references, the ultimate M-references of these words also depend on the references of other words in the context. The context is no idle wheel in the mechanism of M-reference. And, of course, the circumstances in which the speaker finds himself at the moment of speaking may have their influence as well.

Thus, it is misleading to consider only the dependence of the total reference of a complex expression on the references of its parts. Within the field of ACTUAL M-reference, the reference of a statemental or multi-statemental report to states or events, etc., often influences the references of its parts. To be sure, it also depends on the possible M-references of its parts, as well as on their non-referential contributions. But the ACTUAL M-reference of these parts can often only be determined as features of the total situation corresponding to the total statement, or report.

Apart from the nature of the relations of dependence in a special case, I take it that M-reference is reference to all the facts, states and events at issue in a certain piece of discourse, as well as to their special features, in so far as particular words or word combinations can be held contextually responsible for mentioning them. Accordingly, M-referents are everything the relevant piece of discourse can be said to be about. So M-referents may be facts, states, events, actions, processes, developments, etc., as well as the things, persons, periods, areas, qualities, dispositions, relations, etc., involved in them.

This may seem rather promiscuous, but as a matter of fact it is part of the notion of the referential use of language and of the quite plausible view that language may be about very divergent types of referents. Be it noted, however, that so far I have only spoken about the reporting use of language. Other uses of language involve still other referents like fantasies, problems, and solutions.

Hereafter, I shall discuss some implications of this notion of M-reference. Although the notion is in general use, it has not often been thoroughly analysed so far. Current conceptions of reference have been determined mainly by I-reference and in the second place by D-reference. M-reference shows some deviating traits.

Consequently, some of my remarks will clash with some standard conceptions of reference. But they will also to some extent justify the seemingly promiscuous catalogue of M-referents given above. (For convenience' sake I shall sometimes use 'reference' instead of 'M-reference'.)

By way of example, I quote the following statement from the *International Herald Tribune* (Febr. 23/24, 1974): "The Belgian government today froze prices of oil products for two months despite demands by oil companies for an early increase." To begin with, there is apparently an I-reference here to the Belgian government, and thus an M-reference as well. But also a certain decision made by this government is M-referred (although not I-referred) to, viz. the decision to leave the prices of oil products for the present as they are. The description of this decision contains M-references to, at least, oil products and their prices. In the second half of the sentence there are M-references to oil companies, their demands, and to the content of these demands, viz. an early increase (of prices).

So, the sentence quoted shows a rather intricate web of M-references. Its threads, however, have been woven not only by the grammatical form of the sentence, but also by the character of the situation described. Accordingly, we must not assume that all prices of all oil products (nor all oil companies) are referred to, but only those that have to do with Belgium. This remains true even though hardly any reader of this report may have been able to specify exactly (or pick out!) which products and which companies are involved. On the other hand, not each part of the sentence has a referring function. A striking example is the word 'despite': it does not refer to any feature of the events the sentence is about, but it only registers a certain discrepancy between some of these features. So, meaning has not been completely swallowed by M-reference.

However, 'despite' helps to fix the intent of 'early' (in 'an early increase'), among other things; it helps to make clear that an early increase here is an increase much earlier than after two months from now. It helps the reader in interpreting 'early', as well as in finding a more precise reference for 'early increase'.

Generally speaking, I think, one could describe M-reference as a case of 'calling attention to something' (to things, states, events, decisions, locations, and so on). More especially, if an utterance M-refers to something, then it calls the hearer's (or reader's) attention by certain linguistic means to something outside that utterance. I would not say that the converse is true, however. For instance, an utterance may call attention, even by conventional linguistic means, to certain feelings or emotions felt by the speaker without referring to them. And in the above example, 'despite' could be said to call the hearer's attention to a discrepancy without, however, referring to it. The essential notion seems to be the notion of 'about-ness': an utterance calling attention to x M-refers to x only if it is about x. Nonetheless, to realize that M-reference is at least a case of calling the hearer's (reader's) attention helps to clarify some problems.

For one thing, it throws some light on the question whether reference is only possible to something existing in reality. As to I-reference, such a requirement is sometimes made. Recently, however, many authors have acknowledged that identifying reference may be to something existing in the imagination only, or that the question whether the referent really exists does not matter at all.[13] Of course, attention can be directed to imaginary objects. But then attention can also be called to such objects, so that M-reference to nonexisting referents would be possible. Thus a statement may refer to a price increase which is only asked for.

This is not to say, however, that the question whether a possible M-referent exists has no bearing at all on the notion of M-reference. More specifically, I do not think, without qualifications, that every definite description, regardless of its context and the circumstances in which it is used, M-refers to a real or imaginary person, thing, situation, event, etc., falling under the description.

By means of the phrase 'Martini-drinking ghost' one may M-refer to a Martini-drinking man. Normally, one would at the same time call attention to (and even M-refer to) certain ghost-like characteristics of this man. But it is not evident that there would also be a reference to a ghost; theories of metaphor differ as to this issue.[14] This complication does not occur in an example used by Keith Donnellan: 'Who is the man drinking a Martini?', when the man apparently meant is in fact drinking water, and the speaker, in using the words 'a Martini', is simply mistaken, and not speaking metaphorically or ironically. Certainly here too, in the first instance, attention is called to a man who is drinking a Martini; and up to a point there is a corresponding M-reference, among other things, to a Martini in the hands of the man. Given the circumstances, however, this is overruled by a reference to the man *simpliciter*, whether he is actually drinking a Martini or not (he may even be not drinking at all). By calling the hearer's attention to a man drinking a Martini the speaker succeeds in directing the hearer's attention to a person who is not drinking a Martini. So an M-reference corresponding to the words used, strictly interpreted, may be overruled by another M-reference corresponding partly to the words used, freely interpreted, AND to the circumstances.

The above suggests that one could distinguish between two variants of M-reference. On the one hand, the notion of M-reference may be used in such a way that an M-reference to some feature x implies that x is real. This may be called Mr-reference. (The index 'r' has been chosen as the first letter of 'real'.) On the other hand, it may be used without such an implication, while it is taken for granted that by means of his language a speaker is able to refer to something he invents, or incorrectly believes to be the case, or falsely reports. Any object of thought or attention can be made the object of reference, according to this second conception. This variant may be called Ma-reference. (The index 'a' has been chosen as the first letter of 'attention'.)

As I have argued earlier, in general the notion of Ma-reference should be preferred. Of course, the question is largely a terminological one. Even if one does not agree that linguistic expressions may have non-existent referents, one will have to acknowledge that they may be about non-existent things, imaginary events, etc.[15] I do not know why the notion of reference should be unsuitable to cover the latter situation, too. But the above example, taken from Donnellan, makes it clear that the circumstances may be such as to favour Mr-reference rather than Ma-reference. Because of the circumstances, Mr-reference may overrule Ma-reference.

It should be noted, however, that the situation of our example would radically change if the speaker and his (her) hearer, after putting the question and answering it, would go on to discuss the Martini the third man is supposed, by both, to be drinking. Then, after all, there would be M-reference (Ma-reference, to be sure) to something having only an imaginary status. This is especially clear if the two partners in the discussion would turn away from the third man to give free rein to their fantasy.

Moreover, some qualifications are called for in connection with what Donnellan has characterized as the attributive use of a definite description. According to him, "a speaker who uses a definite description attributively in an assertion states something about whoever or whatever is the so-and-so". It is distinguished from the referential use of a definite description where the speaker uses the description to enable his audience to pick out whom or what he is talking about. Donnellan goes on to say that "in the first case the definite description might be said to occur essentially, for the speaker wishes to assert something about whatever or whoever fits that description; but in the referential use the definite description is merely one tool for doing a certain job – calling attention to a person or thing – and in general any other device for doing the same job, another description or a name, would do as well. In the attributive use, the attribute of being the so-and-so is all important, while it is not in the referential use."[16]

So, in 'Smith's murderer is insane' the definite description may be used attributively or referentially, depending on the speaker's intentions. In 'The Republican candidate for president in 1964 will be a conservative', said in 1960, the definite description will normally be used attributively.[17] I do not think, however, that the distinction between attributive and referential use is as clear-cut as suggested by Donnellan. Suppose Smith's murderer has been arrested and has been described and even mentioned by name in the newspapers. Now someone says 'Smith's murderer is insane'. Must it be clear, even to the speaker himself, whether he uses the definite description referentially or attributively, i.e. whether he makes it possible to identify the person he is speaking about by using implicitly the reports in the newspapers, or comments on the act of murder? He may do both things at once, though one more than the other. That is to say, among other things, a definite description may have an attributive function mainly, without being for that reason prevented from specifying the object in a much higher degree than follows from the description alone. Moreover, even in a case in which the use of the description 'Smith's murderer' in the sentence quoted above is completely attributive, it should not be concluded that the description is not referential at all. To be sure, it is not used, supposedly, to enable the audience to pick out the man talked about; let us assume that nothing is known about him, apart from the way he has murdered Smith. But the expression, though not I-referential (contrary to what definite descriptions often are), can yet be taken to be M-referential. For it calls attention to the man (whoever he may be!) who has murdered Smith. And anyhow the sentence is about him. To a certain extent this is even acknowledged by Donnellan, who at the end of his article hesitatingly speaks of "reference in a very weak sense – namely, reference to WHATEVER is the one and only one ø, if there is any such".[18]

But in the last-mentioned case the reference is certainly more vague or indefinite than in a case where it is possible to pick out the referent. This also applies to Donnellan's second example quoted above. The sentence about the Republican candicate in 1964, uttered in 1960, is even more about the Republican party than about its candidate. However, it would be incorrect to say that no attention is called at all to whoever will be the Republican candidate. So, even here the definite description M-refers to a certain degree.

These qualifications amount to the view that reference should be taken as a matter of degree. A complete theory of reference should not treat reference as a matter of yes or no, i.e. present or not-present. M-reference at least allows for comparative statements as to its relative strength and preciseness. "Reference in a very weak sense" (Donnellan) may veıy well be weak reference at the same time (as well as vague reference, for that matter).

The conclusion that M-reference (I-reference not excluded) is a matter of degree in some diverse respects is contrary to the way in which reference has been usually discussed. In view of the foregoing discussion it is not quite unexpected, though. For reference has been characterized above as a case of calling attention, and attention can be called with varying degrees of prominence and preciseness.

Now I would like to discuss a distinction made by P. F. Strawson, which, like Donnellan's, deserves to be taken into consideration here. Commenting upon the statement that 'Jones spent the morning at the local swimming-pool', Strawson suggests that there seems to be a difference as to its truth-value, if an existential condition is not satisfied, between the situation that there is a local swimming-pool but no Jones, and the situation that Jones exists but there is no local swimming-pool. In the first situation we would naturally say that the statement has no truth-value, that it is neither true nor false. In the second situation, however, it may seem natural enough to say that the statement is false; for, 'however Jones spent the morning, he did NOT spend it at the local swimming-pool, since there is no such place'. And Strawson goes on to suggest that the latter intuition might be accommodated by allowing the guilty referring expression, 'the local swimming-pool', to be absorbed into the predicate of the sentence, while such a move would not be suitable in case 'Jones' were the guilty one.[19]

As a matter of fact, Strawson does not quite accept this explanation. As he does not want to deny the intuitive difference between the two situations, Strawson sketches another solution, which is a refinement of the provisional explanation. He says that statements have, in a rather vague sense, topics, or centres of interest: the 'things' they are about. Now, if a certain referring expression is used in the sentence, the specification of the topic of the statement may or may not involve mentioning the object which the referring expression was intended to refer to. So we get statements of Type 1 and statements of Type 2. The original example ('Jones spent the morning at the local swimming-pool') would be of Type 1 relative to 'Jones', having as its topic how Jones spent the morning, and of Type 2 relative to 'the local swimming-pool'. This would explain the difference between the two situations as regards I-referential failure.[20]

Without going into further details one implication will be clear: According to Strawson so-called referring expressions may differ as to their role in focussing the hearer's attention. But this difference is not absolute. It is not that some referring expressions (viz. those relative to which the statement in which they occur is of Type 1) focus attention, and the others do not do so at all. The difference, of course, is one of degree; Strawson's own examples and wordings indicate that only a relative distinction can be made. For instance, take the crucial notion of 'topic'. It is only vaguely characterized, and rightly so. For even with regard to such a clear-cut example as the statement about Jones one has to make certain restrictions. It seems untrue that the statement is not about the local swimming-pool AT ALL; it is only far less about the pool than about Jones. Thus it may be said that in Strawson's example 'Jones' M-refers stronger than 'the local swimming-pool', the statement being more about Jones than about the pool.

The necessity of regarding M-reference as a matter of degree could have been argued in other ways than by appealing to different uses of definite descriptions and to the uses of proper names. Other types of expressions and other uses could have served as well. Thus it could be argued, apart from the consideration of expressions of special types, that the statement taken from the *International Herald Tribune* is more about the decision of the Belgian government as to the prices of oil products than about the demands made by oil companies: the essential information is contained in the first half of the sentence. (But of course this depends on context and circumstances.) Moreover, it will be clear that many utterances only weakly direct a hearer's attention to something outside the utterance through being about it. For one thing, also expressions not belonging to the class of definite descriptions used attributively (e.g., verbs and adjectives) may prove to be rather unspecific if we wish to determine what they M-refer to. Further, in making a statement the speaker often assumes the audience to have a certain knowledge, which may allow for only a weak reference in certain contexts.[21] Attention may primarily be focussed on the utterance itself at the expense of the attention directed to the referent, as happens according to Roman Jakobson in the poetic use of language.[22] Moreover, the utterance may be a matter of routine, or it may be mainly an expression of emotion. Cases like these make it plain that the question whether reference occurs is somewhat misleading, unless connected with the question whether the reference, if present at all, is weak or strong, vague or precise.

In this connection it may be useful, however, to consider two further issues somewhat more extensively, viz. the question of implicit reference and the analysis of the not purely referential use of so-called referring expressions occurring in an opaque context.

When reference is spoken about it is mostly presupposed that the reference is explicit. As regards my own characterization of M-reference, I have stated that particular words or word-combinations have to be present for the reference to depend on. This suggests explicitness, indeed; the same is true of my linking M-reference and mentioning.

Nonetheless, in special cases an M-reference, though dependent on certain particular words present in the utterance and essentially connected with their mentioning function, may involve a process of inference. In such a case the reference can be called IMPLICIT. An example would be the following statement: 'The fluent course of this meeting contrasted sharply with what one was used to.' Next to the explicit reference to one meeting and the way it went off, there seems to be an implicit reference to former meetings as well. The former meetings are not explicitly mentioned; nonetheless, one may say that they are implicitly (or at least less explicitly) referred to. And in our newspaper-example one has to infer that it is prices that oil companies wanted to increase.

Generally speaking, implicit reference will be less strong and/or prominent and/or precise than explicit reference.

Let us now turn to the analysis of the not purely referential use of so-called refering expressions. In the literature on this subject there is a tendency to consider occurrences of expressions which are not purely referential, because they are placed in a context which is referentially opaque, as being not referential at all. Witness Quine. In his well-known essay, "Reference and Modality", he says that an occurrence of an expression in a statement is not purely referential if "the statement depends not only on the object but on the form of the name".[23] This still leaves the possibility that the object IS referred to. Soon, however, it becomes evident that Quine argues as if an occurrence which is not purely referential is not referential at all; and he goes on to use 'irreferential' instead of 'not purely referential'.[24] But given some of his own examples this is not very plausible. In 'Gorgione was so-called because of his size' the name of the painter is patently not purely referential: replacement of 'Gorgione' by 'Barbarelli' changes the sentence from true to false. However, to me it seems absurd to say that the name 'Gorgione' has no reference at all to the painter in the sentence quoted. For the sentence is, among other things, about the painter himself. Essentially the same applies to the occurrence of 'Tully' in 'Philip is unaware that Tully denounced Catiline', since in uttering this sentence it would be implicitly stated that Tully denounced Catiline which would mean that the name 'Tully' IS to a certain degree referential. And maybe it even applies to the occurrence of 'Tegucigalpa' (the name of the capital of Honduras) in 'Philip believes that Tegucigalpa is in Nicaragua'. Only a sentence like ' "Cicero" contains six letters' would give a clear-cut example of a not purely referential occurrence which is not referential at all, insofar as Cicero would be the referent.[25]

Contrary to Quine, Leonard Linsky uses the term 'impure reference' or 'non-pure reference' in cases in which there is no purely referential use; he also uses the expression 'to refer impurely'.[26] With a view to my above argument Linsky's use of these expressions is to be welcomed. So also the discussion of not purely referential occurrences leads to the conclusion that reference should not bluntly be treated as a matter of yes or no.[27]

NOTES

1 John Lyons, *Introduction to Theoretical Linguistics*, Cambridge, 1968, 424. See also 404.

2 Lyons even uses 'reference' here too (Lyons, *Introduction*, 430).

3 Whether a certain definite description is used referentially or attributively is, according to Keith S. Donnellan, "a function of the speaker's intentions on a particular

case" (Keith S. Donnellan, "Reference and Definite Descriptions", *The Philosophical Review*, 75, 1966, 297).

4 J. R. Searle, *Speech Acts: An Essay in the Philosophy of Language*, Cambridge, 1970, 28 (my emphasis).

5 Searle, *Speech Acts*, 27, n.l. The remark is about such expressions as 'a man' in 'A man came'; probably it is also meant to apply to 'plural indefinite referring expressions' like 'some men' in 'Some men came'. – I leave out of consideration Russell's view that even definite descriptions and non-logical proper names do not refer to any corresponding object. One important recent publication on this topic is Tyler Burge, "Reference and Proper Names", *The Journal of Philosophy*, 70, 1973, 425-39.

6 W. V. O. Quine, "Reference and Modality", *From a Logical Point of View*, 2nd ed., Harper Torchbooks, 1961, 139-59.

7 See, e.g., L. Linsky, *Referring*, London, 1967, 118-9.

8 See, e.g., P. F. Strawson, "Identifying Reference and Truth-Values" = Strawson, *Logico-Linguistic Papers*, London, 1971, 75-95.

9 See, e.g., Richard Robinson, "The Concept of Knowledge", *Mind*, 80 (1971), 17, where the remark is made that in expressions like 'suddenly he knew' or 'suddenly I knew', as occasionally used by novelists, there is reference to a mental event.

10 Jan Srzednicki, "Reference and Description", *Theoria*, 36, 1970, 127.

11 Jan Srzednicki, "Reference", 138.

12 P. F. Strawson, *Individuals: An Essay in Descriptive Metaphysics*, London, 1959, 146. It is clear that by a term Strawson understands a non-linguistic item (see also pp. 140-1).

13 See, e.g., L. Linsky, *Referring*, 122-3, and Lauri Karttunen, "What do Referential Indices Refer to?", MIT-paper, 1968.

14 See my essays "Metafoor en vergelijking in de literatuur", *Forum der Letteren*, 14, 1973, 121-57, and "Tenor, Vehicle and Reference", *Poetics*, 1975, forthcoming. These essays also contain some remarks on reference of which the present essay is an elaboration.

15 This has been acknowledged by Nelson Goodman in his essay "About" in *Mind*, 70, 1961, 1-23. In such a case Goodman prefers to say that the discourse is 'X-about' (e.g., 'Pickwick-about') rather than that it is about X. See also Michael Hodges, "On 'Being About'", *Mind*, 80, 1971, 1-16.

16 Keith Donnellan, "Reference", 286.

17 Keith Donnellan, "Reference", 282, 293, 297.

18 Keith Donnellan, "Reference", 303.

19 P.F. Strawson, *Logico-Linguistic Papers*, London, 1971, 87-90.

20 P. F. Strawson, *Papers*, 92-95.

21 Such that it may even be unclear whether there is reference at all. In connection herewith see also Strawson's assertion "that the spheres of (*a*) what a statement addressed to an audience is ABOUT and (*b*) what, in the making of that statement, the audience is assumed to have some knowledge of already, are spheres that will often, and naturally, overlap" (Strawson, *Papers*, 93).

22 R. Jakobson, "Linguistics and Poetics", *Style in Language*, ed. by Thomas A. Sebeok, Cambridge, Mass., 1960, 350-77.

23 W. V. O. Quine, *From a Logical Point of View*, 140.

24 Quine, *From a Logical Point of View*, 141 (ll. 1-2) and 144.

25 For these examples, see Quine, *From a Logical Point of View*, 139-142. Quine himself implicitly acknowledges that by using the phrase 'X is unaware that *p*' one implicitly states that *p* is true (147). Moreover, he says that the quoted sentence about Philip's unawareness (as to Tully and Catiline) "cannot be considered SIMPLY as affirming a relation between three persons" (142; my emphasis), which suggests that (among other things) it does at the least affirm such a relation.

[26] L. Linsky, *Referring*, ch. 7, esp. 102, 104, 106, 108n.

[27] The essays by Donnellan and by Strawson, quoted respectively in notes 3, 16, 17, 18 and in notes 8, 19, 20, 21, as well as the last chapter of Linsky's book *Referring* which is referred to in notes 7 and 13, can also be found in *Semantics: An Interdisciplinary Reader in Philosophy, Linguistics and Psychology*, ed. by D. D. Steinberg and L. A. Jakobovits, Cambridge, 1971, 76-114. See also the review article by P. A. M. Seuren in *Neophilologus*, 57, 1973, esp. 205-10.

IDÉOLOGIE ET SÉMIOLOGIE CHEZ LOCKE ET CONDILLAC: LA QUESTION DE L'AUTONOMIE DU LANGAGE DEVANT LA PENSÉE

HERMAN PARRET

CONNAISSANCE DES IDÉES ET SCIENCE DES SIGNES

On a souvent cité le dernier chapitre de l'*Essai concernant l'entendement humain* où Locke divise les sciences en trois espèces: la *physique* ou "la connaissance des choses comme elles sont dans leur propre existence, dans leurs constitutions, propriétés et opérations", la *pratique* qui "enseigne les moyens de bien appliquer nos propres puissances et actions pour obtenir des choses bonnes et utiles", et la *sémiotique* ou "la science des signes".[1] Cette sémiotique est une *critique* puisqu'elle circonscrit le domaine de l'usage *légitime* des signes; et puisque les mots font la classe la plus ordinaire des signes, la sémiotique peut être appelée également une *logique* ("*logikè* du mot *logos* qui signifie *parole*", ajoute Locke). Une sémiotique se justifie pleinement puisqu'elle a comme objet les grands instruments de la connaissance; la double fonction des signes, l'enregistrement des pensées dans la mémoire et l'entre-communication des pensées, en fait le moyen indispensable de la connaissance. La spécificité de la sémiotique devant la philosophie naturelle (ou 'physique') et la morale (ou 'pratique') découle de la spécificité de son objet qui, à l'encontre des deux autres branches, n'est pas substantiel. Les signes ne sont pas des substances à connaître mais des *moyens* de connaissance, et c'est ainsi que, pour Locke, les *idées et* les *mots* forment ensemble le domaine sémiotique: les idées sont les *signes* des choses et les mots les *signes* des idées. Quand Destutt de Tracy invente le lexème *idéologie*,[2] plus d'un siècle après la parution de l'*Essai*, l'idée et le mot n'auront plus, pour lui, le même statut épistémologique appartenant en fait à deux sciences autonomes, l'idéologie d'une part et la grammaire de l'autre[3]: l'idéologie désigne la science des idées proprement dites, qui sont *un des moyens* de connaître tandis que la grammaire est la science des signes, ce qui signifie pour Tracy qu'elle est la *continuation* de la science des idées sans pouvoir être identifiée avec elle.[4] On devine le rôle capital de la doctrine condillacienne dans ce fléchissement: la 'nouvelle métaphysique' de Condillac, bien que tributaire de l'enseignement de Locke, distingue clairement la fonction représentative de l'idée et la fonction analytico-méthodique du signe, spécialement du système sémiotique priviligié qu'est le langage. Le signe n'est pas le versant extérieur et discret de l'idée, et c'est bien sur ce point que Condillac, ce 'Locke français', s'écarte de son maître. L'ébranlement et la subtilisation de l'ancienne sémiotique englobante (lockienne) sont dûs à la défense vigoureuse chez Condillac, de l'autonomie des systèmes de signes et de la fonctionnalité constitutive des signes dans le déploiement des opérations de l'âme. Cette thèse, qui rappelle singulièrement certaines positions des plus contemporaines, comporte deux présuppositions dont la compatibilité devra être interrogée: signifier et parler, c'est *sentir*; signifier et parler, c'est *calculer*. Le sensualisme de Condillac s'inscrit, bien sûr, dans la longue tradition empiriste inaugurée par Locke; son algébrisme, par contre, indique une rupture et un déplacement à l'intérieur de cet empirisme. Nous nous proposons ici d'étudier le lieu spécifique de la doctrine condillacienne en la confrontant essentiellement avec la position de Locke, surtout en ce qui concerne le rapport du signe à l'idée, de la sémiologie à l'idéologie.

Il est vrai que des traits communs caractérisent toute la pensée du langage aux 17e et 18e siècles: la *Grammaire générale*, des Cartésiens aux Idéologues, ne voit le langage que dans son *fonctionnement* et non pas dans son existence. L'archéologie, proposée par Foucault,[5] démontre le clivage entre la Renaissance et l'âge classique et l'homogénéité des options fondamentales de la *Grammaire de Port-Royal* à la *Grammaire* de Tracy. Le langage *fonctionne* comme *critique* – comme *analyse* et *méthode*, dirait Condillac; la raison en est que c'est le rôle *représentatif* du langage qui est retenu en priorité (de sorte que l'on doit poser au langage la question de la vérité, de sa valeur expressive), la conséquence, que le langage est essentiellement *discursivité*, disposition de signes selon un ordre linéaire. La représentativité et la discursivité du langage marquent la couche archéologique inaugurée par les grammairiens cartésiens et portée à l'apogée dans l'œuvre de Condillac et de ses commentateurs.[6] Si Chomsky a eu 'l'impertinence', pour employer le terme de certains historiens des théories linguistiques, d'incorporer dans la 'linguistique cartésienne' des empiristes lockiens comme Dumarsais, c'est que d'importantes présuppositions communes aux empiristes et aux rationalistes, comme celles décrites dans l'archéologie de Foucault, témoignent d'une profonde solidarité epistémologique.[7] Mais même si l'on admet que le champ épistémologique de la *Grammaire générale* est homogène et qu'on y trouve une délimitation jamais transgressée du domaine linguistique (le langage dans son rôle représentatif, comme discursivité), deux figures théorématiques se dégageront d'emblée. Leur confrontation ne concernera pas l'innéisme (on verra que Condillac démontre l'innéité du langage en s'opposant à l'innéité des idées) ni la nature de l'esprit ou des facultés de l'âme, mais bien le *type de relation* du langage (des mots, des signes) à la pensée. La linguistique cartésienne et la linguistique condillacienne incarnent ces deux figures de l'*épistèmè* classique.[8] Il ne s'agit pas de cerner cette opposition selon que le principe de connaissance soit posé tantôt dans la sensation tantôt dans la raison, comme on le fait traditionnellement dans les épistémologies rudimentaires mais bien selon que le langage soit considéré tantôt comme l'*expression* de la pensée tantôt comme son *déploiement*. Que le langage soit *expression* ou *articulation*,[9] voilà les deux possibilités théorématiques de l'épistèmè de la représentation et de la discursivité. Les théoriciens cartésiens prônent l'indépendance des sphères de la pensée et du langage, et les opérations de l'esprit s'y déroulent en dehors de toute incarnation linguistique. Le grammatical *reflète*, *exprime* le logique: l'expression linguistique n'est jamais constitutive de la pensée, elle est accidentelle, elle affaiblit, par des transformations déformantes, les qualités logiques sous-jacentes. La connaissance ne s'*articule* pas dans et par le langage; la mise en ordre des parties du discours, la structure grammaticale n'est pas autoconsistente puisqu'elle n'est que le versant sensible de 'l'art de raisonner'. L'entreprise condillacienne, exposée d'abord dans l'*Essai sur l'origine des connaissances humaines* en 1746, nuancée et retravaillée dans la *Grammaire* (1775) et surtout dans la *Logique* (1780), achevée dans *La langue des calculs* posthume (éditée en 1798), révolue radicalement le schéma cartésien.[10] Bien que Condillac admette l'existence de la pensée discursive, 'l'*art* de penser' comme ensemble d'opérations intellectuelles, comme créativité de l'esprit, comme progrès de la connaissance, n'est possible que par le déploiement ou l'articulation de la pensée dans et par le langage. Que 'l'art de penser' se réduit à une langue bien faite,[11] que les sciences ne sont que des langues bien faites, ne sera que la conséquence radicale du rôle constitutif que joue le langage dans la formation de la nature humaine, de la culture et de la société. En s'écartant du modèle cartésien, Condillac se rapproche davantage du relativisme humboldtien. Mais il convient de noter que ce déplacement n'est pas dû à Locke qui, comme on le verra, n'accorde nulle part au langage ce pouvoir d'*articuler* de la pensée.

Le lieu original de la philosophie condillacienne se conquiert donc sur deux fronts. Sa 'nouvelle métaphysique' qui se veut nette et précise comme la géométrie et qui veut thématiser les bornes mêmes qui lui sont marquées, s'oppose bien à la tradition cartésienne où le doute méthodique est si vite écarté par de la spéculation excessive. Toute la machinerie lockienne est employée par Condillac contre le paradigme cartésien, mais Locke lui-même, le seul pourtant qui s'est borné à l'étude de l'esprit humain, est mis en cause "parce qu'il a passé trop légèrement sur l'origine de nos connaissances"[12] et surtout parce qu'il n'a pas entrevu "que l'usage des signes est le principe qui développe le germe de toutes nos idées".[13] L'originalité de Condillac tient ainsi à son *générativisme* (il faut expliquer la *génération* des opérations de l'âme, l'enchaînement et l'interpénétration des facultés de l'âme) et à sa *sémiologie* constitutive (le sémiotique est le levier du logique). Quand Condillac se croit obligé de se faire "un nouveau langage" pour échapper "au grand chaos" de l'ancienne métaphysique, à ses mystères et ses hypostases,[14] c'est qu'il se propose de rendre compte de l'*engendrement* des opérations de l'âme et de sa faculté discursive. Ce dynamisme génératif concerne aussi bien le langage lui-même du philosophe-grammairien que le langage-objet reconstruit par la nouvelle science. Ce générativisme qui fait de la philosophie condillacienne une véritable *pratique* linguistique modulant son propre objet comme un univers *sémiotiquement articulé*, ne s'inscrit ni dans le cadre des orientations lockiennes ni, bien sûr, dans la tradition cartésienne. La complexité et la cohérence de la nouvelle science ne cesseront d'étonner. Cette nouvelle science est ni plus ni moins une philosophie du langage, étant elle même un travail dans et par le langage, un travail engendrant aussi bien le *discours* philosophique que son objet qu'est la puissance *articulatoire* des signes et des ensembles de signes. Il n'est pourtant pas facile de pointer exactement le lieu théorématique de l'œuvre de Condillac. La linguistique condillacienne est solidaire de l'*épistèmè* classique, au sens de Foucault, puisqu'elle présuppose la représentativité et la discursivité du phénomène linguistique; elle est solidaire du projet lockien en ce qu'elle tend à la destruction du chaos spéculatif et qu'elle essaie de contrôler le *principe* de la connaissance; mais elle est hautement originale *comme sémiologie* et par sa capacité *générative* en ce qu'elle engendre aussi bien son propre discours que son objet de connaissance, le rapport analytique du langage à la pensée.

LE BESOIN NATUREL ET LE CALCUL ANALOGIQUE

Discourir, c'est sentir et/ou calculer; son principe est double – le sensualisme et l'algébrisme se révèlent, tout le long de l'œuvre de Condillac, concurrents. Le langage est *naturel*, irréfléchi et spontané mais il est en même temps *construit*, inventé méthodiquement; le langage reproduit l'immensité du besoin naturel des hommes mais il est aussi la caractéristique universelle savamment chiffrée. Seul le langage rend possible cette étrange coexistence du sentir et du calculer; c'est donc le langage qui subvertit les épistémologies trop rudimentaires.

Condillac ne dément jamais que "la perception ou l'impression occasionnée dans l'âme par l'action des sens, est la première opération de l'entendement" et qu'"ainsi le premier et le moindre degré de connaissance, c'est d'apercevoir".[15] La génération des facultés et des opérations de l'âme s'appuie sur le fond inamovible des sensations. Condillac publie, quelques années après l'*Essai*, son *Traité des sensations*[16] où l'adage que "dans l'ordre naturel tout vient des sensations"[17] est concrétisé par la célèbre histoire de la statue, "organisée intérieurement comme nous et animée d'un esprit privé de toute espèce d'idées",[18] qui conquiert progressivement toutes les connaissances dès que les sens s'opérationalisent. La perception, la conscience, l'attention, la réminiscence, voilà des opérations qui ne présupposent que la présence de l'objet et son impression dans l'âme. Mais même la *Logique*, rédigée plus de vingt ans plus tard, reprend le même adage, insistant davantage sur le fait que la logique est 'naturelle' dans son commencement: nous devons le progrès de la logique aux premières leçons que la nature nous a données.[19] Le naturel qui se manifeste dans la logique est double: il est dans les deux aspects *aprioriques* de toute connaissance, la relation des sens (et de ses impressions) aux objets du monde, et la faculté de sentir de notre âme qui déploie un art qui a toujours déjà commencé avant qu'on apprenne, avant qu'on en soit conscient. On est donc né "avec sa nature": "c'est cette nature qui commence; et elle commence toujours bien, parce qu'elle commence seule",[20] et "la nature, c'est nos *facultés déterminées par nos besoins*: car les besoins et les facultés sont proprement ce que nous nommons la nature".[21] Que la philosophie du langage, "cette nouvelle et bonne métaphysique", soit une philosophie du désir et du besoin, signifie que le langage est *inné*, qu'il y a déjà un langage d'avant le langage sémiotiquement chiffré. Ce langage-là est thématisé par Condillac sous le terme de 'langage d'action'. Si on accorde tout le poids à l'affirmation condillacienne selon laquelle 'l'action' (les gestes, les mouvements du visage et du corps, les 'accents inarticulés') serait un langage, il faudrait admettre le paradoxe inconfortable que non seulement le *langage* est naturel mais également que la *nature*, dans sa détermination par les besoins, est essentiellement linguistique. C'est bien dans ce sens-là que la philosophie condillacienne du langage n'est pas uniquement une épistémologie sémiologique (brouillant les positions trop faciles de l'axe rationalisme-empirisme) mais qu'elle est, en plus, une 'nouvelle métaphysique'.

Dès lors, il ne faut plus s'étonner que la *Grammaire* débute sa première partie *De l'analyse du discours* par un chapitre *Du langage d'action*[22] et que l'*Essai* fait l'historique de l'origine et des progrès du langage selon le même schéma: d'abord le langage d'action (gestes et danse), ensuite la prosodie, la déclamation, la musique, la poésie qui en conservent le caractère et ne peuvent être imaginées que sur le modèle du langage d'action,[23] et enfin le langage des sons articulés, le plus perfectionné et le plus commode de tous. Cette génération est fondée sur la nature des choses[24], elle échappe au pouvoir créateur des humains: dire que "les langues sont l'ouvrage de la nature" signifie pour Condillac "qu'elles se sont formées, pour ainsi dire, sans nous, et qu'en y travaillant, nous n'avons fait qu'obéir servilement à notre manière de voir et de sentir"[25]; il n'arrive jamais aux hommes de dire *faisons une langue* puisqu'il est naturel que les hommes sentent le *besoin* du langage et de son progrès vers plus d'arbitrarité. Que "les langues, dans l'origine, n'étaient qu'un *supplément* au langage d'action"[26] déterminera la structure même de la grammaire et l'hiérarchie de ses fonctions. La grammaire condillacienne est avant tout, comme le décrit brillamment Foucault,[27] une théorie de la nomination généralisée: le langage est un geste qui désigne et l'origine du langage est dans son rôle de désignation première. Puisque le langage d'action est parlé par le corps, reliant par une genèse le langage à la nature, puisque le langage est le *supplément* du corps, toutes les parties du discours seront des désignations, des *noms*. Tous les mots, même ceux dont on ne perçoit que laborieusement le contenu significatif, comme les prépositions, sont des noms. Comme supplément du corps, le langage est le besoin de représenter les existences que l'on *sent* présentes, en les désignant. Parler, c'est sentir.

Tous les mots sont des noms, excepté un seul. C'est ici que commence le *calcul* linguistique. Le mot *être* (tous les verbes se décomposent en deux parties: *être* plus un adjectif) ne désigne rien: il affirme le rapport des noms en articulant des conglomérats de noms sous la forme de *propositions*. *Etre*, écrit Foucault, est la condition indispensable à tout discours, *être* est le seuil du langage.[28] Ce pouvoir de *liaison* qu'a le langage grâce au travail du mot *être* dans son sein, libère le grammatical de la fonction naturelle de nomination: la syntaxe est autonome parce qu'il y a le jeu, immanent au langage, de l'affirmation ou de l'abnégation de liaison. Ce serait mal interpréter le champ épistémologique de l'intuition condillacienne que de projeter l'autonomie du langage à l'égard des objets désignés, dans l'opération de généralisation ou d'abstraction, ou dans la complexion des idées, même si ces idées sont des archétypes (des idées sans modèle)[29]; la nomination généralisante ainsi que archétypique est tributaire du fond sensualiste et le langage y reste inébranlablement orienté par le besoin naturel. Condillac s'explique sans ambiguité dans sa *Logique* où il s'efforce de prouver que les idées abstraites ne sont que des dénominations: "c'est parce que les idées que nous nommons abstraites cessent de tomber sous les sens, nous croirons qu'elles n'en viennent pas; et, parce qu'alors nous ne verrons pas ce qu'elles peuvent avoir de commun avec nos sensations, nous nous imaginerons qu'elles sont quelque autre chose".[30] Cette erreur, qui compromet bien des épistémologies 'spéculatives', et tout d'abord la cartésienne, détruit la spécificité immanente des systèmes d'expression, c'est-à-dire l'aspect algébrique de leur construction.

Les langues sont-elles *calculées*? La *Langue des calculs*, œuvre inachevée de Condillac et publiée après sa mort, est sous-jacente au projet entier se manifestant, le long du parcours de ses écrits, de plus en plus ouvertement. Pourtant, le principe *naturel* n'est pas trahi: la langue des calculs dans ses commencements est corporelle puisque le premier stade dans la génération des langues algébriques est celui du calcul avec les doigts; et Condillac insiste que tout calcul qui n'est pas engendré à partir de de commencement, ne sera qu'une langue mal faite. Mais où se situe alors le déplacement, l'écart qui fait que la langue ne saurait être identifiée à son origine, à son principe naturel? Où se situe l'*invention* et l'*imagination*, quel est le *second* principe qui domine la créativité méthodique du langage? C'est bien l'*analogie* et "... la langue des calculs est celle où l'analogie se montre davantage. C'est à cela qu'elle doit sa richesse, je veux dire toutes ses expressions, toutes ses méthodes, toutes ses découvertes ...."[31] Il faudra revenir plus tard sur ce concept absolument central d'*analogie* chez Condillac[32] et il suffit ici d'indiquer que c'est exactement la *théorie de la proposition et du verbe être*, composante priviligiée de la grammaire, cette théorie statuant la discursivité du phénomène linguistique, qui présuppose le travail du calcul analogique. La *liaison* des mots (et des idées), rendue possible dans et par la proposition et donc grâce à la puissance originale de *être*, ne saurait être comprise que par son *double* principe: le besoin naturel et le calcul analogique. Ceci constitue, on ne se doute pas, le noeud théorématique génial mais paradoxal de la pensée du langage chez Condillac.

On suit donc Foucault lorsqu'il présume, en analysant la conception du langage de l'*épistèmè* classique, que "la genèse du langage à partir du langage d'action échappe entièrement à l'alternative entre l'imitation naturelle et la convention arbitraire".[33] La désignation et la proposition ne s'opposent qu'à première vue comme l'imitation *contraignante* des existences et l'artifice *arbitraire* des calculs. Il devrait être clair maintenant que cette contrainte et cet arbitraire perdent toute leur pureté – pour se rejoindre, en fin de compte, comme deux 'aspects' du même principe (double, il est vrai, si le principe est déployé en théorème) – puisque, d'une part, l'imitation y est une représentation *discursive* ou, on le verra tout de suite, *analytique* des 'présences' relevées dans et par la sensation, tandis que, d'autre part, la convention algébrique n'y est pas du tout arbitrairement mais *analogiquement* créée. Le langage réalise donc le paradoxe. Comme la nature (le besoin de gesticulation, du cri, de la danse) est constitutive du langage conventionnel des sons, l'inverse est vrai aussi. La 'nouvelle métaphysique' lance une provocation dont les effets subversifs se font sentir de plus en plus: la nature elle-même est langage, convention, signe. C'est dire que la contrainte (naturelle) et l'arbitraire (conventionnel) se définissent mutuellement et ne se présentent plus sous forme d'alternative. Certes, le langage (naturel, c'est-à-dire le langage d'action), pour Condillac, est *discours*, et l'arbitraire est *analogique*. Il est intéressant de suivre l'évolution terminologique à cet égard chez Condillac. Il oppose dans l'*Essai* le 'rapport arbitraire' au 'rapport naturel' et fait, dans un chapitre très important consacré à l'usage des signes, de l'arbitrarité du langage (comme système de signes) le critère distinctif du véritable langage analytico-méthodique.[34] On assiste dans la *Grammaire* à un revirement intéressant développant une plus grande cohérence de la pensée condillacienne du langage dans le sens que nous avons préconisé ici: Condillac y évite le terme 'arbitraire' en faveur de '*artificiel*' pour mieux récupérer ce qu'il en est de la nature du calcul analogique. Il explique: "Remarquez bien que je dis de *signes artificiels* et que je ne dis pas de *signes arbitraires*: car il ne faudrait pas confondre ces deux choses. En effet, qu'est-ce que des signes arbitraires? Des signes choisies sans raison et par caprice. Ils ne seraient donc pas entendus. Au contraire, des signes artificiels sont des signes dont le choix est *fondé en raison*: ils doivent être imaginés avec tel art que l'intelligence en soit préparée par les signes qui sont connus... Alors vous aurez une suite de signes qui ne seront dans le vrai qu'un signe modifié différemment. Les derniers, par conséquent, *ressemblent* aux premiers; et c'est cette ressemblance qui en facilitera l'intelligence. On la nomme *analogie*. Vous voyez que l'*analogie* qui nous fait la loi ne *nous permet pas* de choisir les signes au hasard et *arbitrairement*" (nous soulignons).[35]

Il faudrait recourir à l'admirable relecture de Condillac que Derrida a réalisée dans *L'archéologie du frivole*, pour se rendre compte de l'équilibre difficile et du risque permanent chez Condillac de "donner trop" ou de "donner trop peu aux signes", c'est-à-dire à l'arbitrarité, à la liberté de l'algèbre.[36] Bien que Condillac n'affirme nulle part que le langage (le signe) est premier dans l'expérience en général, il généralise le travail du sémiologique dans tout le domaine du grammatical; bien que le langage n'est jamais posé explicitement au commencement (cf. le *Traité des sensations*), il est toujours déjà dans la sensation, confusément et obscurément, dès qu'elle juge et connaît. Le regret, chez Condillac, d'avoir peut-être "trop donné aux signes" et la peur de dissoudre le paradoxe tout entier en l'homogénéisant, sont à l'origine de la critique de l'arbitrarité sémiologique, à partir de la *Grammaire*. Il est vrai que cette critique *renforce* le paradoxe: le sémiologique, étant enfin défini comme l'*analogique*, et l'illusion libertaire de la pseudo-créativité *ex nihilo* étant dissoute, Condillac peut installer le *double* principe comme un paradoxe: le langage *est* besoin naturel et calcul analogique. La structure du paradoxe n'est *pas dialectique* – il faut penser le rapport des deux termes comme une structure de *supplémentarité* ou de *remarque*: le calcul *supplée* au besoin, ce qui ne signifie pas que le calcul ne soit pas fondé dans le besoin ni que le besoin, en fin de compte, ne soit calculé.

LE TRAVAIL SÉMIOLOGIQUE ET LE LANGAGE ANALYTICO-MÉTHODIQUE

"Il arrive ... que l'*analyse* est, de toutes les opérations, celle dont on connaît le moins l'usage. Combien d'hommes chez qui elle n'a jamais eu lieu! ... De là le chaos où se trouvent les sciences abstraites: chaos que les philosophes n'ont jamais pu débrouiller, parce qu'aucun d'eux n'en a connu la première cause."[37] Si les sciences sont des langues bien faites, c'est que les langues bien faites *articulent* la pensée selon le double principe du besoin naturel et du calcul analogique. On peut considérer les langues comme autant de méthodes analytiques. Cette fonction analytico-méthodique du langage précède en importance sa fonction communicative; elle présuppose la représentativité et la discursivité du phénomène linguistique, qui requièrent pourtant – et ceci est l'originalité de la linguistique condillacienne – la nouvelle connotation *sémiologique*: c'est en élaborant la notion de *signe* que le rapport articulatoire du langage à la pensée puisse être thématisé adéquatement. "Le signe artificiel nous est nécessaire pour démêler dans nos sensations toutes les opérations de notre âme",[38] ce qui indique, bien sûr, l'entrelacement du langage et des sensations dès l'origine, dans la nature des 'présences' et dans notre faculté de sentir. Mais, en plus, "le premier objet du langage est d'analyser la pensée. En effet nous ne pouvons montrer, successivement aux autres, les idées qui co-existent dans notre esprit, qu'autant que nous savons nous les montrer successivement à nous-mêmes; c'est-à-dire que nous ne savons parler aux autres qu'autant que nous savons nous parler. On se tromperait, par conséquent, si l'on croyait que les langues ne nous sont utiles que pour nous communiquer mutuellement nos pensées."[39] Tout langage (communicatif) est d'abord un langage *intérieur*; c'est d'abord au creux de soi-même que l'on analyse les opérations de l'âme et les collections d'idées. Aussi longtemps que l'esprit est comme l'oeil, qu'il embrasse simultanément des multitudes confuses, il n'y aura pas de véritable connaissance[40]; de même qu'il n'y aura pas de langage, aussi longtemps que les collections d'idées ne seront pas décomposées *dans un ordre successif*. La méthode analytique est 'naturelle', elle ne doit être inventée par les philosophes: voilà pourquoi le langage est *inné*. "Analyser, c'est décomposer, comparer et saisir les rapports",[41] et c'est la manière dont on procède spontanément en parlant. Pour mettre en œuvre la méthode analytique en soi-même, il faut se défaire de toutes les spéculations parasitaires qu'autant de siècles d''ancienne métaphysique' ont accumulées: la philosophie sémiologiquement orientée prône le discours naturel, le désir inné du calcul, le bon sens *méthodique*. Le méthode, pour Condillac, n'est pas le *doute* mais le *discours naturel*, la langue bien faite. La seconde partie de l'*Essai* s'intitule *Du langage et de la méthode*, et le livre se termine par une critique féroce de Descartes,[42] qui a pu donner la préférence à la synthèse parce qu'il n'a pas entrevu la fonction analytico-méthodique du langage et son pouvoir constitutif pour 'la recherche de la vérité'.

"Etudier la grammaire, c'est étudier les méthodes que les hommes ont suivies dans l'analyse de la pensée"; "la *Grammaire générale* enseigne les principes que cette méthode (analytique) prescrit à toutes les langues."[43] La *Grammaire générale*, si on reprend la définition de Foucault, est "l'étude de l'ordre verbal dans son rapport à la simultanéité qu'elle a pour charge de représenter"[44]; son objet n'est donc ni la pensée ni la langue, mais le rapport articulatoire du langage à la pensée, c'est-à-dire le *discours* comme suite de signes verbaux représentant (méthodiquement, analytiquement) la simultanéité des idées. L'ordre *linéaire* des signes 'représente', analyse l'ordre *simultané* des idées. Dès que la pensée devient *discursive*, les idées se déroulent en propositions, qui sont, pour Condillac, des unités de l'*énonciation* de la pensée en non plus de la pensée linguistiquement désincarnée. Que le langage est l'analyse de la pensée signifie que l'énonciation introduit le temps (la successivité) dans l'espace (la simultanéité): l'ordre spatial dès qu'il est analysé, devient l'ordre temporel. Cette transition de l'ordre *pensé* à l'ordre *énoncé* est provoquée par la force même du calcul linguistique émanant de la réflexion et de l'imagination, c'est-à-dire par le pouvoir des signes *artificiels*. Que la *Grammaire générale* est plus une philosophie qu'une linguistique découle du fait qu'elle étudie la fonction analytico-méthodique du langage (le rapport articulatoire du langage à la pensée) et que la fonction communicative, beaucoup plus pertinente si l'on aborde le langage dans sa positivité, est considérée comme périphérique (chez Condillac, bien sûr, et non pas chez Locke comme on le verra). Il est sans doute dangereux de qualifier le langage comme *autonome* dans la perspective de la *Grammaire générale*, puisque le langage n'est jamais, pour les classiques, autoconsistent et clos sur lui-même: *comme discours* il *représente* le savoir. L'essence du langage étant dans sa puissance analytico-méthodique, il y aura toujours entrecroisement et appartenance réciproque du savoir et du langage. Le logique et le grammatical ne sont que deux aspects d'une même relation, celle que le langage analytico-méthodique réalise avec la pensée: il n'y a pas de savoir en dehors du langage et si la grammaire est normative et prescriptive, c'est qu'il faut éviter les erreurs dans la recherche de la vérité, au niveau des représentations discursives – les règles de l'art de raisonner se concrétisent dans les langues bien faites. Si le savoir aspire à l'universalité, c'est par l'intermédiaire du langage que le rapport à l'universel doit être projeté: le savoir universel, pour Condillac, est un savoir *encyclopédique* et l'Encyclopédie est le discours de la totalité du pensable. Entrecroisé avec le savoir, matérialisant l'universalité logique dans l'Encyclopédie, le langage se rapporte, dans son essence, *au temps*. Non pas que la *Grammaire générale* juge que les langues sont prises par l'histoire et sont ainsi continuellement transformées de l'extérieur, mais bien plutôt que "le temps est pour le langage son mode *intérieur* d'analyse – ce n'est pas son lieu de naissance"[45]; l'ordre de la successivité du langage analytico-méthodique n'est autre que la temporalité discursive. Il devient clair, dès lors, que, à l'intérieur de l'*épistèmè* classique, le paradigme condillacien conquiert son originalité si l'on considère comment la relation du langage au savoir, à l'universalité et au temps y est thématisée.

Les tentatives de restauration du paradigme cartésien n'ont pas manqué; c'est ainsi que Maine de Biran, en accusant Condillac d'avoir "trop donné aux signes" (ce que Condillac lui-même a pensé à certains moments de sa vie), n'a pas failli d'indiquer les "faiblesses" et les "contradictions" de l'œuvre de Condillac, en proclamant le retour à la primauté du logique sur le sémiologique, au temps extérieur au langage, à l'indépendance de la pensée et du savoir. Ses *Notes sur l'influence des signes*[46] comportent une critique passionnée de la 'nouvelle métaphysique' condillacienne: la double tendance qui caractérise le projet condillacien, le sensualisme et l'algébrisme, est vue par Biran comme épistémologiquement contradictoire et incohérente; il y aurait en Condillac "deux systèmes de philosophie tout à fait différents", l'un menant au psychologisme sensualiste, l'autre à l'artificialisme algébriste. Nous avons soutenu plus haut que ce paradoxe dans l'œuvre de Condillac ne peut être dialectisé et qu'il faut penser cette apparente 'contradiction' selon la structure du supplément ou de la remarque. Que Biran est incapable de penser cette structure en ce qu'elle est épistémologiquement inédite et révolutionnaire, tient à son refus d'admettre toute fonction représentative du langage qui ne serait pas *expressive*. Le détail de ses notes critiques concerne bien le rapport articulatoire du signe à l'idée, et surtout la valeur, constitutive pour la pensée et la connaissance, du signe *artificiel*. Biran admettrait bien une 'sémiologie' à *simple* principe, ce qui réduirait tout signe tantôt au signe *naturel* exprimant le fond obscur des passions, des sentiments et des besoins communicatifs, tantôt au signe *arbitraire* exprimant la créativité inconditionnée et menant, en fin de compte, à la construction idéale d'une caractéristique universelle. Si Biran passe à côté de la spécificité de l'entreprise condillacienne, c'est qu'il n'admet pas la possibilité épistémologique d'une entité *à double principe*. Il faut bien délimiter selon Biran les domaines 'à principe différent' et, entre autre, ce qui appartient au sentiment, d'une part, et au calcul, de l'autre: la morale n'est pas l'algèbre, et il n'y a pas, pour Biran, de réseau identique (représentatif et discursif) de signes qui engendre les deux à la fois. C'est que la morale est inscrite dans l'âme, elle est 'simplement' naturelle et son 'articulation' serait déformante et dangereuse; l'algèbre, par contre, – et la caractéristique universelle qui en est le prototype – n'est niée par aucune 'présence' et elle se développe arbitrairement dans une sphère de liberté désincarnée. La dichotomisation biranienne est, bien sûr, sérieusement dupe de la très classique épistémologie bipolarisée. Et, comme nous avons déjà suggéré plusieurs fois, l'œuvre de Condillac subvertit l'ancienne catégorisation en ce que l'*analogie*, l'*invention*, le *génie* – la *sémiologie* même – ne sauraient être polarisés sur l'axe du sensualisme à l'algébrisme, de l'empirisme au rationalisme, du naturalisme à l'artificialisme.

La perspective générativiste chez Condillac favorise l'idée de *continuité* et d'imbrication des différents stades dans le progrès du langage. Du langage d'action aux "langues formées et perfectionnées",[47] du signe naturel au signe artificiel, il y a progrès continu. "Les langues, dans l'origine, n'étaient qu'un *supplément* au langage d'action"[48] avant de faire de nouveaux progrès menant à la dénomination généralisée et ensuite à la proposition. Il y a bien chez Condillac une téléologie et c'est la possibilité du signe arbitraire qui commande la totalité du progrès.[49] Mais c'est bien là que surgit le regret et l'inquiétude. Condillac voudrait pouvoir thématiser le seuil, la rupture, et c'est pourquoi il accuse lui-même, à partir de la *Grammaire*, l'arbitrarité du sémiologique. Il tend a démontrer que le signe *à double principe* est exemplaire du sémiologique, que la langage 'formé et perfectionné' est la totalité finalisée de tout langage. C'est démontrer toutefois que le tout est dans les parties, la fin, dans les stades successifs, le signe, dans le besoin, le langage, dans la nature; le projet condillacien ne serait alors que l'hallucinante métaphore de l'*identité*. Derrida déduit ainsi que toute philosophie *du langage* – et l'entreprise condillacienne en est une figure priviligiée – est, somme toute, une philosophie *du désir* (de l'identité).[50] Le langage *comme travail* analytico-méthodique, est désir de l'identité, la vraie, celle qui incorpore son seuil intérieur, son supplément. Cette identité (désirée, il va de soi – donc, jamais là) défie le génie – et sa faculté d'invention.

LE GÉNIE ET SA FACULTÉ D'INVENTION

Bien que les considérations concernant l'origine et le progrès du langage ne sont annoncées que pour la seconde partie de l'*Essai* (*Du langage et de la méthode*), le signe et sa fonction analytico-méthodique sont déjà au cœur de la première partie où Condillac présente "l'analyse et la génération des opérations de l'âme".[51] Ces quelques pages, où l'auteur se demande "comment la liaison des idées, formée par l'attention, engendre l'imagination, la contemplation et la mémoire"[52] et affirme "que l'usage des signes est la vraie cause des progrès de l'imagination, de la contemplation et de la mémoire",[53] résument tout le programme condillacien. Quel est l'impact sémiologique sur la génération des opérations de l'âme? L'attention, par son rapport "à notre tempérament, à nos passions, à notre état, ou, pour tout dire en un mot, *à nos besoins*", *cause* la *liaison des idées*: elle forme des espèces de chaînes extensibles autour des idées fondamentales (qui sont les perceptions directes de nos besoins). L'attention, par son implantation dans la nature et par sa dépendance de notre besoin de sentir, possède la force de la *liaison* (des idées aux choses, des idées entre elles). La faculté de lier nos idées produit l'*imagination* (et son incarnation perfectionnée: la *contemplation,* quand la perception ou l'idée se conserve sans interruption même quand l'objet vient de disparaître); dans la *mémoire*, par contre, l'image (la perception) ne doit plus être réveillée pour qu'on ait l'idée présente. Condillac estime donc qu'il y ait une double rupture dans le progrès des opérations de l'âme. Entre l'attention et l'imagination, il faut supposer la *faculté de liaison*, première manifestation du travail sémiologique inchoatif. Entre l'imagination et la mémoire (et ensuite, la réflexion), il faut intercaler la *faculté d'analogie*, seconde manifestation du travail sémiologique plein. L'imagination, d'une part, et la mémoire (ainsi que la réflexion), de l'autre, retirent secours de l'usage des signes. La faculté de liaison se trouve à l'origine des signes *accidentels* "ou les objets que quelques circonstances particulières ont liés avec quelques-unes de nos idées, en sorte qu'ils sont propres à les réveiller" et des signes *naturels* "ou les cris que la nature a établis pour les sentiments de joie, de crainte, de douleur etc.".[54] Avec le seul secours des signes accidentels, l'imagination et la réminiscence pourront avoir déjà quelque exercice. Comme la liaison est l'épiphénomène du besoin, on peut attribuer cette faculté aux animaux, capables ainsi du travail sémiologique inchoatif (signes naturels et accidentels) et donc d'imagination. Condillac définit l'*instinct* comme "une *imagination* qui, à l'occasion d'un objet, réveille les perceptions qui y sont immédiatement liées, et par ce moyen dirige, *sans le secours de la réflexion*, toutes sortes d'animaux"[55]; les animaux ne sont pas de purs automates puisqu'ils possèdent la faculté de liaison, inchoativement sémiologique. Toutefois, la seconde rupture, celle qui instaure la discontinuité entre l'imagination et la mémoire, fait appel au sémiologique pur. "... Aussitôt qu'un homme commence à attacher des idées à des signes qu'il a lui-même choisis, on voit se former en lui la *mémoire*. Celle-ci acquise, il commence à disposer par lui-même de son imagination et à lui donner un nouvel exercice; car, par le secours des signes qu'il peut rappeler à son gré, il réveille, ou du moins il peut réveiller souvent les idées qui y sont liées"[56]; "... ce pouvoir n'a lieu qu'autant que par l'*analyse* des signes que nous avons choisis ...".[57] La mémoire, par quoi l'homme se distingue des animaux, n'est possible que grâce aux signes *artificiels* "ou ceux que nous avons nous-mêmes choisis, et qui n'ont qu'un rapport arbitraire avec nos idées",[58] produits de la faculté d'analogie. Nous voilà, dès lors, dans la sphère du choix, de la liberté et de la domination des dépendances: "aussitôt que la mémoire est formée, et que l'exercice de l'imagination est à notre pouvoir, les signes que celle-là rappelle, et les idées que celle-ci réveille, commencent à retirer l'âme de la dépendance où elle était de tous les objets qui agissaient sur elle".[59] La *réflexion* – suprême opération de l'âme dont l'homme est capable "puisque c'est la réflexion qui distingue, compare, compose, décompose et analyse; ... de là se forment, par une suite naturelle, le jugement, le raisonnement, la conception, et résulte l'entendement"[60] – n'est, dans l'opinion de Condillac, que l'*attention dirigée* de celui qui dispose de la mémoire et donc du libre usage des signes. Tout le progrès des opérations de l'âme – mais également la typologisation de l'univers des idées, comme moyens de connaissance, dans leur dépendance ou indépendance des objets, d'une part, et des signes, de l'autre – manifeste le discontinu créé, d'abord par la puissance naturelle de *liaison* (rendant possible le langage d'action qui est, on le sait maintenant, le langage de l'imagination) et par la puissance calculatoire d'*analogie* (rendant possible le langage 'perfectionné', articulé, qui est le langage de la réflexion). Certes, l'analogie présuppose la liaison comme la mémoire et la réflexion présupposent l'imagination; l'analogie est une liaison dont le pouvoir est *augmenté*, puisqu'elle transcende le naturel et l'accidentel qui déterminent encore ce qui n'était qu'inchoativement sémiologique.

Condillac s'est efforcé, dans *De l'art de raisonner*[61] et dans sa *Logique*,[62] de définir l'analogie comme procédure méthodologique d'acquisition de connaissance. "L'analogie est comme une chaîne qui s'étend depuis les conjectures jusqu'à l'évidence. Ainsi vous voyez qu'il y en a plusieurs degrés, et que tous les raisonnements qu'on fait par analogie n'ont pas la même force. ... On raisonne par analogie lorsqu'on juge du rapport qui doit être entre les effets, par celui qui est entre les causes, ou lorsqu'on juge du rapport qui doit être entre les causes par celui qui est entre les effets."[63] Cette définition, on le voit, est tributaire d'une epistémologie empiriste, construite à partir des catégories de phénomène, d'observation et d'expérience, et appliquée surtout, par Condillac lui-même, aux démonstrations en physique. Son intuition est bien différente dans l'*Essai* quand l'analogie concerne le langage analytico-méthodique, et surtout dans *La langue des calculs*.[64] "La langue des calculs a cet avantage que l'*analogie* n'échappe plus, dès qu'une fois on l'a saisie. Elle est donc la plus parfaite et la plus facile."[65] C'est que, dès qu'il s'agit du calcul du langage (des langues), l'analogie peut être considérée comme une *méthode* non plus de démonstration mais *d'invention*. Condillac suggère, par conséquent, que "la méthode pour *inventer* est ... la même que pour raisonner et *pour parler*"; mais il faut noter encore "que la méthode d'invention n'a pas été créée par des inventeurs ... puisque ce principe (c'est-à-dire l'analogie) a toujours été en nous".[66] Il est faux, affirme Condillac, qu'inventer, c'est trouver quelque chose de nouveau par la force de l'imagination; ce n'est pas l'imagination qui est le partage des hommes de génie, mais l'analyse et donc l'usage d'un langage bien fait. "Qu'est-ce donc que le génie? Un esprit simple qui trouve ce que personne n'a su trouver avant lui. La nature, qui nous met tous dans le chemin des découvertes, semble veiller sur lui pour qu'il ne s'en écarte jamais. Il commence par le commencement, et il va devant lui. Voilà tout son art, art simple, que par cette raison l'on ne lui dérobera pas."[67] *Inventer*, c'est *trouver*; le calcul, prototype de l'invention analogique, est le langage analytico-méthodique par excellence.

Comme "l'analyse et l'imagination sont deux opérations si différentes qu'elles mettent ordinairement des obstacles aux progrès l'une de l'autre",[68] le génie exercera fort l'analyse, en transcendant l'imagination jusque dans la réflexion; il sera comme le géomètre pour qui "l'analogie devient comme un flambeau dont la lumière augmente sans cesse".[69] La faculté *d'invention* par analogie est ce qui distingue le génie du talent: en combinant analogiquement, le génie invente ce qu'on trouve. "Nous ne créons pas proprement des idées, *nous ne faisons que combiner*, par des compositions et des décompositions. ... *L'invention consiste à savoir faire des combinaisons neuves.* Il y en a de deux espèces: le talent et le génie. ... Celui-ci ajoute au talent l'idée d'esprit, *en quelque sorte, créateur.* ... Il donne naissance à une science nouvelle."[70] Le génie ne sait 'créer' ou inventer que selon les possibilités combinatoires du langage. C'est dire que le calcul analogique n'exploite pas la richesse d'une subjectivité inépuisable mais étend, par le travail analytico-méthodique, le champs des combinaisons possibles. Le génie, comme le géomètre, n'exprime pas l'infinité de son âme prédiscursive: l'inventeur génial *est porté* par le langage.[71] Non seulement le besoin naturel et le calcul analogique tendent à l'identité, comme nous avons suggéré à la fin de la section précédente – le *langage* et le *génie*, l'analyste, l'inventeur, celui qui calcule la langue bien faite, se retrouvent identiques. Ici aussi la relation sujet-langage est brouillée par un générativisme qui fait naître les deux pôles en même temps. Dans l'univers condillacien, la distinctivité de *inventer* et *trouver*, exemplairement à l'œuvre quand on hypostasie la soi-disante 'créativité linguistique' (entre autre, 'cartésienne'), disparaît dans l'identité qui n'est que *force* et *désir*.

LA *SEMEIOTIKÈ* LOCKIENNE ET L'ÉCART CONDILLACIEN

Bien que Condillac cite régulièrement, dans l'*Essai* et ailleurs, l'entreprise de Locke comme un modèle, il estime qu'il faut la compléter en donnant plus de substance à la *semeiotikè* (pour la distinguer d'une idéologie purement logique), en rendant la puissance du sémiotique plus constitutive. Locke explique que ce n'est que secondairement qu'il a examiné l'influence des signes sur nos idées: "J'avoue donc que, lorsque je commençai cet ouvrage, et longtemps après, il ne me vint nullement dans l'esprit qu'il fût nécessaire de faire aucune réflexion sur les mots pour traiter sur cette matière. Mais quand j'eus parcouru l'origine et la composition de nos idées et que je commençai à examiner l'étendue et la certitude de nos connaissances, j'ai trouvé qu'elles ont liaison si étroites avec nos paroles, qu'à moins qu'on eût considéré auparavant avec exactitude, quelle est la force des mots, et comment ils signifient les choses, on ne saurait guère parler clairement er raisonnablement de la connaissance qui roulant uniquement sur la vérité est toujours renfermée dans les propositions. Et quoiqu'elle se termine aux choses, je m'aperçus que c'était principalement par l'intervention des mots, qui par cette raison me semblaient *à peine capable d'être séparés* de nos connaissances générales."[72] Que les mots sont *à peine capables* d'être séparés des idées, ne signifie pas que les signes ne soient pas subordonnées aux idées, tout comme les idées sont subordonnées aux effets dans la nature[73]; c'est même le sens profond de toute la thérapeutique que Locke élabore consciencieusement mais obstinément contre toutes les imperfections et tous les abus des mots. Locke seul (et son précurseur Bacon) a connu l'origine et la génération *de nos idées*, avoue Condillac dans l'introduction de l'*Essai*[74]; il faut sous-entendre évidemment qu'il n'a pas compris la portée de la génération *du langage* et de son caractère analytico-méthodique.[75] Locke laissa bien entrevoir que "nous pouvons *à peine* faire usage des nombres, surtout dans les combinaisons fort composées" sans usage des signes,[76] que les noms sont nécessaires pour les idées archétypes puisque "cette union, qui n'a aucun fondement particulier dans la nature, cesserait s'il n'y avait quelque chose qui la maintint et qui empêchât que ces parties ne se dispersassent".[77] Mais la lenteur avec laquelle Locke met à reconnaître la portée d'une véritable *semeiotikè* se déclare exemplairement, dit Condillac, dans le fait qu'"il suppose que l'esprit fait des *propositions mentales* dans lesquelles il joint ou sépare les idées sans l'intervention des mots".[78]

Le quatrième livre (*De la connaissance*) de l'*Essay* lockien illustre la position de l'empirisme *mentaliste* concernant la vérité; c'est comme si ce quatrième livre enjambe le troisième (*Des mots*) qui dégénère ainsi à l'état d'une simple intercalation, pour rejoindre directement et conséquemment le second (*Des idées*). "Pour avoir une notion claire de la vérité," déclare Locke, "il est fort nécessaire de considérér la vérité mentale et la vérité verbale distinctement l'une de l'autre. Cependant il est très difficile d'en discourir séparément, parce qu'en traitant des propositions mentales on ne peut éviter d'employer le secours des mots."[79] Comme le nom se présente plus aisément que l'idée, surtout quand il s'agit d'idées complexes et de substances, les hommes mettent des mots à la place des idées en formant leurs pensées et leurs raisonnements; cependant, "il faut les prier de réfléchir sur les choses elles-mêmes, et de laisser à quartier tous ces mots avec lesquels il est si ordinaire qu'ils embrouillent les autres et qu'ils embarassent eux-mêmes". Il faut surtout, en épistémologie, distinguer entre *proposition verbale* et *proposition mentale* "où les idées sont jointes ou séparées dans notre entendement, *sans l'intervention des mots*, par l'esprit, qui apercevant leur convenance ou leur disconvenance, en juge actuellement".[80] L'inquiétude, qui résonne jusque dans l'œuvre de Maine de Biran,[81] est, bien sûr, que les propositions des plus complexes (archétypes) comme les propositions *morales* ne seraient pas soumises à un critère de vérité autre que leur perfectionnement grammatical. Une 'morale bien faite' ne peut être le résultat que d'une *réformation*, pensent aussi bien Condillac que Locke. Ce dernier veut démasquer la 'frivolité'[82] du revêtement verbal et mettre en évidence les propositions *mentales*; le premier, par contre, tend a réformer le langage lui-même, en le rapportant à son *double* principe, en le purifiant en langage *réfléchi* (la réflexion étant l'opération de l'âme procédant par analogie). Il n'y a, pour Condillac, des propositions que *discursives*; et, inversement, "tout discours est une proposition ou une suite de propositions".[83]

Il n'en peut autrement puisque c'est dans la proposition que la pensée est *articulée*. Foucault remarque que "c'est la proposition en effet qui détache le signe sonore de ses immédiates valeurs d'expression, et l'instaure souverainement dans sa possibilité linguistique".[84] Pour Locke, la proposition n'est *pas* un *signe*; seuls les mots sont des instruments de connaissance et des unités de la *semeiotikè*. C'est ainsi que le langage selon Locke est celui du primitif qui ne parvient pas à parler, bien qu'il prononce des mots qui sont des marques sonores de ses idées, elles-mêmes représentations des choses; l'assemblage de ces mots n'aura jamais valeur de proposition. Le prototype du mot, pour Locke, est le *terme général*; non pas le nom propre, puisque toute nomination passe par l'idéologique, ni, bien sûr, les termes exprimant les relations syntaxiques (e.a. les 'particules'), ni le verbe qui "est emprunté des opérations de choses sensibles" et qui a une signification plus "abstruse" que le terme général.[85] Cette typologie catégoriale est celle de l'empirisme mentaliste: il y a une primauté absolue de l'idéologique – la *semeiotikè* n'est pas encore incarnée –, le langage n'est qu'une existence et non pas un fonctionnement. Les catégories grammaticales sont autrement hiérarchisées chez Condillac. Puisque le langage a une *double* origine, il y aura deux prototypes grammaticaux: l'interjection et le verbe. Leur rapport est semblable à celui du langage d'action et du langage 'formé et perfectionné', du signe naturel et du signe artificiel. Ce n'est donc pas un rapport de discontinuité, mais de *supplémentarité*: dans le hurlement se cache déjà la proposition. La primauté du sémiologique chez Condillac signifie aussi que l'atomisme nominal est transcendé; l'unité centrale de la grammaire est la *proposition discursive*. On constate, en consultant sa *Grammaire*, que Condillac engendre toutes les catégories grammaticales par une analyse (de décomposition) de la proposition; précisément l'inverse se passe dans le troisième livre de l'*Essay* lockien où la typologie atomiste des mots décalque d'ailleurs en plein isomorphisme la typologie des idées. Puisque, chez Condillac, tout le fonctionnement (syntaxique et lexical) du langage est obtenu par une analyse de la proposition discursive, on pourrait dire que la grammaire y est essentiellement une *théorie du verbe*. On a déjà démontré plus haut que le principe *calculatoire* est présent dans le discours comme le fonctionnement de *être* (l'élement qui constitue l'essence du verbe puisque le verbe est le conglomérat de *être* et d'un adjectif)[86]; et c'est la faculté d'*analogie*, source de mémoire et de réflexion, qui rend possible l'*affirmation* du verbe, la formation de la *proposition* et la transformation d'un assemblage de mots en *discours*.

Il n'est pas difficile de déduire de l'analyse que l'on vient de terminer, comment Locke et Condillac vont aborder la question des fonctions du langage. Déjà au tout début du troisième livre, Locke évoque la faculté de parler comme "le grand instrument et le lieu commun de cette société".[87] Mais l'essence de cet instrument ne consiste pas dans le fait qu'il est sonorement sensible, mais bien plutôt que les sons servent "comme des signes de conceptions intérieures". "Dans tous les cas," écrit Maine de Biran, "les mots n'étaient aux yeux de Locke que des moyens de communication entre les hommes, qui leur servaient à s'exprimer mutuellement les idées qu'ils avaient des choses ou les jugements qu'ils en portaient, sans que les noms dont ils se servaient eussent eu aucune influence sur la formation première de ces idées."[88] Locke insiste que l'homme inventa les signes *extérieurs* et sensibles par lesquels les idées *invisibles* puissent être *manifestées* aux autres. La thérapeutique lockienne tend à la *transparence* maximale du langage et privilégie ainsi la fonction de manifestation, d'expression des fragments linguistiques. Ce n'est que par son *expressivité* que la faculté de parler favorise la communication et la sociabilité des hommes. Il est remarquable que Locke accentue l'absolue nécessité de l'*arbitraire* parfait de la signification des mots: "à la vérité, dans toutes les langues l'usage approprie *par un consentement tacite* certains sons à certaines idées et limite de telle sorte la signification de ce son, que quiconque ne l'applique pas justement à la même idée, parle improprement".[89] Opposée à l'extériorité et l'expressivité du langage chez Locke, est l'*intériorité* et le pouvoir articulatoire du langage chez Condillac. On sait maintenant que Condillac ne proclame plus, à partir de la *Grammaire*, l'*arbitrarité* des signes[90]: le langage analytico-méthodique n'est pas arbitraire mais *artificiel*, et la transparence expressive du langage n'est plus souhaitée. D'ailleurs, l'*arbitrarité* (et l'expressivité) est la relation de la pensée au système secondaire et parasitaire des signes tandis que l'*artificialité* (et l'articulation) est la relation du langage à la pensée en continuelle constitution. Le progrès dans les opérations de l'âme et les ruptures qui constituent la spécificité de l'imagination d'une part et de la mémoire (ainsi que de la réflexion) de l'autre, ne sont jamais dûs à des constellations communicatives et intersubjectives. La *Grammaire générale* de type condillacien se déploie sans que l'homme ni le monde interfèrent dans le cercle du langage et de la pensée: le désir de l'identité exclut toute transcendance et toute finalité du fonctionnement linguistique.

L'*epistèmè* classique domine, des Cartésiens aux Idéologues, en ce que l'*idéologie* et la *sémiologie* sont formulées comme les pôles d'une tension universellement reconnaissable en toute pratique scientifique des 17e et 18e siècles: la représentativité et la discursivité marquent la relation épistémique du signe et de l'idée. Le paradigme cartésien et le paradigme condillacien offrent d'importantes variantes à l'intérieur de l'*epistèmè* classique. La question de la relation du langage et de la pensée s'oriente de manière différente selon que l'on considère le langage comme *expression* ou comme *articulation* de la pensée. La *Grammaire de Port-Royal* est une logique amendée, une 'métaphysique spéculative', tandis que la *Grammaire* de Condillac est une vraie philosophie du langage, une 'nouvelle métaphysique'. Si on s'est intéressé au lieu original de Locke dans cette opposition, c'est que la *semeiotikè* lockienne n'est pas une sémiologie comme celle de Condillac. Le mentalisme de Locke, bien qu'il soit encadré par une épistémologie empiriste, ne peut s'accommoder d'une conception du langage constitutif de la connaissance et du raisonnement: en effet, le troisième livre *Des Mots* est 'surajouté' comme le reconnaît Locke lui-même. Condillac, le 'Locke français'? *Encore* moins qu'il ne le pense: son projet s'écarte *essentiellement* de la *semeiotikè* lockienne. Le langage, chez Condillac, *domine*: il n'y a que le langage, il n'y a rien 'en dehors' du langage, si ce n'est sa force articulatoire. Ce 'dehors' -- la *force* d'articuler la pensée – s'appelle peut-être *désir*.

Fonds National belge de la Recherche Scientifique

NOTES

1 J. Locke, *An Essay concerning Human Understanding* (1690). Nous citons l'excellente et importante traduction de P. Coste, *Essai philosophique concernant l'entendement humain ... traduit de l'anglois de Mr Locke, par Pierre Coste, sur la quatrième édition ...* (Amsterdam, 1700). Condillac a pris connaissance de la doctrine de Locke à travers la traduction de Coste; Leibniz, dans les *Nouveaux Essais sur l'Entendement Humain* (1703; première édition en 1765), découpe le texte de Coste en petits morceaux pour le placer dans la bouche de Philalèthe, l'incarnation de Locke dans cet étrange dialogue Locke-Leibniz que sont les *Nouveaux Essais*.

2 Cf. F. Rastier, *Idéologie et théorie des signes : Analyse structurale des Eléments d'Idéologie de Destutt de Tracy* (La Haye-Paris, 1972), 6-20.

3 A. L. C. Destutt de Tracy, *Eléments d'Idéologie* (1803-1804; réimpression photostatique Paris, J. Vrin, 1970): Première Partie: *Idéologie proprement dite*; Seconde Partie: *Grammaire*.

4 A. L. C. Destutt de Tracy, *Grammaire*, 1.

5 M. Foucault, *Les mots et les choses* (Paris, 1966), 92-136.

6 Foucault cite de préférence, dans *Les mots et les choses*, des auteurs généralement classés comme des 'sensualistes' (Condillac, Diderot, Destutt de Tracy, Sicard, Domergue); bien que Cordemoy et Lamy, les deux cartésiens les plus orthodoxes ne soient jamais cités, le rationalisme de l'âge classique y est très présent lui aussi par la *Logique* et la *Grammaire de Port-Royal*.

7 Cf. N. Chomsky, *Cartesian Linguistics* (New York and London, 1966). Cf. aussi A. Joly, "Cartésianisme et linguistique cartésienne", *Beiträge zur romanischen Philologie*, 11 (1972), 86-94.

8 Cf. A. Joly, Introduction à F. Thurot, *Tableau des progrès de la science grammaticale* (Paris, 1970), 28-41.

9 Nous avons étudié cette opposition en rapport avec Saussure et Husserl dans "Expression et articulation: Une confrontation des points de vue husserlien et saussurien concernant la langue et le discours", *Revue philosophique de Louvain*, 71 (1973), 72-113.

10 Nous citons l'*Essai sur l'origine des connaissances humaines* (1746), dans la nouvelle édition de 1973 (Paris, Editions Galilée), précédée de *L'archéologie du frivole* de J. Derrida; la *Grammaire* (*Cours d'études pour l'instruction du Prince de Parme II*), dans l'édition G. Le Roy, *Oeuvres philosophiques de Condillac*, I (Paris, 1947) (*Corpus général des philosophes français*), 425-513; on a dû recourir pour la *Logique* à l'édition des *Oeuvres complètes de Condillac* (Paris, 1822), XV, 317-463; *La langue des calculs* se trouve dans le Tome XVI de cette même édition des *Oeuvres complètes*.

11 *Logique*, 420ss.

12 *Essai sur l'origine ...*, 102.

13 *Ibid.*, 103.

14 *Essai*, 114.

15 *Ibid.*, 115.

16 *Traité des sensations* (1754), dans G. Le Roy, *Oeuvres philosophiques de Condillac*, I, 219-319. L'*Essai sur l'origine des connaissances humaines* est de 1746.

17 *Traité des sensations*, 313.

18 *Ibid.*, 222.

19 *Logique*, 319.

20 *Ibid.*, 325.

21 *Ibid.*, 324.

22 *Grammaire*, 428ss.

23 *Essai*, 200 et 232ss.

24 *Grammaire*, 440.

[25] *Ibid.*, 432.
[26] *Ibid.*, 445.
[27] M. Foucault, *Les mots et les choses*, 119.
[28] M. Foucault, *Les mots et les choses*, 108.
[29] *Essai*, 156-61 et 271-77.
[30] *Logique*, 423.
[31] *La langue des calculs*, 29.
[32] Sous "Le Génie et sa Faculté d'Invention" (cf. infra).
[33] M. Foucault, *Les mots et les choses*, 122.
[34] *Essai*, 128-31.
[35] *Grammaire*, 429; cf. aussi *Logique*, 349.
[36] J. Derrida, *L'archéologie du frivole*, 61-95.
[37] *Essai*, 165-66.
[38] *Grammaire*, 441.
[39] *Grammaire*, 442.
[40] Cf. *Logique*, 330-41.
[41] *De l'art de penser*, Partie 2, chap. 4: *De l'analyse*, dans l'éd. G. Le Roy, I, 769-71.
[42] *Essai*, à partir de la page 280 (§ 32ss.).
[43] *Grammaire*, 443.
[44] M. Foucault, *Les mots et les choses*, 97.
[45] M. Foucault, *Les mots et les choses*, 164.
[46] Dans les *Oeuvres de Maine de Biran*, publiées par P. Tisserand (Paris, 1920), I: *Le premier journal*, 240-309; ces *Notes sur l'influence des signes* ont été probablement rédigées en 1795. Cf. la bonne introduction de P. Tisserand, surtout pp. LXI-LXXV. Sur la réception de la doctrine condillacienne aux 18e et 19e siècles, cf. P. Juliard, *Philosophies of Language in Eighteenth Century France* (The Hague-Paris, 1970).
[47] *Grammaire*, 447.
[48] *Ibid.*, 445.
[49] J. Derrida, *L'archéologie du frivole*, 74-8.
[50] J. Derrida, *L'archéologie du frivole*, 79-95.
[51] *Essai*, 124-55.
[52] *Ibid.*, 125.
[53] *Ibid.*, 128. Cette problématique est reprise et approfondie dans un autre chapitre de la première partie: "De l'opération par laquelle nous donnons des signes à nos idées" (162-6). Le même thème, avec quelques développements, sera traité dans *De l'art de penser* (*Cours d'études*, V), dans G. Le Roy, *Oeuvres philosophiques de Condillac*, Vol. 1, surtout pp. 726-38.
[54] *Essai*, 128.
[55] *Ibid.*, 130.
[56] *Ibid.*, 131.
[57] *Ibid.*, 129.
[58] *Ibid.*, 128.
[59] *Ibid.*, 132.
[60] *Ibid.*, 142.
[61] *De l'art de raisonner* (*Cours d'études* IV, dans G. Le Roy, *Oeuvres philosophiques de Condillac*, I), 683-85.
[62] *Logique*, 456-57.
[63] *De l'art de raisonner*, 683.
[64] *La langue des calculs*, surtout 177-83.
[65] *La langue des calculs*, 181.
[66] *Ibid.*, 177.
[67] *Ibid.*, 179.
[68] *Essai*, 265.

69 *Ibid.*, 263.
70 *Ibid.*, 152.
71 J. Derrida expose admirablement cette lecture dans *L'archéologie du frivole*, surtout 2: *L'après-coup de génie*, 31-42.
72 J. Locke, *Essay*, Book III, Ch. IX, § 21 (dans la traduction de P. Coste, 395-96).
73 Cf. Maine de Biran, *op. cit.*, e.a. 260ss., qui préfère de loin le point de vue lockien à celui de Condillac.
74 *Essai*, 100-103.
75 Cf. e.a. *L'art de penser* (*Cours d'études V*), éd. Le Roy, I, 774; Condillac développe ailleurs une critique de Locke, même pour le domaine de la génération des jugements et des sensations (p.e. dans *L'extrait raisonné* du *Traité des sensations*, éd. Le Roy, 324-25).
76 J. Locke, *Essay*, Book II, Ch. XVI, § 5 (P. Coste, 156).
77 *Ibid.*, Book III, Ch. V, § 10 (P. Coste, 349).
78 *Essai*, 173; cf. aussi *De l'art de penser*, 738.
79 J. Locke, *Essay*, Book IV, Ch. V, § 3 (P. Coste, 474-75).
80 J. Locke, *Essay*, Book IV, Ch. V, § 4 (P. Coste, 476).
81 Cf. Maine de Biran, *op. cit.*, 255-59.
82 J. Locke, *Essay*, Book IV, Ch. V, § 6 (P. Coste, 477).
83 *Grammaire*, 450.
84 M. Foucault, *Les mots et les choses*, 107.
85 J. Locke, *Essay*, Book III, Ch. I, § 5 (P. Coste, 323).
86 *Grammaire*, 458.
87 J. Locke, *Essay*, Book III, Ch. I, § 1 (P. Coste, 322). Cf. aussi Book III, Ch. IX, § 1 (P. Coste, 385).
88 Maine de Biran, *op. cit.*, 275.
89 J. Locke, *Essay*, Book III, Ch. II, § 8 (P. Coste, 327).
90 *Grammaire*, 431-32.

ON PLAGIARISMS IN THE *MINERVA* OF FRANCISCUS SANCTIUS

W. KEITH PERCIVAL

The purpose of this paper is to document a little known fact, namely that the *Minerva* of Franciscus Sanctius (1587) contains a number of obvious plagiarisms. What follows here may be regarded as in the nature of a footnote to Professor Verburg's characterization of Sanctius's feud with the Elder Scaliger as a mere family quarrel,[1] for as we shall see presently the bulk of the plagiarized passages are from Scaliger's celebrated treatise on grammatical theory. Space does not permit me to take up the general question of Sanctius's relations to his predecessors, an issue which I have broached elsewhere[2] but which still awaits more extensive investigation.

Sanctius's attitude to the grammatical tradition was curiously ambivalent. At the very beginning of the *Minerva* he grandly advocates examining all questions on the basis of reason alone without regard to authority: "Itaque nisi te totum inquisitioni tradideris, nisi artis tuae quam tractas causas rationesque probe fueris perscrutatus, crede te alienis oculis videre, alienisque auribus audire" (f. 5^{v}, Book I, Chap. 1).[3] This is, of course, a fine precept in theory but alas far from easy to follow in practice. Even the most uncompromisingly radical thinker owes something to his predecessors and Sanctius, who was much less of a revolutionary than he appears to be at first sight, is no exception to this rule. In any case we must remember that he lived in an age in which appeals to authority, and particularly ancient authority, still carried much weight. It is not surprising, therefore, that in spite of his resolution to be intellectually independent he never fails to assemble scriptural backing for his more radical departures from the grammatical tradition.

A good example of Sanctius's procedure is his defence of the thesis that the category of neuter verbs can be eliminated. (Neuter verbs were traditionally defined as verbs which do not conjugate in the passive voice and were therefore considered to belong in a genus co-ordinate with the actives and the passives.) To combat this view Sanctius appeals to the authority of Aristotle, who maintained that all motion is either action or the undergoing of action ('passion') and that there is no category intermediate between the two: "Quoniam ex Aristotele citavimus omnem motum aut actionem aut passionem esse, nihilque medium quod neutrum possit vere appellari, consentaneum erit verba neutra reicere, quibus videlicet id quod non est in rerum natura velint grammatici nuncupari" (f. 93r, Book III, Chap. 3). To balance this Sanctius also produces a modern authority for the same view. The Elder Scaliger had proposed in his *De causis linguae Latinae* (1540) that verbs should be categorized as either active or passive and Sanctius hastens to quote the relevant passage: "Nobis autem, inquit Caesar Scaliger, satis sit universum verborum ambitum in duo dividere, quae actionem et passionem significent, quem ad modum horum utrumque ad unum quippe ad ipsum EST, quod est utriusque radix et fundamentum" (f. 89v, Book III, Chap. 2).[4]

But as if this were not enough his next step is to corroborate Scaliger's position by appropriate quotations from Aristotle and Cicero: "Hanc Scaligeri rationem sic confirmare possumus: Philosophia, id est recta et incorrupta iudicandi ratio nullum concedit medium inter agere et pati. Omnis namque motus aut actio est aut passio. Immo, si rem penitus inspicias, actio et passio nihil differunt nisi ratione quadam sicut acclive et declive, id quod docet Aristoteles 3. Physic. cap. 3 [202a12-22]. Quare quod in rerum natura non est, ne nomen quidem habebit. Nihil enim agens, inquit Cicero, ne cogitari quidem potest quale sit. Idem secundo De Natura Deorum 'mihi', inquit, 'qui nihil agit esse omnino non videtur' ... An nescis omnem causam efficientem debere necessario effectum producere, deinde etiam effectum non posse consistere sine causa? Quanto rectius Aristoteles qui libro primo de generatione et interitu [Chap. 7] asserit in omni actione alterum esse quod agat, alterum quod patiatur. A philosophis, inquis, ista sumis. Metuebam ne a lenonibus diceres, quasi ulla sit ars quae possit esse a ratione aliena. ... Sed si philosophos spernis, audi etiam grammaticos antiquos" (ff. 89v-90r, Book III, Chap. 2). He then proceeds to quote from Priscian, Lebrija, Scaliger, and, finally (f. 91r), Aristotle again. Thus Sanctius's contention that the class of neuter verbs can be dispensed with is not his own idea and the arguments he marshals to support the contention are all borrowed from other sources also. What we have then is an elaborate network of mutually supporting quotations from both ancient and modern authors.

In the case I have just cited Sanctius is at least good enough to mention the names of his authorities. In many instances, however, he does not choose to specify all his sources. An interesting example of this can be found in his thesis that three parts of speech (noun, verb, and particle) suffice to express everything which needs to be expressed in language: "Cum igitur oratio sit finis grammatici, excutiamus ex quibus haec oratio possit constitui ita ut nihil sit quod per orationem non possimus enuntiare. Sunt autem haec tria: nomen, verbum, particulae. Nam apud Hebraeos tres sunt partes orationis: nomen, verbum, et dictio consignificans. Arabes quoque has tantum tres orationis partes habent" (f. 10r, Book I, Chap. 2).

This passage has led a number of historians to conclude that Sanctius was influenced by Arabic grammatical theory.[5] But as Constantino Garcia has pointed out,[6] there is no other evidence in Sanctius's biography and works of any interest in or reference to Arabic. The sources of this notion are in fact classical, as the rest of the paragraph in which this discussion occurs makes abundantly clear. However, there are in addition two more recent sources for the idea which Sanctius does not mention for us and with which we may assume he was in all probability familiar.

The first of these is the Latin grammar of Juan de Pastrana, which was widely used in the Iberian peninsula in the fifteenth and well into the sixteenth century. This work begins as follows: "Partes orationis quot sunt? Quattuor. Quae sunt? Littera, syllaba, dictio, et constructio. Quot sunt dictiones? Tres. Quae? Nomen, verbum, adverbium. Quid est nomen? Quod declinatur per casus. Verbum? Quod declinatur sine casibus. Adverbium? Quod non declinatur."[7]

Note that Pastrana has the same three parts of speech as Sanctius but he defines them differently, i.e. morphologically rather than semantically. While it is clear that Sanctius was aware of Pastrana's grammar and familiar with its contents,[8] we cannot know for sure whether the passage I have just quoted influenced him.

The second possible source for the notion is Petrus Ramus's *Scholae Grammaticae* (1559). Ramus's discussion of the parts of speech reads as follows: "Aristoteles vocis genera duo: κατηγόρημα καὶ σύνδεσμον: κατηγορήματος species duas: nomen et verbum fecerat, et recte. At grammatici pro duobus generibus eorumque binis partibus alii quinque, alii septem, plerique fere omnes octo, nonnulli decem fecerunt. At, inquiet Aristoteles, generalia generaliter explicanda sunt. Analogia declinationum et generum in pronominibus et participiis nulla specialis est; tota est generalis. Praepositiones et interiectiones, sicut adverbia, sunt velut adiectiva singularum vocum. Sunto igitur genera duo:

κατηγόρημα καὶ συνδεσμός. Categorematis species sunto nomen et verbum, σύνδεσμου adverbium et coniunctio, ceteraeque grammaticae artis regulae ad istam legem καθόλου πρῶτον sunto."[9] Ramus has two major parts of speech: full word and particle, each consisting of two sub-classes: the full word is divided into noun and verb, and the particle into adverb and conjunction. This system resembles Sanctius's in that it lumps together adverbs and conjunctions. Again it may be assumed that Sanctius was familiar with this discussion but we do not know whether he was influenced by it.[10]

In the case of the plagiarisms in the *Minerva*, to which I shall now turn, the sources are likewise not mentioned, but obviously the mere fact of plagiarism presupposes that influence has occurred. I shall make only two general comments on the plagiarisms before enumerating them. First, they are all from modern grammatical writers. Sanctius did not steal from the ancients, quite possibly because he could not have done so without being found out. Second, the plagiarisms are from the three grammatical theorists whose ideas influenced Sanctius most, namely Thomas Linacre, Petrus Ramus, and Julius Caesar Scaliger. Of these three Sanctius's explicit references to Linacre are for the most part favourable (except those on ff. 85^{v}, 156^{v}-157^{r}, 157^{v}, 221^{v}, 223^{r}, and 227^{v}), the bulk of his references to Scaliger are on the other hand violently unfavourable, and Ramus is an author whose name (for obvious political reasons) he did not dare to mention in the *Minerva*.

I shall number the passages cited from the *Minerva* sequentially for easy reference. After each one I shall then quote in full the relevant passage from the plagiarized work. To facilitate quick identification and comparison I shall add an A to the number at the head of the passage from the *Minerva* and a B to the corresponding number at the head of the passage from the plagiarized work.

1A. Ellipsis est defectus dictionis vel dictionum ad legitimam constructionem. *Minerva*, f. 164^{v}, Book IV [Chap. 1].

1B. Est enim eclipsis dictionis ad legitimam constructionem necessariae in sensu defectus. Thomas Linacre, *De emendata structura Latini sermonis libri sex*. London, R. Pynson, 1524, f. XXIII^{r}, Book VI.

2A. Vulgi errorem secutus est Quintilianus. Dicebantur enim quondam grammatici vulgo, qui primis rudimentis pueros instituebant et eis poetas enarrabant, quo in munere subeundo adhibebant praeter grammaticam variarum artium cognitionem. Neque tamen vulgus intellegebat doctorem illum musicae, astrologiae, philosophiae esse peritum. *Minerva*, ff. 8^{r}-8^{v}, Book I, Chap. 2.

2B. Qui error ex imperitae plebeculae (ut de oratore dictum est) errore profectus est. Dicebantur enim quondam grammatici vulgo, qui in litteris pueros instituebant et eis poetas enarrabant, quo in munere adhibenda esset artium praeter grammaticam variarum cognitio. Nec tamen vulgus intellegebat doctorem illum, qui in poetis explicandis varias artes doceret, esse quoque et historicum, et musicum, et astrologum, et philosophum, et rhetoricae peritum, non autem grammaticum tantum. Petrus Ramus, *Rhetoricae Distinctiones in Quintilianum ad Carolum Lotharingum Cardinalem.* Paris, A. Wechel, 1559, pp. 30-31.

3A. Nam qui nomina casu facta contendunt audacissimi sunt; nimirum illi, qui universi mundi seriem et fabricam fortuito ac temere ortam persuadere conabantur. *Minerva,* f. 6r, Book I, Chap. 1.

3B. Alii contra, omnia casu facta nomina, multo audacius affirmant; nimirum quibus universi mundi compago, series, temperatio, casu ac temere orta constituuntur, servantur constituta. Julius Caesar Scaliger, *De causis linguae Latinae.* Lyons, Seb. Gryphius, 1540, p. 120, Chap. 68.

4A. Quae [sc. nomenclatura] si in multis est obscura, non tamen propterea non investiganda. Multa latuerunt philosophos quae Plato eruit in lucem, multa post eum invenit Aristoteles, multa ignoravit ille quae nunc sunt passim obvia. *Minerva,* ff. 6r-6v, Book I, Chap. 1.

4B. Etymologia vero etsi in multis obscura est, superque eadem voce alia alii visa, tantum tamen abest ut tollenda sit, ut tam maxime sit investiganda quam maxime latet. Quid enim occultius veritate? At multis in rebus ea in primis desideratur, neque tamen quisquam tam sit impudens qui eam neget. ... Ita materiae primae natura praeterierat veteres omnes philosophos, donec a Platone inventa, ab Aristotele omnium sapientium principe eruta est in lucem. *De causis linguae Latinae*, p. 349, Chap. 190.

5A. Latet enim veritas, sed nihil pretiosius veritate. *Minerva,* f. 6v, Book I, Chap. 1.

5B. Nihil enim pretiosius veritate, ea enim hominis solius sola meta est. *De causis linguae Latinae*, p. 108, Chap. 63.

6A. Usus porro sine ratione non movetur, alioqui abusus non usus dicendus erit. Auctoritas vero ab usu sumpsit incrementum, nam si ab usu recedat, auctoritas nulla est. Unde Cicero Coelium et M. Antonium reprehendit, qui suo arbitratu, non ex usu loquerentur. *Minerva,* f. 7r, Book I, Chap. 1.

6B. Nam cum hoc interpretandi munus usu, auctoritate, ratione constare dixerint, sane intellegendum est usum sine ratione non semper moveri. ... Auctoritas vero quid aliud quam usus est? Nam quod auctore

M. Tullio dicimus, ex eius usu id habemus. At si ab usu recedat, tum vero auctoritas nulla est. Quare etiam Caecilium reprehendit Cicero, etiam M. Antonium, qui tum aliter quam ex usu loquerentur. *De causis linguae Latinae*, p. 351, Chap. 192.

7A. Verum interest philosophi placitis humanis anteponere rationem. *Minerva*, f. 8r, Book I, Chap. 2.

7B. Verum interest philosophi placitis humanis anteponere rationem. *De causis linguae Latinae*, p. 108, Chap. 63.

8A. Est enim oratorum et poetarum lectio variis artibus referta, quas si magister iste callet, iam non grammaticus dicendus erit. *Minerva*, f. 8v, Book I, Chap. 2.

8B. Est enim oratorum poetarumque atque historicorum lectio differta variis artibus atque scientiis. *De causis linguae Latinae*, p. 3, Chap. 1.

9A. Alii vero dividunt grammaticam in litteram, syllabam, dictionem, et orationem, sive quod idem est in orthographiam, prosodiam, etymologiam, et syntaxim. Sed oratio sive syntaxis est finis grammaticae, ergo igitur non pars illius, quia nulla ars in se versatur. Sic enim aliud est grammatica, aliud grammaticae finis et scopus seu quod Graece dicitur ὑποκείμενον. *Minerva*, f. 9r, Book I, Chap. 2.

9B. Aliud enim est grammatica, aliud grammaticae subiectum dictio sive oratio. Sicut neque verum est quod aiunt alii, qui grammaticae partes quattuor fecere: litteram, syllabam, dictionem, orationem. Neque enim est grammaticae pars oratio, sed totum ipsum argumentum quod vocant ὑποκείμενον. *De causis linguae Latinae*, p. 135, Chap. 76.[11]

10A. Cum artem dico disciplinam intellego, est enim disciplina scientia acquisita in discente. *Minerva*, f. 9r, Book I, Chap. 2.

10B. Sane disciplina est scientia acquisita in discente. *De causis linguae Latinae*, p. 2, Chap. 1.

11A. Fluentes dicimus quarum natura est esse tam diu quam diu fiunt. *Minerva*, f. 10v, Book I, Chap. 2.

11B. Quod Graeci ὄν vocant ... id partim significat res permanentes ... partim fluentes, quarum natura est esse tam diu quam diu fiunt. *De causis linguae Latinae*, p. 124, Chap. 72.

12A. Quid quod individua substantia (ut physice dicamus) melius et peculiarius explicatur per tua haec pronomina quam per nomina propria. Cum enim dico 'ego', neminem alium poteris intellegere. At cum dico 'Franciscus', etiam in alium potest transmitti intellectus. Unde *Franciscus* potius pro *ego* ponitur quam contra. Multo plus errarunt qui loco nominis proprii pronomen posse poni docuerunt. Nam hoc modo *magister*, *rex*, *dux*, *gubernator* essent pronomina, quia pro Pompeio aut Cicerone ponuntur. *Minerva*, f. 12^r (sig. B4^r), Book I, Chap. 2.

12B. Praeterea *ego* et *tu* individualitatem statuunt magis quam nomen Caesaris et Catonis, neque enim cum dico 'ego' potes alterum intellegere neque cum altero communicare. Cum dico 'Caesar' etiam in alterum transmitti potest intellectus, ut non solum non ponatur *ego* loco nominis huius *Caesar*, sed etiam e contrario nomen ipsum *Caesar* per pronomen ad certam substantiam praescribatur. Ut etiam plus errarint qui sic sentiunt *ego* esse pronomen quoniam pro proprio nomine ponitur, sic enim etiam nomen appellativum esset pronomen cum dicam 'homo loquor', poneretur enim pro *Caesare*, sed substantiam meam statim significat non nomen meum. *De causis linguae Latinae*, pp. 256-257, Chap. 127.

13A. Figura dicta est a fingendo, et fingere est exprimere imitatione rem veram. Ita vocamus figuras in tabulis et signis. Hinc ducta est similitudo in re litteraria quando ex duabus vel pluribus vocibus effingimus unam. *Minerva*, f. 13^v (sig. B5^v), Book I, Chap. 3.

13B. Est igitur fingere exprimere imitatione veram rem; idcirco dicta figura in signis et tabulis, atque hinc porro in grammaticis. *De causis linguae Latinae*, p. 161, Chap. 87.

14A. Numerus alius singularis, alius pluralis, neque plures numeri fuerunt necessarii, nihil enim tertium est inter unum et plura, quoniam unum et plura ex uno frequentato facta sunt. Neque rationi consonum est aliquos Graecorum (ut Iones) recepisse numerum dualem, quem Aeoles non receperunt, quos Latini in multis fuere imitati. ... *Minerva*, ff. 15^r-15^v (sigs. B7^r-B7^v), Book I, Chap. 4.

14B. Quare id quoque secutum fuit, ut numerus alius diceretur singularis, alius pluralis, neque enim medium ullum est inter unum et plura, quoniam plura ex uno frequentato facta sunt. Quare Iones non recte fecere, qui dualem numerum a plurali discerpsere, atque idcirco severiores Aeoles neque recepere, neque in Latinos transmisere. ... *De causis linguae Latinae*, p. 139, Chap. 78.

15A. Sed nihil erit impedimento quominus verbum *pluit* primam personam habere dicatur, si modo loquatur Deus. *Minerva*, f. 85^v, Book III, Chap. 1.

15B. Sic nihil impedimento est quominus verbum *pluit* primam personam habere dicamus, si modo loquatur Deus. *De causis linguae Latinae*, p. 224, Chap. 110.

NOTES

1 "Sanctius ... staat met zijn *Minerva seu de Causis Linguae latinae* (1587) aangemerkt als de antipode van Scaliger. Principieel is het verschil evenwel gering; het is een familie-twist, geen fundamentele controverse" (P. A. Verburg, *Taal en functionaliteit*, 165).

2 "Deep and Surface Structure Concepts in Renaissance and Mediaeval Syntactic Theory", to appear in Herman Parret (ed.), *History of Linguistic Thought and Contemporary Linguistics*. Berlin, Walter de Gruyter.

3 Here as elsewhere in this paper I quote from the first edition of the *Minerva* – Francisci Sanctii Brocensis in inclyta Salmanticensi Academia Primarii Rhetorices, Graecaeque linguae Doctoris *Minerva*: *seu de causis linguae Latinae*. Salmanticae, apud Ioannem & Andręam Renaut, fratres, 1587.

4 The original passage in Scaliger's work reads as follows: "Nobis autem satis sit universum verborum ambitum in duo dividere, quae actionem, et quae passionem significent, atque eo cetera omnia tamquam ad signa recipere, quem ad modum horum utrumque ad unum quippe ad ipsum EST, nam tametsi non significat ἐνεργείαν, tamen nota est ἐνδελεχείας, quae est finis actionis et passionis" (p. 221, Chap. 110). I quote from the first edition: Iulii Caesaris Scaligeri *De causis linguae Latinae libri tredecim*. Lugduni, Seb. Gryphius, 1540.

5 See Berthold Delbrück, *Vergleichende Syntax der indogermanischen Sprachen* (Strassburg, Trübner, 1893), vol. 1, p. 16, and most recently Nicolae Drăganu, *Storia della sintassi generale* (Bologna, Riccardo Pàtron, 1970), p. 18.

6 *Contribución a la historia de los conceptos gramaticales*: *La aportación del Brocense* (= *Revista de Filología Española*, Anejo 71), p. 82.

7 *Grammatica Pastrane*. Lisbon, João Pedro Bonhomini de Cremona, 1512, sig. a2[r], quoted from the facsimile reproduction in Manuel II, *Livros antigos portuguezes, 1489-1600, da bibliotheca de sua Majestade fidelissima*, desciptos por S. M. El-Rei D. Manuel (London, Maggs Bros., 1929), vol. 1, p. 231. This same passage is quoted from an (unidentified) edition in the Biblioteca Nacional at Madrid by Felix G. Olmedo, S. I., in his monograph *Nebrija en Salamanca* (*1475-1513*) (Madrid, Editora Nacional, 1944), pp. 33-34.

8 Sanctius mentions Pastrana twice, once disparagingly (sig. A4[r]) and once approvingly (f. 24[r]). The second of these two references proves that he was familiar with the content of Pastrana's grammar. It reads: "Praeclare mihi videtur sentire Ioannes Pastrana cum praecipit omnia nomina in *-us* non significantia vere marem aut feminam posse etiam terminari in *-um*, ut *baculus*, *baculum*, *puteus*, *puteum*" (Book I, Chap. 9).

9 P. Rami *Scholae grammaticae*. Parisiis, apud Andream Wechelum, 1559, p. 12. P. Rami *Scholae in liberales artes*. Basileae, per Eusebium Episcopium et Nicolai F. haeredes, 1569, sig. a2[v].

10 We know for certain that Sanctius was familiar with Ramus's *Rhetoricae distinctiones in Quintilianum* since, as I shall show, he plagiarized from it. This work was Ramus's critique of Quintilian's *Institutiones oratoriae* and it first appeared in 1549 (Paris, M. David). It was later combined with his *Brutinae quaestiones* (first published in 1547) to form the *Scholae rhetoricae*, which appeared as part of the *Scholae in liberales artes* (Basle, 1569). The *Scholae rhetoricae* also appeared separately in 1581 (Frankfurt, A. Wechel) and as part of the *Scholae in tres primas liberales artes* (same printer, same year). Of the *Scholae grammaticae* two editions appeared, the first in 1559 and the second in 1564, both printed by Wechel at Paris. It was later incorporated into the *Scholae in liberales artes* just mentioned. Which of these editions Sanctius had access to is not known. It seems to me a fairly safe assumption that given his interest in Ramus's writings he either took care to obtain a copy of the separate *Scholae grammaticales* or he owned a copy of the *Scholae in liberales artes*. Information

about editions of Ramus's works may be found in Walter J. Ong, S. J., *Ramus and Talon Inventory*. Cambridge, Mass., Harvard University Press, 1958.

11 A possible additional source here is the *Mercurius Maior* of Augustinus Saturnius (Basileae, ex officina Ioannis Oporini, 1546). The second chapter of book I of that work is entitled "Alias esse partes artis grammaticae, alias orationis". Sanctius was familiar with the *Mercurius Maior* and mentions it several times in the *Minerva*. For instance, in discussing his choice of title he says: "At de linguae Latinae causis iam scripserat Caesar Scaliger, quem quia in multis sequor, nonnunquam tamen ab eo disentiens, titulum non abiciendum putavi. Et Augustinus Saturnius suas acutissimas dissertationes in grammatica *Mercurium* vocavit, quem quia minus aliquando probamus, Minervam illi fidum monitorem adhibemus" (ff. 7r-7v, Book I, Chap. 1). According to Luigi Ferrari (*Onomasticon*, Milan, Hoepli, 1947, p. 611) Saturnius died in 1533. It may be mentioned in this connexion that the epistola nuncupatoria in the *Mercurius maior* is signed March 24, 1531. Hence Saturnius's book clearly antedates both Scaliger's and Sanctius's. Whether Scaliger was familiar with it prior to writing his *De causis linguae Latinae* is not clear. I am aware of two editions of the *Mercurius Maior* other than the Basle edition, to which I have access, namely a Venice edition printed by C. de Tridino in 1556, and a Lyons edition of the same year "partagée entre J. Frellon et A. Vincent" (J. Baudrier, *Bibliographie Lyonnaise*. Paris, Louis Brun & A. Picard et Fils, 1901, vol. 5, p. 236).

POSTSCRIPT 1974

Since writing this paper in early 1973 I have discovered more evidence of plagiarisms in the *Minerva*. In this set of instances the source is Petrus Ramus's *Grammaticae libri quatuor*, first published in Paris by André Wechel in 1559. I shall quote here from a copy of the third edition (published in the following year in the same place and by the same printer) to be found in the Biblioteca Nacional in Madrid (Shelf-mark R-1562). The passages in question occur in the section headed "De Partibus Orationis" at the end of the *Minerva* (sigs. *1r-**8v) and also in Sanctius's earlier *Verae brevesque grammatices Latinae Institutiones* (Lugduni, apud haeredes Seb. Gryphii, 1562 and subsequent-editions).

It may be noted in passing that the 1562 edition of Sanctius's *Institutiones* contains a preliminary version of the *Minerva* entitled *Minerva seu de Latinae linguae causis et elegantia* (sigs. F1r-L3r). The existence of this edition was first pointed out by Gregorio Mayans y Siscar in his introduction to the four-volume edition of Sanctius's works (*Francisci Sanctii Brocensis Opera Omnia*, Geneva, Frères de Tournes, 1776, vol. 1, p. 18). More recently it has been described in some detail by Jesús María Liaño Pacheco in his monograph *Sanctius el Brocense* (Madrid, Talleres Aldus, 1971, pp. 11-18). The interested reader may find a bibliographical description of the edition in Palau y Dulcet, *Manual del Librero Hispanoamericano*, vol. 19, p. 286, No. 294853.

I shall number the passages cited as I did in the main body of the article, an A indicating the passage in the *Minerva* (with a page reference to the *Institutiones*) and a B the corresponding passage in Ramus's *Grammatica.* Where the wording in the *Institutiones* differs markedly from that of the *Minerva* I add the relevant passage from the *Institutiones* identified by means of an AA.

The reader will notice that in each such case the formulation in the *Institutiones* is appreciably closer to Ramus's than is the one to be found in the *Minerva.* Consider, for instance, the definition of the conjunction (extracts 22A and 22AA). In the *Minerva* the conjunction is defined as a word which conjoins *sentences* whereas in the earlier *Institutiones* it is defined as conjoining *parts of speech*, i.e. sentence constituents. It is clear that the earlier definition is closely modelled on Ramus's (with the word *multiplicis* omitted), and it may be surmised that Sanctius deliberately changed the definition in the later work.

This supposition is borne out by the fact that in a copy of the *Institutiones* which is at present in the library of the University of Salamanca (Shelfmark 1.ª/11167) and which is known to have belonged to Sanctius, there is a marginal correction in the author's hand above the definition of the conjunction. The words *orationis partes* have been emended to read *orationes diversae* and the revised definition reads: "Coniunctio est vox expers numeri, qua orationes diversae coniunguntur", which is identical in substance with the formulation in the *Minerva.*

Moreover, it seems likely that in this instance Sanctius was bringing his ideas into line with those of the Elder Scaliger. In chapter 165 of the *De causis linguae Latinae* Scaliger criticizes the traditional definition of the conjunction as a word which connects parts of speech, arguing that this connexion is effected by the agreement of the noun and the verb, and suggests redefining the conjunction as a word which conjoins sentences. In the case of a sentence such as *Caesar et pugnat et scribit*, which does not look like a pair of conjoined sentences, there are in fact two sentences *potestate*, i.e. potentially.

The relevant passage reads as follows: "Coniunctionis autem notionem veteres paulo inconsultius prodidere; neque enim, quod aiunt, partes alias coniungit; ipsae enim partes per se inter se coniunguntur. Verbum namque nomini iungitur affinitate numeri et personae. Sed coniunctio est quae coniungit orationes plures, sive actu sive potestate. Nam *Caesar pugnat, Caesar scribit* duae sunt orationes separatae, quae coniunctione in unum coalescent, actu igitur duae sunt. At *Caesar et pugnat et scribit* potestate duae sunt, quoniam *Caesar* bis est repetendus" (*De causis linguae Latinae*, p. 323, Chap. 165).

In this connexion it is interesting to note the remarkable extent to which Sanctius adopted Scaliger's whole approach to this topic in the main body of the *Minerva*, without giving Scaliger any credit whatever: "Coniunctio neque casus neque alias partes orationis, ut imperiti docent, coniungit. Ipsae enim partes inter se coniunguntur, ut nomen nomini, nomen verbo, etc. Sed coniunctio orationes inter se coniungit, ut *Caesar pugnat, et Cicero scribit*. At vero cum dicis *Cicero scribit et vigilat*, duae sunt orationes in zeugmate figura. Item *Cicero et filius valent* figura syllepsis est, ut *Valet Cicero et valet filius*" (*Minerva*, f. 148^{r-v}, Book III, Chap. 14). Thus a careful textual study of variant formulations of the same definition in the *Institutiones* and the *Minerva* can throw unexpected light on the process by which Sanctius blended ideas from different sources.

Finally the question arises as to how one can be certain that Sanctius plagiarized the passages I am about to transcribe, from Ramus's *Grammatica* and not from some other of Ramus's grammatical works, viz. the *Rudimenta* or the *Scholae grammaticae*. A cursory inspection of the relevant passages in these books reveals that the definitions of the parts of speech are virtually identical in all of them. Fortunately for us, however, there are in one or two instances significant stylistic differences between the various formulations. There are some especially noticeable differences, for example, in the way Ramus defined the participle in his various Latin grammatical works. In the *Rudimenta* the participle is introduced in the following way: "*Discipulus*: Oriturne nomen aliquod a verbo? *Praeceptor*: Oritur participium, sic appellatum ideo quod nomen cum sit, partem sui capiat a verbo, significationem quippe et tempus" (*Rudimenta grammaticae Latinae*, Paris, A. Wechel, 1560, p. 17). In the *Scholae*, on the other hand, the topic is discussed as follows: "Ex omnibus verbis personalibus nomina oriuntur verbi significationem et tempus retinentia; participia ideo nominantur" (*Scholae grammaticae*, Paris, A. Wechel, 1559, p. 281). Neither of these versions, however, is as close to Sanctius's formulation in the *Institutiones* as is the version of this definition in Ramus's *Grammatica* (see extracts 20AA and 20B).

I now proceed to transcribe the passages in question, observing the conventions specified above.

16A. Voces omnes aut numeri participes sunt aut expertes. Numerus est differentia vocis secundum unitatem aut multitudinem. *Minerva*, sig. *1^{v}; *Institutiones*, sig. B6^{v}.

16B. Vox enim particeps est numeri aut expers. Numerus est differentia vocis secundum unitatem aut multitudinem. Ramus, *Grammatica* (1560), p. 16.

17A. Nomen est vox particeps numeri casualis cum genere. Ex quibus differentiis oritur declinatio. Casus est specialis differentia numeri nominalis. ... Genus est differentia nominis secundum sexum. *Minerva*, sig. *1[v]; *Institutiones*, sig. B7[r].

17B. Nomen est vox numeri casualis cum genere, atque his e differentiis facta nominum flexio. Casus est specialis differentia numeri nominalis. ... Genus est differentia nominis secundum sexum. Ramus, *Grammatica*, pp. 16-17.

18A. Dividitur nomen in substantivum et adiectivum. Substantivum est quod cum uno genere declinatur, ut *pater*, *mater*. Adiectivum genus non habet, sed terminationes ad genera sub uno fine, ut *felix*, *par*, *oriens*, vel sub duobus, ut *fortis* et *forte*, *dis* et *dite*, vel sub tribus, ut *bonus*, *bona*, *bonum*. *Minerva*, sigs. *1[v]-*2[r].

18AA. Genus dividit nomen in substantivum et adiectivum. Substantivum est quod cum uno genere aut summum duo declinatur, ut *pater*, *vates*; adiectivum quod tribus generibus sub uno fine vel duobus vel tribus, ut *felix*, *fortis* et *forte*, *bonus*, *bona*, *bonum*. *Institutiones*, sig. B7[r].

18B. Nomina substantiva sunt vel adiectiva e differentia generis: substantiva, quae cum unico genere aut duobus summum declinatur, ut *pater*, *civis*; adiectiva autem, quae cum tribus generibus declinantur vel uno fine, ut *felix*, *amans*, vel duobus, ut *fortis*, *forte*, vel tribus, ut *bonus*, *bona*, *bonum*. ... Ramus, *Grammatica*, p. 18.

19A. Verbum est vox particeps numeri personalis cum tempore. ... Persona est specialis differentia numeri verbalis. Ea est triplex ... Tempus est differentia verbi secundum praesens, praeteritum, et futurum. *Minerva*, sig. *2[v]; *Institutiones*, sigs. B7[v]-B8[r].

19B. Verbum est vox numeri personalis cum tempore. ... Persona est specialis differentia numeri verbalis, eaque triplex est. ... Tempus est differentia verbi secundum praesens, praeteritum, futurum. Ramus, *Grammatica*, pp. 49-50.

20A. Participium est vox particeps numeri casualis, tempus et constructionem a verbo ducens. *Minerva*, sig. *3[r].

20AA. A verbo personali nomina verbalia oriuntur, significationem et tempus a verbo ducentia, unde participia sunt appellata. *Institutiones*, sig. B8[r].

20B. A verbo personali nomina verbalia oriuntur, significationem et tempus a verbo ducentia, quae ideo participia appellata sunt praesens, praeteritum, futurum. Ramus, *Grammatica*, p. 52.

21A. Adverbium est vox expers numeri, quae aliis vocibus tamquam adiectivum adiungitur. ... *Minerva*, sig. *3[r]; *Institutiones*, sig. B8[v].

21B. Adverbium est vox expers numeri, quae voci alii adiungitur. ... Est igitur adverbium tamquam adiectivum nominum, verborum, adverbiorum etiam ipsorum. Ramus, *Grammatica*, pp. 77-78.

22A. Coniunctio est vox expers numeri, qua orationes coniunguntur. *Minerva*, sigs. *3r-*3v.

22AA. Coniunctio est vox expers numeri, qua orationis partes coniunguntur. *Institutiones*, sig. C1r.

22B. Coniunctio est vox expers numeri, qua orationis multiplicis partes coniunguntur. Ramus, *Grammatica*, p. 81.

OUTPUT CONDITIONS IN WORD FORMATION?

H. SCHULTINK

In 1. it is explained that in a transformational-generative model of language, word derivation can take place only via transformational rules or in the lexicon. 2. Shows that in a transformationalist approach, the ordering of the relevant transformations presents problems. Chapin's (1967, 1970) 'epicycle hypothesis' does not, as it turns out, solve these problems. In 3. Leitner's (1972) solution is found to be unacceptable too. Output conditions à la Perlmutter (1970, 1971) seem to offer better perspectives.

1. It is not easy to say how derivational formatives are introduced in strings in a transformational-generative model of language. Following in the steps of Chapin (1967:13), Chomsky (1970) distinguishes between a so-called transformationalist and a so-called lexicalist approach to this introduction. The transformationalist standpoint means that derivational formatives are introduced by means of transformations. According to the lexicalists, word formation should be dealt with largely, or even entirely, in the lexicon.

Both Lakoff (unpublished) and McCawley (1973) protest against the dichotomy between lexicalist and transformationalist. Thus McCawley points out that *post*-lexical and *pre*-lexical transformations are lumped together under the heading 'transformationalist'. By prelexical transformations are understood those which precede lexical insertion; postlexical transformations follow lexical insertion. Postlexical nominalization transformations are found in Lees 1960 and Lakoff 1970; Chapin (1967, 1970) also derives words with the aid of postlexical transformations. Prelexical transformations are used by generative semanticists like Gruber (1965) and McCawley (1968). Chomsky utterly rejects the idea of prelexical transformation. This rejection is one of the corner-stones of the lexicalism for which he definitively opts in 1970. A large part of word derivation should, according to him, be handled in the lexicon. Exactly how large a part is specified by Bresnan (1971:269-70). Jackendoff's (1972:13) 'extended lexical hypothesis' extends this to all word derivation. In the meantime, Gruber (1967) had also, in addition to this, dealt with a considerable part of inflection within what he calls his 'translational lexicon'. Finally, Halle (1973:6) does not see any argument at all for describing inflectional phenomena in a different way from derivational phenomena. Accordingly, he accounts for both, without separating them out, in his morphological components.

Apart from transformationally or in the lexicon, in principle, it also seems to be possible to introduce derivational elements with the help of phonological or syntactic rewrite rules. Dik (1967:366), Wurzel (1970:17), and Kiefer (1970:18-20) give as their main objection to the introduction via phonological rules that it fundamentally alters the character of the phonological component. More convincing than their protest is that of Halle. With reason, he wants to restrict the 'more powerful devices' which he needs for word formation to the relevant component and thus not build them into the phonological component. "It is obvious that, in general, one would not wish to replace less powerful by more powerful devices especially when it is known that the less powerful devices are capable of handling a very large part of the task at hand. Under such circumstances, it would be essential to attempt to limit as much as possible the domain in which the more powerful devices may be invoked" (Halle 1973:15).

Finally, we face the possibility that derivational formatives be introduced directly via syntactic rewrite rules. In the discussion about transformationalism versus lexicalism, what have been mainly though not exclusively referred to until now are word-derivational relations of a transpositional nature i.e. derivational relations which involve a difference in lexical category. The reader is reminded of nominalizations like *eagerness* and *refusal*, nouns which correspond to the adjective *eager* and the verb (*to*) *refuse* respectively. An adjective like *readable* corresponds to the verb (*to*) *read* in a similar transpositional manner.

In addition, we find derivations which do not go together with a change in lexical category. Wurzel (1970:83-84), who devotes a good deal of attention to these non-transpositional derivations, mentions German nouns such as *Fuchs-Füchsin*, *Fuchs-Füchslein*, *Berg-Gebirge* and adjectives such as *blau-bläulich*, *gram-grämlich*, *süß-süßlich*. He tries to make it plausible that non-transpositional derivation of nouns and adjectives like this should be dealt with in the base-component, with the aid of rewrite rules. To derive similar formations transformationally from underlying deep structures "wäre eine sehr künstliche und rein technische Lösung" (84). Nevertheless, Wurzel considers it inevitable that the verb *fällen* should be derived transformationally from the verb *fallen*, just as he derives all transpositional formations by means of transformations.

If we take into account Dutch words like *baron* 'baron'-*barones* 'baroness' and *(te) dansen* '(to) dance'-*danser* 'dancer'-*danseres* 'lady dancer' in our investigation, then we ascertain the following. The derivation of *danseres* from *danser*, within a non-lexicalist model, presupposes an earlier transformation of the verb *dansen* to the noun *danser*.[1] As the application of rewrite rules precedes the application of transformations, *danseres* too should be derived from *danser* transformationally. As, moreover, a grammar which derives *danseres* from *danser* in a different way than *barones* from *baron* clearly misses a significant generalization, *barones* also has to be derived from *baron* transformationally. On the ground of similar arguments the transformational derivation of German words like *Füchsin*, *Füchslein*, *Gebirge*, *bläulich*, *grämlich*, and *süßlich* is to be preferred to derivation via rewrite rules. In addition, there is the fact that, by already introducing some derived words via rewrite rules, Wurzel gives a markedly idiosyncratic character to these rewrite rules. In any case, in this way, any assumption "that much of the structure of the base is common to all languages" (Chomsky 1965: 117) is undermined.

2. Anyone who wants to account for derivational elements via transformations has to take into account that transformational rules have to satisfy the demands of asymmetry, transitivity and irreflexiveness within one cycle.[2] Asymmetry means that – given rule X and rule Y – Y can not both follow and precede X. Transitivity means that when – given three rules X, Y, and Z – X precedes Y and Y precedes Z, X also precedes Z. Irreflexiveness requires that no rule precede itself.

In the meantime, Chomsky (1970:212) states: "As is well-known, processes of derivational morphology are applicable in sequence – they may even be recursive." Bierwisch (1967:262) gives examples of this such as *analyticity* and *realizational*. Considering the above, we should not be surprised that Wurzel (1970:90-91) implicitly provides an A-B-A proof that his morphological 'Wortbildungsregeln' are cyclically ordered. For, *Häßlichkeit* and *ganzheitlich* are cases where two suffixes appear now in the order A-B and then in the order B-A. In view of this cyclic applicability, we could have expected formations like *Einheitlichkeit* and *Freiheitlichkeit* reported by Wurzel, in which one and the same derivational affix is added to a root twice with another affix between the two additions. Even if Wurzel does not say this in so many words, it follows from the above that the syntactic transformations that lie at the root of the sequences *lich-keit*, *heit-lich* and *heit-lich-keit*, in his descriptive model, are also cyclically ordered.

Chapin (1970:60-62) has already shown earlier, in the light of English and German material (*organize*, *organization*, *organizational*, *organizationalize*, *organizationalization*; *physical*, *physicalist*, *physicalistic*, *physicalistical*, *physicalisticalist*; *Schade*, *schädlich*, *Schädlichkeit*, *schädlichkeitlich*, *Schädlichkeitlichkeit*), that in both these languages some words need to be derived via cyclically ordered transformations. At the same time, it is not the case that all word derivation rules in English and German are cyclically ordered. Thus, to mention only one, the rule which derives English words in *-less* can not be applied cyclically. Chapin formulates his 'epicycle hypothesis' on the basis of the available material, of which he himself admits there is not much. This 'epicycle hypothesis' is to the effect "that it may be possible to order the rules in such a way that rules which must be cyclically ordered can always be ordered adjacent to each other; that is, that no rule which does not participate in a given cycle need be ordered (...) between any two rules which do" (Chapin 1970:61). Chapin supports this with a diagram

A——B——C——D——E——F——G.

"Assume that A, B, *etc.* are derivational rules and the '' ——are ordering relations, ... Then the proposal under discussion is that cyclical ordering is possible only among groups of alphabetically adjacent rules. Possible cyclical groups would be B-C, F-G, C-D-E, A-B-C-D, and so on; C-D-F, A-E, and so on would not be possible cyclical groups. Thus ... the hypothesis holds that the rules for attachment of *-tion*, *-al*, and *-ize* may be ordered immediately adjacent to each other, with no necessity for the interposition between two of them of some other rules, say the rule of *-less* attachment, which does not enter into the cyclic pattern" (Chapin 1970:61). If the 'epicycle hypothesis' is not falsified, it leads to a theory which is, of course, more powerful than a theory in which arbitrary sets of derivation rules can be applied cyclically.

The 'epicycle hypothesis' can, however, be refuted on two counts. In the first place, the general theory must allow for the possibility of describing derived words with a double suffix. It is undoubtedly a fact that, so far, there are more languages known in which there is no double suffixation than languages in which there is double suffixation (cf. Uhlenbeck 1962:428, Kiefer 1970:23, and Matthews 1972:98 fn. 1). Nevertheless, in a language like Afrikaans, derivations with double diminutive suffixes are to be found such as *stukk-ie-tjie* 'small piece', *pot-jie-tjie* 'small pot', *stomp-ie-tjie* 'small stump', *rekenink-ie-tjie* 'small account', *kramp-ie-tjie* 'slight cramp', *stoel-tjie-tjie* 'small chair', *blaar-tjie-tjie* 'small leaf', *stof-ie-tjie* 'small stove', *vink-ie-tjie* 'small weaver-bird' (cf. Odendal 1963:221-22). Within a transformational framework, these diminutives should be described via a cyclically applicable transformation. A cyclically applicable transformation like this does not, however, have to be one of a group of rules, which is different from what Chapin's 'epicycle hypothesis' suggests ("cyclical ordering is possible only among *groups* of alphabetically adjacent rules", Chapin 1970: 61; italics are mine, H. S.). As appears from Kempen's (1969:591) brief survey of suffix combinations in Afrikaans, the diminutive in that language can be followed by, apart from itself, only the plural *-s*. This *-s*, in its turn, can not precede a diminutive suffix. In Chapin's 'epicycle hypothesis' therefore, provision would at least have to be made for cyclically applicable derivation rules which act independently.

A second, graver objection has, however, been raised against the 'epicycle hypothesis'. Chapin (1970:59-62) argues that the suffixes *-tion*, *-al*, *-ize* and the suffixes *-ist*, *-ic*, *-al*, in English, form cyclical groups. Leitner (1972:240-42), however, shows that this does not explain the grammaticality of words like *organizationalist* and *fictionalistic*. Moreover, he demonstrates that Chapin is forced to order suffixation with *-ory* in English both before and after his cyclical groups (Leitner 1972: 242). Nor is this ordering-paradox solved by the 'epicycle hypothesis'. In short, we are obliged to endorse Leitner's (1972:242) view that Chapin's theory is untenable.

3. We are now still faced by the following problem. "The derivational rules of English as a whole cannot be cyclically ordered. Some subgroups of them, however, must be cyclically ordered. Therefore the derivational rules cannot be linearly ordered as a whole, in spite of the considerable evidence that many individual rules are extrinsically ordered with respect to each other. How are these contrary bodies of evidence to be mutually accomodated?" (Chapin 1970:61).

Leitner (1972:244-50) makes an interesting proposal to break this impasse. He orders his suffixes according to the position which they can occupy in words. Thus, in English, he distinguishes sets of (1) terminal suffixes (*-ly* and Gen.), (2) preterminal suffixes (Num.), (3) prepreterminal suffixes (*-ness*, *-ity*, *-ship*, ...), (4) postcyclic suffixes (*-able*, *-esque*, *-er*, ...), (5) cyclic suffixes (*-ic*, *-al*, *-ize*, *-ion*, *-ist*, *-ism*), (6) precyclic suffixes (*-an*, *-ern*, *-ify*, *-ate*, *-ory*, ...), and (7) suffixes which can never follow another suffix (*-oid*, *-th*, *-dom*, ...), respectively. This ordering of suffixes can be represented schematically. In his table, Leitner spreads the elements from set (7) over the other six sets according to the number of suffixes by which they can be followed. For, his general criterion for ordering is the maximum distance, in terms of suffixes, by which the suffix in question is separated from the end of the word.

(7)	(6)	(5)	(4)	(3)	(2)	(1)
oid	*an*	*ic*	*able*	*ness*	Num.	*ly*
th	*ern*	*al*	*esque*	*ity*		Gen.
dom	*ify*	*ize*	*er*	*ship*		
	ate	*ion*	*th*	*dom*		
	ory	*ist*				
	oid	*ism*				

Only elements from set (5), the cyclic suffixes, can be combined with one another in one and the same word. No mutual combination of elements occurs in any of the other sets. What does occur is a combination of every set S_i and every set S_j, where $j > i$, and in such a way that S_i follows S_j. For the elements from these sets this means, at least theoretically,[3] that every element j from S_j can be combined with every element i from S_i and this in such a way that j precedes i. Under the same conditions, sequences of more than two sets and elements are possible in words.

Affixes are now being handled on two levels. The syntactic component generates their syntactico-semantic structure. They do not get their morphological characteristics until in a morphological component which is situated between the transformational component and the phonological component. In this morphological component rules which are combined into sets, operate. Rules of this kind have little else in common than that every rule from one particular set produces an affix which can occur in only one particular position in a derived word. Which affix is chosen in this particular position does not depend solely on the syntactico-semantic structure mentioned above. The morphological structure and other properties of the stem which is to be affixed also have a part to play in this. Thus, in Dutch, in addition to *goed-heid* 'goodness' and *schilder-achtig-heid* 'picturesqueness', we find abstract nouns derived from adjectives such as *sterk-te* 'strength', *duister-nis* 'darkness', *rijk-dom* 'richness', and *zwanger-schap* 'pregnancy'. There are no derivatives like this, or hardly any, ending in *-te*, *-nis*, *-dom*, and *-schap* from adjective stems which are themselves derived. All of this can even result in identical information from the syntactic component leading to the introduction of affixes which are from different sets. Thus, the English verbal suffixes *-ate* (as in *activ-ate*) and *-ize* (as in *central-ize*) are from sets (6) and (5) respectively.

There are also objections to be raised against Leitner's proposal, which is only extremely briefly reproduced here. One of the things he himself points out is that the non-cyclical suffixes *-ive* and *-ate* are nevertheless combined in two kinds of sequence in words like *migr-at-ive* and *act-iv-ate* (Leitner 1972:247). Moreover, his sets of rules considerably extend the formal universals in the general theory, an extension for which there seems to be no independent evidence.

Perlmutter (1970) makes it plausible that the combinatory restrictions to which affixes are subject in words, should be of the same nature as output conditions on clitic pronouns. These output conditions on clitics are given in terms of a filter which characterizes the grammatical sentences, while every sentence which contains a sequence of clitic pronouns which does not satisfy these conditions will be filtered out, will be discarded as ungrammatical. Thus Perlmutter's (1970:226) surface structure constraint on French clitics is as follows

		me				
Nom	*ne*	*te*	III_{Acc}	III_{Dat}	*y*	*en*,
		nous				
		vous				
		se				

in which Nom stands for *je*, *tu*, *il*, *elle*, *nous*, *vous*, *ils*, *elles*, *on*; III Acc for *le*, *la*, *les*, and III Dat for *lui*, *leur*. For a French sentence to be grammatical it is, of course, not necessary for all seven slots indicated to be filled. The slots which are filled do have to be in the order indicated, while, moreover, every slot may be filled by only one member of the set assigned to this slot.

Perlmutter (1970:250-52) is right when he points out that the notation developed by him reminds us of the 'morpheme order charts' and the 'decade notation' with which we are familiar from the late forties and the fifties. For that matter, also Leitner's (1972:245) table reminds us of this. Therefore, Perlmutter's notation may be appropriate for stating constraints on word formation too. Provision can be made for double affixation as in Afrikaans (cf. Odendal 1963:222) by repetition of the relevant slot, e.g. –Dim Dim– (cf. Perlmutter 1970:216). Perlmutter's proposed universal, however, purposely does not provide for cyclic derivation.

A priori, it does not seem to be at all out of the question to formulate output constraints in such a way that justice is done to the grammaticality of cyclically derived words. Should this prove to be feasible, then the next question is whether this form of description provides an argument in favour of the transformationalist standpoint and detrimental to the lexicalist standpoint. Perlmutter (1970:253) states that the constraint on the occurrence of Spanish clitics "applies to the final output of the syntactic component". He later adds: "The question of whether there are well-formedness conditions which apply at other stages of derivations must be considered open" (Perlmutter 1971:134). Was Halle – within the framework of his own theory – attempting to answer Perlmutter's open question too when he wrote: "In fact, it may well be useful to speak not of 'rules of word formation' but rather, as has been suggested by Lakoff and others, of 'derivational constraints that hold in word formation' " (Halle 1973:15)?

Utrecht, June 1974

NOTES

1 The latter transformation is self-evident even within a lexicalist descriptive model à la Chomsky. For, the type of formation is a productive one; there is a fixed semantic relationship between the verb and the derived agent noun; the syntactic environments in which the two types of word figure are very different. Compare Chomsky 1970:187 for these criteria.

2 We refer the reader to Lehmann 1972 and the literature listed there for other views.

3 The actual combinatory possibilities of separate elements from two combinable sets must be explicitly indicated.

BIBLIOGRAPHY

Bierwisch, M.
1967 "General Problems of So-Called Pronominal Inflection in German", *To Honor Roman Jakobson: Essays on the Occasion of his Seventieth Birthday, 11 October 1966*, I (= *Janua Linguarum*, series maior, 31), 239-70. The Hague-Paris, Mouton.

Bresnan, J. W.
1971 "Sentence Stress and Syntactic Transformations", *Language*, 47, 257-81.

Chapin, P. G.
1967 *On the Syntax of Word-Derivation in English*. Cambridge, Mass., MIT Dissertation.
1970 "On Affixation in English", *Progress in Linguistics : A Collection of Papers*, ed. by M. Bierwisch and K. E. Heidolph (= *Janua Linguarum*, series maior, 43), 51-63. The Hague-Paris, Mouton.
Chomsky, N.
1965 *Aspects of the Theory of Syntax*. Cambridge, Mass., MIT Press.
1970 "Remarks on Nominalization", *Readings in English Transformational Grammar*, ed. by R. A. Jacobs and P. S. Rosenbaum, 184-221. Waltham, Mass., Toronto, London, Ginn.
Dik, S. C.
1967 "Some Critical Remarks on the Treatment of Morphological Structure in Transformational Generative Grammar", *Lingua*, 18, 352-83.
Gruber, J. S.
1965 *Studies in Lexical Relations*. MIT Dissertation (IULC 1970).
1967 *The Function of the Lexicon in Formal Descriptive Grammars*. Santa Monica, Calif., SDC.
Halle, M.
1973 "Prolegomena to a Theory of Word Formation", *Linguistic Inquiry*, 4, 3-16.
Jackendoff, R. S.
1972 *Semantic Interpretation in Generative Grammar* (= *Studies in Linguistics Series*, 3). Cambridge, Mass., and London, MIT Press.
Kempen, W.
1969 *Samestelling, afleiding en woordsoortelike meerfunksionaliteit in Afrikaans*. Kaapstad, etc., Nasou.
Kiefer, F.
1970 *Swedish Morphology*. Stockholm, Skriptor.
Lakoff, G.
1970 *Irregularity in Syntax* (= *Transatlantic Series in Linguistics*). New York, etc., Holt, Rinehart, and Winston.
unpublished *Generative Semantics*.
Lees, R. B.
1960 *The Grammar of English Nominalizations* (= *Indiana University Research Center in Anthropology, Folklore, and Linguistics*, 12). Bloomington, Indiana.
Lehmann, T.
1972 "Some Arguments against Ordered Rules", *Language*, 48, 541-50.
Leitner, G.
1972 "Argumente für eine morphologische Ebene in einem TG-Modell", *Linguistik 1971 : Referate des 6. Linguistischen Kolloquiums 11.-14. August 1971 in Kopenhagen*, ed. by K. Hyldgaard-Jensen (= *Athenäum-Skripten Linguistik*, 1), 236-51. Frankfurt/M., Athenäum.
Matthews, P. H.
1972 *Inflectional Morphology : A Theoretical Study Based on Aspects of Latin Verb Conjugation* (= *Cambridge Studies in Linguistics*, 6). Cambridge, University Press.
McCawley, J. D.
1968 "Lexical Insertion in a Transformational Grammar without Deep Structure", *Papers from the Fourth Regional Meeting, Chicago Linguistic Society*, ed. by B. J. Darden, Ch.-J. N. Bailey, and A. Davison, 71-80. Chicago.
1973 Review of *Studies on Semantics in Generative Grammar* by N. Chomsky (IULC).

Odendal, F. F.
1963 "Limitations of Morphological Processes: A Note", *Lingua*, 12, 220-5.
Perlmutter, D. M.
1970 "Surface Structure Constraints in Syntax", *Linguistic Inquiry*, 1, 187-255.
1971 *Deep and Surface Structure Constraints in Syntax* (= *Transatlantic Series in Linguistics*). New York, etc., Holt, Rinehart, and Winston.
Uhlenbeck, E. M.
1962 "Limitations of Morphological Processes: Some Preliminary Remarks", *Lingua*, 11, 426-32.
Wurzel, W. U.
1970 *Studien zur deutschen Lautstruktur* (= *Studia Grammatica*, VIII). Berlin, Akademie-Verlag.

SEMIOTIC ASPECTS OF THE INTERROGATIVE

A. G. F. VAN HOLK

1. In this article I propose to discuss some aspects of the total interrogative (yes-no questions), using mostly English examples, within a SEMIOTIC MODEL of language. The term 'semiotic' is here taken to refer to a type of investigation which strives to incorporate the linguistic sign function in the analysis of deep structure, and to treat the utterance as embedded in a cultural process,[1] in particular the creation and reception of a literary text and the performance of a dramatic piece in which part of the information-carrying 'substance' is non-verbal (Wienold 1972: 123ff.).

Within such a semiotic perspective the 'upper boundary' of grammatical structure may be described as what has been called the 'syntax of situations' (Ivanov and Toporov 1963: 112), while the 'lower boundary' is formed by the elementary morphophonologic signals (pauses, tone contours, as well as features of grammatical concord), which impart to language as a means of communication its specific discrete character.[2]

The principal task of a semiotically oriented text grammar will accordingly consist of detecting and analyzing the possible structural levels lying between these upper and lower limits. In doing so one will inevitably encounter that level of deep structure of the sentence which is constituted by deep categories or 'cases' in the sense of Fillmore's 'case grammar' (cf. esp. Fillmore 1968; Abraham 1971b). Applying Fillmore's notion of case to the analysis of yes-no questions will require the identification of the semantic primitives entering the deep structure of interrogative sentences; it will be argued that the modal feature of 'uncertainty' common to all yes-no questions can be decomposed into a configuration of deep cases if their grammatical status is reinterpreted, and slightly modified, within the semiotic model proposed in this paper.

2. In accordance with most contemporary views a literary text will be considered here (in first approximation) as a string of sentences

S_1, S_2, ..., S_n, between which there exist certain relations established by means of one or more of the following features:[3]

(i) pronominal cross-reference;

(ii) intonation patterns;

(iii) lexical contiguity.

These relations confer to the text a greater or lesser degree of COHESION (Halliday 1971:143, 160-164; Van Dijk 1972:96-120). Although, as has been pointed out by some investigators, it is possible to establish in this way certain suprasentential narrative units[4] (of the extent of, say, a paragraph), this does not in any way affect the status of the *sentence* as the LARGEST LINGUISTICALLY MARKED unit of utterance, its limits being established on the basis of intonational and other features of the sound form of sentences. This means, on the one hand, that whatever features of content one might be led to ascribe to a literary text (or any lesser suprasentential unit) can only be transmitted at the level of the surface structure of the sentence; on the other hand it means that the sentence is the largest structural frame for a strictly distributional delimitation of grammatical categories: every feature of the thematic content of a literary text must have its origin in a categorial semantic feature defined exclusively by its position inside the sentence.

Every sentence is further supposed to be ultimately representable as a string of MORPHEMES, which can be grouped into words and PHRASES. Moreover, every linguistic expression realizes some conventional pattern of arrangement, here called after De Groot a CONSTRUCTION (De Groot 1964:61-82); the features of arrangement which serve to identify a construction comprise the following:

(i) features of the sound form of an expression, e.g. the place of phrase stress;

(ii) the order of constituents;

(iii) the number of constituents;

(iv) the selection of certain morphemes (concord).

Finally, it is necessary to account for COEXISTING constructions, which are convertible into one another by means of a TRANSFORMATION.[5]

In general, two constructions will be regarded as MUTUALLY TRANSFORMABLE if they comply with the following conditions:

(i) the constructions have a certain configuration of stem or root-morphemes in common;

(ii) the differences in arrangement – which may affect any of the features listed under (i) through (iv) above – are systematic at least in the language of the text (or the body of texts) at issue.

The systematicity of a transformation depends primarily, it would seem, on the extent to which the language of the text has available such morphologic and syntactic devices as operate INDEPENDENTLY of the configuration of stem or root morphemes; thus the nominalizing transformation converting a clause like *her face was white* into the noun phrase *the whiteness of her face* exhibits a great systematicity in that the addition of *-ness* (or any of its allomorphs) is subject to few restrictions; the underlying invariant configuration *her face ... white* can therefore readily be isolated from any sentence in which it might be included. This result can be further generalized by considering that the members of such a configuration are not the individual morphemes, but CLASSES OF EXPRESSIONS of common distribution and morphologic signature.

It should be emphasized in this connection that there may be mutual transformability between a pair of sentences and a single (complex) sentence, as illustrated by embedding by means of a relative pronoun, e.g. *The family was living out in the country. They felt very happy there* beside *The family was living out in the country, where they felt very happy.* For a pair of sentences to be convertible into a single complex sentence it is by no means necessary that they should be adjacent, or even belong to the same paragraph or other suprasentential narrative unit. Suppose the first paragraph of a short story contains a sentence like *The man drove a nail into the wall,* while the last contains a sentence like *He was found hanging on the nail.* These two sentences may be converted into a single sentence such as *He was found hanging on the nail that he had himself driven into the wall.* Since in principle any sentence of a text can be embedded in at least one other sentence of the same text – the transformations required being systematic and therefore independent of the morphologic composition of the sentences at issue – it follows that there always can be found at least one invariant morpheme configuration covering an entire text; such a configuration may be identified as the THEMATIC STRUCTURE of the text (cf. e.g. Horecký 1973).

Thus a configuration must be assumed to have an extremely large latitude of complexity, all the way from the simple clause up to the thematic structure of an entire text. Inevitably therefore the question arises as to the possible structural phases between these extremes, and it is only natural to look for the required data in the systematicity of composition inside relatively small suprasentential units, of the dimensions of an average paragraph. Finally, in the light of the above considerations, the need for finding the ELEMENTARY configurations evidently becomes particularly great.

In what follows an attempt will be made to describe the total interrogative as a particular type of invariant configuration conveying the modal content of 'uncertainty' by determining its ultimate primitive configurations.

3. A suitable starting point for our study are declarative sentences of the equational type, such as the ensemble (1-3) below.

(1) *Edinburgh is the capital of Scotland.*
(2) *A horse is a noble animal.*
(3) *Ivan the Third Dimitrovich was the first to call himself Czar of Russia.*

The common construction of these sentences may be represented as a string of morphologically determined constituents, as in diagram (4),[6]

(4) $NP_1 \quad V_{Cop} \quad NP_2$,

which suggests that the sentences under consideration consist of two noun phrases and a finite form of the copula *be*, in such a way that there is a syntactic relationship between each NP and the verb, but not between the NP's themselves. It is possible to consider the finite verb as designating a semantic relation of 'identity' between the realities denoted by the NP's, while this finite verb at the same time performs a pragmatic function in expressing the attitude of the speaker-observer towards the posited identity, in particular his 'belief in the existence' of such a relation (cf. De Groot 1964:65); this may be taken to be the specific function of the indicative morpheme. In order to ascertain the role of the indicative morpheme in the sentences at issue we first note that the indicative may be modified by means of adverbial adjuncts such as *certainly*, *probably*, *supposedly*, all of which occupy the most peripheral position in the sentences quoted.

We now want to assume by way of a working hypothesis that for any feature of meaning (as coded in natural language) a syntactic structure can be found which renders this feature REDUNDANT, or at least minimizes its information content; Apresjan gives an example of this, where he points out that in the context *A on ego* VERB *palkoj po golove* 'And he VERB him with a stick on his head', virtually any substituted verb will automatically assume the categorial semantic feature 'hit' (Apresjan 1967:29ff.; Kortlandt 1971:56).

The search for a construction which would make explicit in this way the meaning of the indicative morpheme yields a class of expressions of the form Pe V_{Dic} (C) ——,[7] in which any sentence having the indicative feature can be embedded. The superimposed construction is at any rate maximally peripheral with regard to the embedded sentence, and in this respect therefore equivalent with the class of adverbial adjuncts mentioned above.

This may be illustrated as in (5), where the double arrow designates mutual transformability (§2),

(5) Pe V_{Dic} (C) (NP_1 ...... NP_2) ↔ Adv (NP_1 ...... NP_2)

it is supposed that	*supposedly* (...)
I am {*certain* / *sure*} *that* (...)	*certainly* (...)
	surely (...)

The peripheral constituent in (5) refers to what we will term the EVALUATOR. The underlying morpheme configuration of the constructions Pe V_{Dic} (C) and Adv in fact refers to a SPEECH SITUATION, and corresponds fairly precisely to the text-grammatical structure postulated by Abraham for the 'dativus ethicus' in German (Abraham 1971a: 126). Little imagination is needed to foresee the advantage of this representation for a linguistics going 'beyond the sentence' (Hendricks 1967) and aiming at integrating the syntactic structure of the sentence in the thematic macro-structure of a text.

The finite verb *is* in (1) further contains a reference to the moment of utterance or observation, but I am assuming that this reference can be isolated from the rest of the sentence content: the selection of tense obviously depends on factors which remain outside the equational structure of the sentences (1-4); thus *was* will substitute for *is* in a context such as (6).

(6) *Jack always insisted that a horse was a noble animal.*

Outside such a context, however, the selection of tenses is often neutralized in sentences of the equational type. The explanation of this striking peculiarity is probably that the equational structure at issue is equivalent in some respects with an expression dominated by a tense morpheme; i.e. we presuppose an equivalence between the meaning of the indicative expressed structurally and the meaning of the present or preterite tense expressed morphemically. This may be diagrammed as in (7).

(7) Indicative

NP_1 V_{Cop} NP_2 equivalent with (NP_1 V ...) Tense $\begin{Bmatrix} \text{Present} \\ \text{Preterite} \end{Bmatrix}$

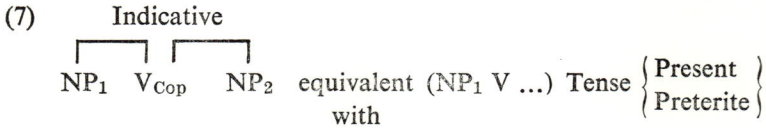

4. We will now take a closer look at the two noun phrases of examples (1-3).

These constituents are similar in that their sound forms culminate in a (high or low) phrase stress, and in that they occupy a position which is characterized by the concordant ending of the verb. In this type of sentence the distinction between grammatical subject and predicate is probably cancelled out, and the copula agrees (in person and number) with both NP's. Outside the equational type, in particular when the NP's are allowed to take different articles, the first NP will normally have the definite article, the second NP the indefinite, so that the symmetry of the equational construction is then destroyed (Van Holk 1963).

However this may be, the NP's are in any case marked off by one stress feature and one position marker each. The semiotic function of the stress feature is to characterize an expression as POINTING TOWARDS a situation; this feature is the basis of word class assignment and may accordingly be called a CLASS MARKER. The class marker is associated with an UNRESTRICTED paradigm, consisting of all the expressions which can carry this high or low phrase stress. The position marker, in our examples, indicates that this unrestricted paradigm figures in the position of a SUBSTANTIVE vis-à-vis the rest of the sentence.[8] Only the combination of a class marker and a position marker constitutes a (linguistic) SIGN (Van Holk 1963). The sign at issue is implemented by the simplest possible morpheme configuration in natural language, as it consists of only one class marker (phrase stress) and one position marker (in our examples any morpheme in the finite verb agreeing with the left and/or right noun phrase). We call this configuration the NOMINATIVE. The construction of the sentences (1-4) may be re-written in terms of the notions developed so far as shown in (8).

(8)

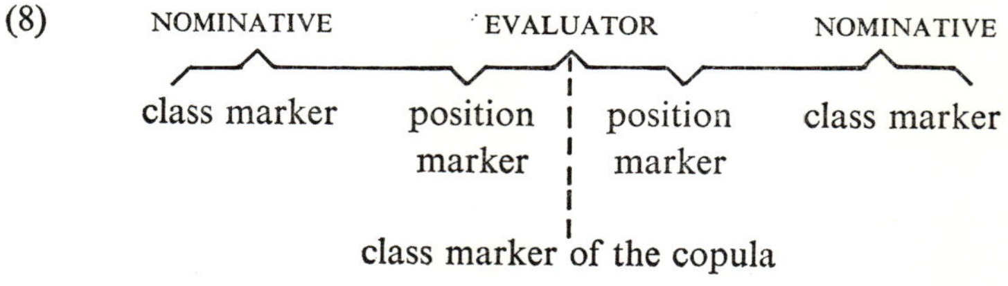

From formula (8) we further see that a morpheme configuration such as NOMINATIVE may be distributed over two or more sentence constituents, so that the internal structure of the NOMINATIVE configuration within the context at issue is 'contextual'; only in the limiting case where a noun phrase is used in 'absolute position' (Bloomfield 1933:170) will its internal structure be 'non-contextual', i.e. the class marker and the position marker combine within the same sentence constituent.

5. We have now reached the problem of the manner in which the interrogative sentence corresponding with (1), namely

(9) *Is Edinburgh the capital of Scotland?*

can be represented, if possible without the introduction of a new, undefined element of meaning such as 'uncertainty'. It can be established immediately that the interrogative sentence (9), just as the corresponding non-interrogative sentence (1), expresses an attitude of the speaker-observer, which therefore may be represented by a peripheral constituent in the same way as the declarative attitude in diagram (5). We should further take into account that a yes-no question is not necessarily addressed to a listener; for example in (10)

(10) *He was asking himself: Is Edinburgh really the capital of Scotland?*

the context denotes doubt on the part of the person indicated by *he*, and points to the absence of a listener. This entitles us to eliminate the attention-drawing function of the interrogative intonation, and to relegate the feature of 'uncertainty' to the word material of the sentence, i.e. to an expression with a statable syntactic structure. We must therefore also examine the use of the same word material as a conditional clause in a sequence of closely linked sentences like (11).

(11) *Is Edinburgh the capital of Scotland? Then that's where we ought to go.*[9]

We find that the clause with inverted word order in (11) has the same function as the first NP (with high phrase stress) in (1), i.e. the clause in (11) functions in its entirety as the 'topic' relative to the rest of the utterance. This clause therefore must contain one class marker less than the corresponding uninverted clause in (1). Nevertheless, the clause in (11) still contains two noun phrases, and the concord relations between these and the copula *is* are the same as in (1).

The most obvious interpretation of these facts is that the clause in (11) does contain the same two position markers as in (1), but has one class marker less; this state of affairs is diagrammed in (12).

(12)
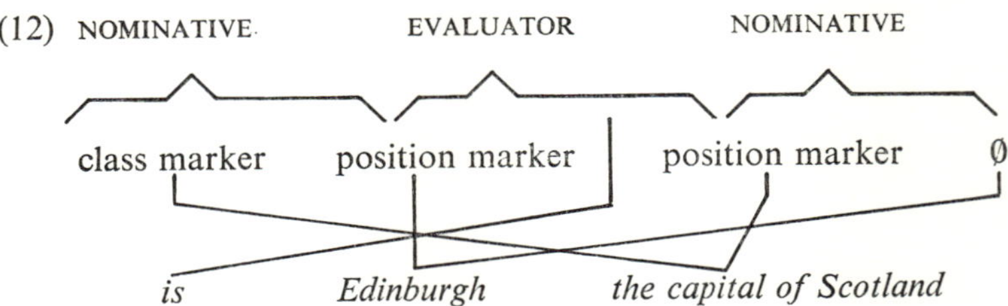

The supression of the topic-comment distinction, appearing as a one-peak intonation contour in the first part of (11), also characterizes the corresponding interrogative (9), which we may describe as a conditional clause in absolute position; only in the latter case there are certain additional intonational features, whose semiotic function need not concern us here.

6. For a correct understanding of the syntactic properties of the interrogative it is further necessary to look closer at the constituent representing the evaluator, which we have assumed to carry the attitudinal component within the modality of 'uncertainty'.

It will have become clear that the expressions representing the evaluator in the sentences under consideration rather neatly comply with Fillmore's definition of the 'dative' as "the case of the animate being affected by the state or action identified by the verb" (Fillmore 1968:24), and even better with his later definition of the same case as that of the "experiencer, the entity which receives or accepts or experiences or undergoes the effect of an action" (Fillmore 1969:116).

Fillmore's treatment of deep categories as primitive components of sentence structure and as 'frame features' for verbs, however, gives rise to a number of questions. First of all we ought to know, what enables us to conclude that a deep category is 'primitive', as Fillmore assumes for his 'cases' when he states: "What is needed is a conception of base structure in which case relations are primitive terms of the theory" (Fillmore 1968:2-3).

I propose here to assume that a deep category is primitive if, and only if, a construction can be associated with it which complies with the following conditions:

(i) the structure is entirely determined by syntactic relations between constituents;

(ii) the structure is built up around a single central position, in which lexical material can be substituted independently, thereby forming an unrestricted paradigm;

(iii) the morphemes participating in an elementary construction all refer to the same entity in the universe of discourse, i.e. they are co-referential ('parallel' in the sense attributed to this term by Ebeling (1954)).

For our present purposes the third condition is particularly important. It may be noted in this connection that the relation of parallelism, defined by Ebeling in semantic terms, can always be turned into a syntactic relation of *congruence* (between morphemes) by translating the original expression into a language with sufficiently developed morphology; thus, in an English expression like *John's hat*, there is a parallel relation between headword and determiner, as appears from the translation into Russian *Ivanova šljapa*, or equivalently, of English *my hat* into Italian *il mio capello*; the possessive construction, represented here by /z/ in English, by /ov/ in Russian, and by /mi/ in Italian, involves two non-parallel (non-congruent) noun phrases (such as *John* and *hat* in English), and therefore cannot be elementary. Only that morpheme or morphologic feature in *John's* that is preserved after substituting the definite article *the* is parallel with the head word (cf. Italian *il capello* vs. *la casa*), and therefore belongs to the same elementary construction. Note also that the definite article in English is the only morpheme to express 'definiteness' all by itself, and in the normal subject position usually cannot even be replaced by an 'indefinite' article: therefore it constitutes an absolutely closed paradigm, of one member.

A second question raised by Fillmore's theory regards the semantic starting point. In line with what has been stated above concerning elementary constructions, I believe that an effort must be made to give a maximally formal definition of deep categories. Various recent studies of the dative construction have revealed that, insofar as we can speak of a single dative construction per language, this construction at any rate possesses considerable latitude, manifesting itself in a wide range of subtypes; in this connection one would mention for example the *to*-dative and the *for*-dative in English, which Jackendoff and Culicover (1971), however, have shown to form a deeper unit than Fillmore initially supposed, insofar as these constructions both feature prior to the passive transformation (the only difference then is that P-deletion is ungrammatical in the case of *for*, cf. **A new wardrobe was bought Mary by John*).

This is not the proper place to discuss the many problems surrounding the dative construction; I must confine myself to commenting that in a 'content-free' approach to these problems, at least the following syntactic properties of the dative construction can be identified:

(i) the construction is made up of one verbal constituent in syntactic relationship with one nominal constituent;

(ii) the nominal constituent refers to a 'person', i.e. it can be the subject of a 'verb of saying';

(iii) the syntactic relation between the constituents is invariant under an indirect-passive transformation, such as is found between *John wrote a letter* and *Mary was written a letter* (by John);

(iv) the position of the nominal constituent is more peripheral than that of the otherwise similar direct object, as appears, in English and many other languages, from the potential use of prepositions to express the verb-noun relation;

(v) an expression containing a dative construction includes any other verb-noun construction; in particular, a dative construction which is 'topicalized' as a subject-predicate expression will be characterized by a *more complex* relation between subject and predicate: thus in *I know that –*, *I believe that –*, etc., the subject-predicate relation appears to be incorporated in a more complex construction by virtue of its systematic transformability into expressions like *it is known to me that –*, *it seems to me that –*, etc.

To sum up, then, we describe the dative category as an ensemble of expressions characterized by a definite degree of inclusiveness as presupposing any other verb-noun construction (to the exclusion of clause-adverbial constructions), and associated with a characteristic verb-noun construction which is invariant under an indirect-passive transformation; each expression of the ensemble, moreover, is made up of morphemes which are parallel (potentially congruent) in the sense explained above, and consist partly of class markers, partly of position markers. This may be diagrammed as in (13).

(13)

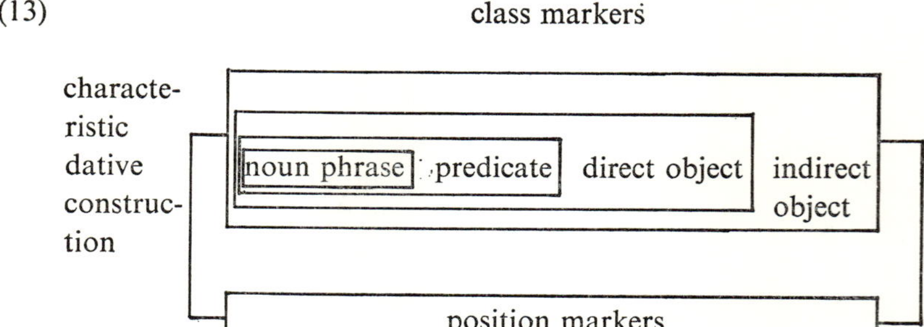

Now it appears from a closer inspection of expressions containing a dative construction that this construction rarely occurs in isolation; more normally we find combinations of the dative construction with one or more other elementary constructions: thus the possessive construction considered above (5) may be decomposed into one dative construction and one objective (direct object) construction. As pointed out before, such constructions are non-elementary if they involve two or more non-parallel (potentially noncongruent) noun phrases, such as the 'possessor' and the 'possessed' in *John's hat*, *John has a new hat*, *John bought a new hat*, *John lost his new hat*, *John got his new hat stolen from him*. Notice that Fillmore's fundamental condition on deep cases prohibiting the combination of two or more identical cases within a single (simple) sentence (Fillmore 1968:21; 1971:38), under the present theory applies only to constructions which are included in a single expression containing only parallel morphemes; otherwise there is no theoretical objection against having combinations of, say, two or more dative constructions. This is in fact what we find on analyzing sentences like *John gave the letter to Mary*, which can be decomposed, following some very interesting suggestions in a recent paper by Daneš,[10] into three elementary constructions:

(i) the dative verb-noun construction in which the noun phrase refers to the 'resultant possessor' (*Mary* in *John gave the letter to Mary*);

(ii) the objective verb-noun construction in which the noun phrase refers to the 'object possessed' (*the letter* in our example);

(iii) the verb-noun construction in which the noun phrase refers to the 'initial possessor' (*John* in the sample sentence); noticing that this constituent occupies the same peripheral position in the indirect passive transformation *Mary got the letter from John* as the indirect object *to Mary* in the original sentence, we identify this construction as another dative.

The identification of the two constructions (i) and (iii) as datives finds strong support in the fact that the 'initial possessor' is in many languages expressed by the same surface features (dative suffix and/or indirect object position) as the 'resultant possessor', e.g. French *Je lui ai enlevé la lettre*, Dutch *Ik heb hem de brief afgepakt* 'I took the letter away from him', while in Russian the 'initial possessor' is expressed by the same surface features as the 'static possessor', e.g. *Ja otnjal u nego pis'mo* 'I took the letter away from him' beside *u nego pis'mo* 'he has a letter'. However, the two constructions (i) and (iii) can be identified only if the DIRECTION of the process is left unconsidered: this comprises both the selection of one or the other possessor as the agent (factor A in Daneš's formula) and the transition from one possessive relation to the next (factor T in Daneš's formula).

Before using the above description of the dative to represent the evaluator in the indicative configuration underlying sentences (1-3) it is necessary to dwell a moment on one pivotal aspect of configurations of constructions. As we have seen, one of the nominal constituents in the interrogative configuration is represented by an elementary construction lacking one class marker, i.e. with ONE EXCESS position marker. This state of affairs suggests that in the corresponding indicative configuration (8) the evaluator should be represented by a constituent containing TWO EXCESS position markers, each being matched by the class marker of a noun phrase. This means that the expression of the evaluator is not simply a dative construction, but rather a dative with performative function, paraphrasable in the usual way as something like 'I declare that –' or 'X is of opinion that –'. Thus in general an 'adverb of saying' in the function of a performative constituent is to be represented by a dative expression with two excess position markers. This leads to a representation of the indicative configuration (8) underlying sentences (1-3) as diagrammed in (14).

(14)

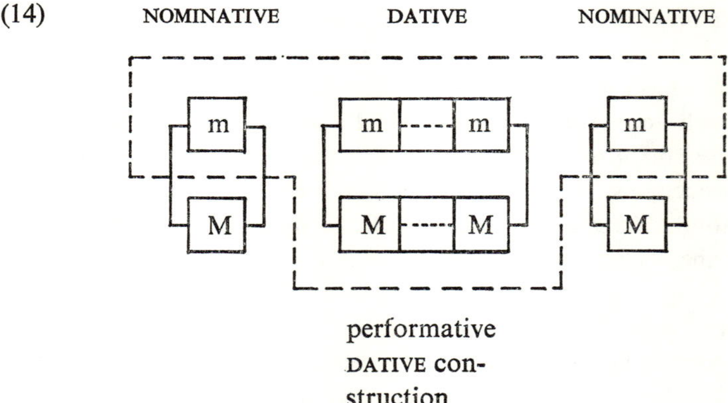

(Symbols M and m indicate class markers and position markers, respectively)

The above representation can also be used for the interrogative construction (12), which will then take the form (15)

(15) NOMINATIVE + DATIVE + m,

using the symbols of (14).

7. The indicative and interrogative constructions described in the preceding sections were shown to consist of elementary categorial constructions corresponding in many respects to Fillmore's 'cases', although their structural status seems to be somewhat deeper, and also differs in allowing the same category to occur more than once within a simple sentence, in accordance with Daneš's proposal (§6). Within the conceptual framework outlined in this paper it seems altogether permissible to interpret the elementary deep categories and their intercombinations as the MOTIFS of folktale analysis (Ivanov and Toporov 1963:112).

It is our contention that the elementary constructions representing elementary motifs constitute a finite (and indeed, it would seem, very limited) set, out of which any complex construction, such as the indicative and interrogative, or the possessive, are obtained in the course of the creative process by which sentences are concatenated into a coherent utterance. Thus the possessive construction and the doubly-possessive construction 'x gives z to y' (§6), when used as the dominant unifying factors of a literary text, both contribute to the expression of the motif of 'man's rapacity', as exemplified by Molière's *L'Avar* or Ostrovskij's *Crazy Money*. The indicative construction is peculiar in conveying the narrator's 'belief',[11] which, regardless of the lexical material inserted in the construction, serves as a particular unifying factor in certain genres of literature (e.g. the 'moral' in a Fontaine fable, or the more sophisticated 'philosophy' voiced in the opening lines of *Anna Karenina*). The total interrogative construction, owing no doubt to its 'incomplete' status as compared with the indicative, does not readily occur as a motif by itself, although it certainly enters as a component into various modal constructions marked by the feature of 'uncertainty', such as the optative and potential moods.

Summing up the outcome of the present investigation we can say that the semiotic approach outlined here departs from ordinary case grammar by incorporating the semiotic distinction of class markers and position markers, and the relation of co-referentiality (parallelism) that connects them, into the description of deep categories. It remains for the future to test the capacity of the approach to account for the combinatorics of motifs in literary discourse.[12]

Slavic Institute
University of Groningen

NOTES

[1] Thus, according to Umberto Eco, it can be said in a first approximation that "die Semiotik alle kulturellen Vorgänge (...) als Kommunikationsprozesse untersucht" (Eco 1972:32).

[2] The delimitation of the field of semiotics in terms of upper and lower boundaries is due to Eco (1972:31ff.).

[3] A more extensive list of such features is presented by Petőfi (1971:209ff.).

[4] An interesting attempt to determine such a suprasentential unit using co-referentiality (cf. § 6 of this paper) as a unifying principle is put forward by Rychner (1971).

[5] See for this notion of transformation Ivanov and Toporov (1963:106ff.), and Harris (1963:11): "Given a sentence S_1 which is a particular grammatical arrangement g_1 of particular morphemes (words) m_1, a transform of it TS_1 is another grammatical arrangement g_2, satisfying certain conditions, of the same m_1. (...) TS_1 is itself either a sentence, or a sequence of sentences with connectors, or a constituent to be included in a neighboring sentence."

[6] This notation is taken from Apresjan (1967:39).

[7] The meaning of the symbols is as follows: Pe – personal noun phrase; V_{Dic} – verb of saying; C – conjunction; Adv – adverb.

[8] Class markers and position markers may be compared with Hjelmslev's 'sémantèmes' and 'morphèmes': in both pairs the former determine the conditions under which the latter are selected (Hjelmslev 1937; Harweg 1968:14-16).

[9] In languages like Dutch, German, and Russian there seem to exist more possibilities for letting a total interrogative enter a complex sentence as a subordinate clause; e.g. Dutch *Regent het, dan gaan we niet uit*, 'If it rains, well, we shall not go out', Russian *Pridet on vo-vremja, nu čtož, to my s nim pogovorim o vašem dele* 'If he comes in time, well, we shall discuss your problem with him'. In English, this type of clause appears to require the use of the modal preterite of an auxiliary, e.g. *Should he call, tell him I am not at home*, which, in addition, is mainly literary (Zandvoort 1972:261).

[10] Daneš distinguishes between the semantic content of a construction and its expression in a specific language; the semantic content of constructions of the form 'x gives z to y' is analyzed into two possessive relations xPz and yPz, connected by a factor T symbolizing the transition from one possessive state to the next, and a factor A (x) which – in the manner of a logical quantifier — specifies the origin of action; the entire formula thus reads A (x) (xPz) T (yPz).

[11] This notion of 'belief' plays an important part in aesthetic theory; cf. e.g. Aiken (1967:146ff.). The special type of belief conveyed by our indicative configuration is closely akin to the "equational proverb" of the form

$$\text{NP} + \text{copula} + \begin{Bmatrix}\text{better}\\ \text{worse}\end{Bmatrix} \text{than} + \text{NP},$$

investigated by Dundes, and discussed by Hendricks (1967:50-51).

[12] A proposal on classifying literary motifs, with applications to the thematic analysis of a text, will be found in Van Holk (1973, 1974).

BIBLIOGRAPHY

Abraham, Werner

1971a "Der "ethische" Dativ", *Fragen der strukturellen Syntax und der kontrastiven Grammatik*, *Sprache der Gegenwart*, XVII. Düsseldorf, Päd. Verlag Schwann.

Abraham, Werner (ed.)

1971b *Kasustheorie*. Frankfurt/M., Athenäum.

Aiken, Henry David
1967 "The Aesthetic Relevance of Belief", *Aesthetic Inquiry: Essays on Art Criticism and the Philosophy of Art*, ed. by Monroe C. Beardsley and Herbert M. Schueller. Belmont, Cal., Dickenson.

Apresjan, Ju. D.
1967 *Èksperimental'noe issledovanie semantiki russkogo glagola*. Moskva, Izd. Nauka.

Daneš, František, Zdeněk Hlavsa, Jan Kořenský
1973 "Postavení slovesa v struktuře české věty", *Československé přednášky pro VII mezinárodní sjezd slavistů (Varšava)*, 129-139.

Van Dijk, Teun A.
1972 *Some Aspects of Text Grammars: A Study in Theoretical Linguistics and Poetics*. The Hague, Mouton.

Ebeling, Carl L.
1954 "On the Semantic Structure of the Russian Sentence", *Lingua*, 4, 207-22.

Eco, Umberto
1972 *Einführung in die Semiotik*. München, Fink.

Fillmore, Charles J.
1968 "The Case for Case", *Universals in Linguistic Theory*, ed. by Emmon Bach and Robert T. Harms. New York, Holt, Rinehart, and Winston.
1969 "Types of Lexical Information", *Studies in Syntax and Semantics*, ed. by F. Kiefer, 109-37. Dordrecht, Reidel.
1971 "Some Problems for Case Grammars", *Linguistics: Developments of the Sixties – Viewpoints for the Seventies*, ed. by Richard J. O'Brien (= *Monograph Series on Languages and Linguistics*, No. 24), 35-56.

De Groot, A. W.
1964 *Inleiding tot de algemene taalwetenschap*. Groningen, Wolters.

Halliday, M. A. K.
1972 "Language Structure and Language Function", *New Horizons in Linguistics*, ed. by John Lyons, 140-65. Harmondsworth, Penguin.

Harweg, Roland
1968 *Pronomina und Textkonstitution*. München, Fink.
1971 "Die textologische Rolle der Betonung", *Beiträge zur Textlinguistik*, ed. by Wolf-Dieter Stempel, 124-59. München, Fink.

Hendricks, William O.
1967 "On the Notion 'Beyond the Sentence'", *Linguistics*, 37, 12-51.

Van Holk, A. G. F.
1963 "Definite and Indefinite in Old Church Slavonic: A Contribution to the Theory of the Linguistic Sign", *Dutch Contributions to the Fifth International Congress of Slavicists*, 93-124. The Hague, Mouton.
1973 "Deep Categories in Ryleev's Descriptions of Nature" (forthcoming).
1974 "Verbal Aggression and Offended Honour in Dostoevskij's *Selo Stepančikovo i ego obitateli*" (to appear in *Russian Literature*).

Horecký, Ján
1973 "Poznámky k metóde analýzy textu", *Slovo a Slovesnost*, XXXIV, 34-38.

Ivanov, V. V., V. N. Toporov
1963 "K rekonstrukcii praslavjanskogo teksta", *Slavjanskoe jazykoznanie, Doklady sovetskoj delegacii, V Meždunarodnyj s''ezd slavistov*, 88-158. Moskva, Izd. Akad. Nauk SSSR.

Jackendoff, Ray S., Peter Culicover
1971 "A Reconsideration of Dative Movements", *Foundations of Language*, 7, 397-412.

Kortlandt, F. H. H.
1971 "The Semantics of the Russian Verb", *Lingua,* 27, 53-81.
Petöfi, János S.
1971 *Transformationsgrammatiken und eine ko-textuelle Texttheorie: Grundlagen und Konzeptionen.* Frankfurt/M, Athenäum.
Rychner, Jean
1971 "Analyse d'une unité transphrastique: La séquence narrative de même sujet dans *La Mort Artu*", *Beiträge zur Textlinguistik,* ed. by Wolf-Dieter Stempel, 79-122. München, Fink.
Wienold, Götz
1972 *Semiotik der Literatur.* Frankfurt/M, Athenäum.
Zandvoort, R. W.
1972 *Handbook of English Grammar,* 12th ed. Groningen, Wolters-Noordhoff.

AMBIGUÏTÉ DANS LE LEXIQUE

WIECHER ZWANENBURG

0. Notre but est de réfuter l'opinion de Katz (1972:68-70) selon laquelle la polysémie et l'homonymie se laissent réduire à des degrés différents de ressemblance sémantique. Nous essayerons de montrer qu'il faut recourir à des facteurs extralinguistiques pour décrire ces notions.

A cet effet nous examinons dans le paragraphe 1 comment la polysémie et l'homonymie sont traitées de façon traditionnelle dans deux dictionnaires récents du français et dans Ullmann (1951, 1952, et surtout 1962). Dans le paragraphe 2 nous étudions les deux types de polysémie distingués par Ullmann, métaphorique et métonymique. Le paragraphe 3 est consacré à la façon dont Katz rend compte de la polysémie et de l'homonymie, et dans les paragraphes 4 et 5 nous essayons de tirer les conséquences de son analyse et de celle de Ullmann pour la description de la polysémie. La conclusion à laquelle nous arrivons dans le paragraphe 6 implique non seulement qu'il est impossible de réduire la polysémie et l'homonymie à des degrés différents de ressemblance sémantique, mais encore que la notion de 'changement sémantique possible' ne saurait être définie sans recours à des facteurs extralinguistiques.

Nous nous servirons de matériaux français, et partout où le contraire n'est pas indiqué, les descriptions des sens sont empruntées à Dubois e.a. (1966).

1. La difficulté de distinguer la polysémie d'avec l'homonymie se constate quand on compare entre eux les deux dictionnaires complets du français qui sont les plus récents, Dubois e.a. (1966) et Robert (1953-1970). Dubois, par exemple, distingue deux homonymes *front* et quatre homonymes *pied*, tandis que Robert ne reconnaît dans les deux cas qu'un seul mot polysémique.

Aussi Ullmann (1962:159) dit-il: "Bien que ... la frontière entre polysémie et homonymie soit parfois floue, les deux types sont si différents qu'il faut les considérer séparément." Et il résume la distinction traditionnelle entre les deux en disant qu'il y a polysémie "quand le même mot a deux ou plusieurs sens différents" et homonymie "quand deux ou plusieurs mots ont la même forme".

2. Là où les deux dictionnaires sont d'accord pour ne reconnaître qu'un seul mot, l'un distingue parfois deux sens tandis que l'autre n'en présente qu'un seul. Comparez:

(1) *bouche*: Dubois: orifice d'entrée du tube digestif, chez l'homme et chez certains animaux
Robert: 1. cavité située à la partie inférieure du visage de l'homme, communiquant avec l'appareil digestif et avec les voies respiratoires
2. cavité buccale de certains animaux

Quand ils sont d'accord pour reconnaître différents sens d'un mot polysémique, les deux les énumèrent souvent sans commentaire. Mais Robert, à l'encontre de Dubois e.a., ajoute souvent une remarque à un sens donné, distinguant ainsi des types particuliers de polysémie. Comparez les descriptions suivantes, prises dans Robert:

(2) *bouche*: 1. cavité située à la partie inférieure du visage de l'homme, communiquant avec l'appareil digestif et avec les voies respiratoires
2. par analogie: l'ouverture, l'entrée de quelque chose
(3) *front*: 1. partie supérieure de la face humaine, comprise entre les sourcils et la racine des cheveux, et s'étendant d'une tempe à l'autre
2. par extension: la tête, le visage
(4) *nez*: 1. partie saillante du visage, située dans son axe, entre le front et la lèvre supérieure et qui abrite la partie antérieure des fosses nasales
2. pris pour: face, figure, visage
(5) *oreille*: 1. l'un des deux organes constituant l'appareil auditif
2. par métonymie: personne qui entend, écoute

Et les commentaires cités dans chaque cas sous le deuxième sens avant les deux points ne constituent qu'un choix limité de ce qu'on rencontre à cet égard dans Robert.

Chez Ullmann on ne trouve pas une réponse directe à la question de savoir quels types de polysémie on peut distinguer. Il nous renvoie à son étude des sources historiques de la polysémie en disant (1951: 118-119): "Les sources de la polysémie sont pertinentes du point de vue synchronique puisque la relation entre les différents sens est perçue par définition par le sujet parlant – sans cela il s'agit d'homonymie, non de polysémie." Nous verrons ci-dessous que cette remarque est erronée en ce sens que distinguer deux sens n'implique pas savoir comment est née la différence entre ces deux sens.

Les sources de polysémie qu'énumère Ullmann (1962:159-167) sont les suivantes: (1) glissements de sens, (2) spécialisation dans un milieu social, (3) langage figuré, (4) réinterprétation d'homonymes, (5) influence étrangère.

Quant au langage figuré, il distingue entre origine métaphorique et origine métonymique d'un nouveau sens. Il décrit ainsi la première, en discutant le sens métaphorique 'muscle' de *musculus* 'petite souris' en latin (1962:213): "La structure fondamentale de la métaphore est très simple. Il y a toujours deux termes en présence: la chose dont nous parlons et ce à quoi nous la comparons. ... Au lieu de formuler explicitement, sous forme de comparaison, qu'un muscle ressemble à une petite souris, on identifie les deux par une sorte de sténographie verbale. En ce sens il est correct de dire que la métaphore est une 'comparaison condensée posant une identité intuitive et concrète'." La métonymie est décrite (1962:163) comme "basée non sur la ressemblance mais sur quelque autre relation entre les deux termes." Pour autant que l'ancien sens se maintient quand le sens métaphorique ou métonymique est introduit dans la langue, on peut dire que ces deux sources différentes de la polysémie sont pertinentes du point de vue synchronique. C'est qu'elles résultent en deux types de relations synchroniques différentes entre les deux sens.

Commentant les glissements de sens, Ullmann dit ceci (1962:160): "Nos mots ont un certain nombre d'aspects différents d'après les contextes dans lesquels ils sont employés. Certains de ces aspects sont purement éphémères; d'autres peuvent se développer en nuances de sens permanentes et, à mesure que la distance entre ces nuances s'agrandit, nous pouvons finir par les considérer comme des sens différents du même terme." La différence d'avec la catégorie précédente est décrite ainsi (Ullmann 1952:202): "La cristallisation des glissements sémantiques en acceptions distinctes est le résultat d'une évolution lente et graduelle. Par contre, la métaphore et la métonymie agissent instantanément: on perçoit une similitude, on évoque un rapport quelconque, et la transposition s'effectue spontanément." Dans la description diachronique il ne semble pas toujours possible de distinguer les deux catégories, témoin cette remarque sur les sens d'un mot polysémique anglais (Ullmann 1962:160): "La plupart de ces sens sont nés par suite de glissements de sens, bien qu'un autre facteur, le langage figuré, puisse y avoir contribué aussi.'' Quoi qu'il en soit, du point de vue synchronique la différence entre les deux catégories ne semble pas être pertinente. Comparez la polysémie de *mortel*, décrite par Ullmann (1952:139) comme résultat de glissements de sens: 'qui cause la mort, qui entraîne la mort' dans *maladie mortelle*, 'qui hait profondément' dans *ennemi mortel*, 'qui est sujet à la mort' dans *l'homme est mortel*. En synchronie ce cas ne se distingue pas essentiellement d'un cas de polysémie décrit par Ullmann (1952, 202) comme dû à un emploi métonymique: *cuisine* 'pièce destinée à la préparation des aliments' et 'art ou manière d'apprêter les aliments'. De même la relation entre les deux sens de *bouche* mentionnés dans (1), pour autant que le second est dû à un glissement de sens, ne se distingue pas fondamentalement, au niveau de la synchronie, de celle entre *patte* 'membre articulé du corps des animaux, jouant un rôle dans la marche, dans la préhension' et *patte* 'jambe, pied', dont le second serait sans doute décrit par Ullmann comme dû à un emploi métaphorique.

De même, les trois autres sources de polysémie citées par Ullmann, spécialisation dans un milieu social, réinterprétation d'homonymes, et influence étrangère, ne sont pas pertinentes en synchronie. En effet, une fois qu'un sens donné a été admis dans la communauté linguistique, il ne présentera pas une relation particulière avec d'autres sens du fait qu'il est dû à un de ces facteurs ou à une combinaison de plusieurs d'entre eux. Ainsi on trouve chez Ullmann (1952, 204) que *dada* 'cheval', dans le langage enfantin ou plaisant, doit son sens 'idée chère à quelqu'un, qui la répète fréquemment' à l'influence de l'anglais *hobby*. Mais ce fait ne distingue d'aucune façon, en synchronie, la relation entre ces deux sens de celle entre *jouet* 'objet dont les enfants se servent pour s'amuser' et *jouet* 'victime d'autres personnes, d'une volonté supérieure, des éléments', dont le dernier est dû à un emploi métaphorique. D'ailleurs dans des présentations parallèles de la classification des sources de la polysémie (Ullmann 1951:118-119 et 1952:200-207) la catégorie (2), spécialisation dans un milieu social, est traitée comme une sous-catégorie de (1), glissements de sens.

Ainsi il nous reste, en synchronie, deux types de polysémie: métaphorique et métonymique, la première fondée sur une ressemblance entre les deux termes, la seconde sur quelque autre relation.

Cette conclusion semble être confirmée par la façon dont Ullmann (1962:211-227) traite les changements de sens. Il distingue quatre types, caractérisés respectivement par la ressemblance des sens (métaphore), la contiguïté des sens (métonymie), la ressemblance des noms (étymologie populaire), et la contiguïté des noms (ellipse). On constate tout de suite qu'il ne s'agit pas d'une classification homogène: dans les deux premiers cas il s'agit de la relation entre l'ancien sens et le nouveau, dans les deux derniers de celle entre la forme du mot qui change de sens et la forme d'un autre mot. Quant à la relation entre l'ancien sens et le nouveau, les deux derniers types se ramènent simplement soit au premier soit au deuxième. En effet, le changement de *forain*, 'étranger' en ancien français, en *forain* 'qui pratique son commerce ou son industrie sur les foires' (*marchand forain*) par étymologie populaire d'après *foire* (Ullmann 1952:288), est un changement métonymique. Et il en est de même de *capitale* 'de toute première importance', devenu *capitale* 'ville où se trouve le siège des pouvoirs publics d'un Etat' par ellipse de *ville*. Ainsi s'explique ce que dit Ullmann (1962:223) sur la distinction entre les quatre types: "Il y a beaucoup de changements sémantiques qui semblent entrer dans plus d'une catégorie. On peut se demander, par exemple, si des expressions comme *un Picasso* pour 'un tableau de Picasso' ou *bourgogne* pour 'vin de Bourgogne' sont métonymiques ou elliptiques. Le plus simple est peut-être de les considérer comme des changements 'composites' dus à l'interaction de deux types d'association différents."

Somme toute, le traitement traditionnel de l'ambiguïté lexicale par Ullmann nous livre deux types, polysémie et homonymie, et pour le premier une distinction entre polysémie métaphorique et métonymique. Les commentaires de Robert comme ceux cités dans (2)-(5), pour autant qu'ils ne se servent pas des termes métaphore et métonymie mêmes, peuvent se ramener à ces deux: ainsi 'par analogie' dans (2) indique une relation métaphorique, et 'par extension' dans (3), 'pris pour' dans (4) désignent une relation métonymique.

3. Considérons maintenant comment Katz rend compte de ces phénomènes dans le cadre d'une grammaire générative.

Katz-Fodor (1963) et Katz-Postal (1964) ne distinguent pas, dans le lexique, entre les deux types d'ambiguïté que constituent la polysémie et l'homonymie, et Weinreich (1966:399-412) leur en fait grief. Il leur reproche de ne pas "distinguer entre l'homonymie fortuite et la polysémie intéressante du point de vue lexicologique". La première serait représentée par exemple par *rock* 'rocher' et *rock* 'se balancer' en anglais, la deuxième par *land* 'pays' et 'terre', *cook* 'cuisinier' et 'faire la cuisine'.

Katz (1972:69) lui répond ainsi: "Supposé que la distinction de Weinreich entre 'homonymie fortuite' et 'polysémie intéressante du point de vue lexicologique' ne soit pas basée sur des considérations d'ordre diachronique, nous pouvons représenter la ressemblance sémantique dans les cas du dernier genre et la non-ressemblance dans les cas du premier genre en terme de marqueurs sémantiques. On n'a pas besoin d'une distinction de forme des entrées lexicales pour présenter les relations sémantiques en question. Les lectures lexicales pour les deux sens de *cook* seront pratiquement les mêmes, excepté que dans le cas où *cook* indique celui qui prépare les repas la lecture lexicale contiendra le marqueur sémantique 'humain', tandis que dans le cas où *cook* indique la préparation elle-même la lecture lexicale contiendra le marqueur sémantique 'procès'. D'autre part, les lectures lexicales pour les deux sens de *rock* n'auront pas de marqueurs sémantiques en commun. Les deux sens de *land* représentent un phénomène qui se trouve quelque part entre les deux, puisque les sens ne sont pas si proches l'un de l'autre que ceux de *cook*, mais pas si différents que ceux de *rock* non plus. De tels faits montrent qu'il n'y a pas de dichotomie simple entre 'des cas de polysémie intéressante du point de vue lexicologique' présentant une ressemblance de sens et des cas d''homonymie fortuite' ne présentant pas de ressemblance de sens. Plutôt, il y a une échelle de ressemblance de sens, dont les cas-limites sont la synonymie d'un côté et la différence de sens complète de l'autre. La terminologie de Weinreich suggère qu'il y a une dichotomie qui demande une bipartition dans la notation de la théorie sémantique, tandis qu'il y a en réalité une échelle de ressemblance de sens qui permet de comparer des paires d'entrées lexicales et d'évaluer leurs différences en degré de ressemblance de sens."

Ainsi les notions de polysémie et homonymie sont réduites à celle de (degré de) ressemblance, que Katz (1972:48) définit ainsi de façon provisoire (nous traduisons par 'ressemblance' le terme anglais 'similarity'): "Un constituant C_i est sémantiquement ressemblant à un constituant C_j pour un sens donné dans le cas où il y a une lecture de C_i et une lecture de C_j qui ont un marqueur sémantique en commun. (Ils peuvent être dits sémantiquement ressemblants par rapport au concept ϕ dans le cas où le marqueur sémantique partagé représente ϕ.)" Et de façon corollaire il définit ainsi la différence de sens complète: "Un constituant C_i est sémantiquement distinct d'un constituant C_j pour un sens donné de C_i et un sens donné de C_j dans le cas où les lectures de ces sens n'ont pas de marqueurs sémantiques en commun." Ainsi la ressemblance est une qualité graduelle, de sorte que "la synonymie est le cas-limite de la ressemblance sémantique: c'est le cas dans lequel deux constituants sont aussi ressemblants que possible, où il n'y a pas de différence sémantique entre un sens donné de l'un et un sens donné de l'autre".

Une fois que la dichotomie constituée par polysémie et homonymie a été éliminée du lexique, la théorie est privée de la possibilité de rendre compte des intuitions qu'ont les sujets parlants sur la question de savoir si, dans un cas donné, on a affaire à un mot ou à deux mots. Et il semble d'autant plus nécessaire de rendre compte de telles intuitions qu'elles sont présupposées par les intuitions qu'ont les sujets parlants concernant l'emploi métaphorique et – peut-être en une moindre mesure – métonymique des mots. Katz ne se prononce pas sur ce problème, mais il semble raisonnable de penser que cette dichotomie fait partie de la théorie de la performance et qu'elle y est à définir entre autres en termes de ressemblance sémantique. C'est-à-dire que dans un type donné de performance il faut un degré donné de ressemblance pour que les sujets parlants estiment qu'on ait affaire au même mot.

Une telle description semble pouvoir rendre compte du fait qu'il y a de si grandes divergences entre auteurs de dictionnaires ou autres sujets parlants quand il s'agit de délimiter polysémie et homonymie.

4. Cela dit, la question se pose de savoir si, pour les sens qui présentent suffisamment de ressemblance pour qu'on puisse dans certaines conditions les considérer comme relevant de la polysémie, les relations appelées métaphoriques et métonymiques par Ullmann doivent être décrites dans un cadre génératif. Dans le cas d'une réponse affirmative, il faudra déterminer quel est le rôle de la théorie linguistique dans cette description.

Comme nous l'avons dit dans le paragraphe précédent, nous pensons qu'il faut rendre compte de façon ou d'autre des intuitions qu'ont les sujets parlants sur l'emploi métaphorique et métonymique des mots. Mais il y a d'autres facteurs qui nous semblent conduire à la nécessité de décrire ces relations. D'abord celles-ci, témoin les remarques de Ullmann à cet égard, semblent devoir jouer un rôle dans la détermination de la notion 'changement sémantique possible'. Et en second lieu ces relations ne se présentent pas seulement entre deux sens d'une entrée lexicale tels qu'ils sont définis dans le lexique d'une époque donnée ou de deux époques successives; elles se rencontrent tout aussi bien entre un tel sens défini dans le lexique et un nouveau sens créé ad hoc dans la performance, littéraire ou non. Or, on aura de toute façon à rendre compte de ce dernier phénomène, qu'on peut appeler métaphore et métonymie originale, par opposition à la métaphore et la métonymie d'usage qui concernent deux sens définis dans le lexique.

Quant au rôle de la théorie linguistique dans la description de ces relations, il nous semble qu'il a été surestimé par Bickerton (1969), qui néglige au fond la différence que nous venons d'établir entre métaphore et métonymie originale et d'usage. Discutant plus particulièrement la métaphore, il propose de prévoir toutes les occurrences de cette figure dans la grammaire en pourvoyant chaque entrée lexicale de marqueurs sémantiques particuliers pour toutes les métaphores auxquelles il pourrait donner lieu. Nous pensons que Matthews (1971) s'est opposé à juste titre à une telle conception en disant: "La distinction, relevant de la performance, entre métaphore et non-métaphore, se caractérise correctement au niveau de la compétence en termes d'une distinction entre phrases sémantiquement déviantes et non-déviantes. Les restrictions sélectionnelles qui présentent l'emploi non-métaphorique général en termes de systèmes de traits lexicaux des mots constituants sont violées dans le cas de phrases déviantes. La présence d'une violation d'une restriction sélectionnelle est ainsi une condition nécessaire et suffisante pour distinguer la métaphore d'avec la non-métaphore, excepté évidemment les cas où les énoncés ne sont pas censés avoir un sens."

Nous pensons cependant que Matthews caractérise ici aussi bien la métaphore originale que la métonymie originale. Et en négligeant la différence entre les deux, il est à son tour amené à sous-estimer le rôle possible de la théorie linguistique dans la description des deux. Il rejette ce qu'il appelle les théories concernant la métaphore qui sont fondées sur la ressemblance. Mais une fois que le critère qu'il fournit lui-même se trouve ne pas différencier entre métaphore et métonymie originales, il faut se demander comment on peut se passer de la notion de ressemblance pour les distinguer. Et cette question s'impose encore davantage pour la métaphore et la métonymie d'usage, auxquelles le critère de Matthews ne s'applique d'aucune façon.

Cela n'empêche que nous sommes d'accord avec Matthews pour dire que la description de la métaphore, de même que celle de la métonymie, relève de la performance. Cela nous semble résulter des conclusions que nous avons tirées de Katz concernant la description de la polysémie, dont la métaphore et la métonymie dépendent. Mais cette solution s'impose en outre dès qu'on veut rendre compte de ce que les figures d'usage et les figures originales ont en commun, puisque par définition ces dernières ne se rencontrent que dans la performance. Reste la question de savoir quel doit être exactement le rôle de la théorie linguistique dans cette description.

5. Cette question nous confronte avec une situation étrange. Nous avons constaté, en effet, que d'une part Katz se sert de la notion de ressemblance quand il s'agit d'opposer (de façon graduelle) la polysémie à l'homonymie. Et d'autre part nous avons vu – et nous venons de le constater à nouveau – qu'on a besoin, de façon ou d'autre, de cette même notion pour opposer la forme métaphorique de la polysémie à sa forme métonymique. Considérons donc de plus près l'emploi que fait Ullmann de cette notion pour opposer ces deux types de polysémie.

D'abord il caractérise le changement de sens métaphorique et métonymique – et par là indirectement la relation métaphorique et métonymique en synchronie – par la ressemblance et la contiguïté des sens, respectivement. Mais une discussion plus détaillée de ces relations (1972:213) l'amène à caractériser ces notions en termes de relations entre choses dans la réalité. Par rapport à la métaphore il dit: "Il y a toujours deux termes en présence, la chose dont nous parlons et ce à quoi nous la comparons." Et le métonymie est dite être "basée non sur la ressemblance mais sur quelque autre relation entre les deux termes" (1972: 163). Ailleurs (1952:277-278) il passe imperceptiblement du niveau des choses à celui des sens en décrivant la métaphore: "On perçoit par exemple une ressemblance entre les *dents* humaines et les saillies d'un peigne. Au lieu de préciser que ces saillies sont *comme* des dents, on les appellera simplement les *dents du peigne*. Ce faisant, on aura transposé le nom d'un organe humain pour désigner un objet inanimé. La ressemblance entre les deux sens nous permet d'appliquer à l'un d'eux la désignation propre à l'autre. Par un acte d'assimilation aperceptive, on conjugue les deux notions en vertu de ce qu'elles ont en commun et l'on fait abstraction des différences."

Evidemment la ressemblance des choses et la ressemblance des sens ne s'excluent pas. Aussi est-il facile de constater, sans qu'on entre dans les détails de la description sémantique, que la première, nécessaire pour qu'il y ait métaphore, peut se combiner avec la seconde. Considérez par exemple le sens métaphorique de *bouche* 'orifice de certaines cavités', comme dans *bouche de métro*; le sens littéral est 'orifice d'entrée du tube digestif, chez l'homme et chez certains animaux'. Même une analyse superficielle révèle qu'il doit y avoir ressemblance des sens du fait de la présence d'un ou de plusieurs marqueurs sémantiques centraux communs: 'orifice de ... tube ...' et 'orifice de ... cavités'. Mais il peut y avoir ressemblance des choses sans qu'il y ait ressemblance des sens. Comparez par exemple *aigu* 'terminé en pointe ou par un tranchant' et son sens métaphorique 'dont la hauteur peut avoir quelque chose de désagréable', comme dans *un bruit aigu*. On ne voit pas en quelle mesure les deux sens peuvent être dits ressemblants. Il y a plutôt une ressemblance dans la réalité qu'on pourrait formuler à peu près ainsi: un bruit aigu peut faire mal aux oreilles comme un objet aigu peut faire mal à n'importe quelle partie du corps.

Quant à la métonymie, la situation est encore plus confuse. Prise à la lettre, la définition de Ullmann nous oblige d'attribuer à deux sens en relation métonymique la qualité de contiguïté, tandis que la caractérisation de la polysémie par Katz nous force en même temps à leur reconnaître un rapport de ressemblance. Or, on pourrait arguer que la description de Katz n'est que provisoire et qu'il faut en venir à distinguer différents types de ressemblance, d'après la place qu'occupent les marqueurs communs dans la constellation de l'ensemble des marqueurs qui constituent les deux sens. Il y aurait alors une ressemblance concernant les marqueurs centraux, correspondant à la ressemblance des sens de Ullmann, et une ressemblance intéressant des marqueurs périphériques, correspondant à la contiguïté des sens de Ullmann. Et une telle proposition semble en effet pouvoir rendre compte par exemple de la relation métonymique entre *côte* 'chacun des os allongés et courbes qui forment la cage thoracique' et 'partie supérieure de la côte d'un bœuf, d'un veau, d'un mouton, etc., avec les muscles qui y adhèrent'. Mais nous avons déjà vu qu'un procédé qui ne se fonde que sur la ressemblance des marqueurs sémantiques est incapable de rendre compte de certaines métaphores. Et en outre il semble que ce que nous venons de proposer ne permet pas de bien différencier métaphore et métonymie. Dans le cas de la relation métonymique entre *poitrine* 'partie du tronc, entre le cou et l'abdomen, qui contient les poumons et le cœur' et *poitrine* 'seins de femme', nous semblons plutôt avoir affaire à deux sens qui ont un ou plusieurs marqueurs centraux en commun, à l'encontre de ce que notre proposition prédirait. Et il en est de même pour la relation métonymique qui explique le changement du latin *coxa* 'hanche' en *coxa* 'cuisse'.

Ainsi c'est la ressemblance ou la contiguïté des choses, plutôt que la ressemblance ou la contiguïté des sens, qui est une condition nécessaire pour qu'il y ait métaphore ou métonymie. Cela est d'ailleurs confirmé par le fait que les noms propres, qui justement n'ont pas de sens (Katz 1972:380-382), peuvent servir de point de départ pour une métonymie; comparez par exemple la relation métonymique qui existe entre le nom du produit *roquefort* et celui de son lieu d'origine, *Roquefort*. Sous ce rapport Ullmann (1952, 287) fait remarquer: "Le rapport de contiguïté qui gouverne la métonymie dépend parfois de circonstances toutes spéciales que seule l'étude historique peut reconstituer. Entre le verbe latin *monere* et le substantif *moneta* 'monnaie', on ne saisit aucun lien sémantique, et en effet le contact entre les deux notions a été purement contingent: la monnaie romaine se fabriquait dans le temple de *Juno Moneta*."

En somme, la théorie linguistique ne peut contribuer à la description des métaphores et des métonymies que dans la mesure où la ressemblance sémantique, dans ses différentes formes, reflète la ressemblance ou la contiguïté des choses. Il nous semble probable qu'il sera possible de conclure d'une forme donnée de ressemblance sémantique à la ressemblance ou la contiguïté des choses, mais pas inversement. Ainsi la théorie linguistique peut contribuer à la description des figures en raffinant la notion de ressemblance sémantique telle qu'elle a été définie provisoirement par Katz. Mais c'est à la théorie de la performance de décrire les conditions nécessaires pour qu'il y ait métaphore ou métonymie.

6. Cela est grave de conséquences pour la description de l'ambiguïté lexicale en général. Dans le paragraphe 3 nous avions conclu provisoirement que les notions de polysémie et d'homonymie font partie de la théorie de la performance et sont à définir dans cette théorie entre autres en termes de ressemblance sémantique. L'exposé de Katz nous a amené à penser qu'un minimum de ressemblance sémantique, définie en termes de marqueurs sémantiques, est une condition nécessaire pour qu'il y ait polysémie.

Dans le paragraphe 4 nous avons argué que les relations polysémiques se laissent réduire à des relations métaphoriques et métonymiques. Nous avons constaté ensuite dans le paragraphe 5 que ces relations peuvent se présenter sans qu'il y ait ressemblance sémantique dans le sens indiqué. La seule condition nécessaire semble être la ressemblance des choses pour la métaphore, la contiguïté des choses pour la métonymie.

Par conséquent les notions de métaphore et de métonymie ne se laissent pas décrire en termes exclusivement linguistiques, et c'est la théorie de la performance qui doit en rendre compte. Mais, vu la façon dont la polysémie d'une part, la métaphore et la métonymie d'autre part, dépendent les unes des autres, il faut conclure de tout cela que la conception de la polysémie développée par Katz ne peut pas être maintenue. On ne peut pas égaler la polysémie, en tant que phénomène de la performance, à un degré minimum de ressemblance, variable d'un type de performance à l'autre. En d'autres mots: un degré donné de ressemblance sémantique n'est pas une condition nécessaire pour la polysémie.

Cette conclusion implique que, étant donné le caractère métaphorique ou métonymique des changements sémantiques tels qu'ils ont été décrits par Ullmann, il est impossible aussi de donner en termes purement linguistiques une définition de la notion 'changement sémantique possible'.

LITTÉRATURE CONSULTÉE

Bickerton, D.
1969 "Prolegomena to a Linguistic Theory of Metaphor", *FL*, 4, 34-52.
Dubois, J., e.a.
1966 *Dictionnaire du français contemporain*. Paris.
Katz, J. J.
1972 *Semantic Theory*. New York.
Katz, J. J., et Fodor, J. A.
1963 "The Structure of a Semantic Theory", *Lg*, 39, 170-210.
Katz, J. J., et Postal, P. M.
1964 *An Integrated Theory of Linguistic Descriptions*. Cambridge, Mass.
Matthews, R. J.
1971 "Concerning a 'Linguistic Theory' of Metaphor", *FL*, 7, 413-25.
Robert, G.
1953-70 *Dictionnaire alphabétique et analogique de la langue française*. 7 volumes. Paris.
Ullmann, S.
1951 *The Principles of Semantics*. Oxford.
1952 *Précis de sémantique française*. Berne.
1962 *Semantics*. Oxford.
Weinreich, U.
1966 "Explorations in Semantic Theory", *Current Trends in Linguistics*, éd. par T. A. Sebeok, 3, 395-477. The Hague.